A graduate of the University of Cambridge and of Birkbeck, University of London, **Lucy Pollard** has been a Trustee of the Association for the Study of Travel in Egypt and the Near East and is a member of the Hellenic Society.

'*The Quest For Classical Greece* is a delightful and immensely readable book, which combines fine scholarship with a refreshing enthusiasm for human frailties. Lucy Pollard's seventeenth-century travellers measure the Parthenon and clamber up Mount Athos. They marvel over Troy (which isn't Troy at all) and explore the Cretan labyrinth (actually a disused quarry), all the time grumbling about the locals, bribing officials and stealing "souvenirs" of their trip. They manage to combine bravery, bigotry and a restless curiosity in a strangely endearing way. I cannot recommend this book highly enough.'

Adrian Tinniswood, OBE, writer and historian; author of *The Polite Tourist: A History of Country House Visiting* and of *The Rainborowes: Pirates, Puritans and a Family's Quest for the Promised Land*

'*The Quest for Classical Greece* is a timely, scholarly, and well illustrated reminder of the early and intimate links between England and the eastern Mediterranean, seen through the eyes of English travellers. Lucy Pollard shows that the Ottoman Empire was an important destination on the Grand Tour, facilitating researches into the classical and Christian sites which so fascinated English scholars. The unpublished diary of John Covel – which Pollard discusses at length – is a major new source, revealing a seventeenth-century English chaplain's views of Greeks and Turks.'

Philip Mansel, writer and historian, author of *Levant: Splendour and Catastrophe on the Mediterranean* and of *Constantinople: City of the World's Desire, 1453–1924*

THE QUEST FOR CLASSICAL GREECE

Early Modern Travel to the Greek World

Lucy Pollard

BLOOMSBURY ACADEMIC
LONDON • NEW YORK • OXFORD • NEW DELHI • SYDNEY

BLOOMSBURY ACADEMIC
Bloomsbury Publishing Plc
50 Bedford Square, London, WC1B 3DP, UK
1385 Broadway, New York, NY 10018, USA

BLOOMSBURY, BLOOMSBURY ACADEMIC and the Diana logo
are trademarks of Bloomsbury Publishing Plc

First published in Great Britain 2015 by I.B. Tauris & Co. Ltd
Paperback edition first published 2021 by Bloomsbury Academic

Copyright © Lucy Pollard, 2015

Lucy Pollard has asserted her right under the Copyright,
Designs and Patents Act, 1988, to be identified as Author of this work.

For legal purposes the Acknowledgements on p. viii constitute
an extension of this copyright page.

All rights reserved. No part of this publication may be reproduced or
transmitted in any form or by any means, electronic or mechanical,
including photocopying, recording, or any information storage or retrieval
system, without prior permission in writing from the publishers.

Bloomsbury Publishing Plc does not have any control over, or responsibility for,
any third-party websites referred to or in this book. All internet addresses given
in this book were correct at the time of going to press. The author and publisher
regret any inconvenience caused if addresses have changed or sites have
ceased to exist, but can accept no responsibility for any such changes.

A catalogue record for this book is available from the British Library.

A catalog record for this book is available from the Library of Congress.

ISBN: HB: 978-1-7807-6961-5
PB: 978-1-3501-9738-1
ePDF: 978-0-8577-2433-5
eBook: 978-0-8577-3799-1

Series: Library of Classical Studies, volume 8

Typeset in Garamond Three by OKS Prepress Services, Chennai, India

To find out more about our authors and books visit
www.bloomsbury.com and sign up for our newsletters.

For Garth, with love

CONTENTS

Acknowledgements	viii
Illustrations	x
Map	xiii
Introduction	1
1. The Logistics of Travel	45
2. Scholars and Texts	65
3. Antiquities, Proto-Archaeologists and Collectors	103
4. Among the Greeks	151
5. Among the Turks	188
6. Conclusion	206
Notes	212
Bibliography	251
Index	265

ACKNOWLEDGEMENTS

This book started life as a PhD thesis, and my greatest debt is to Professor Catharine Edwards for her rigorous and generous supervision.

Conversations with colleagues at ASTENE (Association for the Study of Travel in Egypt and the Near East) have been a great help in shaping my thoughts. Matthew Adams very kindly allowed me to read an unpublished MPhil thesis, and Paul Hetherington and Dr Janet Starkey generously showed me unpublished papers.

The staff at the British Library, the Bodleian Library, Cambridge University Library, Christ's College Cambridge, Friends House, the Institute of Classical Studies and the Royal Society have been unfailingly helpful.

I should like to thank all of the following people for their help: Dr Lindsay Allen, Sonia Anderson, Dr Fred Anscombe, Professor Malcolm Baker, Professor Mary Beard, Dr Stephen Brogan, Dr Christy Constantakopoulou, Professor David Feldman, Dr Mary Gifford, Dr Gordon Glanville, Professor Jean-Pierre Grélois, Professor John Henderson, Professor Carole Hillenbrand, Professor Robert Hillenbrand, Dr Eva Holmberg, Professor Michael Hunter, Sue Kentish, Alexandra Lapierre, Dr Elisabeth Leedham-Green, Dr Marilyn Lewis, Professor Gerald MacLean, Marcos Magarinos, Dr Justin Meggitt, Dr Kate Nichols, Matthew Robertson, Professor Stephen Robertson, Dr Lyn Rogers, Professor Michael Vickers, Dr Matthew Walker and Dr Dyfri Williams. The book's faults are all my own.

Acknowledgments

A version of part of Chapter 2 has appeared in *Classical Receptions Journal* 4/1 (2012), pp. 48–65, under the title 'Every stone tells a story'.

I am grateful to Ed Oliver for making the map. My editors, Dr Seb Manley, Alex Wright and Allison Walker have been a pleasure to work with.

Finally, this project would never have come to fruition without the love and support of my husband, my sons and their partners: Garth Pollard, Dr Finn Pollard, Tam Pollard, Liam Pollard, Eilidh Pollard and Dr Rachael McLennan.

ILLUSTRATIONS

Figure 1. Typical page of Covel's diary, BL MS Add. 22914, 16r (© The British Library Board).

Figure 2. Plant sketch by Covel, BL MS Add. 22914, 44r (© The British Library Board).

Figure 3. Typical page of Vernon's diary, Royal Society MS 73, 45r (courtesy of The Royal Society).

Figure 4. Page of Covel's diary showing a passage in code, BL MS Add. 22912, 189v (© The British Library Board).

Figure 5. Covel's sketch of the route from Constantinople to Adrianople, BL MS Add. 22912, 171r (© The British Library Board).

Figure 6. Vernon's sketch map of Greek islands, Royal Society MS 73, 31r (courtesy of The Royal Society).

Figure 7. Detail of the funerary monument for Finch and Baines, Christ's College Chapel, Cambridge (photograph: the author).

Figure 8. Wheler's sketch plan of Delphi, *Journey into Greece*, 313 (photograph: Tam Pollard).

ILLUSTRATIONS   XI

Figure 9.   Wheler's plan of Ephesus, *Journey into Greece*, 253 (photograph: Tam Pollard).

Figure 10. Covel's plan of Ephesus, BL MS Add. 22912, 45r (© The British Library Board).

Figure 11. Wheler's plan of Athens from the south, *Journey into Greece*, 338 (photograph: Tam Pollard).

Figure 12. Wheler's plan of Athens from the north, *Journey into Greece*, 340 (photograph: Tam Pollard).

Figure 13. Wheler's drawing of the Parthenon, *Journey into Greece*, 360 (photograph: Tam Pollard).

Figure 14. 'Heaps of ruins', *Journey into Greece*, 271 (photograph: Tam Pollard).

Figure 15. Drawing of Didyma (from Covel's diary but not in his hand), BL MS Add. 22912, 307v (© The British Library Board).

Figure 16. Page of Covel's diary showing his recording of inscriptions, BL MS Add. 22912, 275r (© The British Library Board).

Figure 17. The 'Sarcophagus of Achilles': Covel saw parts of it in the Gate of Persecutions at Ephesus (photograph reproduced by kind permission of the Duke of Bedford and the Trustees of the Bedford Estates).

Figure 18. Covel's sketch map of Mount Athos, BL MS Add. 22912, 335r (© The British Library Board).

Figure 19. Drawing of Mount Athos by Covel, BL MS Add. 22912, 336r (© The British Library Board).

Figure 20. View of Mount Athos today (photograph: Marcos M. Magarinos).

Figure 21. Covel's sketch of the Galata Tower, BL MS Add. 22912, 163v (© The British Library Board).

Figure 22. View of the Galata Tower today (photograph: the author).

Figure 23. Typical page from Covel's diary, BL MS Add. 22912, 180v–181r (© The British Library Board).

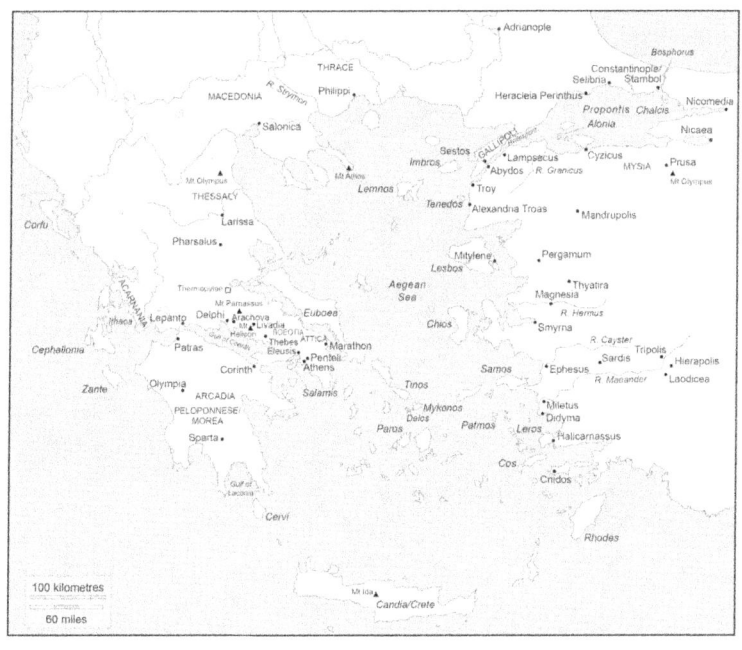

INTRODUCTION

Caelum non animum mutant qui trans mare currunt.
(Travellers change their environment, not their nature.)
                              Horace, *Epistles*, 1.11.27

We cross the seas, and 'midst her waves we burn,
Transplanting lives, perchance, that ne'er return;
We sack, we ransack, to the utmost sands
Of native kingdoms and of foreign lands;
We travel sea and soil, we pry, we prowl,
We progress and we prog from pole to pole.
  Francis Quarles, *Emblems Divine and Moral*, Book 2, Emblem 2

The sure traveller
Though he alight sometimes, still goeth on.
                   George Herbert, *The Church Porch*, stanza 57

Travel literature has been fertile ground for poets and other writers for much longer than it has been the subject of academic study, and the physical journey has a long history as a metaphor for spiritual, emotional and intellectual voyages, in particular for the cradle-to-grave progression that every individual has to make. Travel from one place on the globe to another is always, to some extent, a journey between two different worlds, that of home and that of abroad, but it may involve antitheses other than this too: familiar and alien, bodily and 'armchair', the physical landscape and landscapes of the imagination. An imaginary landscape can itself be both a point of departure and a destination: for John Covel and his fellow countrymen in the Ottoman Empire, on whose writings this book is based, the classical world offered layers of meaning which encouraged them to look both backwards and forwards. It presented them with the past, not only in terms of Graeco-Roman history, but also on a more personal level, as the world of their childhood and youthful education; it also promised a world they could look forward to discovering, or rediscovering, intellectually as well as physically, as they journeyed through it. Their travels involved a constant mental oscillation between their intellectual and emotional understanding and their observations, stimulating them to interpret classical sites in the light of the ancient texts that many of them knew so well, and to reinterpret those texts in the light of what they saw on the ground. Travellers carry with them not only their trunks but also their emotional, social, cultural and educational baggage. Their backgrounds and their particular interests inform both their expectations and also what they actually observe, as well as what they make of their observations; at the same time, they may be changed by their experiences of other cultures. They bring home the foreign and exotic (habits, tales or actual objects),[1] as well as taking the familiar (habits of mind no less than physical luggage) abroad. Horace's dictum, quoted above, tells only part of the story.

This book is about the Levant Company chaplain John Covel, and his contemporaries George Wheler, Paul Rycaut, John Finch and others, whose work or interests took them to places in the Greek world in the period after the Restoration in England, and also about some of their predecessors. They travelled in the area that is now Greece, and to Constantinople and the Aegean coastal area of what is now Turkey, where the Greek population was considerable in the seventeenth century. Much of what we know about them comes from their own writings, including published accounts, formal diplomatic letters, and private letters and diaries. In recording their experiences in various different ways, these travellers were not only working out their views of the places and people they encountered, but also making or remaking their own identities. On a personal level, a traveller's view of the world, which might change as he saw more of it, contributed to his sense of his place in it and of himself. Wheler, for example, confirmed his status as a gentleman by the acquisition of the qualities that go to make up 'civility': not only polish, but also a certain familiarity with the civilised world and its inhabitants, and the ability to deal with all sorts and conditions of men without compromising his English origins.[2] A man's civility was manifest in the way he presented himself to others, and therefore an essential part of his individuality, and it was enhanced by his experience of self-definition among foreigners. In this respect, the men I am writing about prefigure the Grand Tourists of a few decades later. More will be said later about the absence of women from this story.

Furthermore, in the years after the Restoration, at a time of religious instability when fear of Catholicism, and specifically fear of crypto-Catholicism within the English court, as well as distrust of dissent, was rife at home,[3] Anglicans abroad wore their Anglicanism with pride, although they had to tread carefully in their relations with Muslims. Anti-Catholic sentiment is common in travel writing, but it has more to do with the fear of Catholicism that was embedded in English society than with the writers' reactions to the Catholics they met on their travels. At the same time, travellers were – partly by virtue of their experiences abroad and in particular their encounter with the Ottoman Empire – beginning to see themselves as part of an English nation rather than of a broader Christendom. Perceptions of the Ottoman Empire in the seventeenth century were an important factor in the emergence of aspirations to an English empire.[4] In addition, the discovery and colonisation of the new world that were going on at this time gave travellers a different perspective on the possibility of empire, and affected attitudes to the old world.

Yerasimos has written that travel texts begin from a world view in which the traveller is the centre, and his journey takes him towards the periphery.[5] In the case of travel to the Ottoman Empire, some English visitors at least began to see that, in Blount's words,

Turks had 'an other kinde of civilitie, different from ours but no lesse pretending'.[6] They began to sense that there might be other centres of gravity than their own. By contrast with Turkey, travel to Greece was on one level a return by Englishmen to their own cultural origins.

It is impossible to consider western encounters with Islam without reference to Edward Said and the debate about orientalism. The emphasis in this book is on Greece, and attitudes to the ancient Greek past as well as to its surviving remains and to the contemporary Greek people. But travellers' experiences of the Ottoman Empire can be used as a foil against which to examine these attitudes. While some of the characteristics seen by westerners as typical of 'the orient' (licentious sexuality, for instance) are prefigured in the seventeenth century, I suggest that in this period the relationship between Europe and the Ottoman Empire was more porous: I cannot agree with Lewis's statement that:

> The struggle [between Islam and Christianity] [...] began with the advent of Islam [...] and has continued virtually to the present day. It has consisted of a long series of attacks and counterattacks, jihads and crusades, conquests and reconquests.[7]

We need to look behind what Brotton has called 'the powerfully divisive discourse of Orientalism',[8] which is sometimes read backwards into a period earlier than the one that Said was writing about, but which depends on a view that only comes into gradual focus alongside the colonisation of the new world.[9] It took time before the old world was seen through the eyes of successful colonisers and empire-builders, even if the English were already aspiring to an empire. However, this is not to deny the Eurocentricity of much that is to be found in seventeenth-century travellers' accounts, and even more so in authors who wrote about the Ottoman Empire without visiting it. A graphic example is found in Richard Knolles's history of the Turkish Empire, which was first published in 1603 and went into many subsequent editions: he complains that the Turks have given *'strange and barbarous names of their owne devising'* to cities, rivers, and so on. To sort these out would require 'No small travell and paine'.[10] For him, the 'real' names of places were the classical ones.

The ancestry of travel

The roots of travel are found in many different soils. From the classical world, Odysseus provided the most potent example of a resourceful adventurer who acquired wisdom through his journeying.[11] The beginnings of recorded history and geography, the works of Herodotus and Strabo among others, were well-known to those who had had a classical education. Strabo was extensively used by Covel and other antiquarians in Greece, and Herodotus, although surprisingly not much mentioned in travellers' accounts,[12] is an obvious model for the descriptions of other people's customs that are found in many travel 'relations'.[13] Covel was a classical scholar, but many other writers about travel were also eager to assert their classical authority: Bishop Joseph Hall, for example, writing anonymously, flags this up by describing himself on a title page as an 'English Mercury'.[14] Edward Leigh (a writer on travel though not himself a traveller) also alerts his readers on a title page to his credentials, citing Cicero's view in the *Tusculan Disputations* that the wise man has nothing to fear from exile: in this passage Cicero quotes Pacuvius (a second-century BCE playwright), who himself is quoting Aristophanes, to emphasise the idea that men are citizens of the world.[15] Exile was a fact of political life in the ancient world; a subgenre of philosophical writing, *consolatio*, aimed at assuaging the pain of the death of loved ones or of exile (itself seen as a kind of death) grew up.[16] Englishmen educated under a school curriculum in which Cicero played a prominent part would have been familiar with the idea that the wise person needs little, and that that little (i.e. knowledge) can be carried anywhere. They may also have known Seneca's *Ad Helviam*, which asserts that travellers take their virtues with them: writing about Caesar's rival Marcellus, Seneca reformulates Ovid's dictum more positively by stating that his change of place did not alter anything in his mind.[17]

The early Christian and mediaeval practice of pilgrimage is another important strand in the ancestry of travel, and a comparison can be drawn between pilgrims who mapped their spiritual journeys on to the physical landscape of the Holy Land and classically educated travellers who mapped their intellectual and cultural inheritance on to the topography of Greece. In each case they attached appropriate quotations, biblical or classical, to the sites they visited on their journeys. The word 'pilgrim' is not common in travel texts, probably because of its connotations of 'popery', but visiting sites in Greece was nevertheless a kind of secular pilgrimage for those with a love of the classics.[18]

The debate about travel and its purposes

During the seventeenth century, there was an ongoing debate about travel, its purposes, benefits and disadvantages, in which both travellers themselves and thinkers at home participated. The physical exploration of the wider world had been an important part of English life since the sixteenth century, and the first colony in the new world was founded in 1607. The accuracy of maps was increasing, and they were no longer simply representations of a world view in which Jerusalem was assumed to be at the centre, but were gradually relating more closely to the physical world.[19] The intellectual world was also in the process of change: books about geography and travel were increasingly popular. The first edition of Hakluyt's huge collection of travel accounts appeared in 1589, followed by his successor's *Purchas His Pilgrimage* in 1613. Peter Heylyn's historical–geographical work appeared in the third decade of the seventeenth century, going into many further editions. By the end of the century, a number of translations of continental travel accounts had been made into English.[20]

The development of Baconian inductive science played another crucial part in raising awareness of the possibilities of travel. Bacon himself, who had spent time in France in the 1570s, saw travel as an opportunity for education for the young and an experience for older people; he recognised the importance of learning languages ('else young men shall go hooded and look about little'), and of mixing with natives rather than with one's compatriots.[21] The precursor of the Royal Society, the Experimental Philosophy Club, was active in Wadham College, Oxford, from the late 1640s; when the Royal Society itself was formed, under the patronage of Charles II, with the purpose of 'study[ing] nature rather than Books', it began to issue instructions for travellers on what kinds of information to collect.[22] A new genre of writing, that of books of topographical and/or moral advice for travellers, began to appear, from Dallington (1605?), for example, through Palmer, Cleland, Greville, Essex, Neale, Howell and Blome to Leigh (1671).[23] Sometimes such works took the form of advice to a younger person, but they could also be much more formal. Palmer's, for instance, is set out as a series of tables in the style of family trees:[24] thus it was to be seen as a learning device that offered two parallel pathways to the student, the text itself and the physical routes to which the text acted as a guide.[25] Advice was also sometimes included in travel 'relations' and other works such as Peacham's *Complete Gentleman*; another work, Lewes Roberts's *Merchants Mappe of Commerce* (1638), incorporated an extraordinary mix of information[26] about different areas of the world, and was aimed at gentlemen and diplomats as well as merchants.

Alongside the many expressions of encouragement to travel abroad, there were also anti-travel arguments, and here religion became crucial to the debate, since the principal objection to travel was often the potential for corruption by 'papists'. One of the most vociferous of the anti-travel writers was Bishop Joseph Hall, whose view was that the only two legitimate excuses for travel were trade and business of state.[27] Even those who went to spas for their health, he alleged, risked having their souls poisoned by papistry without their bodies being cured.[28] However, the main targets of his diatribe were those 'that professe to seeke the glory of a perfect breeding, and the perfection of that, which we call Civilitie, in Travell'. On the contrary, he writes, they return 'empty of grace' and full of 'words, vanitie, mis-dispositions'.[29] It was to the 'Travell of curiosity' that he took greatest exception, mainly on the grounds that it was on the whole the young who undertook such journeys, and they might as easily learn evil as good: 'may not anything bee written upon a blanke?'[30] Young travellers were in danger of being introduced to 'Antichristianisme', since 'those parts which are only thought worth our viewing [i.e. the only parts thought worth viewing], are most contagious [i.e. Catholic]'.[31]

Hall thought that the English colleges abroad were skilled at enticing English travellers with a welcome that led to subtle attempts at conversion, starting with the easier doctrines and tailoring their arguments to their hearers: 'Doe we take pleasure to make them rich with the spoile of our soules, and because they will not come fast enough to fetch these booties, doe wee go to carry them unto their pillage'.

So the traveller must 'stop up his eares with waxe against these Syrens', because 'No fisher lets down an emptie hooke, but clothed with a proper and pleasing bait'.[32] In his view, there was nothing 'in all the knowne world, which mapps, and authors, cannot instruct a man in, as perfectly as his owne eyes'.[33] One of the reasons for his attitude was what he regarded as the perfection of England:

> The double praise which was of old given to two great nations, That *Italie* could not be put down for armes, nor *Greece* for learning, is happily met in one Iland. Doe we make a prison where God meant a Paradise?[34]

Perhaps it was easier for one who had never left England to be confident of the superiority of home than for those who saw the Ottoman Empire for themselves and had to recognise that it had some virtues. An anxiety about English society is manifest in some travellers' accounts but is entirely absent from Hall's work. That his ideas continued to carry weight years after his death in 1656 is shown by the publication in 1674 of a single sheet listing his 56 precepts against the travel of curiosity.[35]

Henry Peacham, employed by the Earl of Arundel (who was responsible for bringing many antique marbles to England) as tutor to his children, looks from a slightly different perspective when he reminds his readers that the antiquarian riches of England make foreign travel less crucial:

> our English travellers in foreign countries [...] curious in the observation and search of the most memorable things and monuments of other places, can say [...] nothing of their own, our country of England being no whit inferior to any other in the world for matter of antiquity and rarities of every kind.[36]

INTRODUCTION 9

This reflects the antiquarian activity, stemming from the work of Camden, Cotton, Selden and others, in England at the time, which took the forms of both investigations on the ground and the gathering of objects into cabinets of curiosities.[37]

Even the apologists for travel found it necessary to address the religious argument. Thomas Fuller, a popular collector of apothegms, writing during the Civil War, linked religion and climate (as indeed Hall had done) when he advised the traveller to be 'well settled in thine own Religion, lest, travelling out of England into Spain, thou goest out of God's blessing into the warme Sunne'.[38] Peacham too reminds the traveller to be constant, like a compass, to his own religion.[39] Fuller in any case thought that no one should venture beyond the Alps, quoting with approval Ascham's comment that in nine days in Venice he found 'more liberty to sinne, then in London he ever heard of in nine years'. At least, however, Fuller did see a positive purpose to travel, with his recommendation to 'Labour to distill and write into thy self the scattered perfections of several Nations'.[40]

In fact, the pro-travel writers could list numerous advantages to be gained from it. In the first place, it was crucial for trade and diplomacy,[41] and Covel as well as Rycaut, Dudley North, Finch, Thomas Smith and John Luke all worked for the Levant Company. Men went to the Ottoman Empire not just for personal reasons but also to benefit their country, both by carrying on open commercial and diplomatic activities and by spying. They expected to be better equipped by their activities abroad to fulfil roles in public life when they came home.[42]

However, the argument most frequently emphasised by both the pro-travel writers and the travellers themselves was that nothing could be compared to experience. Travel contributed to a man's education,[43] it delighted his senses,[44] it taught him civility,[45] it satisfied his curiosity about the world beyond his native shores. People were anxious to see the world with their own eyes, not just to read about it in books. According to James Howell, whose practical guide appeared in the 1640s, and who added a section on Turkey to a later edition, travel was the true 'Peripatetique School'.[46] He thought that islanders were the very people most in need of travelling, though he presumed that he was writing for an audience of men who had studied religion at university and would therefore be unshakeable in their faith. Howell, like Bacon, stressed the importance of learning languages and mixing with local people. Travellers must observe, listen (it is better to 'go fifty miles to heare a wise man than five to see a faire Citty') and reflect (because 'by seeing and perusing the volume of the Great World, one learne[s] to know the little [i.e. oneself]'). He countered the religious anti-travel argument by saying that the purpose of travelling to Turkey was to understand the errors of Christianity's greatest enemy.[47]

Heylyn demonstrates the educational value ascribed to travel in his dedication to Prince Charles: 'Those parts which other Princes have visited onely in a Map, you have honoured with your owne survey, and seene more than they have read'.[48] Evans has shown how the enforced exile of Charles II was 'spun' after the Restoration as a kind of grand tour designed to fit him for monarchy.[49] Travel in books and physical travel were seen as complementary by several writers: according to Essex, for example, men of action need to study the real world as well as books.[50] Phrases such as 'eye-witness' crop up constantly, an emphasis that has obvious links with the new inductive science. Wheler stressed his 'ocular observations', Rycaut wrote that he saw the seven churches of Asia 'with [his] own eyes', and Ellis Veryard, a doctor, emphasised the need to see things; the latter, however, envisaged travellers as actors in the theatre of the world, which suggests that there is not always a simple contrast between books and 'reality'.[51] For Lassels, the world was itself a book, which travellers might read.[52]

Another motive that is expressed over and over again by travellers is curiosity. Thomas Coryate had a 'burning desire' to see the world, though he was surprised by how far his curiosity eventually took him, that is to India;[53] it was curiosity which led Wheler, whose wish to travel dated from his teenage years, to 'hobble [...] over broken stones, decayed buildings, and old rubbish';[54] and Covel described his 'Meer curiosity of learning some things abroad' about which he thought there was 'but a slight account at home'.[55]

INTRODUCTION   11

This is not to say that the dangers and hardships of travel were not recognised: Lassels thought that it taught toughness as well as wisdom and humility,[56] and Neale wrote that its purpose was to harden the body and improve the mind.[57] Edward Browne, as a way of placating his father, Sir Thomas, who did not altogether approve, confessed his 'rashnesse and obstinate folly' in undertaking his journey.[58] Veryard began to think his curiosity 'dear-bought' when he was under threat of being captured and sold into slavery.[59] Lord Winchilsea, Daniel Harvey's[60] predecessor as ambassador and a cousin of John Finch, beset by homesickness, expressed envy of anyone who had the opportunity to travel to study in the book of the world, but was nevertheless personally glad to be leaving Constantinople with its plague, earthquakes, loneliness, fires, avanias (trade agreements), indecency of religion, pride of the residents, thieving servants, cheating dragomans, impertinent Turks and stupid Greeks.[61]

Several other motives for travel should also be mentioned. Whatever Christians thought about Islam, they were generally, except in the case of Quakers, wary of attempts to convert Muslims. But many showed an interest in Islam, and in the varieties of Christianity which were to be found in the area: Covel had been deputed by a group of Anglican divines to research the beliefs of the Orthodox Church.[62] The collection of antiquities and manuscripts was the prime reason for some journeys, for example those of Edward Pococke and John Greaves in the 1630s, and Covel was not alone in collecting in a modest way, and in making a record of classical inscriptions wherever he had the opportunity. Several travellers, again including Covel, had a strong interest in natural science, particularly botany: Wheler's book is full of enthusiastic accounts of his 'simpling' activities, with drawings.[63] Of course it is also true that Covel and other employees of the Levant Company went to the Ottoman Empire to take up salaried posts, not just to enjoy travelling.

John Covel and his diaries

In this book, I have chosen to focus particularly on John Covel. Covel was born in 1638 near Bury St Edmunds in Suffolk, and educated at the grammar school there before going on to Christ's College, Cambridge, where he was later elected to a fellowship; he continued to hold his fellowship during his years in Constantinople in the 1670s.[64] On his return from the Levant he briefly held livings in Essex and Leicestershire, was chaplain to the princess of Orange in the Hague for a few years, and, briefly again, was chancellor of York. In 1688 he returned to Cambridge, where he spent the rest of his long life, serving as Master of Christ's (and for two spells as vice-chancellor) from then until his death in 1722.[65]

As an example of a traveller to the Greek world, Covel is both typical and distinctive. He belongs among a group of scholarly travellers, men with a classical education behind them who were often particularly interested in the Greek Church and in seeking out and assiduously recording ancient remains, men who were collectors not on a grand scale but in a modest way, often acquiring coins or manuscripts, as well as transcribing inscriptions. Luke and Pococke, like Covel, went on to have subsequent academic careers. Others, such as Greaves, Rycaut, Francis Vernon and to some extent Wheler, can be linked with this group in terms of their scholarly and antiquarian interests. Unlike all of these except Vernon, who died abroad, Covel published nothing until over 40 years after his return from the Ottoman Empire, but the manuscript accounts we are left with have an informality that give them a particular character, as well as providing an immense amount of detail about his life and travels in the empire.

A traveller and writer from earlier in the century, George Sandys, described his 'doubled travels; once with some toyle and danger performed, and now recorded with sincerity and diligence'.[66] There is always, to a greater or lesser extent, a gap between the experience itself and the written account of it. Covel's experience is mainly recorded in his diaries, which were never published (though he intended to publish them, and we do not know why he never did):[67] this means that they lack polish, and tend to ramble, but have the advantage of a greater immediacy. Other extant manuscripts include letters both to and from him, a commonplace book, and a list of the contents of his library towards the end of his life.[68] The only book he ever published was his voluminous work on the history and doctrine of the Greek Orthodox Church, which appeared in 1722, the year of his death, when he was in his eighties.[69]

The diaries not only give us a uniquely detailed picture of the kind of life he led in the Ottoman Empire in the 1670s, but also paint an intimate portrait of the man and his interests. The longest of the three volumes[70] consists of nearly 400 closely written folios, with sketches, maps, diagrams and copies of inscriptions. Some sections are numbered in Covel's own hand, but the volume was bound and the pages renumbered in 1875. There are differences in paper quality and size in the different sections. Some maps, drawings and pages cut from printed books have been bound in, and some pages are written in other hands. In many places, Greek and Latin quotations, sometimes with line references, have been added, either in the margins or in gaps left in the text; while some of these were probably added later, when Covel had access to a more extensive library, others may have been written in at the same time as the rest of the text, since they fill the spaces left for them so neatly. The fact that mistakes appear in some of the quotations and attributions[71] suggests that in those cases Covel was relying on his memory. Some sections are in note form: for example, notes on Ephesus (which are crossed through) look as if they have been jotted down on the spot for writing up later.[72] One section has been divided into numbered chapters by Covel himself,[73] apparently with a view to publication. Another section appears to have been written in the form of an extended letter to an unnamed friend,[74] probably his Christ's College friend Robert Huckle (although there is only occasional evidence of the paper having been folded as a letter would have been); this is suggested by his reference to 'our chappel',[75] for example, and by his words at the end of the section: 'I cannot read these papers over to correct them, you are my Freind for your sake I have scribbled them a full Gallop'.[76] In places the ink has run so badly that the hand is no longer legible.

This volume includes Covel's account of his journey from England to Constantinople, his account of some of the many trips he took while he was there, his description of the court ceremonies he witnessed in Adrianople, his description of Constantinople itself (based on other such descriptions), part of his account of Mount Athos, and an account of his time in Italy on his way home. The other two volumes of his diaries[77] cover the rest of his account of Mount Athos, his trip to Nicaea and his journey home to England. Although the diaries are not organised or polished in the way that they would have been for publication, they have much in common with contemporary published travel writing, which developed over the course of the seventeenth century not as a homogeneous genre but in different forms, sometimes closer to fiction than to fact, and with an emphasis on information or entertainment in varying proportions.[78] Particularly when the remains of the classical world are under observation, fact and fiction, or history and myth, are not distinct, but overlie each other: as Henry Blount wrote of the ruins of Troy, 'so hath that famed *Towne* now put on *immortalitie*, having no *existence* but in *Poetry*: whose fictions by complying with the fancy of man, uphold themselves beyond the *Realitie* of their *Subject*'.[79]

Writing up one's journey was part of what MacLean has called 'doing-being' English.[80] The writer uses the process of writing it down as a way of fixing his (in most cases) own identity.[81] Blount (writing at the beginning of the century) is an interesting example of the complexities involved here. He valued the fact that he travelled as the only Christian in a group for two reasons: that the 'errors' of other Christians could not 'draw either hatred, or engagement' from him – that is, that he could not be held responsible for anything anyone else might say about Christianity – and that it allowed him freedom to answer questions in his own way.[82] This line of argument suggests that, for his own clarity of mind, it was important for him not to depend on any kind of group identity. On another occasion during his travels Blount was deliberately obfuscatory about who he was, pretending – to a Turk who virulently attacked the English – that he was a Scot, 'a name unknown to them'. He excuses this to his readers, to whom, he assumes, the appellation 'Scot' is familiar, as being not a 'quitting of my Countrey, but rather a *retreat* from one corner to the other'. When questioned further by the Turk, he tells him the truth, but speaks 'in the old obsolete Greeke, and Latine titles, which was as darke to them as a discourse of Isis and Osyris'.[83] In this way he builds up his identity both by dissembling to Turks[84] and by assuming a shared understanding with his readers.

Travel writing seems to have been very popular with readers: Blount's work, for example, went through some six editions in the 35 years after it was published.[85] Many accounts of travel, as well as works of history, geography, languages and antiquities, are found in the handlist of Covel's library which was compiled a few years before his death.[86] The range of types of published travel writing was wide: 'relations',[87] which themselves varied from the relatively straightforward to elaborate literary constructs such as that by Sandys;[88] works such as Rycaut's which took the long historical view and were overtly educational and moral;[89] more polemical works with a religious or political slant;[90] practical guides for merchants; Coryate's works designed partly to achieve a social position at home; and even Kenelm Digby's fantasy novel, based on his courtship and marriage.[91] As evidence for what it felt like to be English in the Ottoman Empire in this period there are also unpublished sources, including Covel's diaries and letters, official letters such as John Finch's ambassadorial reports, and other private letters. Although this book concentrates on the post-Restoration period, I have drawn on sources from the earlier Stuart era and the Commonwealth as well.

While Covel's own diaries are relatively straightforward, it is still necessary to bear in mind the gap between the person and his persona as projected in writing.[92] Authors situate themselves differently in their texts: William Biddulph, for example, an earlier Levant Company chaplain, hid behind the invented 'Theophilus Lavender' as a way of feigning modesty and reluctance to publish, and in order to be able to make accusations against another traveller without appearing to do so from personal animosity.[93] Coryate deliberately presented himself as a buffoon, though an adventurous one, using self-mockery both to amuse his readers and, as a country boy, to achieve a place among the London wits.[94] This is reinforced by a picture of himself seated on an elephant which he uses on his title-page. The extraordinary achievement of walking most of the way from England to India is treated as a picaresque adventure.[95] William Lithgow also uses illustrations to create the image of the traveller avid for experience and willing to suffer for it: on his frontispiece he stands proudly wearing Turkish dress, including a huge turban, surrounded by Trojan ruins; elsewhere we see him bound to a tree by robbers, and chained while awaiting interrogation.[96] Both Coryate and Lithgow belie Chard's assertion that the idea that the 'traveller will experience travel as an exciting and dangerous adventure of the self' only appears at the end of the eighteenth century.[97]

With any travel writer, the question of veracity arises: is this author a person who can be believed? Or is he what Adams has called a 'travel liar'?[98] It is not easy to make this judgement on objective grounds: Covel comes across as a reasonable observer, but he certainly had his own agendas, as will be clear when I come to discuss his attitude to Greeks in particular. Like all of us, he was a person of his time: although there are moments when the reader of his diaries may feel that he is our contemporary – when he describes experiences and expresses feelings similar to ours – at other times he can seem immensely remote. However, much of the evidence he provides for the way of life of a foreigner in Ottoman Constantinople is corroborated by other sources, such as the writings of Finch, Winchilsea, Rycaut and Wheler. It should also be remembered here that what we would call 'plagiarism' was to some degree at least acceptable in the seventeenth century. As Yerasimos has suggested, successive travellers went through a process of tracing on the ground the steps that they had already taken in their heads through their reading, with the result that many texts repeat descriptions of sites in the same or similar terms.[99] In the words of Hemmerdinger Iliadou:

> It should be understood that the use of these texts poses various problems [...] One must be extremely careful in using the information provided by these accounts, as well as making a range of comparative studies, which are the only means of distinguishing between what is true and noteworthy and what

is legend, folklore or a product of the imagination. These accounts are frequently either compilations or simple copies of earlier sources which served as guides.[100]

In the case of Covel, much of his diary consists of notes made at sites which he visited, and he is often at great pains to stress that the opinions he puts forward are just that – his personal opinions; however, the reader does need to be aware of the way in which his anti-Catholic bias coloured much of what he wrote. The complexities of his attitude to Greeks and to Greek orthodoxy will be discussed later.

One intriguing aspect of Covel's diary should be mentioned here: some 20 short sections (usually not more than a sentence long, sometimes only a phrase)[101] are written in code. The code is based on one symbol per letter of the alphabet, plus a single symbol for 'and' and the Greek letter alpha for the indefinite article. Covel also uses crescent symbols, singly or in pairs. Some, at least, of the symbols appear to be based on a Masonic alphabet. The words are written continuously; the letters in each word are in reverse order, and the breaks in words are indicated by a dot inside the symbol that represents the final letter. It would have been cumbersome to write, hence the short passages. After I had (with help[102]) worked on deciphering the code, I discovered that this had already been done by J-P. Grélois in his edition of part of Covel's diary.[103] I agree with most of his transcriptions, with a few small changes (Covel was quite careless in his use of the code, and it is not always possible to decipher every word). However, I think he is wrong about the meaning of the crescent symbol, which he transcribes as 'the Turks'. This is obviously logical, but it does not take into account the fact that Covel sometimes uses a single crescent and sometimes a pair. In addition, although 'the Turks' fits with the pieces of code which Grélois transcribes, there are other sections where it does not fit. I think myself that the symbol stands for 'my Lord(s)', and refers to Sir John Finch, the ambassador, and his companion Sir Thomas Baines (both, like Covel, graduates of Christ's). For example, in a description of Baines's discussion with the mufti comes the following passage:

'THE DRUGERMAN SAIES NO SUCH MATTER HE SWORE TO ME HE DURST NOT FOR HIS HEAD SPEAKE MANNY THINKS [i.e. THINGS] WHICH [CRESCENT] BID HIM TO'.[104] This is confirmed by the fact that 'the Turks' is spelt out in other coded sentences, for example 'WE HAD BEEN MAD TO MENTION BUSINES AT FIRST VIEW [CRESCENT] BEGAN TO TALK AL[L] IN ITALIAN THE DRAGERMAN ADJURED [CRESCENT] TO SPEAK ENGLISH MANY TURKS UNDERSTAND ITALIAN IT HAD NOT BEEN SAFE'.[105] The words 'my Lord' or 'ambassador' are never spelt out.

The contents of the coded passages are generally quite unexceptionable, apart from some mildly uncomplimentary remarks about (I suggest) the ambassador. As this part of the diary appears to have been written with a particular (unnamed) friend in mind, I wonder whether the code may be something the two had invented, perhaps when they were students, and used for fun. This is confirmed by the existence of a letter, signed simply with the initials 'R. H.', written from Christ's to Covel in Constantinople on 18 December 1674.[106] On the back of the letter, in Covel's hand, the name 'Huckle' appears. The evidence suggests that this is Robert Huckle, who matriculated at Christ's in 1656 (two years after Covel) and was later Burrell lecturer in rhetoric: the initials with which the letter is signed are clearly in the same hand as Huckle's signature in the university's subscription book.[107] The letter itself, which is mainly about college and university business and gossip, includes several passages in the same code. One such piece reads: 'AM VERY SORRY TO FIND SUCH A CHARACTER OF [CRESCENT] WHOM I TOOK TO BE A GENEROUS PERSON', which appears to refer to Finch. It seems that relations between Covel and his boss were not always of the warmest kind, although when Covel left Turkey Finch made him a generous present of money to buy books in Italy.[108]

There is one aspect of Covel's life in Constantinople that receives surprisingly little attention in his diaries, and that is his work as a chaplain.[109] Apart from a reference to prayers and a sermon on the morning of the departure of the ambassador and his retinue for Adrianople,[110] where the Sultan was holding his court, we hear almost nothing about his professional duties, although his contemporary Vernon records hearing a sermon by Covel on the subject 'we shall have sorrow in this world'.[111] There is little evidence of the kind of pastoral work undertaken by his predecessor Thomas Smith, who visited the Seven Towers prison to give communion to Protestant prisoners,[112] although Covel's letters suggest that later in his life his pastoral care for students at Christ's was valued: there is an exchange of letters between him and Wheler about Wheler's third son, who was being educated at the college.[113] From other letters, however, we get an idea of some of the administrative difficulties Covel was obliged to sort out in connection with the death of his first ambassador, Daniel Harvey.[114] There was a gap of 16 months between Harvey's death and the arrival of his successor John Finch,[115] during which Covel records no trips away from the city. After Covel's return to England, Finch's companion Baines wrote to him to ask for help in finding a secretary for the embassy, perhaps implying that Covel's administrative skills were missed: in Baines's words, life has been 'vexatious, stormy & troublesome. It hath bin Intractabile Coelum, No Anchor, No Cable, would hold, No Sayl could be manag'd'.[116] The diplomatic problems of dealing with the Porte are confirmed by Rycaut.[117]

It may have been precisely because his official duties were not usually so onerous that Covel was able at other times to indulge his taste for trips away, one of which, to Prusa/Bursa, he himself describes as a 'frolic'.[118] In his own words:

> I will see Nice [Nicaea], Nicomedia, Cyzico, Mount Athos, Lemnos, Lesbos, Chios and what else lyes in my way before I leave ye countrey [...] from hence to Aleppo, and all about Ancyra, and on ye other side in Caria &c, are the stateliest things in the world, and in very great numbers; he that thinkes them worth his labour and expence and hazard let him go fetch them, yet I confesse I have an itching after them.[119]

During his seven years in the chaplaincy, he did in fact manage to see many of these places, leaving descriptions that are fascinating for the breadth of his interests and the amount of detail that he includes. His curiosity about people, antiquities, language, customs, plants and many other things makes him a uniquely valuable witness to the world in which he moved during this period of his life. With the honourable exceptions of Leedham-Green and Grélois, modern scholars have not given him the attention he deserves, perhaps partly because of the unwieldy nature of the material, and perhaps also because his subsequent life lacks the measurable achievements that might have been expected of a young man of such apparent promise. He is a particularly fruitful subject for the investigation of how a traveller's mental furniture both influences and is influenced by the experiences that travel provides, and specifically because his writings offer us an insight into the ways in which he knitted together his deep love and knowledge of the classics with the Protestant Christianity of which he seems to have been a sincere and faithful adherent.[120]

Covel's diaries also tell us something about the character of the man himself. His enormous curiosity about all sorts of subjects was combined with a nostalgia for home demonstrated by frequent references to and comparisons with the landscapes and buildings of his native East Anglia.[121] Perhaps in doing this he was also reassuring himself by using his memories of home to anchor the emotions he was experiencing in a strange world. His interests included history, antiquities, language, botany and the Church, as well as medicine and music. As regards theology, he had been commissioned by a group of Anglican divines to look into the question of whether the Greek Orthodox Church believed in the doctrine of transubstantiation, and right at the end of his life he produced a rambling and unwieldy volume on this subject that even his friend Wheler thought was of less value than it would have been had it appeared 30 years earlier. A less charitable comment was that an abridgement might have been of some use.[122] Covel's own excuse for the delay was the pressure of college business,[123] but perhaps he had too many interests to be able to focus on any single one. Another question that arises is why the book was eventually published, so long after the research on which it is based was done. The explanation for this may have something to do with the non-jurors, who continued to hope until well into the eighteenth century that a union between the two Churches might take place. Negotiations were carried on during the second decade of the eighteenth century, but foundered on the issue of transubstantiation, and it may be that Covel (not a non-juror) published his book in that context.[124] Whatever the fortunes of the book, Covel's concern for the Greek Church – a concern shared by his contemporaries Smith and Rycaut – is demonstrated by his journeys to the sites of the seven churches of Asia, and in particular also to Mount Athos, which he was probably the first Englishman to visit,[125] as well as by many comments in his diary.

It is impossible to know much about Covel's personal religion. He was probably at the more liberal end of the Anglican spectrum, influenced by having spent some of his formative years in the milieu of Henry More, the Cambridge Platonist, at Christ's.[126] There are moments in the diary when he adopts a more introspective tone or when the reader catches a glimpse of personal feeling, for example when he imagines a Turkish khan as the scene of Christ's nativity,[127] or when he thanks God for preserving him from many dangers.[128] During his visit to Rome en route to England at the end of his chaplaincy, he was disturbed to hear a rumour, which he thought could not refer to anyone but him, that an English minister had converted to Catholicism; this he fiercely refuted in a letter to the English consul in Naples, in which he avers 'my own integrity and constancy in my faith and Religion': he is 'immoveably, a true Son of the protestant church' in which he was bred and hoped to die, and utterly opposed to some Catholic doctrines.[129] His dislike of Catholicism runs right through his book on the Greek Church. There is no doubt that he was fascinated by other sects and religions, though Games's phrase 'Covel's ecumenism' is perhaps overstating the case.[130] Entering a church in Malaga on his way east, he records being asked whether he was not afraid to go into an 'Idol Temple'; his reply was that idols were nothing to him: 'God the searcher of hearts knowes, that I do not do it to joyn in their way of worship, but onely to se[e] it and be the better able to discourse of it as an eye witnesse'.[131] He also wrote that if he was in the Indies he would want to go into such idol temples, in order to see them with his own eyes.[132]

One characteristic that horrifies our modern sensibilities, though in this he is a man of his time, is his attitude to Jews. Writing of his visit with the ambassador to Adrianople, he implied that Jews were not even human beings:

> The house we first were allotted, was ye damnedest confounded place that ever mortall man was put into. It was a jewes house, not half big enough to hold half my Ld's family, a meer nest of fleas and cimici [bugs], and rats and mice, and stench surrounded with whole kennels of nasty beastly Jewes.

One end of the town had no decent houses, 'being all Jewes, crouded two or three families into a house that hath not more roomes':

> If the old Jewes were such poisonous beasts I must needs allow their frequent washings, and think they needed not touch a dead body to be unclean, for they could not touch a living one without being so.[133]

It is evidence of deeply ingrained prejudice that whereas, as will be seen, Turks are praised for their cleanliness, Jewish washing is seen as an indication of unnatural dirtiness. Yet there is ambivalence too: Covel himself, waiting for the departure of the ship that was taking him away from Constantinople on his return home, wrote a sympathetic account of a heterodox Jewish sect among whom he had a 'particular acquaintance' in a letter to his colleague at Christ's, Henry More. It is almost as if he was only able to sympathise with them because they were at variance with orthodox Jews. One of the aspects he stressed was their greater willingness to eat with Christians.[134]

Covel's breadth of interest is attested to by the range of subjects covered in the library that he had built up by the end of his life.[135] He was a skilled linguist, in later years corresponding with other scholars in French, Italian, Latin and contemporary Greek.[136] Although, on the evidence of the diaries, he may not have been able to write Turkish, unlike Luke, whose diaries are peppered with words and phrases in Arabic script,[137] he probably did learn to speak it: in one letter he mentions the ease of learning both Turkish and 'vulgar' Greek.[138] His interest in the latter was not merely practical: on one page of his diary he lists, with a diagram, the Greek names for the parts of a ship.[139] He was fascinated by the pronunciation of Greek, which was a live issue in English education,[140] and by etymology, regretting that he did not have the work of John Cheke, the sixteenth-century Hellenist, to hand to help him in this. A friend eventually procured this work for him, though there is no record that it arrived in Constantinople.[141] On the island of Lemnos, he came across salt-making, which led him into a digression about the etymology of the Greek word ἀυγαρυοὶ (Covel's spelling).[142]

Apart from languages and antiquities, Covel was also a keen botanist and had a serious interest in medicine and in geology. The first pages of his diary are full of the geological observations he made on the English coast when the ship taking him to the Levant was delayed while the captain waited for a fair wind.[143] It has been suggested that he may originally have intended to study medicine, but I have found no independent evidence for this.[144] On Chios he helped a sick woman, creating a queue of potential patients;[145] he certainly had some knowledge of drugs, as is demonstrated by a letter he wrote in April 1674, asking for supplies of medicine for the treatment of plague.[146] When his friend John Cary died, he kept a daily record of the progress of the illness over the 13 days of its duration that reads more like a doctor's case notes than the reflections of a friend or spiritual advisor.[147] In a village on the coast of the Sea of Marmara he dissected a shark, thinking it might be pregnant but finding that this was not the case.[148] When the customs officials rifled through his trunks after his arrival in Constantinople, the only book to go missing was a medical one, which he had replaced in his library by the end of his life.[149] His love of plants was shared with Wheler: at Mount Olympus near Prusa/Bursa, Wheler writes, 'the Mountain was almost covered with curious Plants; which made

Dr *Covel*, who is a great Lover of them, as well as my self, long to go and ransack it'.[150] Because their stay in the area was prolonged by Cary's illness, they were able to do as they wished. Covel's commonplace book provides further evidence of his scientific interests.[151] Both in these fields and in the field of antiquities, he was always careful not to claim certainty: 'all this is but an Hypothesis or *meer Guess* still; and only *a Probability* at last is the very height of all that the wisest Naturalist [...] can arrive at'.[152]

He was anxious to give the investigation of antiquities the time he felt it deserved, and was frequently irritated by the haste of his companions: the phrase 'the hurry we were in' is scribbled across one page of archaeological notes, without any context. At Ephesus, he constantly felt that he was being hurried by his companions: 'the strange importunity of our Company (which were ever in hast) hinder'd us from finding any certain *Ichnography* [ground plan] [of one ruined building]', and there are other such comments.[153]

Given his breadth of knowledge, it is perhaps surprising that Covel's concrete achievements, at least as far as we can tell from the evidence we have today, do not reflect his apparent knowledge and abilities. Even in his own day he was something of a footnote, dining out on the reputation of his glory days in the east: Evelyn records in his diary for 23 November 1695 that he had dined with 'the great oriental traveller' John Covel. His contemporaries were not impressed with his one published work. He seems to have been overwhelmed by college business, and there was a rather querulous correspondence between him and Humfrey Wanley (librarian to Lord Harley), about ten years before Covel's death, about the possible sale of Covel's collection of manuscripts.[154] He had put together a substantial library of some 3,000 items, some of which were auctioned after his death.[155] The information that he gathered from his visit to the monasteries of Mount Athos is invaluable for our knowledge of the Holy Mountain at that date; Covel expanded and in some cases corrected the account given by Pierre Belon in his work of 1554, as well as providing the basis for Rycaut's later description.[156]

Covel was not a man to wear his learning lightly, rarely using one word when ten would do, and conscious of his status as a man of the cloth. On Chios, he grew a beard and dressed in black, thereby gaining the respect of the people, presumably because he looked like a Greek priest.[157] He was extremely irritated to be excluded from Finch's audience with the Sultan at Adrianople, in spite of having been promised that he would be of the party.[158] In the case of a social superior such as the French ambassador to the Porte, the Marquis de Nointel, his dislike of Catholicism seems not to have impeded their friendship: the two of them discussed religion as well as antiquities. Covel writes of de Nointel, 'I shall not blame him for shewing his Zeal for his Religion, for he would always candidly give me leave, civilly and freely to defend my own.'[159] However, although Covel could be both pedantic and snobbish, he also had many attractive qualities. One of these seems to have been physical bravery: in his letter about plague remedies, he states that he 'was not at all afraid' when surrounded by the sickness,[160] while on one of his journeys he and his servant took a detour away from the main party, causing the rest some anxiety: 'I could persuade no man to accompany me, fear of theives and a calf with a white face disheartened them all; away went my man and I'.[161] On the voyage out, when an encounter with hostile ships was in prospect, the captain suggested that Covel go below for safety, but he replied that he could pray as earnestly on deck as below; the captain told him his behaviour was a great encouragement to the sailors.[162]

He was not without a sense of humour, even about himself, writing to his unnamed friend in Cambridge, in connection with a learned exposition about maps and their faults, 'You se[e] how parsonlike I write to you'.[163] In Cyzicus, searching for a spring mentioned in Pliny that was said to cure the pangs of love, he found two possible candidates: 'I drank of both to see if I might find ye cure mention'd in Pliny wrought upon myself: perhaps neither is [the right one].'[164] He also had a taste for scatological humour: he was amused by the identification of little hillocks on the road to Adrianople as marking places where the Sultan had 'eased himself [...] in plain english pist'.[165]

One striking quality is Covel's humanity. Hearing of a Turkish soldier executed for a sexual misdemeanour, he writes, 'his good service in ye Field of Mars might have interceded for one Spasso in ye Courts of Venus',[166] and a later stage of his career, when he was chaplain to the Princess of Orange in the Hague, was abruptly terminated because of an unguarded letter he wrote about the Prince's unkindness to his wife.[167] In Malaga, on his journey out to Turkey, he came across a convent where women could leave their babies without identifying themselves, on which he comments: 'though at first thought they may indeed seem a kind of encouragement for lewd persons to commit wickednesse; yet, undoubtedly, they save the lives of many poor innocent Babes'.[168] Another Levant Company chaplain had less sympathy: Charles Robson, finding that brothels were lawful in Pisa, thought it would not be surprising if 'all our [...] drunkards and whoremasters' were to convert to Catholicism, because any bastards would be cared for.[169] Covel recognised that marriage between non-Christians need not be any less loving and faithful than that between Christians.[170] One of his contemporaries, Isaac Milles, wrote that Covel 'had the repute of one of the gentilest, and best-temper'd, and most obliging Youths he had ever heard of. And being a little acquainted with him, he found him such'.[171]

In the field of religion, he was less judgemental than many: in spite of his views on Jews and Catholics, he stated unequivocally that behaviour mattered more than belief, and that it is only God who knows whether a person is good.[172] Inward and spiritual worship matters more than any outward signs, and Jews and Turks 'Believe and Worship, the same God, *the Father*, as well as we.'[173] He agreed with Erasmus that the only way for Christians to convert Muslims was by their lives, not by arms – and perhaps, though he does not say this explicitly, not by doctrine.[174]

Covel was also well-disposed to animals, having a dog in Constantinople, about which he recorded that during an earthquake he 'trembled and came and lay [by him]'.[175] In his book on the Greek Church, he discusses how dogs show their joy when they see their masters, and concludes that the Greek word for 'worship' may be etymologically linked to the word for 'dog'.[176] He was distressed by cruelty to horses – a contrast to North's story of cutting up a dog with a scimitar, and indeed to some of the experiments conducted by fellows of the Royal Society in its early years.[177]

As far as relationships within expatriate society go, Rycaut records his debt to Covel for providing him with information about Mount Athos, and a letter from Rycaut is filed by Covel under the label 'particular freinds'.[178] After his return to England Covel kept up his friendship with Wheler, who shared his botanical as well as his archaeological interests, corresponding with him when Wheler's third son Granville was a student at Christ's and Covel was master there. One of Wheler's letters is addressed to 'Revd. Sr. & Dear Hellen. Traveller'. After Covel's return from Turkey he corresponded with Wheler's companion Spon, whom he had tried to visit in Lyon on his way home, only to find that he was absent.[179] Covel's friendships with North and with John Finch were perhaps rather more ambivalent. Covel and his friend 'R. H.' are both mildly critical of Finch (in code),[180] and criticism of Covel's behaviour is implied in the biography of North.[181] There may also have been tension between Covel and North over arrangements after the death of Daniel Harvey.[182] Finch's companion Baines, however, wrote warmly to Covel in 1679, and Finch himself made Covel a generous present of money on the latter's departure from Constantinople. This was to be spent on books, in which Covel was to write that they were a gift from Finch.[183]

There is another question that arises in connection with Covel's attitude to Finch and Baines that, given our contemporary attitudes to and understanding of homosexuality, is probably impossible to answer, although it has been sensibly and sensitively written about by Bray and others.[184] From the vantage point of today, Finch and Baines certainly look like a gay couple. That they were accepted as in some sense a couple is clear, particularly from their correspondence, although Winchilsea wrote sarcastically to his cousin Finch about a 'wanton marriage' between two women.[185] North referred to the time when 'Sir John Finch (and, as must be understood, Sir Thomas Baines)' was ambassador.[186] That the two men saw themselves as inseparable is obvious both from Finch's dedication of the notebook he kept after Baines's death[187] and from the marital imagery of their joint tomb in the chapel at Christ's. They should probably also be seen as belonging in the mediaeval tradition of chivalry, which had not yet completely disappeared in the seventeenth century. While we have to remember that buggery was illegal (and Covel explicitly expresses his disgust at it),[188] we cannot make any judgement about whether this particular relationship was sexually expressed. Close male friendships could be emotionally significant, and might also involve physical expressions of affection.[189] However, it is just possible that the slight ambivalence of Covel towards Finch, detectable in his coded remarks, has something to do with Finch's relationship with Baines.

As a fellow of Christ's, Covel was required to be celibate, but he clearly found women attractive. He admired the Chiot women, with their 'great lovely black eyes', who were both 'familiar' and 'courteous', as well as more 'freely merry with strangers' than others were. Although most of them were 'extream modest', some girls were accustomed to sit spinning at their open windows, letting their spindles swing out into the street so as to 'play with any wanton that passe by and offer to catch it'.[190] It was also on Chios that Covel was invited to a wedding party, where he sat cross-legged beside the papas until 'a peevish cur that had a handsome wife rose up and made his wife rise and said he would not stay if [they did]'. Covel tactfully went back to bed until summoned again, to be told that 'ye coxcomb yt [that] began ye embroil was gone'.[191] There is no suggestion of impropriety on Covel's part, but he obviously noticed pretty women, and was not always completely candid in his diary: in Adrianople in a neighbouring garden he caught sight of 'a couple of very lovely women' in the care of 'one poor silly old man': '[They] ramp and play the rogue like little sprites; but more of that between ourselves'.[192] The death from plague of the daughter of his Adrianople landlady, with whom he used to 'prattle', saddened him deeply.[193] On the other hand, he was not above having suspicions of others, as when he saw a good-looking young woman talking to a 'lusty' young monk: when Covel came on the scene, the pair vanished, and he was told, but by implication did not believe, that she had been making her confession.[194]

Like other travellers, Covel stressed the importance of seeing with his own eyes.[195] A general tendency to be critical of religious superstition (Catholic, Orthodox or Muslim) can exist alongside ambivalence or credulousness, sometimes even in the same person. Myths were repeated from one writer to the next: Lithgow, Sandys, Thomas Gainsford (one of Ambassador Glover's retinue in the first decade of the century) and Veryard all tell a story about 900 camels removing the pieces of the Colossus of Rhodes;[196] a tale about a dragon skin with the entire works of Homer written on it occurs in Biddulph and Sandys.[197] It was not always the best-educated men who avoided credulity: for John Finch the fact that one of his teeth fell out a few days before Baines's death confirmed him in his belief that the loss of a tooth presages the death of a friend.[198]

In Covel we find both ambivalence and irony, illustrated by his reference (already mentioned) to Pliny's *fons cupidinis*, his attitude to which seems a bit like some present-day attitudes to horoscopes, mocking but not entirely dismissive; at times he could be sceptical, at others credulous. He was capable of scorn, thinking, for example, that the Ragusan ambassador had been taken in by two Jewish women who alleged that they could identify a thief by suspending a key over an Old Testament open at Psalm 51.[199] On the other hand, he seems to have believed that some Tokay grapes had golden stones, although only because of the analogy with pearls in oysters.[200] He doubted that a stone floor at the monastery of Great Lavra on Mount Athos had been worn away by St Athanasius's knees, as the monks told him,[201] but gives credit to the story (repeated by Randolph) about how the *Plymouth*, holed by rocks near Chios, was saved by a piece of rock getting jammed into the hole, so that she was able to continue her voyage home safely. The piece of rock in question, only discovered when the ship was back in dock, 'is now kept in the K[ing]'s closet'. This story may well have had some basis of truth.[202] A striking, because more than usually introspective, illustration of Covel's mixed feelings is found in his reflections on the attitudes of Turks to fate, which they believe is in some way written on people's foreheads:

> for my part I am not so Calvinized as to say our Fate or Fortune is wrote in our foreheads, but this I will say, I think verily it was

God alone that hath preserved me from so many Death's [sic]. Some that know me I beleive may wonder what the Devil bewitch me to stay in this Hell of a place [i.e. plague-ridden Adrianople], and in good earnest I have wonder'd at myself; but that Fate (I think indeed) was written in my heart.[203]

Here he both rejects the idea of fate, whether Muslim or Calvinist, and allows himself to accept it by reformulating it as the will of God, written in his heart.

The Ottoman Empire

The geographical area covered in this book comprises what is now Greece, the coastal areas of Asia Minor (where there were both a substantial Greek population at the time, and also the remains of many ancient Greek cities), and the city of Constantinople, which had a Christian population (Greek and Armenian) of approximately 34 per cent in the late seventeenth century.[204] Most of Greece at this time was subject to Ottoman rule,[205] but it was only in the course of the sixteenth century that many areas had been wrested by the Turks from Venetian control. From the time of the fall of Constantinople to the Turks in 1453, the Balkans suffered in a tug of war between Venice and the Ottomans. The island of Crete remained Venetian until 1669, Tinos was not conquered by the Turks until 1714, and Venice managed to retain the Ionian islands of Zante, Cephallonia and Corfu, which were indispensable to its Mediterranean trade, as to England's. As well as areas under 'normal' Ottoman administration, Athens, Chios and Rhodes were private appanages of the Sultan: several travellers, including Covel, comment on the comparative freedom allowed to Chiots under this arrangement. We are told by the merchant Bernard Randolph, who was there in the 1670s, that many Catholics (Jesuits, Capuchins and Dominicans) continued to live there, as they did also on Rhodes and Crete.[206] In 1687 the Venetian Morosini, having captured the Peloponnese, forced Athens too to surrender to Venice, but the city was abandoned to the Turks again almost immediately.

Ottoman organisation was based on religious, not ethnic, groupings ('millets'),[207] and the Orthodox millet was to some extent governed by the patriarch, who was based in Constantinople.[208] Alongside the jurisdiction of the patriarch were those of a hierarchy of Ottoman officials, civil, military and religious, to which the non-Muslim populations were subject. In the rural areas of what is now Greece, Greeks remained the predominant ethnic group, but many towns acquired a substantial Muslim population.[209] Christians and Jews were free to practise their religion, the Turks generally preferring to collect taxes rather than to make converts,[210] and many probably felt less threatened by Islam than they had by the Latin Church,[211] but they were never equal citizens with Muslims. According to Covel, 'The *Turk* forces no man to profess Mahometanism; *Greeks*, *Armenians*, *Jews* [...] *Papists*, *Protestants*, all are tollerated', and even Persians can trade freely. However, he adds, each of these religious groups is apt to try to get the others into difficulties with the authorities: Muslims let Greek Christians alone, but Catholics do not.[212] By the middle of the century French and Italian Jesuits, Franciscans, Dominicans and Capuchins had established churches in the city. In Covel's view, their purpose was the conversion not of Muslims but of unlettered Orthodox Christians.[213] However, the only Christians who dared to try openly to convert Muslims were English Quakers, who were sometimes a thorn in the side of the diplomats.[214] Most travellers recognised, like Covel, that 'Wisdom and caution' should be employed in Muslim countries, and that it was unsafe to be 'too warm a Disputant'.[215]

There were substantial Jewish communities in Constantinople and Salonica, as well as smaller groups elsewhere, whose members worked particularly as interpreters, merchants, tax farmers and doctors, and were also heavily involved in the running of slave markets.[216] The number of Jews had been augmented by refugees from the Iberian peninsula after 1492, many of whom settled in Salonica and became hellenised.[217] A note of ambivalence sounds insistently through the comments about Jews made in travel accounts, owing both to religious conditions at the time and to the fact that in the first half of the seventeenth century in England (in contrast to the Ottoman

Empire) few people would have had the opportunity to knowingly meet Jews. Admiration for the Old Testament, and the growing interest in Hebrew studies, were not usually linked to contemporary Judaism.[218] In a climate of demonisation of Jews, Purchas appears to have been unaware of the irony of referring to 'this ISRAEL of great Brittaine' in which God had spoken to his chosen people through 'our Jacob', James I.[219]

English trade with the Ottoman Empire had been growing since the foundation of the Levant Company in the 1580s:[220] the main export from England was cloth of various kinds, but clocks and 'perspective glasses', knives and military hardware were also included; among the goods travelling in the other direction were silk and currants.[221] The non-Muslim sections of the population, as well as expatriate western merchants, were highly important in the field of trade. Covel himself had permission to trade in cloth on his own account, but I can find no evidence for Runciman's assertion that he made a fortune this way.[222] The French and the Venetians were both significant trade rivals of the English, and the western European communities in the trading centres sometimes socialised with each other.

One significant result of the Ottoman conquest was the impoverishment of Greek intellectual life, owing to the fact that many scholars fled to Italy: this is borne out time and again by comments in English travel writing. A small number of Greeks also came to England: Dowling and Fletcher have given an account of a few individuals who did so in the first half of the century, and of the small Greek merchant community that established itself in London, where a church was built for them, from the mid-seventeenth century. In the 1670s and 1680s there was an attempt to establish a college in Oxford for young Greek theologians, but this did not last long.[223] These initiatives are linked to attempts to unify the Orthodox and Anglican Churches, in which cause Covel was asked to look into the attitude of the Orthodox Church to transubstantiation.[224]

Education

Most of the Englishmen who made it to Greece and Turkey in the seventeenth century had received the conventional (for gentlemen or people of 'the middling sort') academic education: grammar or public school (or perhaps private tutor), followed by Oxford or Cambridge, followed (for some) by a spell at one of the Inns of Court. This was a period when the book trade was expanding,[225] so it was easier than it had been for young men to contribute to their education through their own private reading. Edward Browne and Covel both amassed substantial and wide-ranging libraries during their lifetimes, although unfortunately we do not know at what stage particular books were acquired.[226]

Between the accession of James I and the death of Charles I, 142 new grammar schools were established: education was valued highly because equipping people with the means to read the Bible for themselves contributed to the security of Protestantism. Although the intention was not to increase social mobility, that was one of the effects of the spread of educational opportunities.[227] The curriculum consisted almost entirely of the study of Latin, which the boys were also required to speak. At King Edward VI School in Bury St Edmunds, for example, where Covel and North were both scholars, 'The Master and Usher shall oft admonish their Scholars to speak Latin both in the school and out of it'.[228] Some boys certainly emerged from school with an excellent and flexible command of Latin as a living language, which stood them in good stead if they wished to participate in the international republic of letters, the epistolary network of scholars, philosophers and scientists that had arisen out of the culture of humanism: it is clear from the correspondence of Henry Oldenburg, secretary of the Royal Society, for example, how crucial this was for the scientific community in the late seventeenth century.[229] It was probably useful for merchants, too, to be able to communicate in Latin with speakers of other languages. The usefulness of the language was emphasised by Matthew Hale, Lord Chief Justice to Charles II, who wrote to his grandsons that while they were at grammar school he expected them to be able to 'read, understand and construe any Latin author, and to make true and handsome Latin', and added, 'though I would have you learn somewhat of Greek, yet the Latin tongue is that which I most value, because almost all learning is now under that language'.[230] It was not only that Greek texts were available in Latin translations, but that Latin was the international language of the learned and professional worlds.

The study of Latin involved learning grammar, reading and translating the Roman authors, reading 'colloquies' (parallel text dialogues about everyday life), writing epistles and 'themes' (essays), and might also include verse composition, learning by heart, and acting.[231] Thomas Baines used a system of taking notes on his reading that he probably learnt at school or university.[232] One of the most important activities was the collection of passages from the Roman authors into commonplace books, arranged under topics, which could be used as a source when writing themes.[233] To look at Covel's diaries, with their multiple quotations from a wide range of authors, is to see the results of this activity in action later in life. It is an activity that has a long history: for example, Erasmus's *Apophthegmata*, which was very popular in schools, was based on Plutarch's *Lacaenarum apophthegmata*. The Renaissance produced numerous anthologies (*florilegia*) of extracts from poems or prose works, sometimes arranged by author and sometimes by subject. The subject of travel is not particularly popular, though it does appear: Neuhusius, for example, includes a section on 'peregrinandi', and Dadré has 'peregrinatio' (and also 'curiositas').[234]

It is not easy to judge how much learning by heart went on: Gailhard, in *The Compleat Gentleman*, thought that a gentleman should learn something by heart every day, but his book is a guide to what should happen rather than an account of what does.[235] Wheler comments that it is difficult for travellers who pass only briefly through places to identify ancient sites, unless they 'should suppose them to have so many of the antient *Greek* Authors almost by heart'.[236] At Winchester, boys in the upper forms learnt 12 lines per week of Ovid's *Metamorphoses*.[237]

Translation exercises appear usually to have involved word-for-word translation, but there were exceptions: at Winchester the boys translated 'in grosse', that is following the general sense,[238] and Pococke (educated at Thame Grammar School, which followed the Winchester curriculum) in his translations from the Arabic tried to convey the sense rather than giving the literal meaning.[239] Problems of translation are surprisingly little referred to by travellers, but Sandys, who visited Greece in the early seventeenth century, was to become a significant translator of Ovid and Virgil. The work that came out of his journey contains a huge range of translated passages; a comparison of these with his later versions shows that he continued to be exercised by the art of expressing the Latin of Ovid and Virgil in contemporary English.

Robert Mathew, a mid-century scholar at Winchester, has left us evidence of the practice of verse composition in his poem 'De collegio Wintonensi',[240] and both Latin and Greek verse composition were practised at Westminster:[241] Evelyn was 'wonderfully astonish'd' by the 'Theames & extemporary Verses' produced by the scholars there.[242]

Latin was learnt not only for its usefulness in communication, or in homage to the ancient world: the Roman authors were read for their content and for morality as well. The question of morality was a difficult one, since there might be a conflict between Christian and pagan values. Although the choice of texts was wide, there was some expurgation by teachers, so that boys' minds should not be corrupted. Brinsley, in his guide for masters working in 'poore Countrey schooles', stresses the importance of cutting out 'filthy' passages and keeping to morally appropriate contents, though Gailhard, rebutting the argument that heathen authors ought to be avoided, thinks they should be read for their wit, learning, language and 'sometimes good Morality'.[243] Virgil's fourth eclogue was a popular text because it could be given a Christian interpretation,[244] but it is surprising that there were not more objections to texts on grounds of unsuitability. While schools maintained a firmly Christian ethos, they taught an enormous range of pagan authors: in the scheme suggested by Erasmus, which was one of the foundations of the grammar school curriculum, the most important authors were Pliny the Elder, Cicero and Quintilian, but Virgil was also widely taught. Among the other authors who figured in schools we find Caesar, Sallust, Tacitus, Livy, Terence, Plautus, Ovid, Horaee, Lucan, Silius Italicus, Valerius Maximus and Juvenal.[245] The 1665 statutes of King Edward VI

School, Bury St Edmunds, also include Catullus, Tibullus, Propertius, Martial and Persius on the list of authors to be studied.[246]

Greek, taught in Latin, was also on the curriculum in some schools. The primary text in this case was the New Testament, but Homer, Hesiod, Theognis, Isocrates, Demosthenes, Aesop, Xenophon, Euripides and Sophocles were among the classical authors taught.[247] The Bury St Edmunds school list includes Plutarch, Theocritus, Pindar and Aristophanes as well.[248] Peacham particularly recommended the Greek historians.[249] Pepys helped his brother with a speech in Greek, which he was to make at St Paul's School.[250] It is clear that Covel had a good knowledge of Greek, but we do not know how much he learnt at school and how much at Cambridge. Hebrew and Arabic were also taught at some schools (at Westminster, for example, where Vernon, whose linguistic skills were admired by Browne, was educated),[251] with the religious purpose of better understanding the Bible and of having a stick with which to beat Muslims.[252] Covel's work on the Greek Church demonstrates his knowledge of Hebrew. There was also a scientific reason for the study of Arabic, because of the ancient Greek texts such as the works of Aristotle that had been transmitted to the west via Arabic translations.

However, during this period the overwhelming dominance of the classics in education was beginning to be challenged, at least by the theorists. Confidence in the English language and its expressive possibilities was growing, so that by the 1690s Locke was writing that, while he was not against the study of Greek and Latin, the language that a young man 'should critically study, and labour to get a facility, clearness and elegance, to Express himself in, should be his own'.[253] Milton's proposed curriculum aimed to educate the whole person, and he included, for example, exercise, music and diet in his suggested scheme,[254] while Hobbes thought the study of classics positively dangerous, since men found arguments in the classical historians to support 'their disputation against the necessary Power of their Soveraigns'.[255] Watson has shown in detail how a much wider range of subjects began to be introduced into the grammar school curriculum:[256] at the same time, there were schools offering a more practical education for merchants and others.²⁵⁷ Jack Verney (who went out to the Levant as a merchant), having failed to show much interest in or aptitude for Latin at grammar school, was sent at the age of 18 to a school specialising in commerce and accounting.²⁵⁸ North, who was intended from boyhood for a mercantile life, went from Bury St Edmunds to a 'writing school' in London,²⁵⁹ though it is also likely that many merchants had little schooling and learnt on the job.

Covel and most of his English contemporaries who travelled in the Ottoman Empire had studied at Oxford or Cambridge. It is less easy to determine the curriculum followed by any particular undergraduate than is the case with schoolboys, and the university statutes provide an incomplete guide. In the first place, the statutes imply that the course was still entirely scholastic,²⁶⁰ whereas in fact, in this period, it had moved nearer to humanism.²⁶¹ Secondly, individual colleges and tutors had a huge influence on what a student studied. Not only was private reading encouraged by tutors,²⁶² but the general ethos of the college made a big difference: at Christ's, Cambridge, for example, where Covel, Finch and Baines all studied, neo-Platonism was pervasive during the fellowship of Henry More.²⁶³ Students coming from grammar school could be expected to be fluent in Latin, but might need some tuition in Greek. All subjects were studied in Latin (or Greek), so that even when other subjects were taught they were transmitted through the medium of classical texts.²⁶⁴ Thus Aristotle was crucial for his content as well as for his language,²⁶⁵ although with the rise of the new science in the second half of the century, Aristotelian science began to lose ground; the study of history consisted in the study of the ancient historians.²⁶⁶ As at school, students were expected to make commonplace books for themselves of phrases which they could use to aid them in the formation of their own classical Latin style.²⁶⁷ There was a heavy emphasis on grammar and rhetoric, as well as logic and ethics, all taught through the classical authors.²⁶⁸ As Burrow has written: 'all writers who had a rhetorical training – and up to 1700 that was all writers – knew that their style was immeasurably indebted to the works of pagan antiquity'.²⁶⁹

There is some evidence about the prime importance of a tutor in the personal as well as the academic life of an undergraduate. Twigg mentions a student who entered Emmanuel College in 1649, who recorded that a tutor might visit his students' rooms several times a week, and examine them every night on what they had learnt during the day.[270] The correspondence between Sackville Crow (ambassador to Constantinople during the Civil War), his son of the same name and his son's Oxford tutor Arthur Mansell in the 1650s[271] demonstrates the close relationship between tutor and student. The father writes to the son that he should not go anywhere without his tutor's permission, and should not on any account stay out late, 'for Visits in the darke are not Convenient for young men, under Tuition'. If this seems over-protective, we need to remember that boys generally matriculated at a much earlier age than today's students, often at about the age of 15, but sometimes even younger. This particular young man, though a beginner in Greek, was well-grounded in Latin and French, which his tutor was to read with him. He was instructed to concentrate on logic in the mornings and history and his own writing in the afternoons, with natural philosophy and mathematics to follow as time went on. Texts mentioned are Tacitus, Plutarch, Thucydides and Seneca. When Crow junior reads a book, he is required to give an account of it to his tutor. Mansell writes that the course he usually follows with students whose aim is the Inns of Court or travel covers Latin and Greek and sometimes Hebrew, logic, natural and moral philosophy, civil law, mathematics and the use of globes. This last subject suggests the beginnings of a wider curriculum: Ralph Verney, father of Jack, learnt astronomy, history and geography at Oxford as early as 1629–31.[272] Wheler tells us in his autobiography that he learnt mathematics, geography, astronomy, optics and some anatomy at Oxford, as well as grammar, rhetoric, logic, Aristotelian natural philosophy and classical authors. He also read 'Cartesius and the Moderns'.[273] The vocational subjects – law, medicine and theology – were more systematically studied at postgraduate rather than undergraduate level.[274]

While we do not know the details of the curriculum followed by Covel at Christ's, where he went after leaving grammar school in Bury St Edmunds, we do know that his interests extended to natural sciences (especially botany), medicine and music, as well as theology and all things classical.

A number of men went, or went on, to study on the Continent. For medical training, the most significant centre was Padua: Finch and Baines both enrolled there, as did John Evelyn.[275] For oriental languages, Leiden was an important centre.[276] Another recognised route was through the Inns of Court, where Wheler, for example, spent some time.[277] Here, although the principal subject was law, students are thought to have continued their private reading in the humanities and in a range of subjects such as anatomy, astronomy, geography, history, mathematics, theology and languages.[278]

Covel's interest in the sciences has already been mentioned. When he was due to sail for Constantinople, he spent the fortnight of delay while they waited for the wind to change investigating the way pebbles are shaped by the action of waves and the presence of worms in the sand; his diary has a long discussion of coastal erosion and accretion, as well as another about the etymology of place names.[279] His commonplace book consists mainly of annotated drawings of insects, fish and plants.[280] In Asia Minor in the 1670s, he was part of a group of travellers who, following in the footsteps of men such as Camden in England, began to evince a more systematic attitude to the investigation of ancient monuments. While there was some scientific teaching in the universities, the beginnings of the Royal Society in the 1660s, and its precursors in the previous two decades, were of crucial importance to this change in attitudes, as was Bacon's inductive method, with its emphasis on the collection of data. Finch and Baines (unlike Covel, who never lived in London) were among the early members of the society,[281] although when John Dodington tried to find out from them about a purported Greek chemical manuscript in the library of the Duke of Florence, he could obtain no satisfaction:

> When I applied myselfe to Sr John Fynch in this matter, with Great hopes of some light from him & doctor Baynes: I was answered alla Fiorentina, with two Convulsions in their faces & three shruggs of their shoulders. Both averred to me, they

never heard a word of it, nor know of any such book, so I came away re infecta.[282]

James Crawford also found Finch unhelpful in the provision of information, but Vernon, by contrast, provided the Royal Society with letters describing his travels in Greece.[283] The lectures at Gresham College in London,[284] where the Royal Society had its first home, also helped to raise scientific awareness and interest. The passion for collecting, in which travellers were closely involved, encompassed not only classical remains and manuscripts but also specimens of natural history.[285] Scientific knowledge in the broader, seventeenth-century sense of the word 'science' was transmitted back to the Royal Society by numerous travellers.[286] The desire for such knowledge also affected attitudes to some classical authors: the atomism of Lucretius, for example, was attractive to natural scientists such as Kenelm Digby, but caused anxiety in Thomas Browne, who, though he used atomic imagery himself, had moral reservations about his son reading Lucretius.[287] The Cambridge Platonists also worried about the effect atomism might have on Christian belief.[288]

Typically, however, travellers to Greece and Asia Minor had been immersed in Greek and Roman literature, with the result that many of them, Covel included, had what has been called an 'emotional commitment' to the classics,[289] a commitment that was not undermined by the interest some of them had in science. It was still possible at this date to see the body of extant knowledge as something that a man could master in its entirety, but through the seventeenth century the emphasis was shifting in various ways. At the beginning Bacon was already separating scientific from religious knowledge, and by the end Locke was insisting on the educational primacy of the English language over Greek and Latin.[290] We do know of at least two travellers who recognised that their education had not entirely fitted them for an understanding of Ottoman ways. Blount at the beginning of the century wrote, '[I want to see] [f]rom mine owne eye not dazled with any affectation, prejudicacy, or mist of education, which preoccupate the minde';[291] and North, whose livelihood in the mercantile world depended on finding ways of working with Turks, and who, according to the rather adulatory biography by his brother, was a gifted negotiator, wrote: 'But to apprehend these diversities [of legal practice] one must have a strong power of thought to abstract the prejudices of our education and plant ourselves in a way of negotiating in heathen remote countries'.[292]

Nevertheless, Covel is a good example of those classically educated men whose emotional commitment to the classics remained a crucial element in their view of the world, and contributed in a major way to their ability to make sense of the classical sites.

Elsner and Rubiés describe how Palestine was seen as 'a series of scriptural mementoes';[293] similarly, Greece was seen as a series of classical mementoes: travellers such as Covel classified what they saw by what they had read, attaching tags from ancient authors to appropriate sites. Even those who had not had a classical education, such as the merchant Randolph, often made references to classical history or myth, showing that a certain level of classical knowledge was common currency. Interestingly, the library of the English factory or trading post in Smyrna, for which a handlist is extant for the year 1702, included at that time several classical texts as well as biblical and theological works, geography, mathematics, and grammar and lexicography.[294] In an undated letter to Covel, Robert Huntington, chaplain at Aleppo, writes that the report of a great library at Aleppo (he was presumably referring to the factory library there) had dissuaded him from bringing his own books with him – though in fact he seems to have been disappointed with what he found, and in another letter sent Covel a list of titles to look out for in Constantinople.[295] But the presence of at least some classical texts in factory libraries suggests that merchants, too, might have had an interest in such reading.

***

The experiences of Covel and his contemporaries provide evidence of the multi-layered way in which, then as now, we define our places in the different worlds which we inhabit and in relation to the different people we meet. The boundaries of cultures are indeed porous, and there can be constant interaction not only between countries that are widely separated geographically, but also between physical and imagined worlds. By reading between the lines of travellers' accounts we can see some of the processes of the formation of identity taking place, for example in their mixture of pride in and anxiety about England. An exceptionally important part of the mental baggage they carried was the education in the classics that, to a greater or lesser extent, they had all undergone. One of the principal players in this book, Covel, is particularly striking in this respect; but he is also important because during the time of his stay in Constantinople, in the period after the Restoration, attitudes to antiquities underwent a change: he and his contemporaries were instrumental in this shift to what might be called 'proto-archaeology', the beginnings of a more historical and scientific approach to the physical remains of the classical world that exercised such a strong emotional pull on these men.

The reinvention of self, or the seeing of oneself in a new light, is an experience common to travellers to foreign countries, whose personalities and views may be changed, or at least thrown into relief, by their experiences of the other. Coryate is an example of someone who used his travelling as a way of projecting a very particular image of himself to his friends, and to the friends he aspired to gain, at home: he was the indefatigable wearer out of shoes, the gobbler-up of unusual experiences (one of his books is entitled *Coryats crudities*), the witty buffoon. At the site of Troy, he underwent a mock ennoblement, which has been brilliantly deconstructed by Baker as both a kind of half-joking representation of English power and England's supposed Trojan origins, and at the same time an acknowledgement of the reality of Ottoman power.[296] For Coryate, the personal and the political were inextricably linked. That he was not alone in connecting his sense of self to his sense of England is demonstrated by the numerous mentions of the state of the homeland in travel writing. The emergence of England as a nation owes something to the experiences of returning travellers: self-definition and national identity are related.

Covel's case is rather different: although, as with Coryate, his self-revelations are sometimes coloured with humour or irony, it is more often the case that they are made inadvertently, and there is certainly no sense that he was inventing a complete persona for his readers, as Coryate did. No doubt this is partly because of the nature of his writings, a collection of texts written at different times, for different purposes and audiences, and in differing circumstances. His personal identity as a Christian adherent of a middle way, neither Catholic nor Calvinist, is confirmed by his encounters with, and sometimes even admiration for, Turks. On the other hand, in spite of the informal character of his diaries it is rare for the reader to feel that he is writing straight from the heart, so that when he does do so it is all the more striking. The day on which he left Constantinople for the last time, which happened to be his 39th birthday, was clearly a day of deep emotion:

> This day in the year 1638 I was born at 2 a clock in the morning being Monday, and it pleased me to se[e] so many things meet this day, whereby I may reckon it my second birth [...] This day I left Stambol [...] It pleased God I was wth more respect then I deserved treated by all at my parting, and finally accompanied by my freinds to the seaside wth a kind of painfull joy and brought as it was to a new life, just as my Mother in [throes?] and pangs, had a mixture of joy when a son was borne into the world.[297]

Paradoxically, the experiences that he had hungered for had made him into a new person with new friends, yet at the same time the prospect of returning home from an alien to a familiar world was a complementary kind of rebirth. Perhaps it should not be regretted that this urbane and complicated man never published his diaries himself, as the writing might well have lost some of the immediacy and liveliness that it has in its extant form.

William Dalrymple, discussing understanding across cultural boundaries in a different context, that of nineteenth-century India, writes:

It is through the human stories of the successes, struggles, grief, anguish and despair of all these individuals that we can best bridge the great chasm of time and understanding separating us from [... a] remarkably different world.[298]

Covel's world is also remarkably different, yet at the same time his diary offers us some contact with the private person, whose emotions are similar to ours. As we attempt to get a sense of his reactions to and understanding of cultural differences, in the contemporary world in which he was working and in the classical world of his emotional allegiance, his story highlights both the similarities and the differences between our world and his.

CHAPTER 1

LOGISTICS OF TRAVEL

> ye way up is very bad, difficult and dangerous especially descending, not only by being extream steep, and many times broken, but ye path itself is for ye most part so narrow as a horse cannot set both feet together to stand even, and on either side you are most part wall'd in by sloping banks of stone that if your horse fall right down it is difficult getting him up, if sideways you hazard your legs; we scaped well though not wthout a fall or two.[1]

So John Covel described in his diary in October 1675 his climb up Mount Olympus in Mysia, near the town of Prusa/Bursa, now in Turkey. The descent from the mountain was made even more difficult because by this time it was dark, but Covel was a feisty traveller. He was 36 years old at this time, learned in classical languages and theology, and had been ordained to the Anglican ministry. This was a particularly good time for English travellers to visit the Greek world, between the end of the Ottoman siege of Crete (1669) and the coalition of Austrians and Venetians against the Turks (1684). Those who went to Athens, like Covel's contemporary Wheler, also saw the Parthenon before the explosion of 1687, in which it was badly damaged.[2]

Covel's prime motive for taking the Levant Company chaplaincy seems to have been his curiosity about the Ottoman world and about the state of Greece and the remains of its classical civilisation under

Ottoman rule. He himself described his desire to see t‌
'meer curiosity',[3] and on arrival in Smyrna he confided to
'All things being so quite different from our own way of li
very much surprise me wth wonder and delight.'[4] He had a
commissioned by a group of Anglican divines to look in
question of whether the Greek Orthodox Church believed ‌
doctrine of transubstantiation – if it did, this would be a ‌
breaker for those Anglicans who looked to the possible un
between the Church of England and the Orthodox Church.[5]

At the time he climbed Mount Olympus, Covel had been in th‌
Levant for some five years, as chaplain to the English diplomatic and
mercantile community in Constantinople. On the evidence of his
diary, his work as chaplain seems to have been the least prominent of
his many interests. Above all, he was an intrepid traveller, hating to be
hurried as he collected measurements of and inscriptions from ancient
ruins, or botanical specimens. Travel at the time was usually, in the
words of a traveller from the beginning of the seventeenth century,
'dangerous, troublesome and tedious' as well as full of interest.[6] There
was a choice of several routes from England to the Levant: overland all
the way, or by land to Venice and then by sea, or – the route which
Covel took – by sea all the way.[7] None of these routes went by way of
Athens, which helps to explain why few western visitors included
Athens on their itinerary. In any case it could take weeks or months:
Covel left Plymouth in the *London Merchant*, in a large convoy that
included nine Levant-bound ships, in late September 1670, after a
three-week delay in Deal, where he joined his ship, because of
unfavourable weather. He was comparatively lucky in that he was in
the Aegean by the second week of November.[8] He showed his mettle
during the voyage: on 10 November, near the western end of Crete,
Algerine ships were sighted, and the captain suggested that Covel
should go below with the surgeon, where he would be safe. However,
he preferred to remain on deck, praying for success, which the captain
said would be an encouragement for the sailors. Other passengers
followed suit, and they were all provided with arms and stood on the
quarter deck in readiness, but in the event the ships proved to be
French and not a threat.[9]

During the second half of the period he spent in the Ottoman Empire, Covel took advantage of every opportunity to travel outside Constantinople. He was not to be defeated by the petty difficulties of getting about or finding the way. His climb up Mysian Mount Olympus has already been mentioned, and on another occasion, journeying between Adrianople and Constantinople, determined not to miss a chance and scornful of superstition, he set off with his servant on a detour via the sea shore: it was on this occasion that his companions were frightened that they might encounter thieves, and deterred by the bad omen of a calf with a white face.[10] Having arrived at his post in December 1670, after visiting the ruins of ancient Ephesus on the way,[11] he did not record in his diary any journeys outside the city until 1674. In the first year or so, he was probably getting used to the job, but then in August 1672 the ambassador, Daniel Harvey, died, and his successor, John Finch, did not arrive until 1674.[12] During this interregnum, Covel's duties seem to have been quite heavy,[13] but in the next three years he made several trips: in September 1674 to Heraclea Perinthus (in Thrace, on the Propontis); from May to September 1675, with John Finch, to the Sultan's court at Adrianople; in October 1675, with Wheler and his companion Jacob Spon, to the islands in the Sea of Marmara and Prusa; in late 1676 to Smyrna, Magnesia (under Mount Sipylus) and Prusa; in February 1677, at the end of his Levant chaplaincy, to Nicaea and the island of Chalcis; and in April to Cyzicus, Lemnos and Mount Athos.

He was an enthusiastic sketcher of maps and plans, filling a gap for himself that many travellers noticed. Although atlases such as those of Mercator and Ortelius from the sixteenth century and Blaeu after 1662, based on exploration, were gradually supplanting maps such as Ptolemy's, which presented a schematic and symbolic depiction of the world, there was still some way to go in terms of practical guides for travellers,[14] and atlases were not in any case very portable. Covel used Ptolemy, Ortelius and the seventeenth-century French mapmaker Sanson, but on one of his journeys wrote trenchantly, '[I am] resolved to set down every water run, that (if possible) I might give light to your antient Geographers.'[15]

He regretted that he had no sea compass to help him, unlike his friend Wheler, another enthusiastic mapmaker, who in turn was sorry not to have a quadrant.[16] In Ephesus, Wheler proudly recorded, 'I observed the Situation of all that I have hitherto described; and [...] marked them on a Paper; from which I have transferred them to your view.'[17] Another contemporary traveller, Edward Browne (a physician like his father, Thomas), complained that 'he that travels in *Macedonia*, will never be able to reconcile the positions of Rivers and Towns to their usual Descriptions in Maps, although not long ago there have been large ones published of *Greece*'.[18] In his view, the best available maps were those made by Turkish imperial messengers ('chiauses').

In some ways, travel in the Ottoman Empire was easier and more comfortable than it was at home. The facilities for travellers, in particular the khans or caravanserais and the fountains, are frequently praised by western Europeans. In some places there was a wide choice of accommodation: in Constantinople, for example, more than 20 places could be found in the vicinity of the bazaar, and one of the city's khans, built in 1651, could hold 3,000 people.[19] Khans were built round a courtyard or a series of courtyards, and each room had a raised platform round the edge where travellers could spread their bedding and cook their meals, while in the centre animals were tethered to rings in the walls. There might be hooks for clothes (though travellers tended not to undress to sleep), chimneys to allow the smoke to escape, shops for provisions, and even hot baths. The disadvantages were fleas and bugs, as well as noise and lack of privacy, for which reason some travellers thought English inns were preferable.[20] Sometimes, for privacy, safety or comfort, travellers stayed in private houses, but these were not necessarily better: Covel complained bitterly about the fleas and bugs in a house in Adrianople,[21] although, as has already been mentioned, this particular house belonged to a Jew, and Covel is making a point here about his disapproval of Jewish dirtiness.

Tents were an alternative to khans. Covel describes how, on one of his journeys, the wagons were arranged in a circle round the travellers, a fire was lit, and men were set to watch by turns. He adds,

> I have been used to the fashion of the country of lying in my clothes, which I did both outwards and homewards, and once in a frollick to Prusa baths I came not in a bed for 8 weekes together [...] I carried a little sea bed with me which I lay on at Adrianople, and upon the road we first spread a carpet on the ground and then lay'd our beds or quilts upon it, and so tumbled down upon them booted, cloak't &c as we rode.[22]

When Wheler crossed from Lepanto to the Peloponnese on his way between Zante and Athens, his next lodging place left much to be desired:

> we were forced to make a vertue of Necessity, and content our selves, to take up our Habitation in a place not much bigger or better than a Tomb, like the Madman mentioned in the Gospel: Which was a Brick Building, arched over, of six foot broad, and fifteen foot long; and the Floor digg'd two foot deep below ground. It had two such holes, one a top, and another below, as would neither let out the Smoak, nor let in the Light: But cold enough. This Room served us for all the Offices of a spacious House; the worst was, when it came to its turn to be made a Kitchin: not but that we might well enough have endured the Fire, if our Eyes could have agreed as well with the Smoak. Our Patron of the Barque lent us his Sail to spread on the Floor; on which laying our Quilts, we made but a bad shift, the Place being very damp. But the Wetness producing good store of Rushes thereabouts, I taught them at last to be Matt-makers, by tying handfuls of long Rushes together, with Pack-thred we had by us. These we laid under our Quilts, and to stop out the Cold.[23]

The most usual method of getting about the empire was on horseback, and Covel's account of descending from Mount Olympus suggests he was a competent horseman. Long-distance journeys were sometimes made by night, to avoid the scorching heat, but on at least one occasion all those in Covel's party got sunburnt on the left-hand sides of their faces.[24] The French traveller Jean-Baptiste Tavernier describes a trip made to Ephesus from Smyrna in the spring of 1657: the party consisted of 12 Europeans, together with three janissaries, and three extra horses to carry provisions. They departed at three in the afternoon, stopped for supper in a village, and continued their journey until midnight.[25] Churches sometimes offered a cool place to rest.[26] There were also unexpected hazards in hiring horses: Wheler once got into difficulties because the horse he had hired came without saddle and bridle, which he had unfortunately failed to specify.[27] Near the Hellespont, Wheler and his companion were unable to find horses at all, ending up with 'a conceited [i.e. ingenious] Chariot, or, to tell the truth, a Cart', with solid wheels and wicker sides, pulled by buffaloes.[28] Food for the journey may have been carried in tin-lined boxes.[29]

The little 'sea-bed' that Covel carried was not his only item of luggage. The first thing he did when he arrived in Constantinople on 31 December 1670 was to collect his trunks full of books from the customs officers:

> [the officers] ript open my Trunks and boxes and searched and rifled everything; however at last I mist nothing but *Niceron's Thaumaturgus opticus*, which I shrewdly suspect was filch't from me by one, who was indeed call'd a Christian but had not it seems the honesty of a common Turk.[30]

Presumably this so-called Christian was one of his fellow-travellers on board ship: perhaps he assumed that only a westerner would be interested in this book, but it is unclear how a fellow-passenger could have got access to the trunks before they were ripped open by the Turkish officials. We do know that Covel was interested in medicine, and he had replaced this volume, which was one of many medical works he possessed, in his library by the end of his life.[31] We cannot tell what other books he had brought with him: his diaries are littered with quotations and references from the classics, but some at least of these may have been added later, and some quotations may have been inscribed from memory. We can only identify some titles that he wished to have but did not. In several places he asks a friend (probably his Cambridge friend 'R. H.' – Robert Huckle) to check something for him, for example in works by the Cambridge Hellenists John Cheke and Ralph Winterton: 'Bestow a minute or two for my sake in consulting your authors which I want [i.e. lack] [...] You and your books know better then I.'[32]

Apart from books, Covel must have carried paper and writing implements with him on his jaunts, since although much of the diary was probably written up after the event, there are notes, maps and sketches that he must have made on the spot. Other travellers refer specifically to writing materials: Wheler and his companion, for example, were relieved to be able to find a goose-quill replacement when they lost their pens.[33] A particularly useful item was a 'perspective glass', which Covel evidently had with him sometimes, as he describes using it to look at plants in a gulley, but on other occasions he regretted not having one because without it he was unable to read inscriptions high up on buildings.[34] Travellers found it convenient to carry small objects which might be given away as expedient, for example knives, scissors, small European coins, 'perspective glasses', mirrors, spectacles and gloves (of which the two hands of one pair might be given away separately).[35] Covel presented 'a Tunbridge knife', which he had in his pocket, to a Peloponnesian who looked as he imagined Hesiod might have done, with whom he tried to converse in ancient Greek; the man seemed all innocence and helpfulness, but betrayed the ship's company by alerting bandits to their presence, so that when they ventured up into the mountains they were set upon – the diary does not record whether the knife was used.[36]

Among the more formal gifts that were made by European ambassadors to the Sultan were clocks, mirrors, silverware and guns.[37] Although clocks were to be found in the Ottoman Empire (Covel saw one on Mount Athos), they were rare and highly valued. Ordinary people told the time of day by the muezzin's calls to prayer, and Covel counted the duration of various ceremonies at court by his pulse.[38] Apart from the knife that he gave away, we do not know whether he himself generally carried any weapons on his travels, but on one occasion he put his servant's sword to the peaceful archaeological use of clearing away the earth from an inscription.[39] Wheler carried a mattock with him for the same purpose.[40] Greaves designed and took with him a sextant and a large quadrant, to help him determine the latitudes of Constantinople, Rhodes and Alexandria.[41]

Of course, the traffic in gifts and souvenirs was not only one way. Then as now, travellers bought souvenirs to take back with them, in Covel's case several cheap and pretty 'knackes', including coins, intaglios and some 'petrified' mushrooms. He probably also fulfilled the request of his friend 'R. H.' for a Turkish letter-case,[42] but he does not seem to have emulated his ambassador, John Finch, who arrived home in Dover in 1682, after living for some years first in Tuscany and then in Constantinople, with 60 trunks, 19 chests of books,[43] 23 chests of Italian pictures, lots of wine, and jars of olives, oil, anchovies and capers. Finch had already sent home wine, horse furniture, a Chian quilt, a Turkish knife, a set of china bottles, some handkerchiefs, and an 'eagle's stone' (presumably a fossilised egg), 'for the virtue and rarity of it'. He also expected to be able to send an Egyptian mummy.[44] Rycaut was shown a wall full of bones in Philadelphia, and took a piece away.[45]

Franks (as the Turks called foreigners) in the Ottoman Empire regularly wore local dress, and Covel was no exception. He mentions that villagers in Christian villages were sometimes frightened when they saw him approaching in Turkish dress, until he reassured them that he was a Christian by making the sign of the cross.[46] Wheler had a similar experience near Delphi, causing the Greek priest of the village where he was arriving to run away and hide 'among the Rocks'.[47] Wheler did not want to climb after him, so sent his Greek servant, and eventually the priest's wife called him down, and he showed them his church. On another occasion, when Wheler arrived near Smyrna, his party was met by the consul, Rycaut, and many of the English merchants from the colony there: they came 'with good Horses, and well trapped according to the *Turkish* Fashion; as the rest of their own Habits also were, only their Hats excepted, to distinguish them from the *Eastern* Nations'.[48]

Wheler goes on to say that here, about three miles out of town, they were provided with a 'Collation', and drink in which to toast his majesty's health, before marching 'in order, two by two' into Smyrna. Food and wine were important to many English visitors or residents in the Levant, not least to Covel. Much of what he and others describe is familiar to those visiting Greece and Turkey today: fish, chicken, lamb, rice, bread, olives, cheese, nuts and citrus fruits. Covel also mentions sour milk or 'youwort', and 'little bits of broiled fleshe which they call kebob, but whole joints nowhere'.[49] On his visit to Mount Athos, he enjoyed 'the best monkish fare', with plenty of wine.[50] In his book on the Greek Church he mentions that he ate many times in Turkish households; he does not give any details of the kind of food he ate, but it may have been similar to what Wheler described:

> our Supper was *Turkish* Pasties, that were made of Meat minced fine, Marrow, Bread crummed, and Sugar; baked between two Leaves of Paste in Tin-pans. The next dish was *Dolma*; which is a Compound of meat, Suet, Onyons and Spice, made up like Sausage-Meat wrapped in Cabbage, or Vine-leaves, and are either boiled or fried; and then served with a little Vinegar on them, and are both very good. The third was a chief Dish among the *Turks*, like to *Pilau*, which is ordinarily made of Rice; but this was Wheat, or barley, peeled, and boil'd with a Hen, or other Meat. They call it *Tragana*. Afterwards we had a Banquet of Sweet-meats, made of boiled Wine.[51]

Shipboard food could be awful, and the provision of fresh water was sometimes problematical. However, travellers had good experiences too, and once Covel had dealt robustly with his sea-sickness he enjoyed the food, such as the melons, pomegranates, salad herbs, dates, oranges, limes and pumpkins, as well as fish and meat; the latter came from live animals that they had taken aboard in North Africa.[52] While his ship lay off Smyrna for five days before continuing its course for Constantinople, one of the party 'kill'd a little Owl not much bigger than a [q]uail [...] It was very fat and the flesh purely white, and it eat as well as any Chicken'.[53] At that size, it cannot have gone very far.

Covel liked his wine as well as his food, regarding it as 'a very necessary comfort upon the Road' – but not only on the road – and it was, surprisingly in a Moslem environment, not difficult to come by. En route to Nicaea, he was entertained to a good meal by the Metropolitan of Nicomedia, who, though he did not himself drink, told his guest to have whatever he pleased,[54] and on Chios he was delighted to compare the 'sort of Amber muskadine' he drank to the sparkling wine mentioned by Homer.[55] He was served good wine at Mount Athos too, although unlike the bread it was kept locked up.[56] In Constantinople he found no shortage of wine: although it was officially forbidden by Islam, and taverns were closed down from time to time,[57] the prohibition does not seem to have been universally observed, and in any case Christians were exempt. Pera, the suburb of the city where Franks lived, was a vine-growing area: all of Finch's official dispatches from his embassy are addressed from 'The Vines' at Pera.[58] It was there that an early seventeenth-century traveller, Coryate, had helped Greeks to gather and tread their grapes, commenting that Turks drink must if not wine itself, an observation also made by Browne.[59] Covel's experience was that the janissary aga[60] received large sums in bribes from wine-making villagers in the area: the official arrived in one particular village many times 'in show of severity', but always with advance warning. Even the Vizier's aga entertained Covel and Finch with wine.[61]

Another drink that fascinated foreigners in the Ottoman Empire, and that had found its way to England in the 1630s,[62] was coffee, which had arrived there from Yemen during the sixteenth century.[63] Finch, describing the correct way of brewing coffee, writes that the grounds should be used twice, the first time for friends and the second for 'ordinary people'.[64] It was drunk in private houses, in public spaces and on ceremonial occasions. Coffee houses sprang up everywhere,[65] though they were not always approved of by the authorities. Covel mentions coffee houses near Magnesia which were 'not yet put down' by officials, and which accommodated up to 100 people and were open until midnight because it was Ramadan.[66]

Rycaut thought that the Grand Vizier regarded them as worse than taverns for the fomenting of sedition, and Finch called them 'mints of mutiny',[67] but Covel for one enjoyed them, especially one at Mytilene on Lesbos that overlooked the sea and served good cheap wine as well. His experience was that they were frequented by all sorts of people without any disturbances arising.[68] Along with sherbet, coffee was offered at meetings between Ottoman officials and European diplomats: on one occasion, described by Covel in code, Finch was so nervous in an interview with the Vizier that his hand shook and he spilt his coffee.[69] Wheler sat on a sofa (another item that eventually arrived in England from Turkey) to drink coffee with the Archbishop of Athens.[70] Sometimes coffee was offered to Ottoman officials as a sweetener: Wheler mentions the anger of one in the Peloponnese who had been sent sweetmeats rather than coffee by the English vice-consul.[71] In Gallipoli, the customs officer treated Covel courteously to a meal, but would not let him pass without the payment of an oke (nearly three pounds' weight) of coffee.[72]

Such bribes were in addition to the official permits or passports that travellers had to carry. Covel's contemporaries Luke and Rycaut both mention 'commands' from the Sultan that allowed them to travel safely,[73] but sometimes such documents were provided by ambassadors and consuls rather than directly by the Porte. In Patras, Wheler obtained a new passport from the consul there (he does not explain why he needed a new one), and he later refers to the 'Consul's patent from the *Grand Signior*, to travel where we pleased'.[74] The pass used by Covel to go to Mount Athos, signed by the Marquis de Nointel, the French ambassador, is still extant.[75] It appears that sometimes these documents might be recycled: Covel's predecessor as chaplain, Thomas Smith, presented the local legal official in Sardis with a pass he had been given by two other Englishmen, to make 'the best use' he could of it.[76] An early seventeenth-century ambassador, Thomas Roe, was even brave enough to alter 'three tymes after it had ye signature of ye Grand Signor' the pass he had obtained allowing William Petty (agent for Thomas Arundel, one of the earliest collectors) to look for antiquities.[77] It is unclear what alterations he needed to make.

Covel came to the Ottoman Empire to work, but his work figures much less in his diary than his other interests. Like other expatriates, he enjoyed his leisure, and spent much time on a country estate about 12 miles out of Constantinople.[78] One Turkish activity to which Europeans took a liking was picnicking – sometimes a pleasure shared between Turks and Franks. Covel describes spending time in a 'kiosk': 'we oftentimes after our *Spasso* (that is, our rambling in fishing or shooting or the like) if it was not taken up, have recreated ourselves there'. Wheler, meanwhile, describes the shady woods near the village of Belgrade, a few miles north of Constantinople, where 'Persons of Quality', both Turks and Franks, enjoy the fresh air and hunting, especially when the city is oppressively hot. This place evidently had good facilities, namely 'kiosks', cisterns for drinking water and tents.[79] En route to Adrianople, Covel saw an enormous plane tree under which, in summer, many people took their 'spasso' and sat on carpets to eat, drink and smoke.[80] For Turks, such shared activities were perhaps a way of indulging in behaviour that might not have been acceptable in other circumstances: according to Robert Bargrave, a merchant and Levant Company secretary, the English had a country 'palace', surrounded by gardens and woods for hunting, where Turks brought concubines and eunuchs and entertained the English with 'Dauncing, Leaping, & roaring like wild persons let out of a prison'.[81] On one occasion in the course of his travels, Rycaut was not only given carpets and cushions under a tree, with food for himself and his horses, but was also provided with his breakfast, wrapped up in a linen cloth.[82]

Travel, and meeting local people, offered Europeans both an opportunity and an incentive to learn languages. Covel himself was a decent linguist: he spoke Latin, Greek and Italian, the last of which, in its Venetian form and with the addition of words from Spanish, Arabic and Turkish, formed the basis of the *lingua franca* spoken throughout the Mediterranean area.[83] During the course of his stay in the Levant Covel also learned at least some Ottoman (a mixture of Turkish, Arabic and Persian that was spoken among the administrative elite and was regarded as a finer language than Turkish),[84] though probably not how to write Arabic script: there is no evidence in his diary that he could. Here there is a contrast with Luke, whose diary is full of phrases in Arabic script, and who went on to become professor of Arabic at Cambridge.[85] An earlier traveller, Pococke, who in 1636 was the first appointee to the chair of Arabic at Oxford established by Laud,[86] was able to make the Moroccan ambassador on a visit to England laugh when he made a joke in Arabic.[87] By the end of his stay at least, Covel was also fluent in contemporary Greek, so that he was able to correspond with Orthodox churchmen in their own language over the rest of his life.[88] His book on the Greek Church also demonstrates his knowledge of Hebrew. He frequently comments on philological and etymological matters, and on the question of the pronunciation of ancient Greek, which was a live issue in academic circles at the time.[89] His interest in language is also demonstrated by his use of code. Another traveller whose facility in languages was admired by his contemporaries was Vernon, who was murdered in Persia before he could write up his journey; in 1668, before he himself reached Turkey, Browne shared lodgings with Vernon in Amsterdam, and wrote admiringly home to his father about Vernon's mastery of Latin, Spanish, Italian, Dutch and French.[90] According to Spon, Vernon spoke seven or eight languages.[91]

Whether or not you shared a common language with the people you met or had dealings with, dragomans (interpreters) were likely to have been of crucial importance to you. Interpreters were often Greeks (who had sometimes been educated in Italy), but sometimes Poles, Hungarians, Jews, Armenians or Italians,[92] though not Turks: according to Georgirenes, archbishop of Samos and subsequently resident of London, Turks thought it dishonourable to learn Christian languages.[93] Wheler came across a Polish dragoman who, he said, spoke 17 languages.[94]

Diplomats in particular, in their negotiations with the Porte, used dragomans even when they themselves had some knowledge of Ottoman: the task of diplomatic interpretation was fraught with problems. An interpreter who worked for the English embassy was required to swear loyalty to the king, promising to conceal nothing relevant and to be a faithful interpreter and bearer of messages,[95] but the danger of divided loyalties always lurked. Rycaut, who would have liked to see a seminary for English candidates to study as interpreters, found that, not surprisingly, dragomans were reluctant to question the Grand Signor in the matter of capitulations (trade agreements).[96] When an argument arose between the Grand Vizier and the French ambassador over the positioning of the ambassador's stool, the dragoman trembled as he transmitted messages back and forth.[97] And when Finch's companion Baines met with the Vani Effendi (a senior religious official) to discuss religion, the interpreter said he was afraid to translate Baines's remark that he was too set in his ways to convert to Islam, even though the Vani had told Baines that he could say what he liked, and 'nothing should be taken amisse'. We know of this from one of the coded references in Covel's diary, in which the dragoman expresses his fear of saying what Baines has asked him to.[98] According to North, a Levant Company merchant contemporary with Covel and Finch, Finch put a delay in being received by the Sultan down to the dragoman.[99] Much was required of an interpreter, and sometimes his role verged on that of a spy: on one occasion, Winchilsea instructed his man to 'enquire underhand' about a matter.[100] When Finch was trying to sort out some trouble involving the pasha of Tunis, he was aware of the importance of reading the Vizier's mood right: 'if the Vizir does not mention [the capitulations] my Druggerman has order unlesse he finds Him [i.e. the Vizier] out of Humour[,] to mention it Himselfe'.[101] However, Finch also thought that there were many things that had to be concealed from the dragomans themselves.[102]

Covel recounts (again in code) another instance of worry over language and interpretation, in this case in the context of an audience with the Grand Vizier: when the ambassador began to speak in Italian, the dragoman begged him not to use that language, on the grounds that it was understood by many Turks.[103] The complication of a dragoman's life is indicated by Covel's comments on the Greek Panagiotes, who, he had been 'credibly inform'd', was in the pay of both the German Emperor and the Sultan, but who played his game well enough to die in peace.[104]

While foreigners sometimes felt themselves at the mercy of dragomans, the latter could also use their influence with great kindness, as an earlier traveller, Thomas Dallam, found. Dallam was an organ-builder, and at the very end of the sixteenth century he accompanied the organ he had built on behalf of Queen Elizabeth as a gift to the Sultan on its voyage to Constantinople. On his overland journey home, he had cause to be extremely grateful to his dragoman:

> we weare doged, or followed, by 4 stout villans that weare Turks. They would have perswaded our drugaman, which was our gid, to have given his consente unto the Cuttinge of our throtes in the nyghte, and he did verrie wisely Conseale it from us, and delayed the time with them, not daringe to denye ther sute; and so theye followed us 4 dayes over Parnassus; but our drugaman everie nyghte give us charge to keepe good watche, espetialy this laste nyghte, for theye did purpose to goo no farther after us, and our Turke, whome I cale our drugaman, had premeded [permitted] them that that nyghte it should be don. Now, after he had given us warninge to kepe good watche, he wente unto them and made them drinke so much wyne, or put somethinge in there wyne, that theye weare not only drunke but also sicke, that they weare not able to attempte anythinge againste us to hurt us, for the which we had verrie greate cause to give hartie thanks unto Almyghtie God, who was our chefeste savgaurd.

It is only at the end of this account that Dallam tells us that the interpreter came from Chorley in Lancashire, and was named Finch. The appellation 'Turk' given him by Dallam refers to his religion and not his race.[105]

Apart from misunderstandings due to language, another hazard of life for foreigners in the Levant was sickness, in particular plague, which was endemic in the cities. While Roe was ambassador, in the 1620s, plague had killed a thousand people a day,[106] and half a century later it was little better. Wheler and Spon felt it was unreasonable to go into English houses in the Frank quarter of Constantinople, since their curiosity led them 'everywhere, without consideration of Danger': presumably they thought they might be carriers of plague, so instead they chose to stay with a Jew, whose life they evidently took to be of less account.[107] When Covel travelled with Finch to the court at Adrianople, he stayed in a village outside the town in order to minimise the risk. He wrote that he thought no more of seeing a human corpse than that of a calf.[108] Both Winchilsea[109] and Covel sent home for remedies. In the case of Covel, who shows a strong interest in medicine and may possibly have studied it before being ordained,[110] the requests are very specific: he asked for *bezoarticum animale*, and would also have liked to replace the vitriol (dilute sulphuric acid), of which he had had a supply in a glass bottle which broke on the journey out. He tells us that the English mostly used this to treat plague, and, as a prophylactic, chewed 'zeduary' (*curcuma zedoary*) or drank wormwood or punch. He had a poor opinion of Turkish doctors, although Jewish doctors held high positions at court.[111] However, death was an ever-present threat: Covel recorded his friend Cary's last illness in detail, and he tells us how the renegade Baccareschi, with whom he shared some activities in Constantinople, died of plague, having eaten at the English ambassador's table when he was already ill.[112] Vernon's travelling companion Giles Eastcourt died of a fever near Lepanto.[113]

Covel says that early in his stay he himself suffered from a dangerous fever which lasted for 17 days, and was treated by the Greek Alexander Mavrocordato.[114] The French ambassador teased him about this, suggesting that his sickness was a convenient fiction to allow him to avoid a difficult meeting between the French and the English ambassadors about whether the Orthodox Church did or did not believe in transubstantiation;[115] however, since he had been specifically charged with finding out about this subject, it seems on the face of it to be unlikely that he would have deliberately absented himself from the meeting.

Randolph, a merchant and contemporary of Covel's, shows us a glimpse of a world that is mostly hidden from us, that of women, when he describes how, on Crete, he made the acquaintance of a group of 'doctoresses'.[116]

There is a coda to the story of health and sickness: although there were burial facilities for foreigners,[117] there are several instances of embalmed bodies being brought home, sometimes a considerable period after death. When Covel's first ambassador, Harvey, died in office in 1672, his body must have been preserved, as it was not until April 1674 that Covel accompanied it from Constantinople to Smyrna for its passage home by sea.[118] He also tells us that the bodies of the wives of two previous ambassadors, Lady Wych and Lady Bendish, were taken home in ships flying black flags.[119] According to Anne Bendish's husband, in a letter home dated 24 November 1649, her body was lying in a lead coffin under the chapel, prior to being returned to their native Essex for burial.[120] The body of yet another ambassador's wife, Anne Glover, was preserved in 'brawne' (bran) and kept in the buttery at the end of the cellar, although the men in whose correspondence this is discussed, John Sanderson and John Kitely, did not approve of the delay to her burial, which eventually took place in Constantinople in 1612.[121] Winchilsea wrote to Finch about how he had packed up the body of the deceased Venetian ambassador and sent it away secretly; to deflect suspicion, he had some coffin-like chests packed up for shipping, which the customs officer opened, to find nothing but bacon inside.[122] Finch himself records in his notebook that he had Baines's body embalmed by Jenkins the 'chirurgeon' and Cranmer the ship's surgeon, paying them each 28 zecchini (Venetian coins) for the task.[123] Baines and Finch were eventually buried together in a tomb in the chapel of Christ's College, Cambridge.

On a more cheerful note, Franks living and working in the Ottoman Empire, enjoyed a range of activities in their leisure time. Their enthusiasm for picnicking has already been mentioned, while their interest in what might be termed 'proto-archaeology' will be discussed later. North was a keen swimmer in the Bosphorus;[124] swimming and boat trips are also mentioned by Bargrave, secretary to Thomas Bendish, ambassador during the Interregnum.[125] The diplomatic party was allowed to use the summer-houses along the shore when their owners were absent. There were indoor pastimes too, such as playing cards, visiting Turkish houses and amateur dramatics, especially the performance of comedies.[126] Bargrave composed a masque, probably designed to be performed in the garden of the English palace outside the city, in the village of

Belgrade, for the wedding of his boss, James Modyford, to Bendish's daughter. Since the match was called off, it was never performed, but Bargrave did teach some of the tunes to the prospective bride.[127] In a passage excised from Roger North's printed life of his brother, he describes how Dudley and a companion used to enjoy throwing stones down the mountainside, setting land-crabs to race each other, and once cut a dog to pieces with a scimitar, writing '[by which] you may perceive that ye boy was Not quite worne off'.[128] It is hard to imagine that Covel would have enjoyed this last: we know that although he was not squeamish about dissecting a shark, he certainly had some sympathy for animals (he was distressed by cruelty to horses) and owned a dog during his time in the east.[129]

Observers of court life in Constantinople or Adrianople found much to fascinate them, and Covel was no exception. While the ambassador and his retinue were in Adrianople for the ceremonies surrounding the circumcision of the Sultan's son and the marriage of his daughter, the visitors were treated to performances of various kinds, such as acting, tossing weights, fireworks, wrestling with bears, weight-lifting, magic tricks, horse-racing, hunting with hawks and spaniels and a procession of decorated floats. The last included a waxwork garden with clockwork fountains, about three yards square, carried by slaves 'managed by galley whistle'. There were 'apish tricks with cream and custards', as well as acrobatic tricks of a kind he had seen less well done in England. The ambassador had brought, as a gift for the Sultan, a large English mastiff which in a fight proved a match for the biggest bear. Covel evidently enjoyed himself a great deal, and appreciated the courtesy with which the foreigners were treated, even if he did think it was more about showing off than about the feelings of the guests: 'we found ye greatest civility imaginable, and were severall times treated with sherbet of lemmons together with coffee and sweetmeats'.[130]

Although Covel frequently makes comparisons with places at home in England, he does not seem to have suffered from homesickness, as some travellers did. Winchilsea, who was extremely ambivalent about the 'barbaritie refined' and the 'rudenesse [...]

mixed with art' that characterised Ottoman society, in the same letter in which he calls the Turks barbarians also writes of their kindness to him. The list of things he was glad to leave behind when he left the Ottoman Empire has already been given. The personal difficulties he underwent during the period of his embassy – his wife almost died in childbirth and his 14-year-old son, left behind in England, was tricked into an unsuitable marriage – as well as diplomatic problems, are perhaps reflected in this catalogue of miseries. He was also in debt.[131] But perhaps the most poignant of all cases of homesickness is that of Anne Bendish, ambassador's wife, a relation of the Pepys family, who had accompanied her husband to Constantinople with one son and five daughters.[132] Ill as well as mourning the death by drowning of one of her sons, she wrote to her mother in Essex that she had written 40 letters home but had only received four in reply. Six weeks later, her husband wrote home to give an account of the death of 'the light of my life, the joy of my heart'. In his misery, he adds that he has 'undertaken the most troublesome dangerous and ungratefull imployment that ever man had [... owing to] the wicked turbulent spirits of our English nation [i.e. the merchants], who are not nor will be at peace among themselves'.[133] Travel in the seventeenth century was a dangerous business, though many travellers seem to have taken the risks for granted and not been much troubled by them.[134] Neither Coryate nor Vernon returned from the east, Thomas Sherley spent years in prison, and Lithgow suffered torture by the Inquisition; Bendish lost his beloved wife through sickness. Courage and stamina were required, and the successful achievement of a journey to distant parts was a matter of pride. The family of one man, Humfrey Coningsby, who spent 13 months in the Levant some 70 years before Covel, and who died abroad on a later trip, was proud enough of his achievement that it was recorded in detail on his funerary monument, which stands in the south transept of the church in the village of Neen Sollars in Shropshire:

HE WENT INTO TURKEY, NATOLIA, TROY IN ASIA BY
SESTOS AND ABYDOS THROUGH THE HELLESPONT

AND INTO THE ISLES OF ZANT, CHIOS, RHODES, CANDY, CYPRUS, AND DIVERS OTHER PLACES IN THE ARCHIPELAGO. HE VISITED SUNDRY ANTIENT AND FAMOUS PLACES OF GREECE, AS ARCADIA, CORINTH, THESSALONICA, EPHESUS AND ATHENS, WENT OVER THE PLAINS OF THERMOPYLAE BY WHICH XERXES PASSED INTO GREECE AND SO ARRIVED AT CONSTANTINOPLE IN THE REIGNE OF MAHOMET THE 3RD EMPEROR OF THE TURKS WHO TO DO HIM HONOUR GAVE HIM A TURKISH GOWNE OF CLOTH OF GOLD AND HIS MOTHER THE SULTANA EBRITA GAVE HIM ANOTHER RICH GOWNE OF CLOTH OF SILVER AND 50 CHEQUINS IN GOLD.[135]

CHAPTER 2

SCHOLARS AND TEXTS

The deep educational immersion in classical, and particularly in Latin, literature experienced by many men in the seventeenth century has been discussed in the introduction, but given the growing market both in classical texts and also in translations and bilingual editions,[1] it was not only grammar school or university educated men like Covel but also a wider social range who had access to this body of literature. In their use of references and quotations, travellers wove together their 'ocular' experiences with the experiences that they had assimilated through their reading. Covel is only one of many travel writers whose works display a high level of citationality. In addition, their reading of classical texts also contributed to the way travellers made sense of a changing world, in which political and religious stability must often have seemed precarious. Rycaut, for example, in whose attitude we find both religious hopefulness and political cynicism, uses Tacitus to distance himself from and put into perspective his views of the Ottoman Empire, and by implication of the Stuart monarchy too. In many of the accounts written about their experiences by travellers to or residents in the Greek world, classical quotations or references are used, to a greater or lesser extent, to illustrate, embellish or amplify their texts. Sometimes it is a case of mere decoration; sometimes quotations offer the reassurance of signposts to an unfamiliar cultural world from one that was familiar to both writer and readers; at other times, as with Rycaut, they are one of the ways in which the writer reflects on the worlds he inhabits. They may also be used to lend a (perhaps sometimes spurious) intellectual weight to the work in question. Cleland (not a traveller but a giver of advice to travellers) is disarming – but maybe falsely modest – about this: 'so have I covered my selfe [...] under the buckler of famous Authors to shoote my darts against Ignorance'.[2] Of course, these aspects are not mutually exclusive, but can be combined in different ways and proportions: Covel is perhaps the best example of how wide-ranging a writer's usage can be; Wheler and Rycaut were both also prolific quoters.

Writers' use of quotations is often evidence of their past reading and of their store of remembered (or, particularly in the case of poetry, learnt by heart) texts rather than of their current reading, a point that is confirmed by occasional misquotations and wrong attributions. It may also be highly dependent on individual collections of quotations in commonplace books: a single such book would have been much easier to carry around than large numbers of printed texts, though perhaps from our twenty-first-century perceptions we overestimate the convenience. Covel arrived in Constantinople with a trunk full of books, and almost his first action was to extract it from the hands of the customs officers.[3] His contemporary Vernon, though not given to quoting, does provide us with a day-to-day record of what he was reading as he travelled round Greece and Asia Minor. Between 19 September and 8 November 1675, when his journey took him from Patras to Athens, he read Pausanias, Ovid, Strabo (on the Morea, Attica, Boeotia, Thessaly and Acarnania, the areas he was visiting), Vitruvius and Pliny the Elder among ancient authors, as well as Church Fathers Athanasius and John Chrysostom and the early modern authors Johannes Meursius (1579–1639) and Guillet de Saint-George (1624–1705). Between 16 November and the end of January the following year he read Ovid, Virgil, Quintus Curtius Rufus, Pliny and Strabo, and also Justin and notes on Justin by Isaac Vossius (1618–89) and others. About once a week (not always on Sundays, unless he was very careless about dates) he read the Bible: was this perhaps more of a duty than a pleasure? Other books mentioned in his inventory of 25 January 1675/6 include works by

Herodotus, Ptolemy, Theophrastus, Dioscorides, Pierre Gilles (follower of Erasmus; 1490–1555), Pierre Belon (1517–64) and the mapmaker Johann Laurenberg, plus an 'Arab' dictionary and grammar: his next planned destination was Isfahan in Persia, but both Ottoman Turkish and Persian contain many Arabic words. Between 4 January and 12 March, while he travelled between Smyrna and Constantinople, he read Vitruvius, Pliny, Strabo, Homer (in translation, whether in Latin or English is not specified), Eratosthenes, Hipparchus, Poseidonius (as regards the last three, he is presumably referring to what Strabo says about them) and 'Animalibus' (probably Aristotle). In the same period he also read Pietro della Valle (1586–1652), Rycaut's books on Turkish history and the Greek Church, Thomas Smith's book on the seven churches of Asia, and George Sandys's travel book.[4]

The classical poets

When it comes to quotations from the poets, there are lines that had become almost like proverbs – well-known quotations whose origins were not necessarily known by the writer who quoted them. Perhaps the most prevalent of these among travellers to the Levant, because so many of them either visited the supposed site of Troy or saw it from their ships, and because the name and concept of Troy conveyed such a powerful image to men brought up on Homer and Virgil, is Ovid's line 'iam seges est ubi Troia fuit'.[5] In just a few words, Ovid suggests how the cycle of building and decay is seen to reflect, and eventually to revert to, the natural cycle of the seasons. Covel was an educated man, and had certainly read his Ovid, but he reinforces the familiarity of the line by altering it to apply to Carthage instead of Troy.[6] On another occasion, visiting the ancient city of Cyzicus, he quotes the line again but leaves it unfinished: '(corn now growes where –)'.[7] That the line was part of common currency is also suggested, for example, by its use by John Oglander, who wrote of his visit to Quarr Abbey on the Isle of Wight in 1607 that one Fr Penny showed him where the church had been, 'corn now growing where it stood'.[8] Writers may have known the original texts, but they may also have copied each other's allusions, and phrases like this are likely to have been well-known among the reading public. To use them was part of a strategy of creating a sense of community between the author and his readers. 'Touristic repetitiveness' is an apt phrase here, and at this date such repetitiveness had not become the source of anxiety that it was to be later. Such repetitiveness, as Yerasimos suggests, was both a way of emphasising that the writer in question had actually been to the sites he was describing, and also a demonstration that he had read on the ground what he had previously read in the texts.[9] It was almost *de rigueur* to use Ovid's line as part of a description of Troy, a site which had a long history of evoking a particularly strong sense of nostalgia, and reflection on the instability of civilisations.

The use of this line is an example of the way in which writers of travel accounts anchored their references to places that their readers had probably not visited in familiar literary, historical or mythical contexts. The author assumes knowledge of the legendary Troy with which the reader may link the description of the contemporary site given in the text. However, there is often another level of allusion too: in this case the stress on the abandoned and ruined state of a city that was once great suggests an implicit reminder that great cities and empires do have a tendency to fall. There is a moral lesson here about hubris. Even in the period after the Restoration, alongside thankfulness for restored stability in England, memories of the Civil War were raw, and for some of these writers the golden age of Troy may have exemplified both a time of greater security and less uncertainty than their own and at the same time the inevitability of the passing of any golden age. Burrow has written that post-Dante poets often sympathised with Virgil's moments of 'less than total confidence in the *imperium sine fine* which Jove promises to the Trojan exiles',[10] and it may also be that one reason for the popularity of the Roman epic poets was their concern with the political problem of succession, a problem that became acute at several moments in seventeenth-century England.[11] Travellers who had read Lucan knew that both Alexander the Great and Caesar had visited Troy, and could imagine how the site might have evoked in them reflections on the temporality of power.

The cultural currency of classical quotations is neatly demonstrated by a phrase used in 1669 in Richard Baddeley's life of the Protestant scholar Thomas Morton: Morton apparently thought that the suppression of the true religion was the worst of the '*Iliads of evills*' that had fallen on England since the Civil War, in other words a horror both vast in scale and long-drawn-out. It is not clear here whether the phrase is Morton's or Baddeley's, but 'an *Iliad* of Miseries' appears in the English translation (from the Latin) of the letters from Constantinople of Busbecq, sixteenth-century Austrian ambassador to the Ottomans, where the Latin phrase used by Busbecq is 'malorum agmen' ('a troop of miseries').[12]

Another frequently quoted line, this time not tied to a particular location, is Horace's 'caelum non animum mutant qui trans mare currunt':[13] this was evidently so familiar that Lithgow on one of his title pages needed only to quote the first three words of the line.[14] Lithgow, who had had a grammar school but not a university education, assumed that his readers would be able to complete the line for themselves. Generally, however, lines of poetry are used as identity tags for particular places: the context of the line is sometimes relevant, but on other occasions it is ignored, or may even be at odds with the seventeenth-century text, functioning simply as literary decoration. Virgil's lines about Crete:

Creta Iovis magni medio iacet insula ponto,
mons Idaeus ubi et gentis cunabula nostrae.
centum urbes habitant magnas, uberrima regna[15]

are a straightforward description of the island. The first of those lines appears appropriately as a title on Ortelius's maps of Crete, and all three are quoted by Ellis Veryard, in relation to his visit to Crete in 1686. Rycaut, on the other hand, who rarely quotes poetry, uses a line of Ovid's to fix the city of Philippopolis in Thrace (modern Plovdiv) in its geographical setting, entirely ignoring the original context of the line, which refers to Phyllis's description of the place where she first met Demophoon.[16]

Another contemporary of Covel, Edward Browne, demonstrates by his use of classical references that his interest lay in history rather than literature or myth, and in the relationship of the sites he visited to historical events that had taken place there: in his discussion of the battle of Pharsalus (in Thessaly, where Caesar defeated Pompey in 48 BCE) he quotes lines of Lucan's about the city of Larissa, which Lucan describes as being the first to share Pompey's defeat while remaining bloody but unbowed ('nec victum fatis caput').[17] However, Browne was also interested in the factual accuracy of ancient writers' descriptions: discussing Mount Olympus, and stressing the difference between the north and south sides of the mountain, he quotes again from Lucan, and in addition queries the appropriateness of an epithet used by Homer.[18] Covel on the other hand approved of Homer's description of Chiot wine: 'if I might spend my judgement I would pronounce this Homers wine, and deserves the title αἴθοπι οἴνω [sparkling wine]'.[19]

As these examples show, many references to classical texts arose out of the particular itineraries followed by individual travellers, but there are also other reasons for their use. Sometimes they amplify or explain the traveller's experiences: Covel, in the context of a meeting on the island of Cervi (in the Laconian Gulf, off the Peloponnese) with a Greek to whom he spoke in ancient Greek, which the man unsurprisingly did not understand, quotes Virgil[20] on Sinon, the Greek who caused the Trojan horse to be admitted into the city of Troy. Covel was inclined to think that the man was simply stupid, but the ship's captain assured him: 'believe me, Greeks are Greeks still; for falseness and treachery they still deserve *Iphigenia*'s character of them in Euripides, *Trust them and hang them*, or rather hang them first for sureness'.[21] The captain, and Covel in accepting the captain's assertion, are here doing exactly what Aeneas asked the Carthaginians to do with reference to Sinon, that is to say deducing the nature of all Greeks from the crime of one ('crimine ab uno/disce omnis').[22] There is evidence that some parts of Covel's diary were intended to be read by Robert Huckle, also a person of scholarly interests and a fellow member of the republic of letters, who would understand and take pleasure in sharing learned references.

Occasionally, writers use quotations to make descriptive passages more vivid. One of Covel's early seventeenth-century predecessors as a Levant Company chaplain, Biddulph (or his alter ego, the purported author of his preface, Theophilus Lavender), enhances his account of a storm at sea by repeating Ovid's lines:

> me miserum, quanti montes volvuntur aquorum!
> iam iam tacturos sidera summa putes.[23]

It may be that the unspoken message here is that Biddulph felt himself an exile like Ovid, although we know so little of his life that this cannot be more than speculative. A few pages later, he quotes from the beginning of Aeneas's narration of his story to Dido,[24] where the Trojan speaks of the almost unbearable renewal of his grief through the telling; 'Lavender' writes that he can get no account out of Biddulph about his return journey, because it involved the worst of his trials, of which he did not want to speak. It seems likely that this is not entirely straight-faced, but that there is a level of irony involved. Certainly Biddulph was not above deliberate obfuscation – witness his disguising of himself as 'Lavender' – though this may not be strong enough evidence to deduce a capacity for laughing at himself.[25]

John Finch, the ambassador under whom Covel served most of his chaplaincy, was not given to quoting classical authors, but there is one significant exception to this, when he described the death in Constantinople of his beloved companion Thomas Baines. In the course of his eulogy for his friend, Finch quotes from Virgil's description of how Aeneas, preparing to descend to the underworld, longed to meet his dead father Anchises again:

> ille meum comitatus iter maria anima mecum
> atque omnis pelagique ruinas caelique ferebat,
> invalidus, vires ultra sortemque senectae.[26]

The effect here is to raise the emotional temperature of the text, all the more so as it is a departure from Finch's usual practice. Interestingly, in a letter to the Earl of Conway written about four months earlier, Baines mentions the description of Aeneas's journey to the Elysian fields as well as quoting the lines in which Jupiter promises 'rule without end' to the Romans:[27] perhaps Finch and Baines had read or talked about these passages together, about the relationship between Aeneas and Anchises, or about what might happen if one of them predeceased the other. For them as Christians, the only true rule without end could be in heaven.

A creative use of quotation, or in this case adaptation, occurs on the title page of Neale's *Treatise of Direction*, where several lines attributed to Petronius are printed, in English. This turns out not to be a straight translation, although it is closely based on one of Petronius's poems: Neale has expanded it so that it takes up ten lines instead of six (the usual practice in translation being to try to keep the pattern of lines as close as possible to the original),[28] adding references more appropriate to his own readers, for example *'let it not suffice/To see th' adjoining France'*. He also adds a reference to the wisdom of Ulysses, the archetypal traveller, which is not in the original.[29]

Rycaut's classical references are mainly to Tacitus, but he does occasionally mention Latin poets; when he does so, he uses them in a reflective way, to muse on his historical and political themes. At the beginning of his *History of the Present State of the Ottoman Empire*, he quotes Horace's famous 'ship of state' ode in order to make an extended comparison of the way that 'the various motions of good Government' leave little trace on history. Horace's poem describes how winds and seas may force a ship back to sea just when she is apparently reaching harbour, and it may be that Rycaut had personal experiences of sea voyages in mind as well as metaphorical journeys.[30]

Although there are references to Greek poets and playwrights as well as Roman ones in travel writing, there are far fewer actual quotations than from Latin authors, at least in printed works, probably not only because there was less familiarity with the Greek language, so that Latin would have reached a wider audience, but also because of the lack of, and greater difficulty in setting, Greek type.

Sandys, writing in the second decade of the century, created a work in which a wide range of quotations, some of a considerable length, made an integral part.[31] Many of these come from Homer, but they are invariably quoted in English, with Latin versions in the margins, rather than in Greek. In Sandys's case, the prime reason for this was his interest in translation: in his later career he translated the whole of Ovid's *Metamorphoses* and the first book of the *Aeneid*. Covel, of course, was not constricted in his manuscript diary by the need for Greek printing type, and if we include his records of inscriptions the majority of pages have at least a word or two of Greek on them and often many more. Aside from actual quotations there are also hundreds of references to Greek texts, including occasional misattributions, suggesting that he did not always have the text to hand, but was quoting from memory.

Classical authors seem to have been in the forefront of Wheler's mind, too, although in his autobiography he deprecated his own ability in Greek.[32] On Corfu, where the Homeric gardens of Alcinous were supposed to have been sited, he wrote, 'Here we were full of Homer, especially his relation of the Kings daughter Nausica's adventure.'[33] He also discussed the identification of Homer's Ithaca at some length, and in Smyrna mentioned that according to Strabo the people of Smyrna were very insistent that Homer had been born there.[34] He was aware of the Greek playwrights too, who are not frequently mentioned in other seventeenth-century travel accounts: he noted that what he thought was the theatre of Bacchus (Dionysus) at Athens was 'antiently adorned with the Statues of their *Tragedians* and *Comedians*; of these [the comedians] *Menander* only was illustrious: but of the *Tragedians*, many; among which *Euripides*, *Sophocles*, and *Æschylus*'.[35] His other references to Euripides and Sophocles imply that he had not read their works himself. In some cases, he relied on the superior classical knowledge of his French companion, Spon, a doctor and antiquarian.[36]

The prose writers: texts as guide-books

Covel, Wheler and their contemporaries cite a wide range of prose authors as well as poets, usually without giving actual quotations;

one reason for this is that in the case of prose authors the purpose of the references is generally to elucidate the history, geography and topography of the terrain they found themselves in, and in particular of the ancient sites and ruins, rather than to give colour to their writing. Prose texts were frequently used in much the same way as modern tourists use guide-books: the key authors here were Pausanias and Strabo, and to a lesser extent Ptolemy and Pliny the Elder, though many others (Greek and Latin) are mentioned. Of these four, only Pliny is found on the grammar school curriculum, but in the field, at a time before there had been any systematic study of classical sites, when visitors were likely to be faced with a confusing jumble of ruins, they were a crucial aid. Herodotus does not figure prominently, probably because the first complete English translation, Isaac Littlebury's, did not appear until 1709; however, in the popular seventeenth-century genre of instructions to travellers, the range of aspects of life abroad that is covered owes much to the ethnographical tradition that originated with him.[37]

One reason for using classical texts as guide-books was the dearth of more recent texts to supplant them. The best of these, such as they were, were descriptions of the Greek world by Pierre Gilles and Pierre Belon. The work of the latter, who was a botanist, was published in 1554; it meanders through history and antiquities as well as covering the flora, and includes a useful account of Mount Athos. Gilles's two books about Constantinople and the surrounding area, published in 1652, are careful topographical and architectural surveys, based on a wide range of sources.[38] For Athens (which was not on the itinerary of most travellers, but where Wheler spent a month),[39] travellers might have recourse to the book by the Jesuit Fr Babin, published in 1674, which like Gilles's work was similar to modern cultural guides, or to the unreliable book by Guillet de St George.[40] But the ancient authors remained an essential *vade mecum* for the visitor interested in history and antiquities.

English visitors looked to Pausanias, Strabo and other authors to verify what they saw on the ground, and generally regarded them as authoritative. However, Covel and his contemporaries, travelling in the decades after the Restoration, were just beginning to be able to challenge these ancient sources when what they saw did not fit with what they read, or when the sources were in conflict with each other. A more complex and nuanced dialogue began to develop, involving question and argument as well as assent. In Wheler's case, this dialogue extends throughout his book: we know that he borrowed the English consul's copy of Pausanias to carry with him round Attica and the city of Athens.[41] The beginning of a critical attitude to ancient historians is a reflection of the gradual change in the teaching of history in the universities that was taking place in the seventeenth century, so that it no longer took the form simply of a commentary on the ancient historians but moved towards their reinterpretation as part of a broader understanding: the texts become part of the evidence rather than being the definitive narrative.[42] Travel writers also understood that monuments described by Pausanias, for example, were already falling into disrepair when Pausanias was writing: Edward Leigh, in his 'diatribe' (a word that had none of the pejorative connotations of modern usage) on travel of 1671, mentions Diodorus Siculus, Strabo and Arrian, but singles out Pausanias for 'that excellent book of the Monuments and Antiquities of *Greece*, remaining in his time'.[43]

What may be called the 'guide-book' use of references in travel accounts sometimes takes the form of a simple mention of a place, a historical event, or a fact that the seventeenth-century writer uses to anchor his text. The most frequently cited ancient author here is Pliny the Elder, of whose *Natural History* one modern scholar has written that it 'continued to be a standard reference book and an object of scholarly dissection until well into the seventeenth century'.[44] Both Covel and Veryard, at Cyzicus on the Sea of Marmara, mention Cupid's fountain, described by Pliny.[45] Spon and Wheler opened their door one morning in the Peloponnese and found a pelican, which Spon identified by reference to Pliny.[46] It is no surprise to find Wheler, a passionate botanist, recognising a strawberry tree (*arbutus*), by reference to Dioscorides.[47] While Wheler and Spon were travelling in Asia Minor, they thought they had identified the city they called Pliny's Mandrapolis, though in fact it is Livy, not Pliny, who refers to the city of Mandrupolis in Mysia.[48]

Thomas Smith, also in Asia Minor, used Strabo to identify a mountain on the mainland opposite the southern end of Lesbos as the ancient Aegae,[49] and Rycaut, travelling among the cities of Asia Minor, used both Strabo and Pliny.[50] Clearly there was often a great deal of confusion about both topography and nomenclature, which is not surprising given that the seventeenth-century travellers were using texts dating from centuries earlier. Lithgow's indication of his own (and Strabo's) confusion about the island of Cephallonia is a typical example of this: 'The Ile of *Cephalonia* was formerly called *Ithaca* [...] Secondly, by *Strabo* it was named *Dulichi*: And thirdly, by auncient Authors *Cephalonia*.'[51]

Another ancient author, Cicero, is cited with reference to a specific event, in this case by Veryard, although here the event is mythical rather than historical, putting Veryard closer to those writers who embellish their work with poetic quotations: he repeats the story that the temple of Diana at Ephesus was burned down on the night of Alexander the Great's birth, something that could only happen because Diana, goddess of midwives, was away from home attending the birth.[52] In terms of factual accuracy, Veryard, following Cicero, does not explicitly distinguish between the fire and the goddess's absence, though of course it is almost certain that as a Christian he thought of Diana as mythical. He did not always accept his sources unquestioningly: at Lemnos, he thought Pliny had got some of his measurements wrong, at Paros he comments that there is supposed to be a fountain 'if we may credit *Pliny*', and he also held the general view that Pliny himself was 'too credulous' in many things.[53] In the case of the Ephesus story, Cicero ascribes it to Timaeus (a Greek historian of the fourth to the third centuries BCE), and implies that he (Cicero) is sceptical about the reason for the fire; but it is impossible now to be certain who believed what.

On occasion, reading a text suggested to travellers what to look for: Covel and his party would have liked to see the labyrinth at Lemnos, which Pliny described as having had 150 columns and being similar to the Cretan, though in his time there were only remains to be seen; Covel was disappointed to find nothing but a grotto.[54] When Blount, in the fourth decade of the seventeenth century, was at Philippopolis, in Thrace, en route from Sofia to Constantinople, he read Caesar's account of the battle of Pharsalus in *De bello civili*, a copy of which he carried 'on purpose [...] to conferre upon the Place, for the better impression'. There is a lot of confusion here, since Blount seems to have thought that the battles of Philippi and Pharsalus, and maybe also the battle of Thermopylae, had been fought near the spot where he was, whereas in fact he was not at the site of any of the three battles. Thermopylae is in Locris, Pharsalus in Thessaly, and Philippi in southeastern Macedonia. He also believed he had identified the river Strymon, which in fact is well to the south-west of where he was, nearer to Philippi.[55]

It was unusual for text and ground to corroborate each other as neatly as they did for Veryard near the site of Sparta: he saw a bas-relief of Agesilaus, the inscription on which indicated that it had been erected after the subject's death. Veryard points out that according to Plutarch, Agesilaus refused to have a likeness of himself made during his lifetime: 'this makes good a passage in *Plutarch* [... that] he would not suffer himself to be represented by Picture or Statue, but left Monuments of his Mind to all. However, the Citizens, after his death, erected this Piece'. Veryard was clearly pleased to be able to match the text with the evidence before his eyes.[56]

Mostly, the fit was much more awkward, but this in itself was an encouragement to take issue with the classical authors. Some examples of a critical attitude to the ancient texts have already been given. Perhaps it was easier to take such an attitude when the texts did not agree with each other. On the Ionian coast, in the vicinity of the Maeander River, Wheler comments: 'Although *Strabo* here brags to be so exact in his Geography; yet he and *Ptolemy* do not agree concerning the Bounds of *Ionia* and *Caria*.' He goes on to say that while these two do agree about the position of Mount Latmus, on this point they both differ from Pliny.[57] The archaeological evidence that would have helped Wheler and Spon to make a further judgement was simply not available to them: all they had was what they had read and what they could see on the ground. In another instance of an emerging critical sense, Wheler, unusually among his contemporaries, expresses disquiet about the pagan rituals of the Greeks. At Eleusis, he reminds his readers,

> *Pausanias* pretends to be forbidden to write of her Mysteries, by a Dream [...] but *Minutius Fœlix* [a Christian apologist of the third century CE] knew them, and shews them to have been horribly wicked, and Diabolical; which was the reason of their Secresie.[58]

Wheler also, in spite of his great admiration for the monuments of ancient Athens, disapproved of the city as 'The Seminary of superstitious Temples, and false Worship; of which *Pausanias* gives an ample Description'.[59]

Covel visited Ephesus in December 1670, on his way to take up his post in Constantinople. In his long description of the site (some pages of which are unfortunately illegible) he makes use of a range of texts, Strabo, Pausanias, Herodotus, Pliny, Ptolemy and Homer, in order both to understand what he was seeing on the ground and to contribute to his discussion of etymologies and meanings of Greek words. His reliance on these sources underlines the fact that he had few more recent ones available to him, though he does mention Palladio, who he assumes was himself using Vitruvius, as well as Rycaut and Spon.[60] He makes explicit his knowledge that the site of the city had moved several times, sometimes gradually, and sometimes, as after the flooding caused by Lysimachus, hastily. He gives a detailed account of how he tried to relate Strabo's account of these moves to the extant ruins and to the topography of the landscape. He provides two maps or pictorial diagrams of the area,[61] very similar in style to other such maps in his diary, but annotated in a different hand, possibly that of his friend Jerome Salter or Saltier, a member of the Smyrna English community, whose general help in connection with Ephesus he acknowledges. He frequently orientates his description by reference to the sea, but it is not entirely clear whether he understood the extent to which the coastline had altered since early antiquity, although he knew from Pliny about the silting up of the river Cayster. We know from the early pages of his diary, written when he was waiting for his ship to sail to the Levant, that he had a great interest in coastal erosion, but he specifically tells us that for lack of time he did not go down to the sea at Ephesus.

His historical sense was strong enough that he understood how the city had undergone many stages of construction and destruction, and he was well aware that he did not have enough evidence, either in the texts or on the ground, to give a detailed explanation of this process. He writes, 'I do by no meanes pretend to be anything near the exact truth, but according to that idea that remain'd in my mind after our hasty view', offering 'a meer confused guesse at best'. This attitude applies not only to the city and its site as a whole, but to individual buildings, and to periods after those described in the sources: 'There is no doubt but the buildings were increased and altered much after *Strabo* and *Pliny*'s time [...] yet we have but a poor and uncertain account of what the Romanes afterwards did do.'[62] He did not find the ruins of the temple of Artemis, which were not discovered until the mid-nineteenth century, partly because he was looking in the wrong place, that is among the ruins of the Roman city rather than on the site near the modern Ayasuluk, although he did explore the latter area, and made notes about the castle, the so-called Gate of Persecutions and the Basilica of St John.

Covel's use of Homer in the context of Ephesus demonstrates the extent to which his mind was stocked with the works of the classical authors. Thinking about how to identify the areas that Strabo calls 'Tracheia Acte' and 'Lepra Acte', he remembered that Homer uses the word τρηχεῖα to describe a rocky coastline, and wondered – though he had not been to Ithaca – whether the landscape he was seeing at Ephesus might be similar.

Nicaea, like Ephesus, posed problems because the ground did not bear out the text. According to Covel, one gate 'seemes to stand entire [,] conformable to the platforme in Strabo'. This led him to assert, 'I could be easily induced to beleive that ye city in Strabo's time lay square, as farre out as this pick't ground plot, if I had found the footsteps of any old walls to warrant it.'[63] He understood that if he was to trust the text completely he needed to find corroboratory evidence on the ground. At Cyzicus, on the other hand, he found 'a great deal of satisfaction' in seeing ruins that so well matched the description given by Strabo.[64] An almost triumphant note creeps into the tone of his comment on this frustratingly rare experience.

Wheler, who spent more than six months in Constantinople, Asia Minor and Greece (September 1675 to April 1676), mostly in the company of the French doctor and classicist Spon, mainly used ancient sources to guide him. Although he mentions his contemporary Thomas Smith a number of times,[65] usually with approbation even if they were not in complete agreement, and is (like others) dismissive of Guillet de Saint-George,[66] the texts he relied on as he investigated classical sites were Strabo, Pliny and Ptolemy for Asia Minor, and Pausanias for Attica. It seems likely that the two men carried texts of some of these authors with them on their travels. In a typical reference to Strabo, Wheler writes that of the 13 cities mentioned by the ancient geographer only three remain 'either in Name, or tolerable Being. But most of them are easily known where they were, by their Ruins, and the Description that *Strabo* giveth of them.'[67] He recognised that there were sometimes conflicts between the accounts of Pliny, Ptolemy and Strabo, but was generally content to leave it at that, though he also thought that mistakes had been made by 'the Interpreters and Commentators' of Strabo.[68]

Sometimes Wheler and Spon themselves disagreed with each other over the interpretation of Strabo, for example over whether the modern Mount Aleman was the ancient Mount Mimas or not.[69] Wheler was sometimes prepared to doubt whether a received text was faithful to the original: he found the description of the Boeotian lakes, Copais and Hylike, and how they might be fed, extremely confusing, and concluded that 'those that have good skill in the Greek Tongue, may be able to understand that very defective place in *Strabo*, where he speaks of these two Lakes, and restore it again'.

Pausanias too wrote about the origins of Lake Copais: Wheler is prepared to argue with the story he tells (not, incidentally, Pausanias's own view), but is unable to move away from the mythological frame, even though in other places he expresses disapproval of pagan beliefs: '*Pausanias* saith, that the ancients believed that *Hercules* made this lake [...] I rather believe, that *Hercules* stopped [...] the Passage under the Mountains.'[70]

Pausanias is in some ways a more puzzling author than Strabo to deal with in that the religious dimension of his work was probably not well understood in Wheler's day, and the modern reader has the impression that Wheler does not always know quite how to take him. As Elsner puts it in his discussion of Pausanias's description of Eleusis: 'Here, before the sacred which cannot be described, the text's experiential emphasis breaks down. The reader who does Greece *with* Pausanias, in his order, at his pace, along his roads, is left *outside* the sacred wall'.[71]

Pausanias was exploring his own identity as a Greek in the Roman world, and as an initiate: as Pretzler has put it, his writing blurs what was actually visible with his imaginative recreation of the past,[72] and this makes his text less easy for a tourist to follow as a guide-book, as Wheler was doing both for purposes of identification and also for historical and mythological background. As with the Hercules-Lake Copais story, he was not always willing to accept him uncritically, but in many instances found him detailed and helpful. At Delphi, he was able to identify the Castalian spring, and with the aid of both Strabo and Pausanias he and Spon confirmed that the modern village of Salona was the ancient Amphissa, not the ancient Delphi; this recognition led them to Castri, which they realised was the true site of Delphi.[73] Other cases were more confusing: in Patras, they simply 'could not find the *Theater*, nor the *Odeum*, nor many other Temples, which *Pausanias* speaks of'.[74] On the Athenian acropolis, Wheler writes, 'But whether this [a large square building] was [...] that Building, which *Pausanias* saith, is on the left hand of the *Propylaea*, full of Pictures, or painted Work, is hard to say'.[75]

He does not blame Pausanias here, though when it comes to the oracle of Trophonius, in Boeotia, that author 'is not so clear as might be wished': Pausanias gives an extended description of what was involved when a man wished to consult this oracle, but Wheler and Spon disagreed about the exact location of the entrance to the oracle's cave.[76] There are frequent references to times when Pausanias was an invaluable guide, of which the account of the Athenian Erechtheum, easily recognisable 'by two Marks out of *Pausanias*', that it was a *'Double Building'* and that it contained a well of salt water, is typical.[77] In this case, however, what Wheler saw was not Pausanias's well, which Levi thinks might have been a Mycenaean cistern, but probably the cistern later cut into the rock by Christians.[78] If Wheler disagreed with his companion over a particular identification, Pausanias could also be a useful ally.[79]

Early modern writers such as Covel and Wheler (and others who did not profess to be classical scholars) were locating their work within a network of ancient texts that would also have been familiar, to a greater or lesser extent, to their readers. It was a way not only of explaining the 'other' in terms of what readers would have understood, but also of positioning themselves and demonstrating where they stood in relation both to their intellectual and cultural environment and to the society in which their works would be read. The relationship was complex, because by the very activity of visiting classical sites and seeing with their own eyes they were putting themselves in the position of being able to challenge the textual authority of the ancient sources with the knowledge of personal experience, while at the same time being dependent on those same sources. As Grafton, writing about the effect of knowledge of the new world on that of the old, has expressed it:

> The texts provided European intellectuals not with a single grid that imposed a uniform order on all new information, but with a complex set of overlapping stencils [...] These produced diverse, provocative, ultimately revolutionary assemblies of new facts and images.[80]

While this is not so obvious in the case of the old world as in that of the new, we nevertheless see the beginnings of a similar process, particularly in the rise of experimental science, and also – of particular relevance to travellers – of archaeology.

There is no doubt, however, that there was a general appreciation of what the classics had to offer, nor is there any hint of the notion that the ancient authors might be out of date as guides, even if they could be doubted on particular points. It is also true that, in the absence of archaeological evidence, these authors offered the best chance to visitors of understanding what they were looking at.

Rycaut and Tacitus

Rycaut's use of Tacitus is in a different category from the 'guide-book' use of writers such as Strabo and Pausanias, not least because he actually quotes from the Roman historian, rather than just referring to him. In his *The Present State of the Ottoman Empire*, some 18 quotations (more than three-quarters of the total number) are taken from Tacitus, whom he greatly admired and to whom he was compared by some of his contemporaries.[81] He knew the writings of ancient historians well, modelling his style on Thucydides and Livy as well as Tacitus, and was later to translate Plutarch's *Life of Numa Pompilius*.[82] Rycaut uses his knowledge of the Roman Empire and its chroniclers to make constant comparisons between that empire and the Ottoman, viewing both through a lens of irony, sometimes even cynicism, which he shared with Tacitus. Early in his book he quotes Tacitus's phrase 'ludibria rerum mortalium' ('the mockery of human affairs'),[83] adopting a tone that recurs throughout the work. It may have been this quality that the more down-to-earth North (according to his earliest editor) so much disliked, although ostensibly North's criticism was on the grounds of superficiality and factual errors.[84] The quotation about the mockery of human affairs occurs in a passage in which Rycaut is reflecting on the reasons for the success of the Ottoman Empire, coming to the conclusion that it can only thrive through supernatural intervention, and that God allows it to succeed in order to punish Christians for their bad ways. The state of Christendom, or specifically of England, is often implicit in comments on the Turkish Empire by Rycaut and others, and is sometimes made explicit.

Many of the Tacitus quotations are introduced for the purpose of commenting on and moralising about the Ottoman court. Thus the German chieftains' habit of surrounding themselves with bands of chosen youths (in Tacitus) is compared to the way in which those in the ascendancy in the Ottoman court are surrounded with specially trained boys.[85] Corruption under the sultans is compared to that of Fabius Valens, a legionary commander in the Roman province of Germania Inferior.[86] Reflecting on the flattery, capriciousness and uncertainty of life which characterise the Turkish court, Rycaut quotes three times from Tacitus, underlining the messages that friendship and influence between sovereign and subject may come to an end in various ways, that it is human nature to look unfavourably on the good fortune of others, and that nothing in human affairs is so unstable as the fame attached to a power that is not founded on internal strength.[87] According to Tacitus, even the Roman emperor Tiberius, though he did not want public liberty ('qui libertatem publicam nollet'), became weary of his grovelling slaves.[88] The same emperor, however, is contrasted by Rycaut with the grand viziers at the Ottoman court: Tiberius 'held to his rule of manipulating foreign affairs by policy and cunning, without resorting to arms' ('destinata retinens consiliis et astu res externas molire, arma procul habere'), whereas the Sultan's grand viziers could only hold on to power by getting their master to concentrate on war.[89] It is not a matter of simply comparing Ottomans and Romans: the comparisons shift, and they are not usually directly stated but implied by the quotations, suggesting that Rycaut expected a high level of knowledge of Tacitus in his readers.[90]

It is not only Turks who come under scrutiny from Rycaut. He criticises the Greeks and Armenians at the court for adopting Turkish dress, like the Britons under Roman rule who were lured into wearing Roman clothes because they regarded them as a sign of distinction when in fact they were a sign of their servitude ('cum pars servitutis esset').[91] Rycaut had lived through, and been horrified by, the execution of Charles I,[92] and although all his overt references are to circumstances which are distant in time or place from contemporary England, the covert message to the reader is surely about the state of his home country. Did he see himself as a second Tacitus, a detached observer, standing back from but deeply concerned by the chaos of history? He certainly uses Tacitus not only to lend weight to his arguments, but also to suggest that he takes a long historical view. Although he makes no specific reference to this, the second chapter of the first book of Tacitus's *Histories* could be a description, *mutatis mutandis*, of England during the Civil War. Tacitus (and to a lesser extent the other Roman historians) seems to have been his constant companion in his reflections on the state of affairs around him. Musing on the fact that even in the uncertain world of the court there have been some grand viziers who have survived for as much as 19 years in office, he asks himself, following Tacitus, whether we have free will or are ruled by fate.[93] Similarly, to illustrate the signs he perceives of the 'declension and decay' of the empire, he quotes Livy's view that 'you will find everything turned out well for those who obeyed the gods, badly for those who ignored them' ('invenietis omnia prospera evenisse sequentibus deos, adversa spernentibus').[94] He was alert to the idea of the cyclical rise and fall of empires which was a common theme of the time, expressed for example by the early seventeenth-century historian Knolles at the end of his *Generall historie*: 'The greatnesse of this Empire being such, as that it laboureth with nothing more than the weightinesse of it selfe, it must needs (after the manner of wor[l]dly things) of it selfe fall, and againe come to nought'.[95]

While England had not yet acquired an empire, Rycaut (alongside other travellers) was part of the expansion of English interests and influences which would eventually lead to the acquisition of one. Certainly he demonstrates a sustained interest in, and sensitive antennae towards, the workings of power in the Ottoman world.

The fall of empires, or of cities, was a theme often associated with human mortality and the transience of human affairs; Rycaut, again, articulates these ideas in his discussion of the seven churches of Asia: God 'casts down one [empire], and raises another', while the sight of tombs at Hierapolis 'put us in mind of our own mortality, as well as of the period and subversion of cities'.[96] In another passage, observing and reflecting on the Ottoman Empire from a background of extensive knowledge of the Roman Empire, and probably with England at the back of his mind, he discusses the *ius civitatis* and the importance of citizenship as the glue that holds an empire together.[97]

Very occasionally, Rycaut uses a quotation to enhance the descriptive qualities of his prose, as when he expresses the horror and confusion of the Turkish–Hapsburg battle in 1664 by comparing it to what happened to Germanicus (Tiberius's nephew), caught with his troops in a flood, when neither words nor mutual encouragement were of any avail.[98] And on one occasion he lightens the tone of his heavyweight political reflections by comparing the Sultan's relationship with subjects whose loyalty he suspects to that between the cuckoo and the little birds, as described by Plutarch after Aesop.[99] However, these references are outside the usual pattern of his allusions.

History and myth

Apart from references to and quotations from ancient authors, travel writers sometimes mention historical events or mythical topics, with or without specific textual references. Of the former, the exploits of Xerxes are the most popular, in particular his crossing of the Hellespont by a bridge of boats and his cutting through the Mount Athos peninsula. Rycaut was sceptical about the extent of the latter feat: 'the story of *Xerxes* cutting this Mountain [...] seems a Fable, occasioned perhaps by opening and enlarging that Ditch or Channel, which to this day appears from Sea to Sea'.[100] Although he does not specifically say so, he presumably thought that the channel was originally a natural one. Covel, in his account of his trip to Mount Athos, refers to Herodotus here: being on the spot and able to survey the lie of the land, Covel repeats Herodotus's assertion that this was a show of power by Xerxes rather than a practical necessity, though he suggests that the ships could easily have sailed round, while Herodotus thought they could have been dragged across at the narrowest point. He also played down the extent of the feat: 'I question not but that Xerxes did not cut ye mountain, but onely ye low Isthmus, and that onely by a little trench big enough and deep enough to let a galley passe, which may very well have since by degrees been grown up again'.[101]

Wheler was reminded of Xerxes at various places connected with the Persians: he mentions the battles of Marathon and Plataea, and tells the story based on Herodotus of how Xerxes built a silver throne from which to watch the battle of Salamis, the Greek victory leading, according to Wheler, to the king's eventual escape in a small boat.[102] The naval chaplain Henry Teonge also knew of Xerxes's bridge of boats over the Hellespont, as did Veryard, although the latter refers to it as Darius's bridge.[103]

Alexander the Great is another name that crops up from time to time. According to Browne, he was popular with Turks; this may go back to the idea that Mehmed the conqueror saw himself as successor to a line of classical heroes and had visited Troy in Alexander's footsteps.[104] A work by a fifteenth-century Greek historian, Michael Kritoboulos, dedicated to Mehmed, has the comparison with Alexander as a main theme, and it is known that Mehmed possessed Arrian's *Anabasis*, the standard life of Alexander, in a manuscript written by the same scribe as his copy of Kritoboulos, probably Kritoboulos himself.[105] The French historian Michel Baudier, in 1635, wrote that 'some *Sultans* have taken delight to read the life of Great *Alexander*, and some others have caused *Aristotle* to be expounded unto them'.[106] Given Rycaut's interest in the history and politics of empire, it is not surprising to find Alexander's conquests referred to as an example of an empire that, unlike the Roman or the Ottoman, resembled a ship with much sail and no ballast, or a tree with boughs too laden for its trunk to support, so that it 'became a windfal on a sudden'.[107] Wheler writes with admiration of Alexander, describing the river Granicus in north-western Asia Minor as 'the first Theatre of *Alexander*'s great Glory. For here he overcame *Darius* his Governours, and with them all *Asia* within *Taurus*, unto the River *Euphrates*'. But Wheler was more sympathetic to defeated Greeks than some of his contemporaries, and described them, the Athenians in particular, as reduced by the Macedonians to

> such a degree of Subjection, as to disarm them of their very Tongues, by restraining them from talking in their Publick Meetings; by so much, no doubt, more grievous to them, by how much they naturally loved, and used the Liberty of that Member. For who such Wits in all *Greece*, as the *Athenians*? who such Talkers? who so Pragmatical and busie in all Affairs?

And, to give many of them their due, none so Eloquent and Learned.[108]

Browne, who spent most of his time in the Larissa area, remembered reading about how Alexander's father, Philip of Macedon, climbed Mount Haemus (the range of mountains extending westwards from the west coast of the Black Sea), from whose summit it was said both the Adriatic and the Black Sea were visible. The source for this is Livy, who recounts how, when Philip came down, having disproved the story for himself, his party 'did nothing to dispel the popular opinion' ('nihil vulgatae opinioni degressi inde detraxerunt').[109]

The Romans tend to be mentioned in connection with general ideas rather than with particular events or people, though Hadrian's building programme was of interest to Wheler.[110] Roman education, for example, was a topic of interest to Englishmen who saw themselves as in some sense heirs of the Romans: North's biographer, his younger brother Roger, comments that Roman youths 'made it their ordinary exercise to bear the extremes of heat and cold and all sorts of fatigues',[111] the implication being that North, who swam in the Hellespont as he had done in the Thames, was indeed a worthy successor.

Hovering in the background in several travel accounts are the Greek myths,[112] stories of Odysseus and the Trojan War being the most popular subject, followed by myths connected with Crete – the labyrinth, Theseus and Ariadne, Daedalus and Icarus. When Rycaut was exploring the ruins of Ephesus and descended some steps into what he took to be the foundations of a building, he needed a 'Clew of Thread' to find his way: he expected his readers to know the story of Ariadne in Crete without mentioning her name.[113] Covel jokes about the scale of the ceremonies celebrating the circumcision of the Sultan's son by comparing them to the Trojan War – 'the story of ye walls of Troy and their jibby horse is to [the circumcision ceremonies] as Tomthumb to Bevis of Southampton'[114] – but it may be that he was also thinking of the Trojan horse as being less of a marvel than the highly decorated horses in a Turkish ceremonial procession. Covel is also unusual in providing an example of linking myths across different cultures, in that he compares the stories of St George and the dragon, Hercules and the hydra, Apollo and the python, and Eve and the serpent;[115] this suggests that in the period after the Restoration we may be seeing the beginnings of a more analytical attitude to the classical past. When we come to look at attitudes to ruins, we find more evidence of such a shift. The anonymous author of *A Description of Candia* (1670), a mercenary whose work is largely an account of the day-to-day progress of the Turkish siege of Crete, also shows a robust (if not analytical) attitude to myth, referring to 'the various Poetical Fictions and Fabulous Stories of Doting Antiquity' about Crete.[116]

Wheler has a rather different way of using myth: besides linking myths with specific places, as others do, he also uses them to explain the buildings and works of art he saw. When he visited the temple of Nike on the Athenian Acropolis, he was under the impression, following Pausanias and the tenth-century encyclopaedia known as the Suda, that it was dedicated to a wingless Victory: 'It was therefore stiled *Without Wings*; because the fame [of Theseus's victory over the minotaur] arrived not at *Athens*, before *Theseus* himself brought it. For otherwise, Victory used still to be represented *with Wings*.' In fact, Pausanias simply says that it was from this place that Theseus's father leapt to his death: he does not link the Victory's lack of wings with this story. Presumably, neither Pausanias nor Wheler saw the winged victories carved on to balustrade slabs of this temple, possibly because of the fact that they faced outwards.[117] Wheler identified a statue as representing Ceres, the goddess who showed the Greeks how to grow corn, by the basket of wheat-ears and flowers on her head. He sometimes failed to distinguish between history and myth, for example when he identified a spring near Eleusis as the one beside which Ceres sat down to rest during her search for her daughter, and in his summary of the history of Greece, myth and history are run together.[118] This is not necessarily evidence that he did not know the difference, but rather that his mind was peopled with the characters of Greek myth, as is illustrated by a story he tells of his own experience as a traveller. One night, during his final journey from Athens to the Corinthian Gulf, where he was to embark for home, the ignorant guide was unable to find them a place to stay. However, they came across some oxen, which they followed 'as Cadmus did a Heifer, by direction of the Oracle to the building of Thebes', arriving in due course at a hut belonging to a shepherd, who directed them on to a village where they were able to find lodging for the night.[119]

The Bible

Surprisingly, perhaps, since Covel was a Christian minister (as were John Luke, Henry Teonge and Thomas Smith),[120] the Bible does not figure largely among travellers' cultural references. Part of the explanation for this lies in the fact that the places they were exploring were mainly classical sites, but on the other hand Covel, Smith, Luke and Rycaut also visited the sites of the seven churches to whom St Paul had written his epistles. The more compelling explanation is the degree to which these men had been immersed in the classics from the time of their earliest educational experiences. Their writings rarely express any sense of tension between the pagan classics and the Christian scriptures, and there is little evidence that they regarded biblical references as conveying greater moral authority than those from classical literature.

To the extent that the Bible is cited, it is used in the same way as the classics. In the first place, biblical tags are employed to identify sites: almost all those who went to the seven churches, for example, refer to the Book of Revelations,[121] and a visit to Patmos usually evokes a reference to St John.[122] Similarly, Paul's epistle to Titus is sometimes mentioned to underpin the assertion that all Cretans are liars.[123] Sometimes mistakes are made: Veryard was under the impression that Paul had written a letter to the Rhodians, whose alternative name (he believed) was Colossians, after their Colossus.[124] Rycaut, on the other hand, complains that other (unspecified) sources have confused the Island of Birds, or Phygela, a coastal promontory near Ephesus, with Miletus, from where Paul summoned the elders of Ephesus.[125]

Paul was in the forefront of the minds of those following in his footsteps: Wheler describes his conversion of the first Christians in Athens, and mentions him in his discussion of the sad state of Christians in Corinth, where 'few Marks [...] of St *Paul*'s Preaching, Pains, or Care of this famous Church [...] are now to be observed';[126] Teonge too makes several references to Paul's missionary journeys, and jokes that before he himself boarded his ship he tried to retrieve the cloak that he had 'left long since' at the pawnbroker's, not at Troas, where St Paul had left his.[127] Rycaut, as usual, is more reflective, using references to Paul's epistle to the Romans to illustrate and amplify his arguments about the state of the Greek Church and the relationship of the Greeks to other gentiles and to Jews.[128]

In Covel's diaries we find another example (not here linked with the identification of a particular place) of a rather more discursive treatment of a biblical passage, in this case a rare mention of an Old Testament story. On his journey to Nicomedia, Covel came across a stream which was regarded as having miracle-working properties, and heard of a man whose ulcers were said to have been cured by washing in it. He was reminded of Naaman, the leper cured after following Elisha's instructions to bathe seven times in the Jordan, which led Covel to reflect on the medicinal benefits of washing.[129] On Chios, his observation that every Turkish gentleman owned a vineyard reminded him of Isaiah.[130]

In several instances, Covel demonstrates a more academic use of biblical references than is found in most travel accounts. In his description of a visit to Lemnos, discussing salt-making, he includes a learned digression about the use in St Matthew's gospel of the Greek word ἀγαρεύω, meaning 'to compel': 'Whosoever shall compel thee to go a mile, go with him twain.' This arises from his noticing that the Turks who oversee the salt trade are still described by the word ἀνγαριοὶ (Covel's spelling), which is etymologically close to the word for 'compel', presumably implying that the salt-makers are treated like slaves.[131] This is only one example of Covel's interest in etymology. Elsewhere, he links the biblical story of Eve with stories from other cultures, adding with a suggestion of triumph that he can be obstinate in his opinion about this now that Dr Heylyn is dead. Evidently there was an academic controversy over this point.[132] Another such connection is traced by Veryard with reference to the people of Arcadia, who were thought by some to be more ancient than the moon and for that reason to wear moonlike ornaments on their shoes. Veryard opines that such ornaments are likely to have been marks of status, and that it is those same ornaments that are referred to in a passage from Isaiah that he thinks the translators have misunderstood.[133] Such comparisons are part of the culture of curiosity, in which educated gentlemen might make collections both of objects from diverse cultures and of facts about people from different parts of the globe.

Another purpose for which biblical references might be employed is the pointing of a moral, and it is here that their scarcity in comparison to classical references is most surprising. Among few such instances is Wheler's account of his visit to Corinth, where he suggests that the reason for the poor state into which the Corinthians have fallen is their failure to understand the epistle that Paul wrote to them; the implied moral here, that we should pay attention to the scriptures, is also drawn, by Smith in particular, in relation to the seven churches, whose adherents should have paid attention to the call to repentance made in Revelations.[134]

Teonge, as a naval chaplain, recorded in his diary on the first of his two journeys to Scanderun and back the texts he chose for some 40 of his weekly sermons. Some of these texts are appropriate to the particular day, for example Christmas or the king's birthday, but more than half of them cluster round two themes: he gave a dozen sermons on the subject of the Lord's Prayer and another dozen on Exodus 8.1–7, a passage that tells the story of Moses and Aaron and the plague of frogs. It is difficult to imagine how anyone could write, let alone sit through, 12 sermons in six months about the plague of frogs![135]

Finally, there is an example of Covel's recognition of the poetic quality of the Psalms: on the island of Alonia in the Sea of Marmara, he gives colour to his description of rocks covered with rabbits by quoting 'the rocks [are a refuge] for the conyes'.[136]

Christianity and the classics

The potential tension between Christianity and the classics has already been mentioned. What was the attitude, conscious or unconscious, of Covel and other classically educated men of the seventeenth century towards paganism and its relationship to Christianity? Thomas has described the 'tangled inheritance of incompatible ideas – classical, Christian, and chivalric' that formed the mental landscape of educated men of the period, and Green, in his detailed analysis of education and Protestantism in early modern England, refers to 'the idea that the pagan past and the Christian present were indistinguishable'.[137] It seems to have come naturally to men steeped in classical literature to interweave the classical with the Christian: Spenser wrote of Christ as the 'Great Pan',[138] and Milton, who makes the same identification,[139] also uses the term 'Muse', with its classical connotations, alongside Christian imagery in the first section of *Paradise Lost*.[140] Classical texts were seen as a repository of moral wisdom,[141] even in the unlikely location of a sermon: in the funeral sermon preached for Anne Glover, ambassador's wife, classical quotations and references from Euripides, Homer, Plutarch, Seneca, Ennius, Cicero, Lucan and Virgil are found alongside biblical ones.[142]

Covel is an example of a product of the kind of education that privileged classical over Christian texts: he seems to have seen no conflict between his Christian beliefs and his deep love of the classics, the lines between them being blurred rather than sharp. His description of Ephesus[143] is relevant in this context: he was much exercised by his sense that the site had changed constantly over a long period, and that there was layer upon layer of ruins to be deciphered, but he never stresses the break between pagan and Christian. In his long description of the bas-reliefs he saw, he mentions (and firmly rejects) the interpretation that they represent a scene of Christian persecution, but the subject is suggested as one possibility among other (classical) ones.[144] He comments on the Christian significance of the ruins only as a coda to his description of the classical remains, although contemporary travellers were very conscious of the city as being the location of one of Paul's seven churches. It is of course true that there *was* continuity across what we see as the dividing line between pagan and Christian, but it might have been expected that a Christian minister would have signalled the shift. Covel was certainly aware that some buildings might be Christian, identifying one near Nicomedia as such by the crosses on it,[145] and also on the grounds that the column capitals were not of fine enough work to be classical Greek. His contemporary, Rycaut, unlike Covel, refers to the New Testament in his description of the sites of the seven churches, but also moves easily and without comment between Christian texts and classical ones.[146]

There is no sign in Covel of the slight unease about paganism that can be detected in Wheler.[147] In the preface to his *Journey*, Wheler saw the need to explain his interest in ruins by curiosity, and he described the mysteries of Eleusis (after the third-century writer Minutius Felix) as 'wicked, and Diabolical'. Evidently their secret nature, and the stress laid on this characteristic by Pausanias, troubled him.[148] There is probably a temperamental difference here.

Although in Covel's own writings there are no conscious attempts to reconcile the two traditions, he belonged to a world in which such attempts were made: on a small scale, Virgil's fourth eclogue and parts of Ovid could be read as Christian allegories,[149] and Sandys, earlier in the century, was attracted by the sibyls because he saw them as foretelling Christ, though he recognised that there were later accretions in the texts of their prophecies.[150] In Spon's discussion of the Gate of Persecutions at Ephesus, he notes that Hecate triformis can be seen as 'une ombre ou un crayon' ('a shadow or sketch') of the Christian trinity.[151] On a larger scale there was neo-Platonism,[152] which influenced Sandys,[153] and, in its Cambridge form, Covel, Finch and Baines.[154] Ayres has argued that after 1688 there was a strong connection between political free-thinking and admiration for the Roman Republic: he has described a 'God-acknowledging philosophical cast of mind' that was out of sympathy with versions of Christianity that emphasised doctrine.[155] While such a view is not articulated in the Stuart period, its roots can be found there, with Roman 'virtue' being stressed over Christian 'grace'.[156] Camden's work on England's Roman remains also had an effect.[157] More generally, classical authors were recognised as positive sources of moral (if not religious) lessons: Sandys, for example, added moralising comments in the notes to his translation of Ovid,[158] and little emphasis was laid on the differences between classical and Christian morality. One educationalist, however, John Colet, had constructed the curriculum at St Paul's School with the express purpose of combining classical style with Christian morality, for example by teaching Lactantius[159] in place of Cicero.[160] The socio-religious group that at home was most likely to object to the use of the classics as a guide to morals, the Puritans, is barely represented among travellers.

In the final section of his argument about the relationship between the classical and the Christian as part of the mental furniture of educated seventeenth-century men, Green asks whether we can conclude that for the educated laity classical and Christian morality were interchangeable. He answers his question indirectly by illustrating the ways in which the two strands were linked in various areas: in the use of classical precedents to explain or illuminate contemporary events; in artistic and architectural imagery; and in the importance of good works and being a good citizen rather than faith or doctrine.[161] In all these areas, supporting evidence can be found among the Levant travellers. Rycaut provides an example of the first, with his use of Tacitus; the double tomb of Finch and Baines in Christ's College chapel in Cambridge is an example of the second; and the way in which some travel accounts, of which Covel's is one, recognise and give credit to Turkish/Muslim good qualities supports the third.

Post-classical literature

Travellers' accounts provide us with some evidence, too, for their reading of later authors. In most cases, since we are dealing largely with printed works, the books in question may have been consulted at home, where there was access to a range of libraries, after their journeys were over, but we also (particularly in the cases of Vernon and Covel) have some knowledge of what books they actually took with them in their luggage.

Vernon's reading while he was abroad included a number of the Church fathers, various of whom are also mentioned by Covel, Wheler, Smith and others, and whose work was particularly relevant to those visiting the sites of the early Christian churches.[162] Dictionaries, commentaries on classical texts and humanist works are other commonly mentioned categories: the name 'Suidas',[163] for example, crops up regularly in Wheler's book.[164] Covel was particularly interested in the pronunciation of Greek, and refers the recipient of his diary to Ralph Winterton's notes on Hesiod and the work of John Cheke for elucidation, in this case making it plain that he did not have these volumes with him: 'you and your books know better than I'. Other books that we know he did not have access to in Constantinople were the *Lexicon* of Nicholas Lloyd and the *Historia Byzantina*: in reference to both of these he asks his friend, 'bestow a minute for my sake in consulting'.[165] Covel certainly did have a substantial number of books with him: almost his first act on arrival in Constantinople, on New Year's Day 1670/1, was to go and collect his trunks from the customs officer, who to his horror had rifled through them.[166]

Books were of prime importance to him, and he felt deprived when later, during the plague in Adrianople, he was forced to rely on the books lent him by the Metropolitan from his 'small library'.[167] In 1689, some years after Covel's return to England, Thomas Coke of the Levant Company wrote to him from Constantinople to ask him to send some Greek books from England for the Patriarch. He also wanted maps and globes, as well as the Byzantine historians in 22 or 24 volumes (well-packed).[168] It was rarely possible to obtain the reading matter you wanted on the spot.

The merchant Jack Verney may have been typical in carrying a Bible and a few devotional books with him to Aleppo,[169] but some books were available in the English factories (trading houses). Luke asked for help from the Levant Company to form a library at Smyrna, in response to which the governor sent a copy of the polyglot Bible; the governor's widow later presented other books. Luke also asked for a quarter of his salary to be spent on books to be sent out to him from England.[170] Merchants leaving for the factories were also provided by the company with travel and devotional books.[171] Although the Smyrna library was destroyed by fire in 1688,[172] an extant catalogue dating from 1702 shows how it had been built up again, and the range of subjects it covered: more than 100 volumes, in the fields of theology, history and antiquities, geography, medicine, mathematics, law, literature and language.[173]

That it was possible to buy manuscript books in Constantinople, mainly in Arabic and Persian, in the areas especially of history and science, is attested to by Wheler: he met a Scot in the city who told him about the bazaar where they were available, although adding that there were dangers for Christians in frequenting it.[174] During the pre-Civil War period, at a time when the study of oriental languages was growing in England, oriental manuscripts were collectors' items. English scholars such as Basire (a royalist exile) contributed to the knowledge of local languages, and North compiled a Turkish dictionary. Unfortunately, according to North's brother and biographer, this was 'pirated out of his house and he could never find who had it; perhaps it may be now in England, in the hands of Dr Covell'.[175] Basire used contemporary Greek, Arabic and Turkish translations of the catechism during his travels.[176] Robert Huntington, Covel's counterpart in Aleppo, wrote to Covel in Constantinople to ask him to source Arabic, Persian and Hebrew texts for him.[177] A Greek printing press had been set up in Constantinople in 1627, by a Greek who had been in England, but according to Thomas Smith, Covel's predecessor, it had got into difficulties with both Catholics and Turks, and was dismantled.[178]

Historical and geographical books and maps relevant to the region were obviously important to travellers. Leigh gives a list of recommended books, among them those of Blount, Biddulph, Coryate, Lithgow and Greaves, all of whom had visited the Levant in the first half of the century. According to Leigh: 'I suppose Travellers may furnish themselves with the best writers of those parts of the world, whether [i.e. whither] they intend to go, either to instruct them about those places before they go, or to carry with them'.[179]

Howell recommended taking 'Tropographicall [sic]' books, and in particular the epitome of Ortelius (the sixteenth-century mapmaker).[180] Both Covel and Wheler used Ortelius, though without much faith in his accuracy.[181] They also used Philippe Ferrarius's *Lexicon geographicum*, dating from the 1650s, as did Rycaut and Vernon, the latter noting, 'Abbe Beaugrands Lexicon Geographicum (by whose care, Ferrarius is much enlarged) is at last come forth, & I believe will not bee unwelcome to the World.'[182] Another mapmaker, Johann Laurenberg, was also used by Wheler, but as has already been suggested the inadequacies of the available maps are a regular refrain in several texts.

The most popular guide-books were those by Pierre Gilles and Pierre Belon. The latter was a botanist, but also wrote about antiquities, and visited Mount Athos.[183] His sprawling account meanders between plants and animals, local customs, history and myth, and antiquities (those of Troy and Nicomedia, for example), but his account of Mount Athos is useful. Greaves thought he was correct in his view that manuscript hunters would find little to tempt them there, a view later confirmed by Covel's description of his visit to the holy mountain, though Covel made minor corrections to Belon's list of the monasteries.[184] Wheler, whose great passion was the collecting of 'simples', used him as well as John Gerard and a French herbalist called Merchant to help identify plants.[185] Pierre Gilles, who collected manuscripts for François 1er, wrote two books (often bound together) which were invaluable for travellers to Constantinople and the Bosphorus: *De topographia Constantinopoleos* and *De Bosphoro Thracio*.[186] His work is much more coherent than Belon's: the account of Constantinople is a careful topographical survey of Byzantine buildings, based on a wide range of sources, and including, like a modern 'cultural' guide-book, sections on history and myth.[187] Coryate, an adventurer who travelled in the early seventeenth century, is known to have carried his copy with him, because he lost it en route:

> Samuel Purchas [...] gave me a description of Constantinople, and the Thracius Bosphorus [...] by [...] Petrus Gillius: which Booke, when I carried once in an after-noone under mine arme, in walking betwixt our English Ambassadors House in

Pera [...] and the Flemish Ambassadors house, I lost it very unfortunately to my great griefe and never found it againe.[188]

Covel comments on instances of both accuracy and inaccuracy in Gilles's text, to a level of detail that suggests that he too had a copy to hand on the trip he made from Constantinople to Adrianople.[189] Heylyn wrote two books of world history that might also have been a useful companion, but both Covel and Rycaut took him to task for mistakes.[190]

The best account of Athens was that written by Fr J. P. Babin, a Jesuit based in Smyrna.[191] In this Spon criticises previous writers on Athens, such as Ortelius, who 'avec une temerité digne d'un Geographe [...] croit de voir et de mesurer toute la terre sans sortir de son cabinet'.[192] Babin used ancient sources, and his book, like Gilles's, is similar to a modern cultural guide; written specifically to counter inaccurate accounts by earlier writers, it included descriptions of both pagan and Christian antiquities, giving especially high praise to the Parthenon sculptures. Spon and Wheler used Babin's work (which Spon had edited and for which he had written the preface),[193] although not always uncritically, during their stay in Athens,[194] but their main source of help was the verbal information given by Jean Giraud, who intended to publish an account of the antiquities of Athens but never did so.[195] There was another book about Athens, Guillet de Saint-George's *Athènes ancienne et nouvelle*,[196] which purported to be based on the personal research of the author's brother, Guillet de la Guilletière, but was in fact 'an ingenious fabrication from borrowed materials',[197] and Wheler takes every opportunity to correct its mistakes.[198] One of Guillet's sources was Meursius's *Athenae atticae* (1624), a work that both Vernon and Wheler used for the identification of antiquities.[199] Wheler was also familiar with the publication by Selden of the marbles collected in the early seventeenth century by Thomas Arundel.[200]

Vernon too was anxious to discredit Guillet's work:

> Monsieur de la Guilliotiere in that Book he hath written of Athens, hath made a Cut of a Theatre, which he calls that of

Bacchus, which is a meer fancy and invention of his own, nothing like the Natural one, which by the Plan, he has drawn of the Town, I judge he did not know. I give you this one hint, that you may not be deceived by that Book, which is wide from truth; as will appear to any body who sees the reality, though to one who hath not seen it, it seems plausibly written.[201]

The 'cut' in Guillet's book is indeed entirely fanciful, though his map (reproduced in Laborde's book of 1854) is based either on one that had been made by the Capuchins or on information supplied by them, and bears at least some relation to the facts.[202]

The two big collections of travel literature were those of Hakluyt and Purchas. I have found no mention of copies of Hakluyt being taken to the Levant, but his book was large and expensive, and it is unlikely that it would be carried about. The same is true of Purchas, though Ambassador Roe did have a copy of *Purchas His Pilgrimage* with him on his voyage to his earlier posting in India.[203] The list of books owned by Covel in 1715/16 includes Hakluyt among an extensive range of travel books.[204] It is notable that many of the travellers to the Levant knew the work of their predecessors and contemporaries: Wheler records that, leaving aside authors such as Pietro della Valle, Belon, Gilles and Jean de Thévenot, there were enough of his 'own Country' who had described the Turkish Empire for the benefit of travellers, in particular Sandys, Rycaut and Smith.[205] Covel says that he will refrain from describing Constantinople because it has already been done by Belon, Gilles, 'our Mr Sands' and the 'incomparable' Rycaut,[206] while Wheler defers to Smith and Rycaut in the matter of the state of the Greek Church.[207] Covel valued Spon both for his work and for the man himself, remarking on their intimate acquaintance and the fact that they corresponded after their meeting.[208] As far as Rycaut goes, a lone dissenting voice among his contemporaries is that of North: 'the book of Sir Paul Rycaut, of the religion and manners of the Turks, was very superficial, and, in multitudes of instances, erroneous'. He noted the mistakes in the margins of his copy, but the book 'was purloined from him'; Covel is not mentioned here, but the words recall North's accusation that Covel had taken a Turkish dictionary without permission.[209]

In one household, however, Rycaut's work was highly valued. In November 1679, Thomas Browne recommended one of Rycaut's books to his son Edward, who was living in London, some years after his journey to Greece, and two months later wrote to him, stating:

> Since I last writt unto you I have found out a way how you shall receave Ricaut's historie without sending it by the carts [...] I would not have you borrowe it because you may have it allwayes by you [...] you having seen the grand signor now raygning, you may do well to know as much of his historie as you can.[210]

In the period between these two letters, Edward's sister Elizabeth had read the book aloud to her father.[211]

It is almost unknown to find English poetry quoted for the embellishment of travel writers' prose. Covel was not given to enhancing his writings like this anyway, even with classical quotations, and at the end of his life he owned few books of English literature,[212] but there is an interesting departure from his usual style in his book on the Greek Church, where he quotes Chaucer: 'MEN SHOULD NOT KNOW OF GOD'S PRIVICE.'[213] In fact, Covel is using Chaucer's words to make a moral point rather than for any stylistic reason.

Notwithstanding the readiness of English authors to praise one another, travel literature had its shortcomings, not the least of which from a modern perspective was the inclination of one author to perpetuate the mistakes of his predecessors. It will be argued in the following chapter that the 1670s saw a new breed of more scholarly, 'archaeological' travellers than there had been up till that date, men such as Covel who were anxious to view antiquities with a more scientific outlook. The frustration with the quality of information available to them is expressed by a man who was not a scholar but a merchant, Lewes Roberts, who (writing in 1638) perhaps speaks for scholars too:

I have been constrained oftentimes in this *Desert* to travell without a certaine *guide*, and not seldome to navigate by anothers *Compasse*, having not in any Language or Countrey met with any *Author*, that could either totally conduct me, or truely rectifie my steps when I went astray; yet I must confesse I met with some that shot at the marke I aymed at; but it was at randome, and came not home to my proposed blanke; and I found *some* that tooke up stuffe upon trust, and a *second* followed *him*, and a *third* that *second*.[214]

CHAPTER 3

ANTIQUITIES, PROTO-ARCHAEOLOGISTS AND COLLECTORS

Travellers to the Greek world in the seventeenth century did not go with an open mind about what they might see. The classical education that many of them had received, whether to grammar school or to university level, gave them certain expectations about what awaited them: they carried the weight of their knowledge and background with them, and the story of their travels is partly the story of their continuing dialogue with the classical world. As discussed in the previous chapter, Covel and other scholars littered their works with quotations and references from classical texts, but even merchants such as Lewes Roberts made references to familiar myths and episodes from Greek and Roman history. Many travellers were also clergy, with an interest in the Christian sites: Smith and Covel were among those who were anxious to see the seven churches of Asia, which they knew from St Paul's epistles. While they made little explicit distinction between classical and early Christian remains as physical phenomena, in the moral sphere, the ruined Christian sites and the sad state of eastern Christianity were seen as both a punishment for Christian backsliding and, at the same time, a result of the cyclical rise and fall of empires. Classical 'virtue' (courage or manliness) contributed to their moral framework no less than Christian grace: the 14th Earl of Arundel, for example, believed that the study of the arts was an incentive to virtuous behaviour, while Ambassador Roe, who helped Arundel to acquire his collection of antiquities, attributed to works of art 'a kind of lay humanity, teaching and inciting devotion to morall vertue'.[1] Unlike Catholicism, paganism was not a political threat, and unlike Islam, it was already a part of travellers' mental landscape.

The first decades of the century were also the period in which the collecting of antiquities, led by Charles I and aristocrats such as Arundel and the 1st Duke of Buckingham, became a matter of competitive importance among their circle.[2] Although Covel and many others who went to the Levant were men of the middling sort rather than of the aristocracy, they lived in a world in which collecting was an increasingly desirable activity for those who could afford it, and those who could not aspire to a house full of ancient sculptures might still collect in a more modest way, specialising in coins or manuscripts, for example, or putting together a cabinet of curiosities. In October 1671, John Evelyn went to visit the well-known doctor Sir Thomas Browne, in Norwich, and found his 'whole house & Garden [...] a Paradise & Cabinet of rarities [...] especially Medails [coins], books, Plants, natural things'.[3] It was in this household that Edward Browne, Thomas's son, who travelled to Greece in 1668, was brought up. Henry Peacham, tutor to Arundel's children, whose *The Complete Gentleman* was first published in 1622 and went through several editions, added a chapter on antiquities to the 1634 edition, telling his readers that although the best examples were to be obtained in Rome, where they were 'daily found and digged for', they were so 'extremely affected and sought after' that the authorities had made it a 'felony to convey them thence without special license'. For this reason, he encouraged would-be collectors to look to Greece, although he never went there himself:

> But in Greece and other parts of the Grand Seigneur's dominions (where sometime there were more statues standing than men living, so much had art outstripped nature in these days) they may be had for the digging and carrying.[4]

The latter half of the century also saw the rise of interest in inductive scientific studies, as is shown by the foundation and activities of the Royal Society and its predecessors.[5] This too is relevant to the study of attitudes to antiquities: several travellers spent time and energy measuring ancient monuments, sometimes under difficult circumstances. The correspondence of Henry Oldenburg, secretary to the Royal Society, contains many references to such attempts to make exact records of classical ruins.[6] 'Scientific' interests extended well beyond what we would now regard as science: the group of men involved in the society had a great enthusiasm for observing, measuring and classifying all kinds of aspects – historical as well as scientific – of the world in which they lived. In November 1675, Crawford (the English resident in Venice) wrote to Oldenburg, '[Vernon] promised [...] to give me a particular account of the Greek church wch I would gladly have at present'.[7] Rycaut, a proud member of the society, who was to bring out his first history of the Ottoman Empire in 1666, wrote (also to Oldenburg) in February 1666/7: 'where I make my iournies, if any [antiquities or paintings] occurre, I shall not only give you a description of them, but also a rude coppy[8] to communicate to the R. Societie'.[9] It was not unusual for members of the Royal Society to know their classics: for example, in a letter of 21 June 1672 to Oldenburg the physicist Huygens referred to the competition between the painters Protogenes and Apelles over who could paint the finest line (a story told in Pliny's *Natural History*).[10]

The study of antiquities at home in England also became more widespread during the late sixteenth and early seventeenth centuries. Camden, whose *Britannia* was first published in 1586, made use of artefacts such as coins and inscriptions, as well as texts. There were moves towards fieldwork and the study of monuments *in situ*.[11] All of this helps to demonstrate the importance that the prospect of seeing antiquities had as an incentive to travel. Smith made it explicit when he referred to 'the love and respect' he had for antiquity, which he went on to imply were particular qualities of Englishmen: it was the English gentlemen of Smyrna who were the first to visit Ephesus 'to see the remainders of that magnificence, for which those *Cities* were so renowned in the Histories of ancient times'.[12] As will be seen later, there was a good deal of rivalry between the English and the French when it came to the acquisition of antiquities, although there are also examples of co-operation and the sharing of knowledge. While some travellers went with the prime purpose of collecting (Arundel, for example, sent a succession of employees, of whom William Petty was the most significant, to search pieces out for him), the love of antiquities was a secondary motive for many of those who went primarily for other reasons, which might be diplomatic, mercantile, religious or military. Blount, who went in 1629 with the aim of finding out about the way the Ottoman Empire was run, borrowed Lucan's words to express his expectations when he referred to the islands of Greece as 'those islands so voiced [famed] for Antiquities – *Nullum sine nomine saxum*'.[13]

The state of the Greek world

What did travellers find when they arrived in the area? The overwhelming impression of the landscape in Greece and in the Aegean coastal area of Turkey was, to English eyes, of what Byron called a 'chaos of ruins':[14] the words 'confused' and 'heaps' occur repeatedly in their accounts. Veryard saw Halicarnassus as 'a confused heap of Ruins' and wrote of Cnidos: 'amongst the vast Ruins of this famous City, we observ'd nothing very considerable but the Rests of the famous Temple of *Venus*'. Ephesus was 'a vast heap of Ruins' and Troy 'a meer heap of Ruins', with 'old walls, pieces of Arches, Pillars, and Statues, with divers Portico's still standing'.[15] Wheler described the temple of Ceres at Eleusis as lying 'all in a confused heap together: the beautiful Pillars buried in the Rubbish of its dejected Roof and Walls'.[16] Randolph wrote in his account of Crete that

> there are several other places that have had the name of Citys, which are now heaps of ruins; many hundred stately Pallaces there were that now have only some Walls, and those most fallen down.[17]

Covel and Smith travelled widely among the Greek cities of Asia Minor, both recording similar scenes of desolation. At Sardis Smith found standing and fallen pillars 'in a confused heap' and at Tripolis 'huge massy stones lying confusedly in heaps'. Hierapolis was 'now utterly forsaken and desolate', and in the cities of the seven churches he found 'scarce one stone left upon another'.[18] Covel likewise described the scene in Iznik/Nicaea: 'the stones are peices of pillars, pedestals, Architraves, and other parts of old buildings which they raked together and minded not how they placed them'.[19] The vocabulary chosen by these men may well have been influenced by their knowledge of the King James version of the Old Testament, where the word 'heaps' is used in several places to describe the ruins of cities whose inhabitants have not lived up to the standards demanded by Jehovah.[20] The same word was also used by Charles Cotton to emphasise the contrast between the state of England at the Restoration and what had gone before, when he wrote that Charles II's throne was not 'raised upon heaps of Ruine' – although, paradoxically, it may have seemed to some of his readers that the opposite was the case:[21] both the dissolution of the monasteries and the Civil War had of course left England with ruins of her own.[22] Lithgow, who visited Greece and other areas of the Levant in the second decade of the century, specifically compared the ruins of Troy, Tyre and Thebes to those of religious buildings in his native Scotland.[23]

Ruins were sometimes seen almost anthropomorphically: Luke speaks of tombs 'bewailing in desolation their Ancient splendour', and Rycaut of ruins 'unwilling to lose the memory of their ancient Glory'.[24] Spon (after Cicero) referred to the ruins of Ephesus as the 'cadavre' ('corpse') of a city.[25] In using these words, the writers are transferring to the architecture they are observing not only their own emotions but also those they imagined might have been felt by the sometime inhabitants of the ruined places. Ruins may also be seen as presenting a warning, and here an etymological link has been made between the word 'monument' and the Latin verb 'moneo' ('to warn'):[26] Sandys, for example, described ruins as 'threatening instructions' to the world.[27] It is also apparent that several travellers understood that there was not simply a question of past and present, but that they were faced with evidence of layers of history. At Nicaea, Covel saw walls which he took to be in the same position as those described by Strabo, though they had been 'ruin'd and repair'd over and over', as he 'fully concluded by the difference of mortar, brick, stone and manner of building long before [he] saw any inscription to make it out'.[28]

Robson, looking for the famous church in Smyrna, found that it was 'not now to be found in the now *Smirna*, all buried under the beastly new Turkish *Smirna*, so that the novelties have swallowed up the antiquities, and the very ruins of old *Smirna* are ruined'.[29] In these observations Robson privileges the past over the present, an attitude that will be shown (in the next chapter) to be common in relation to the people of Greece, as well as to its antiquities. Similarly, when Sandys was at Memphis in Egypt, he commented that 'The very ruins [are] now almost ruinated [...] Why then deplore we our humane frailty?'[30] Sandys goes on to quote Ausonius: 'mors etiam saxis nominibusque venit'.[31] Another familiar quotation that might have come to mind here, since Lucan was a popular author, is his line 'etiam periere ruinae' ('even the ruins have perished').[32] Sandys's comment also provides an example of another common reaction to ruins, the recollection of human mortality and the closely linked idea of the rise and fall of cities or empires. Coryate read Troy as a reminder of 'the inconstancie and mutabilitie of fortune', and Rycaut in Asia Minor was 'put [...] in mind of our own mortality, as well as the period and subversion of Cities'.[33]

A slightly different note was struck by Veryard when he remarked of ancient building expertise that 'so solid and firm was the Work of former Ages beyond what is erected now-a-days',[34] and there is plenty of evidence that travellers recognised the beauty of ancient architecture and sculpture in spite of the dilapidated state in which most of it was. Wheler, for example, referred to 'A wonderful Portico of Marble' on Delos, of which 'the beautiful parts Bury each other in as great confusion as time and bad Fortune could reduce them to',[35] and Smith at Hierapolis felt a mixture of awe (at the magnificence) and horror (at the decay) when looking at remains 'so glorious and magnificent, that they will strike one with horror at the first view of them, and with admiration too; such walls, and arches, and pillars of so vast a heigth [sic], and so curiously wrought'.[36] According to North, 'all the spite of time and the Turks cannot raze out of the country the marks of great and admirable structures, as fountains, aqueducts and temples'.[37]

For Wheler, as for many modern travellers, the Parthenon was the acme of architectural beauty, and in spite of the Turkish change of use from temple to mosque, his verdict was that 'transform'd from *Minerva*'s Temple to the use of a *Mosque*, [it] is, without comparison, the finest in the World'.[38] He and Spon were lucky, of course, to see it before the explosion that damaged it so badly in 1687. Although his attempts to draw the building were crude, when Stuart and Revett came to do their detailed drawings a century later they expressed their gratitude to Wheler and his companion and their admiration of the work of their predecessors. They were quick to excuse the faults in the drawings, because Spon and Wheler were untrained, had no good draughtsman with them, and stayed only a short time (and that in February, when the days were short): all travellers were indebted to them for 'their diligence, their sagacity, and the genuine truth of their relations'.[39] Although a number of French travellers went to Athens, perhaps because of the presence of Jesuits and Capuchins there, many of the English missed it out of their itineraries, unaware of the treasures still to be seen in the city. The Capuchins, who had established themselves in the city in 1658, ran a guest house for Christian visitors. They had a strong concern for ancient monuments, and made themselves indispensable to tourists looking at antiquities by producing one of the earliest maps of the city.[40]

One site that had a special resonance for all sorts of travellers was Troy, the setting of Homer's *Iliad*. Even those who did not land there were likely to have seen it from the sea (or at least to think that they had seen it, since the visible ruins were not Homeric) on their voyages to Constantinople, especially as there was often a delay while ships waited for the right winds in order to be able to enter the Dardanelles. Teonge, a naval chaplain and older contemporary of Covel's, described seeing Aeolis and Mysia from a distance:

[There] did stand Ilium and Troy, whereupon, or rather close under a great hill, which appeared to us very green through our prospectives, some heaps of pieces of rocks might be perceived, which were (as it is related) the ruins of Troy town.[41]

Teonge was not much interested in classical things, but others were more so, and the area had many visitors, particularly in the early years of the century. Thomas Sherley records that

the ruines of olde Troye are yett to bee seene; they are 30 myle in lenghthe, between Gallipoli & the castell at the mouthe of those streyghtes. The walles are in somme places a yarde highe, in others even with the grounde, & manye foundations of townes are yett extante, & a greate parte of Helens pallas standeth.[42]

There was often emotion at the thought of standing on 'Homeric' ground – as we have seen, several travellers quoted Ovid's line 'iam seges est ubi Troia fuit'[43] – but there is also some evidence for a more sceptical attitude to the physical remains than that displayed by Sherley. The merchant Roberts 'in Anno 1620 [...] hardly saw the reliques of this *mightie fabrique*', though he 'traced it for many miles, and gave eare to all the ridiculous fables of those poore *Grecians* that inhabite thereabouts';[44] however, his scepticism about the fables did not stop him from giving casualty figures for the Trojan War. Sandys recognised that the ruins he was looking at were not those of the Homeric city, on the grounds that the site did not match Homer's description. He thought that the remains visible from the sea were those of the city built by Constantine; in fact, they were those of Alexandria Troas, originally founded in the fourth century BCE. Sandys pointed out that the tombs of the heroes were 'not at this day more than coniecturally extant'.[45]

Lithgow, characteristically, did not mince his words: his guide showed him many Tombes [...] mighty ruinous [...] of *Hector, Ajax, Achilles, Troylus*, and many other valiant Champions, with the Tombes also of *Hecuba, Cresseid* [...] I saw infinite old Sepulchers, but for their particular names, and nomination of them, I suspend, neither could I beleeve my Interpreter, sith it is more then three thousand and odde yeares agoe, that *Troy* was destroyed.[46]

Wheler, like Sandys using Strabo as his authority for believing that this was Alexandria Troas rather than the Homeric city, thought that nothing he saw was older than Roman, and was particularly scathing about Pietro della Valle, an early seventeenth-century traveller, who fancied 'every great Tree a Hector, or Achilles, or an Aeneas'. Of some of the ruins he recorded that he found it impossible to determine whether they had been a castle, a temple or a Christian church.[47] Veryard was of a similar opinion, agreeing with those who 'will have these to be the Ruins of the *Novum Ilium*, which *Strabo* speaks of, and not the Antient, which they esteem fabulous and purely poetical'.[48]

Ruins carry a powerful emotional and moral charge: they are paradoxical in that they offer evidence of both transience and endurance.[49] Greece evoked ambivalent feelings in its visitors as they reacted to the combination of observed decay with the knowledge of past greatness, and their sense that the decay might be the result of either pagan or Christian sinfulness. Krautheimer quotes a poem about Rome (significantly, a Christian city with a pagan past) by the eleventh-century poet Hildegard Lavandin in which the line 'quam magna fueris integra, fracta doces' ('your ruins themselves bear witness to your past glory') occurs.[50] Such ideas were extensively developed by Spenser in his *Ruines of Rome*, based on du Bellay's *Antiquitez de Rome*,[51] and here there is another strand of thought that is relevant to travellers to Greece: did they, when they looked at classical ruins, also hope that their own writings might be more durable than buildings, as they perceived the works of classical authors to be?[52] This kind of permanence is a theme found in Ovid and Horace,[53] and was also expressed in 1605 by Bacon:

For have not the verses of *Homer* continued 25. hundred yeares, or more, without the losse of a sillable, or letter: during which time, infinite Pallaces, Temples, Castles, Cities have been decayed, and demolished?[54]

It is a theme that would have been familiar to many visitors to Greece.

While one of the prime causes suggested by travellers for the state in which they found Greek antiquities was the ravages of time, the other was the behaviour of the Turks. Time and fortune are frequently cited as explanations for ruins: there was a strong consciousness of what Wheler, perhaps echoing Herodotus,[55] called 'the Instability of humane things', which (much influenced by what had happened in England during the period of the Civil War and Commonwealth) he saw as teaching a moral lesson. The state of Greece was in his view

> a Lamentable Example of the Instability of humane things, wherein Your Majesties Discontented and Factious Subjects, if their own late Calamities will not sufficiently instruct them, may see the Miseries that other Nations are reduced to, and behold, as in a Picture, the Natural Fruits of Schism, Rebellion and Civil Discord.[56]

There was also, for Wheler, a strong connection here with the righteousness of the Anglican church; similarly, Smith's view of the state of the seven churches of Asia was that their fallen condition was the result of their not having followed the true path of Christianity: recalling the exhortation to the Ephesians in Revelations Chapter 2 ('Remember therefore from whence thou art fallen, and repent'), he offered the present state of Ephesus as an example to contemporary Christians of what might happen to them. Veryard thought that Ephesus offered 'convincing Arguments [...] of the Mutability of Fortune', and wrote of Cyzicus that 'of all this State and Splendor there only remain some few and obscure Footsteps, the rest being swallow'd up by devouring Time'.[57]

It is unusual to find any explicit recognition of the part played by the weather as a cause of the defacement of ancient buildings, though there are instances in Covel, and Wheler at Troy noted pillars, walls and foundations 'scaled by the weather, and eaten by the Salt-winds'.[58] It was common, however, to blame Greeks as well as Turks. The Greeks, as will be seen more clearly in the next chapter, were widely regarded as ignorant slaves, who knew nothing of their great heritage and were careless of its remains: Smith, writing about the seven churches, attributed their neglect to 'the unpardonable carelessness of the *Greeks*, (unless that horrid stupidity, into which their slavery has cast them, may plead some excuse therein)'. At Thyatira, he wrote, the Greeks were 'prodigiously ignorant of their own Antiquities';[59] and Vernon described Patras as having 'several massive Ruines, which few there know how to give any account of'.[60]

It should be said here that any appreciation of ruins as having an aesthetic value belongs to a later period. It is not, however, the case that there was no aesthetic appreciation of natural landscapes. While it was only in the eighteenth century that ruins began to be seen as making a contribution to the beauty of a landscape,[61] there were early modern travellers who were responsive to the aesthetic qualities of scenery. On his visit to Prusa, Covel climbed the citadel and enjoyed the view of the plain with its variety of trees, bordered by hills: 'we se[e] all the plain in ye semicircle from W. by N. to ye E. as if this was ye pulpitum of A theater'.[62] An anonymous traveller, possibly John Luke, a year or two earlier, mentions 'many a long look from the snowy tops of several hills',[63] showing that he was not entirely indifferent to the natural landscape. Of their contemporaries, the one whose appreciation of scenery is most in evidence is Rycaut, who wrote of his night-time journey between Smyrna and Adrianople that

> Neere the top the mountaine beganne to bee exceedingly pleasant, the highest part being a greene plaine with trees even and equally planted; the prospect of the country on the one side and of the sea on the other, the prodigious precipices and the delightful confusion of the rockes appearing with the dim light

of the moone and the silence of the night, rendered everything there a most pleasing object of the eye.[64]

It is also Rycaut who gives us a description of the terrain of Mount Athos, although he did not himself go there. He owed his information about the mountain to Covel, and perhaps also partly to Belon,[65] and although it cannot be proved it is plausible to imagine that he asked Covel about its physical landscape. According to Rycaut

> it is covered with Trees, Shrubs, and Boscage; and produces many Plants and Herbs of admirable Vertue: It is a place full of little Springs, Rills and Rivulets, that there can be no part so barren and unfruitful in the whole circumference of the lower parts of this Mountain, which may not be capable of great and singular improvement; and in every corner thereof, there are so many Cells and little Recesses, partly framed by Art and partly by Nature, that it seems a place of such stupendious solitude, as if the situation thereof had been designed for the retirement of *Monks* or the Cells of *Anchorites*.[66]

Although this has more detail than is found in Covel's account (or in those of Smith or Georgirenes), Covel also uses the word 'boscage', and refers to the rills that are to be found all over the promontory.[67] Neither Smith nor Georgirenes refers to the terrain.[68]

Rycaut also admired the winding courses of two rivers in Asia Minor, the Maeander and the Pactolus, as seen from above.[69] Looking down on a scene from a height has a long history: the τειχοσκοπία from the walls of Troy in Homer's *Iliad*, Moses at Pisgah and the temptation of Christ,[70] for example, would all have been familiar to educated men. Petrarch is sometimes said to have been one of the first people to climb a mountain in order to enjoy the view.[71] A Latin poem by Maffeo Barberini (b. 1568) describes the landscape as seen from the summit of a hill.[72] Such activities combined aesthetic pleasure with practical benefits: Coryate, in Milan, climbed the cathedral tower, where he was not only delighted with the view but also found it a substitute for a map, because it made clear to him in which directions various other cities lay.[73]

Although the primary meanings of the words 'scenery' and 'landscape' in neither case refer to the natural world, the first meaning theatrical backdrop and the second landscape painting,[74] aesthetic appreciation of that world grew alongside appreciation of its representation in art.[75] The way in which travellers looked at natural scenery as a kind of art, or as material for art, is illustrated by the comment of Bargrave (who arrived in the Levant in 1647) on looking at 'as shady a large Grove of low Trees [as he had seen]: so lovely, as if Nature had sett them for a Patterne of Plantation, to pose Art with'.[76] This can be compared with passages from Ovid, whom we know to have been one of the most popular of the Roman poets in the seventeenth century: in book three of the *Metamorphoses*, for example, he describes a valley where 'simulaverat artem / ingenio natura suo'.[77] The pastoral poetry of Theocritus, Virgil and Horace was also part of the mental furniture of classically educated travellers, as were the paintings of Claude, which were popular at the time.[78]

There was a market at home for drawings, as well as verbal accounts, of what travellers had seen.[79] Hand-drawn or engraved prospects were common, and valued both for themselves and for their practical use alongside, or in the absence of, maps; some so-called maps in travel accounts are closer to what we would regard as pictorial representations.[80] As one guide-book put it:

> What a *large* scope of severall *objects*, are dayly offered to delight the wearied *travailler*, when with true *judgment*, he behold the *variety* of Nature and the *Artifice* thereof, within the *Landskip* of his *Horizon* in a well chosen *Prospect*.[81]

When Peacham was a student at Cambridge, he was able by his own account to draw 'the map of any town according to geometrical proportions'. He also went so far as to list the landscapes he thought most beautiful for the artist to choose from, including Constantinople and the view from Mount Ida in Crete, though he had not seen these views for himself.[82] Burton praised the view from

Acrocorinth 'from which *Peloponnesus*, *Greece*, the *Ionian* and *Aegean* seas were *semel & simul* at one view to be taken'.[83] His pleasure in this view is likely to have been based on engravings or drawings. Although it is true that mountain landscapes specifically tended to inspire terror rather than admiration, as they did in Evelyn when he crossed the Alps,[84] the author of two works on landscape, Edward Norgate, was interested in wild mountain scenery.[85] Both Bargrave and Winchilsea preferred the scenery of plains to that of mountains,[86] but it is overstating the case to say that before the eighteenth century 'landscapes as such gave [Englishmen] no satisfaction whatever'.[87] Landscape painting (by Claude, for example) was admired well before the middle of the seventeenth century, and it is likely that the appreciation of painted landscapes and of the natural landscape went hand in hand. Although travellers to Greece provide no evidence of viewing ruins as contributing to their aesthetic pleasure in the landscape, those who visited Italy in this period, and indeed armchair travellers who saw the engravings that were made from Claude's paintings, were beginning to be made aware of the artistic possibilities of the combination of ruins with natural landscape forms, initiating a shift from ruins viewed as moral lessons towards a more pictorial appreciation, while nostalgia, sentiment and awareness of the poignant contrast between past and present remained important ingredients of observers' responses.[88]

Re-use of buildings and spolia

As far as the ruins in the Greek world are concerned, Turks were no better than Greeks, because as well as converting churches into mosques when it suited them they regularly looted stone from ancient buildings for re-use. Their religious practices are mentioned by some travellers as being inimical to the preservation of antiquities, one reason being the prohibition on the representation of humans in religious art, mentioned by Peacham.[89]

The most obvious reason for the contemporary state of ancient structures, pointed out by many travellers, was the frequent re-use both of whole buildings (usually temples or churches converted into mosques: the Parthenon is only the most famous example) and – even more prevalent – of building materials. Turks and Greeks alike were inclined to re-use any stone that was available to them. Sherley, at the very beginning of the century, saw in Constantinople the mosque 'whiche was St. Sofies Churche in the Christian tyme',[90] and Randolph on Crete in the 1670s saw two churches 'which seem to have been Temples'.[91] At Pergamum, according to Smith, ancient stone buildings were still to be found in use as 'the ordinary dwelling houses of the *Turks*'.[92] More unusually, Covel found a former Greek church that was used by Turks for a Friday porridge-kitchen for the poor, to which he saw people coming on foot and on donkeys.[93]

As far as materials go, stone was re-used for all kinds of public and private buildings. It was Randolph again who recorded that at Athens the houses were 'patcht up with the Ruines of old Pallaces, and in most Walls are abundance of old Inscriptions', and that at Cos the large plane tree later known as Hippocrates's was supported by '12 very stately Marble pillars [...] but it appears they were for a Temple, for part of a wall is yet remaining'.[94] The character of Athenian houses is confirmed by the Jesuit Babin, according to whom, instead of the glories of ancient architecture in Athens,

> l'on ne voit que des rues étroites sans pavé, que des maisons sans aucune magnificence, faites des ruines anciennes, ayans pour tout ornemens quelques pieces de colomnes de marbre mises dans les murailles sans ordre, & à la façon des autres pierres; ou queslques degrez de marbre marquez de croix, qui ont servi autrefois sur les portes ou fenêtres des Eglises ruinées.[95]

Wheler described a khan in Boeotia that incorporated 'ancient Pillars and Fragments of Antiquity'.[96] Sandys mentioned that in the Troad ruins of tombs and of what he thought had been a Christian church 'beare not altogether that forme [that they did], lessened daily by the *Turkes*, who carried the pillars and stones unto *Constantinople* to adorne the buildings of the Great *Bassas*'.[97] The re-use of tombstones, like the conversion of churches to mosques, raises the question of respect, or lack of it, for the dead. Rycaut made no comment on the sepulchre he saw used as a garden ornament or cistern in a Turkish garden,[98] but Covel reported that at Nicaea, men had 'rob'd the dead to preserve ye living', in spite of 'being ashamed of such a misfortune'. By this he probably meant that he thought the Turks in question had a sense of doing something wrong: elsewhere he saw tombstones that had not been taken, although they would have been useful.[99]

It is evident that Constantinople and its surroundings were the destination of a great many pieces of stone, including some with relief carvings or inscriptions, making the Greek cities of Asia Minor more vulnerable in this respect than the mainland or islands of Greece. The inhabitants of Cyzicus reported to Veryard that many statues, pillars, pieces of marble and inscriptions had been taken away, with others daily being found,[100] and Covel wrote that

> round Stambol for many miles, the Turkes have taken almost all the fair stone they could find to rayse their buildings in the city, so that little is to be expected of inscriptions or monuments of antiquity, especially in Thrace, or anywhere near ye shore of ye *Propontis*, from whence caryage by sea is easy; nothing remaining in a manner but the inward part of ye walls of old buildings [...] ye case or outside if it was of good stone being pull'd down and disposed of.

It may have been because of their belief that it was profane to allow any 'reliques of ye ancient learning' in their religious buildings that the Turks had constructed the mosque at Selibria from stones which they either turned inwards or from which they cut out the inscriptions, as Covel noticed.[101] Rycaut confirmed this habit, noting 'antient inscriptions that I have found in Greeke, engraved in stones, being as it were purposely beaten out wth hammers, & placed in walls of new buildings wth the letters subverted'.[102]

Esch has suggested that in Mediaeval England pagan pieces might be neutralised by being incorporated into Christian buildings, and the same might be true, *mutatis mutandis*, for pagan stones used in Islamic buildings.[103] However, as both Greenhalgh and Kinney have warned, we need to be very careful about attributing motives to the users of *spolia*: very often it may just have been the case that there were useful materials to hand that the builders took without any motive other than pragmatism.[104] It does seem, however, that occasionally stones were appreciated either for their aesthetic value or as status symbols, and were taken for the adornment of property rather than for structural use: Wheler recorded that one of the principal Turkish inhabitants of Thyatira had Roman marble gateposts with inscriptions, and that the best inscriptions he saw at Lampsacus were in a Turkish garden.[105]

Obstacles to antiquarian investigation

The state of the visible remains of antiquity was only one of the difficulties encountered by those travellers who wished to identify what they were looking at and to link it to the textual knowledge they had of ancient Greece. It is never easy to (in Allen's phrase) 'flesh a history onto the bones of the directly experienced architecture'[106] on a site, but it was particularly hard for early modern visitors; it was only in the 1670s that classically educated travellers began to try to give systematic accounts of the sites and monuments they visited, but even then, although some of them attempted to use sources such as Strabo and Pausanias, they were hampered by having no accepted architectural or archaeological chronology to guide them. There was no systematic attempt to construct a chronology of classical art until Winckelmann in the mid-eighteenth century published his *History of the Art of Antiquity*, an extraordinary achievement described by Potts as involving

> two key constructs, a notion of historical process that construed the larger history of Greek art as a systematic evolution through rise and decline, and a theory of artistic style or modes of visual representation that gave this abstract model a distinctively visual character. Winckelmann was also the first to question the label 'Greek' as given to works of art that were in fact Roman copies.[107]

Some travellers, even in the later part of the seventeenth century, simply made vague references to age. Browne, a doctor, brought up in a highly cultured home with a father whose wide interests included archaeology, was reduced to the vaguest of comments: in Skopje, on his way to northern Greece in 1668, he saw 'some handsome Sepulchral Monuments', 'an Arch, which seemeth to be Ancient', 'a large Stone also, which seemeth to be part of a Pillar', and 'a noble *Aqueduct* of stone, with about two hundred Arches [...] a handsome Antiquity'.[108] It should be said that his interests were not so much in material remains as in the linking of geographical sites to historical events, though he did show an appreciation of art when he could see it as art. But the achievement of the post-Restoration travellers – Rycaut, Covel, Wheler, Smith and Vernon in particular – is that they begin to show evidence of trying to place remains into a historical chronology: Covel, for example, saw a building at Ephesus which he realised, on the basis of a Latin inscription, could not be the temple of Diana, as he had at first thought, but must be Roman. Covel's legacy was not so much his knowledge as his method, his careful attempts to identify buildings through the evidence of his eyes.[109]

Aside from the gaps in their knowledge and the state of the evidence on the ground, other difficulties encountered were physical and administrative. The Turkish authorities were not always helpful: Wheler and Spon had problems getting permission from the local aga to see the Athenian acropolis, though a gift of coffee (two measures to the aga himself and one to the soldier who mediated the deal) helped as a bribe.[110] Roe had to use all his diplomatic skills to avoid being taken for a spy, and advised Arundel that obvious attention to ruins was apt to suggest the possibility of treasure to local people.[111] In Athens, Wheler was unable to take measurements of the supposed theatre of Dionysus (Bacchus) from fear that the Turkish authorities would disapprove. He obtained the measurements from the consul, Giraud, and from Vernon, but this was not without its problems, as Giraud used the French foot and Vernon the English.[112] The ignorance of local guides was also a hindrance, and local workmen were not always as hard-working as their foreign employers desired. One reason why Roe valued Petty so highly was that in his skill and industriousness he was such a contrast to the locals.[113] The terrain could be inhospitable, though some of these men were certainly tough. Crawford wrote that Vernon said he had 'well examined the ruines of the Temple of Delphos [Delphi] and all that is remarkable at Thebes, Corinth, Sparta, Athenes, etc.' and had 'been clambering up most of the mountains celebrat by the ancients as Helicon, Pernassus, etc.'.[114] Covel, examining a vaulted room at Ephesus, found the bats very troublesome, as well as being anxious about thieves; he knew that he and his party were not the first visitors from the hoof-prints and the remains of a fire they found.[115]

Sometimes conditions did defeat them. Spon and Wheler looked for an inscription near Delphi, which they knew about from another inscription, but Wheler wrote that they were unable to locate it: 'my Comrade [Spon] found it not, although he went with a Candle up to the Knees in Water [in a fountain], to seek for it'.[116] It was also at Delphi that they copied those inscriptions that 'were not out of the reach of [their] Eyes'.[117] Time could be a constraint too. According to Wheler,

> All these things [e.g. the site of the Delphic oracle] want good Search, and Examination; and are not easily to be found out by Travellers, that stay but a little while in a Place; unless we should suppose them to have so many of the antient *Greek* Authors almost by heart.[118]

Human error could of course also be an issue: Wheler remembered that he had measured the dimensions of the gymnasium in Athens, but could not find them among his papers when he came to write his book.[119]

Attempts at identification of sites and monuments
In spite of these difficulties, a number of travellers who made their journeys in the two decades following the Restoration tried extremely hard to measure and identify monuments and to make sense of sites: Rycaut, Vernon, Covel, Smith and Wheler had all, to a greater or lesser extent, had a classical education, but the two books

by Randolph from the 1670s show that he too was influenced by the more investigative and scientific studies of these men. He had been in Athens with Vernon in 1675, and his description of Athens is based explicitly on Wheler's.[120]

There are two interesting earlier examples which prefigure the activities of the 1670s group. Greaves, who went to Constantinople in 1638 with the express aim of collecting manuscripts and books, also made measurements of Haghia Sophia, using 'a line of 10 English yards' for the purpose. The notes in which he mentions this survive in a transcription by his protégé Smith.[121] The second example comes from Sandys, whose journey began in 1610. He had an extensive knowledge of classical literature but was not usually particularly observant on the ground. However, he gave this description of a carved stone chair he saw on Chios, which was said to have been a sibyl's throne:

> The rock there riseth aloft, ascended by staires on the West side; cut plaine on the top, and hollowed with benches about like the seates of a theater. In the midst a ruined chaire, supported with defaced Lyons, all of the same stone [...] But the relicke in my conceit doth disprove the report. For there are the shape of legs annexed to the chaire, the remains of some Image, perhaps erected in her honour, (though I never read of a *Chian Sibyl* [...]).[122]

Sandys was clearly looking closely at the object in front of him, and making deductions to challenge the accepted view, as well as bringing his reading to bear.

The 1670s travellers used a variety of methods and aids to help them come to conclusions about what they saw, the most important of which (as with Sandys) was their knowledge of classical texts. The classical education they had received, and the notable extent to which they quoted classical sources in their published and unpublished works, have already been discussed. Wheler referred constantly to Pausanias, evidently carrying a borrowed copy with him for at least part of his journey, and Covel attempted to describe the geography of

Ephesus by reference to Strabo.[123] At Nicaea, Covel described walls which he believed stood 'much in the same place [...] as they did in Strabo's time, though they have been ruin'd and repair'd over and over'.[124] A knowledge of Greek and Roman myths was useful in the identification of scenes on relief sculptures, even if these 'proto-archaeologists'[125] did not always get it right. Spon clearly did his homework: Wheler refers for example to his having consulted a manuscript collection of drawings of Athenian monuments made by Francesco Giambetti, a fifteenth-century architect, in Cardinal Barberini's Library.[126] Other Renaissance sources such as Belon and Gilles have already been discussed. Rycaut's two books on the history of the Ottoman Empire, which first appeared in 1666 and 1678, were well-known and widely consulted among his contemporaries, as was Knolles's book.[127] Covel, Smith, Wheler, Rycaut and Vernon had contact with each other in various ways, and knew, or knew of, each other's work. Knowledge acquired by other expatriates was also available to them: Jean Giraud was of great assistance to Wheler and Spon in particular, providing both information and guides.[128] Wheler remarked that Vernon had put Giraud 'to a great deal of care and trouble for his safety, being gone out alone, a foot, and without a Guide'.[129] Travellers could be quick to criticise sources that they judged to be unreliable: the work of Guillet de la Guilletière was refuted in many instances by Wheler, and Spon followed up the first three volumes of his published work with a fourth, published a couple of years later, as an answer to Guillet's criticisms of his own work.[130] In spite of rivalry when it came to collecting, other Franks could give valuable assistance: when they were in Constantinople together, the French ambassador, the Marquis de Nointel, showed Wheler the drawings he had commissioned, probably from Jacques Carrey, of the Parthenon sculptures.[131]

Local guides and dragomans, and other local people, were also a necessary source of information; although they were frequently regarded as not being of much help, there were exceptions, such as the one provided for Wheler by Giraud to show him and his companion the Peloponnese. At Corinth, Wheler recorded, this guide had learnt his lesson so well that he would run ahead to see whether there were any inscriptions to be seen, calling out '*Scrittione, Scrittione*' to alert his employers if there were.[132] An earlier traveller, Blount, who had a particular interest in the Jews and other subject peoples in the Ottoman Empire, got much of his local information from 'a learned *Jew*' on his journey east of Sofia.[133]

When Spon and Wheler studied the Parthenon sculptures, Wheler made a striking use of his knowledge of coinage, of his interest in which his book gives ample evidence in its illustrations: he triumphantly though wrongly named the two figures in the corner of the west pediment (now usually regarded as representing a mythical Athenian king and his wife or daughter, ancestors of fifth-century BCE Athenians) as the emperor Hadrian and his wife Sabina, 'whom I easily know to be so, by the many Medals and Statues I have seen of them'.[134] Since Spon gave the same identification in his book (although Giraud believed the relief sculptures of the Parthenon to be by Pheidias),[135] but did not mention coins, it may be that this was one of Wheler's personal contributions to their joint effort.[136] Wheler was not the first to use coins as evidence: the idea of identifying statues of emperors went back to Peacham at least, and Wheler may also have known the work of William Camden (in whose *Remaines Concerning Britain* there is a whole section on coinage),[137] John Aubrey and Thomas Browne. The importance Aubrey attached to coinage is indicated by the constant references in his work: in 1666, for example, he recorded the digging up of two urns of Roman coins near Taunton, and sent a request to a local rector for information about the identity of the emperors depicted on them.[138] Browne showed a surprisingly modern attitude to excavation in his description of the burial urns that were found in Norfolk in 1658 and 1667, recognising the importance of the physical context from which artefacts were unearthed as well as of the combination of objects found together, especially coins, and commenting that the fact

> That they buried a piece of Money with them, as a fee of the *Elysian* Ferryman, was a practice full of folly. But the ancient custome of placing Coyns in considerable Urns, and the present practice of burying Medals in the noble Foundations of *Europe*,

are laudable ways of Historical discoveries, in Actions, Persons, Chronologies; and posterity will applaud them.[139]

Joseph Addison (1672–1719) drew links between coinage and ancient texts,[140] and in 1689 Evelyn wrote to Pepys suggesting the value of coins for the study of architecture, history, geography and chronology.[141]

Wheler knew some of Hadrian's buildings in Athens, so it is perhaps not surprising that he supposed the pedimental figures to represent that emperor and his wife. There was another occasion too on which he used coins as historical evidence, when he was in Pola, in Croatia, on his way to Greece and found that coins with Greek lettering were still being minted, deducing from this that Pola must have been a Greek colony.[142] Probably these were in fact coins based on Byzantine types. Wheler also used Athenian archon lists to help identify inscriptions, comparing them as a dating device to the *didascaliae* or production notices at the beginnings of Terence's plays, which allow them to be precisely dated by the consul names.[143] Transcriptions of inscriptions themselves figure large in the writings of Smith, Wheler, Vernon and Covel, though Covel complained that the letter-carvers had not always taken care to avoid mistakes.[144]

One monument that was of great interest to travellers was the so-called 'Pompey's Pillar' on one of the Cyanean Rocks, called the Symplegades in antiquity, on the European side of the northern end of the Bosphorus. According to Peter Mundy (a merchant) in the second decade of the century, this had been erected by Pompey to mark the boundary of his conquests, and was a place where merchants went from Constantinople 'for recreation'.[145] It appears to have been known to Gilles, who, though he does not mention Pompey's name, describes a marble column with a carved base and Corinthian capital, which he thought were the only remains of a Roman altar described by the second-century CE writer Dionysius of Byzantium.[146] Biddulph and his party wrote their names on it.[147] Wheler and Spon saw it later – it is illustrated in Spon's book – and recognised that the base and the column did not belong together; they also concluded from the inscription that it had nothing to do with Pompey.[148] Its later history is problematic: the base, probably an altar, was seen by Count Andréossy in the 1820s, and according to one modern guide-book is still there.[149] The column itself seems to have fallen into the sea at the end of the seventeenth century, but there is a puzzle surrounding this: a Flemish traveller visiting in the summer of 1680 reported that it had fallen,[150] while Veryard records that in 1686 'On a Rock which runs into the *Euxin Sea*' he saw 'an antient Marble Column of a considerable height, placed on a Pedestal, and call'd *Pompey's* Column, being said to have been erected by him after the defeat of *Mithridates*'.[151]

A site that intrigued travellers with less specialised classical knowledge was the Cretan 'labyrinth'. Lithgow described it as the labyrinth of Daedalus, but did not dare to enter it because nobody in his party was equipped with a candle: 'There are many hollow places within it; so that if a man stumble, or fall, he can hardly be rescued: It is cut forth with many intricating wayes, on the face of a little hill, ioining with mount Ida'.[152]

Randolph also visited it, telling the story of a reclusive king who lived there. He and his party did enter, using Ariadne's method of 'a line to direct [them] out again' as well as 'two torches, and candles in Lanthornes'. The line was 80 yards long and they used all of it.[153] Veryard used a different method:

> we lighted our Torches, and entring in found the Passage in some places narrow, and in others broad and supported with Pillars; but the ways were so strangely intricate, that had we not made a provision of Boughs to mark out our way back, by dropping them at convenient distances, I dare say we might have taken up our lodging there, at least for that Night.

As they continued, it became so much more difficult, with supporting pillars and the sides of passages fallen in, that the guide became very anxious.[154] The minotaur is not mentioned by any of these authors. As for its real nature, either they did not know of Belon's obviously correct assertion that it was a quarry, or it spoiled their story.[155]

Another site that had a particular fascination for travellers was the supposed tomb of Cicero on the island of Zante, which was a regular stopping-place on the sea journey to Constantinople. Cicero's tomb is on the Appian Way outside Rome, but there was a story, going back to one Zuallardo, that his body or his ashes had been brought to Zante for burial.[156] It is not impossible that Cicero's friends or family brought his remains across the Adriatic in order to keep them safe from Antony, whose agents had murdered him. Sandys, acknowledging Zuallardo as his source, recorded that the tomb had been found when the Annuntiata monastery was being built about a mile and a half from the town of Zante in 1550. According to him two urns were found, one containing ashes and the other water, and an epitaph that identified the tomb as Cicero's.[157] Further information appears on the back of a map of Crete (I cannot explain why Crete should have been chosen, except that ships often sailed from Zante to Crete) by Ortelius, but if anything it increases the confusion, reading 'Adamus Tefellenius Lovaniensis in his Journal [...] writes that on this island [Zante] in the year of Christ 1550 he handled the bones of Cicero, and read on his tomb this epitaph: Ille oratorum princeps [...]'.[158]

To muddy the water even further, Coryate thought that he had seen the site of the tomb on the island of Cephallonia: 'I saw a very remarkable Monument [...] the Sepulchre of Marcus Tullius Cicero.' It did not have any 'Sepulchrate or Titularie stone', but he knew from an inscription he had read in a house near St Mark's in Venice that the monument itself had been taken by the Italians. Perhaps when he came to write up his work he just made a mistake about where he had seen the tomb.[159] Wheler wrote that the church of St Helias on Zante was 'remarkable for the fame of Cicero's Tomb, which (as some have written) hath been found there', but in his time only the base of a porphyry urn remained, and he could find no one to tell him what had happened to the rest.[160] Veryard also told the story, without apparently having seen the remains, and with a degree of scepticism:

> In the Tomb [found during the excavation for the foundations of a monastery on Zante in 1544] were two *Urns* of Glass, one

fill'd with Ashes and the other fill'd with Water, with these words on the bottom of the former,

AVE. MAR. TUL.

Which induc'd divers People to believe that one contain'd the Ashes of *Cicero*, and the other the Tears of his Friends. They who speak of his Assassination tell us not what became of his Body; so that 'tis conjectur'd it might have been burnt, and the Ashes carried off by his Adherents, who, tis likely, fled to avoid the same blow, and secur'd themselves in this Island; hindring likewise by that means his Body from being expos'd to publick Ignominy.[161]

It is no longer possible to tell whether there is any foundation to the story.

To return to the more scholarly concerns of Covel and his contemporaries, they are to be seen against the background of the Royal Society and its range of interests, which included the historical as well as the scientific, but were solidly based on the principle of inductive rather than deductive reasoning, and emphasised the study of objects rather than texts. Charles II's interest in science and patronage of the Royal Society may also have contributed to an atmosphere in which antiquarian studies could flourish. In this he offered a marked contrast to James I, who had shut down the Society of Antiquaries because he suspected it was hostile to the Crown, and Charles I, who had closed Cotton's library, an important research tool for scholars.[162] Puritans, too, had tended not to favour antiquarian studies, but after the Restoration such studies began to attract a wider social range.[163] All of these factors, together with the general sense of relief that accompanied Charles II's return, may have played a part in altering the environment for antiquarian/archaeological researches. In Spon's case, his medical training may have influenced his approach to the study of antiquities.[164] Changes in education, too, in the second half of the century, involving for some students a shift towards practical subjects such as navigation, are likely to have affected travellers, particularly merchants.[165]

This situation helps to account for the emphasis on measurement, some examples of which have already been mentioned. Smith, at Laodicea, counted and measured the seats of the theatres and circus, giving the height of the seats in the largest theatre as one and a quarter feet, with a breadth (i.e. from back to front) of three feet. He also measured fallen marble pillars at Ephesus that from their location he took to belong to the temple of Diana/Artemis (although in fact this temple was not rediscovered until the nineteenth century), giving the diameter of the pillars as 7 feet and the height as 40.[166] Vernon, who was an active member of the Royal Society, spent two months in Athens and made three visits to the Acropolis to measure the Parthenon and count the number of pillars, in spite of the difficulties caused by Turkish suspicion of his activities. He also measured other buildings in Athens.[167] Covel spent much time on his journeys sketching, measuring, recording inscriptions and making maps and diagrams: he was particularly interested in what he called the 'ichnography', or ground plan, of a building, and was constantly frustrated by the inadequacy of available maps.[168] His usual method of calculating the size of a building was by pacing it out. However, it was not always only a matter of numbers: Vernon also took note of the sculpture adorning the Athenian temples, recording of the Parthenon that:

> about the Cornice on the outside of the Temple of Minerva is a basso relievo of men on horseback, others in Chariots, and a whole procession of people going to a Sacrifice, of very curious sculpture. On the front is the History of the Birth of Minerva.

Vernon also noticed the depictions of the battle of the centaurs and the 'Prowesses of Theseus' on the so-called Theseion: 'all his postures and looks are exprest with great art'.[169]

Vernon was an indefatigable, if not always successful, seeker after historical remains, not afraid to take risks: he went on from Greece to Persia, where he was murdered. Crawford's letter remarks that his courage was above his strength, but that he has spent some time on the brinke of the River Alpheius where he did with much diligence search for the stadium Olympium but could find no vestigies of it [...] at Corinth nothing but utter desolation, except the Castle [...] he did particularly observe that place of the Istmus where they thought to have made a communication betwixt the two seas.[170]

Wheler was a less adventurous investigator, but he and Spon used Strabo, Pliny the Elder and Pausanias to help them identify various ancient monuments and sites. The care they took to try to get things right is illustrated by their identification of the village of Castri as the ancient Delphi. Others, Wheler says, had assumed that Salona was Delphi:

> But because this [Salona] agreed not with the *Idea* we had of the Situation of that Place [Delphi]; we made strict enquiry, whether there were no old Stones with writing upon them, about the Town.

Hearing that there was something at a nearby church, they were eventually able, after some difficulty caused by the priest being frightened by their Turkish dress, to read the inscription on the stone, which turned out to be a copy of an epistle from a Roman consul addressed to the citizens of Amphissa. In addition, the situation of Salona agreed exactly with Pausanias's and Strabo's accounts of Amphissa. Over a glass of excellent white wine, they gathered from the priest that there were lots of ruins at the village of Castri, on the road to Livadia, so they set off in that direction. 'We no sooner approached, but we concluded, that it was undoubtedly the Remainder of the famous City of *Delphos*'. In case any doubt should remain, they found a stone with an inscription mentioning the name of Delphi, which Wheler eventually took back to Oxford. They saw the site of the stadium, but could not find the temple of Apollo, though they thought it might have been where the church of St Helias stood. A monk in a nearby monastery confirmed that he had read 'some book' that confirmed the identification of Delphi.

Wheler commented sadly that Delphi 'remains Great, at present, only in the Writings of the Antients'.[171]

Wheler alleged that Thyatira, one of the seven churches of Asia, had been wrongly identified by 'ignorant Greeks' until the true location was discovered by the 'Curiosity, and Piety' of Rycaut. There, looking at inscriptions, they caused a stir among the locals:

> a great many *Turks* came staring upon us, to see what we did; who, when we told them, That that stone [a statue pedestal] had on it the antient Name of the City, in the time of the Pagans, and was called *Thyatira*, wondred at the News.[172]

Smith, too, was concerned with the identification of the site of Thyatira:

> the description of the Ancients and the several inscriptions that we found there put it out of doubt, that this is the true *Thyatira*: though the *Greeks*, who are prodigiously ignorant of their own Antiquities, take *Tyreh*, a town twenty five miles to the South-east of *Ephesus*, to be the place.

He, like Wheler, also excited interest among the Turkish inhabitants, 'great enemies of Learning and Antiquity' according to Smith, who thought him quite mad for coming 'to look upon a few old stones', which as far as they were concerned were useful only as building materials.[173] The antics of western visitors evidently provided much local entertainment.

Wheler's own descriptions are frequently confused and difficult to follow, partly owing to his sources. Pausanias 'is not altogether so regular in his Descriptions of Places, as it might be wished' and sometimes 'doth but obscurely mention' buildings that Wheler wanted to investigate. Using the lexicographer Hesychius (fifth century CE) and the Suda (tenth-century CE encyclopaedia) as well as Pausanias, he tried to make sense of the area west of the Athenian Acropolis, including the Areopagus and the monument of Philopappos, concluding that if his conjectures, 'touching the

Areopagus and Fountain there, be good, it will make a great alteration in the Names, which Travellers have hitherto given to sundry Antiquities in *Athens*'.[174] On the monument of Lysicrates, which at that time was known as the Lantern of Demosthenes, he thought that the sculptures represented the labours of Hercules, when they are now identified as Dionysus and the Tyrrhenian pirates.[175] Wheler's book is full of drawings and diagrams, and he was a keen mapmaker: on one occasion he climbed a steep hill near Athens, using this as a vantage-point for plotting places on a map he was making, and looked over the Ilissus river to see the stadium built by Herodes Atticus to the east of the Acropolis, beyond the temple of Olympian Zeus.[176] On the other hand, if we compare the illustrations in Wheler's and Spon's books with, for example, the contemporary engravings of the buildings of Rome by Desgodetz, the latter are in an altogether different class, making Wheler's look sketchy and out of proportion.[177] The beginnings of Greek archaeology and architectural history were a long way behind the equivalent studies in Rome.

What none of these travellers was able even to begin to do, because as yet no one had begun to work out a chronological framework, was to put buildings or works of art in any kind of time frame. Wheler did have some sense of historical chronology, which he used at the beginning of his description of Athens, giving an account of the history of the city from mythical to early Christian times, but he was unable to differentiate between myth and history, and his assignment of buildings or works of art to any particular historical period was both partial and erratic.[178] When Covel visited Ephesus, and tried to use Strabo to work out the history of the site, he recognised not only that the topography had changed between ancient times and his own day, because the coastline had altered, and that the ruins he saw did not all come from the same period, but also that his conjectures about the site were just that – guesswork: 'I do by no meanes pretend [them] to be anything near the exact Truth' and it is 'a meer confused guesse at best, whatever we conjecture of things as we now find them'.[179] Perhaps there is a new appreciation here of the size of the task of identification.

When Smith was at Ephesus – a favourite place for Englishmen interested in antiquities because of its easy access from Smyrna, where there was a thriving English factory (trading station) – he noticed 'vaults built arch-wise'. He thought that what he was looking at was the temple of Diana with a church built in its ruins, but nowhere did he comment on the use of arches, which though used occasionally in Asia Minor in buildings of the Hellenistic period were very rarely used by the classical Greeks.[180] Nor have I found any comment on the use of arches for building elsewhere in travel writing of the seventeenth century. Covel at least knew Vitruvius, though there is little about vaults or arches in Vitruvius and almost nothing in Strabo. He was also familiar with some of the nomenclature of architecture, referring to Doric, Ionic and Corinthian column capitals, and to metopes and triglyphs.[181] Smith saw a building that he thought might have been St Paul's prison, or alternatively a watch-tower, as well as a large porphyry font: he did consider what the date of the latter might have been, since he observed that in the 'sad times' (for Christianity) of Domitian and Trajan baptism would have been a secret ritual and therefore such a large font was unlikely. Evidence that he looked closely at the physical remains is clear: at Pergamum he identified the theatre by 'the marks of steps still remaining' and at Smyrna he noticed stones with V-shaped cuts in them that some people thought indicated 'Vespasian' but that Smith more plausibly thought were cuts used by the stonemasons for joining the stones together.[182]

At Nicaea, Covel was excited by seeing '6 vaults yet remaining and ye vestigiums of two more which have been destroy'd':

> I must confesse [them] to be so glorious and admirable a sight, as I thought it worth my labour and paines and expence only to have seen them. They are made in forme of a coffin: the roof sloping down, and ye floor diminishing towards ye lesser end [...] Every one had at bottome a little hole or doore for a water sink.[183]

He measured and sketched them, thinking that they were tombs; in fact they were the entrances (*vomitoria*) of the Roman theatre.

The possibility of excavating for antiquities buried underground begins to appear in a few sources early in the seventeenth century. In 1627, Ambassador Roe wrote to Arundel, 'there is enough under ground, if our licences would extend to digge'. He thought that some antiquities had been hidden to keep them safe from Turks, although if this were the case there must have been some Greeks who cared more for their past than most travellers would have had their readers believe.[184] One manuscript surviving from this period gives advice to antiquity-hunters: digging should take place near the sites of ancient cities, as indicated by visible ruins; marble blocks for repairing damaged statues should be looked for; small fragments found near statues should be carefully collected; diggers should wear poor clothes, so as to suggest to Turks that the purpose is curiosity rather than the expectation of valuable finds; and tobacco and knives should be carried as presents for Turkish officials.[185] A more problematical story is included by Rycaut in his *Ottoman Empire*, in this case of a Greek who obtained permission to dig at Philippopolis, but his excavation caused the earth to fall in, killing 70 people. The choice of site was determined by little round hills that were supposed to be the graves of Roman legionaries and that the local people may have suspected would yield treasure, but even so this sounds like an operation on an unlikely scale, unless perhaps the digging caused the collapse of a village and the 70 people were 'collateral damage'.[186]

Souvenir-hunting and collecting

The Greek world did not remain a museum, to be observed and studied unaltered by travellers: it was changed by their activities of souvenir-hunting and collecting.[187] There was no sense at this date that antiquities should remain *in situ*, an argument that was only systematically articulated in Napoleonic France, when Quatremère de Quincy complained about the removal of works of art from their original sites to fill the Palais du Louvre.[188] Breaking off small pieces of marble from monuments was not uncommon: Coryate at Troy wrote, 'I brake of[f] certaine stones to carrie with mee into my

Countrey, and to reserve them in my safe custodie for memorable Antiquities while I live.' They were also to be 'some kinde of guerdon or remuneration' for his pains.[189] It is interesting that the argument about the safety of antiquities as a justification for removing them, which was to be so crucial for later collectors such as Lord Elgin, was already appearing. Smith used it a few decades after Coryate and on slightly different grounds when he found a marble statue at Pergamum: 'we caused [the statue] to be removed by a poor *Christian*, this being the only way to preserve it', in this case because of the Muslim dislike of human representation in art.[190] The French ambassador to the Porte at the time of Wheler's journey, de Nointel, wrote that sculptures would be safer from the Turks in the French king's galleries, because, in his view, Turks regarded the disfigurement of figurative statues as a good deed.[191] Coryate also sent the antiquary Robert Cotton an excited message that he had taken possession of 'a very curious white marble head of an ancient Heros or Gyant-like champion. Found out very casually by [his] diligent pervestigation amongst the ruines of the once renowned City of Cyzicum.'[192]

The safety argument was perhaps only an optional extra, rather than the real reason for taking treasures home. Wheler 'prevailed with the Pappa' to remove a bas-relief from a wall at Salamis; he gives no reason, but presumably he just coveted it.[193] Smith reported that at St Polycarp's tomb in Smyrna *'Western Christians* [...] break off pieces of marble and carry them away as reliques'.[194]

Among more portable souvenirs, coins were popular. Browne had acquired some Roman coins which he gave away to the imperial librarian in Vienna: 'because [...] he is a good Antiquary, I presented him with some old Roman Coynes which I procured at Lene in Hungary formerly a Roman station'.[195] Covel showed Wheler and Spon his collection of drawings, intaglios, coins and other such easily manageable souvenirs.[196] Rycaut acquired a collection of coins dating from the third century CE which had been found in the wall of the old theatre at Smyrna.[197] Smith sent a present to Pepys of a copy of an old Egyptian 'curiosity', apparently an inscription, of which the original was in Oxford, having been brought out of Egypt by Robert

Huntington, Levant Company chaplain in Aleppo from 1670: 'I thought it would not bee an unacceptable present to a person of your great genius and comprehensive knowledge, and who is delighted with [antiquityes?] of all kinds.'[198]

It was not, though, simply a matter of souvenirs: there was also collecting on a much more serious scale. This had begun near the beginning of the century, in the aristocratic circles around the court. The person who more than anyone else was responsible for the great vogue in collecting classical antiquities was Thomas Howard, Earl of Arundel, whose employee Henry Peacham attested to the value the earl attached to such pieces, even if they were damaged, when they were still 'venerable for their antiquity and elegancy'. Arundel's great rival, James I's favourite Buckingham, on the other hand, preferred his statues to look perfect.[199] Aesthetic appreciation was certainly a large part of the appeal for Charles I, of whom it was said that he admired 'the tongueless eloquence of lights and shadows, and the silent Poesie of lines, and [...] living Marbles'.[200] For Arundel, they seem to have had a value simply for their associations, as Roe recognised when he sent back a stone which had no beauty but only 'the antiquity and truth' of coming from a building in Troy.[201] Ironically, of course, it probably did not come from Homer's Troy at all. The collection at Arundel House, open in accordance with Arundel's will to 'all gentlemen of Virtue', became deservedly famous.[202] In the 1630s it was said to contain 37 statues, 128 busts, 200 inscriptions and sarcophagi, as well as manuscripts, paintings, coins and gems.[203] In 1663, after his travels, Edward Browne spent Christmas with one of Arundel's grandsons and recalled in his journal early the following year that

> these things were [...] collected by the old earl of Arundel, who employed his agents [...] to buy him up rarities [...] especially in Greece and Italy, where hee might probably meet with things of the greatest antiquity and curiosity.

[...]

Antiquities, Proto-Archaeologists and Collectors 137

> I went to Arundell House where I saw a great number of old Roman and Grecian statuas, many as big again as the life, and divers Greek inscriptions upon stones in the garden. I viewed these statuas till the approaching night began to obscure them, beinge extreamly taken with the noblenesse of that ancient worke, and grieving at the bad usage some of them had met with in our last distractions [i.e. during the Interregnum].[204]

There were other collectors with immense buying power, notably Charles I and Buckingham. These men used agents to acquire sculpture for them, sometimes people sent out specially for the purpose, such as Arundel's Petty, and sometimes people who were on the spot anyway, such as Ambassador Roe. Louis XIV was a formidable rival to English collectors, and there may have been an element of national rivalry involved, as well as the greed of kings. The French diplomat the Marquis de Nointel collected avidly,[205] both for himself and for his sovereign, although when he got seriously into debt and had to sell 'all his books, plate and furniture', he was reported to have said, perhaps disingenuously, 'with tears [...] That others carryd away mony and jewells, but he nothing but marble stones of antiquity'.[206]

Roe and Arundel prefigured Elgin and the Parthenon in their attempts to remove the 'Golden Gate' reliefs from the Seven Towers in Constantinople. The reliefs, set high up on one of the prison gates and representing Hercules among other classical subjects, were seen and admired by Roe. With his assistance, Petty went to immense trouble to try to get permission to have them brought down, but was unable to accomplish this. A blow-by-blow account can be read in Roe's correspondence. Some of the reliefs were still there for Covel, Spon and Wheler to see in the 1670s, but all have since disappeared, and although de Nointel was said to have intended to have drawings made of them, if these were ever done they too have disappeared.[207]

By the time of Covel and Wheler, after the dispersal of Charles I's collection during the Interregnum, collecting had become an activity to a certain extent open to persons of the middling sort as well as to the aristocracy. Those who could not afford statues might collect on a smaller scale, perhaps choosing coins, inscriptions or books. Wheler showed from the illustrations that preface his book, as well as from references within the text, that he had a particular interest in coins. He did, however, also collect some marbles, probably mostly inscriptions. He refers in his preface to *'Divers Medals* [i.e. coins] *and other Antiquities I have by me, since sent from Athens to me'*.[208] When he returned home, he proudly presented his marbles, which included an inscription from Delphi, to his alma mater, the University of Oxford, where 'they have the honour to be placed among the famous *Marmora Arundeliana & Seldeniana'*, though he kept a few figures and bas-reliefs, such as an image of Ceres, which is illustrated in his book.[209] It was clearly not all about personal aggrandisement: private collections were made available to visitors, and generous donations were made to institutions, though, of course, the opening of a collection to visitors of itself conferred personal glory on the owner. In Smyrna, Wheler bought some rare coins, but also saw more 'in the Cabinet of an ingenious Merchant [...] who designs his Collection for the *University* of *Oxford'*.[210] De Nointel, who had a collection of inscriptions in his Constantinople garden, showed Wheler and Spon about 30 marbles, inscriptions and bas-reliefs when they visited him, as well as drawings of the Parthenon sculptures he had commissioned, and they were allowed to make sketches, although unfortunately these do not appear in Wheler's or Spon's books.[211] North, who was in Smyrna and Constantinople in the 1660s and 1670s, had visited the Duke of Florence's gallery, where 'Another room is full of relics of antiquity of all sorts, as statues, old ironwork, and pictures, which they say had their being very long ago and are the works of the first professors of that art'.[212]

The most serious difficulty faced by collectors, especially those who were attempting to remove large-scale works, was transport. In Athens, when Wheler was looking to send his marbles back to England, the consul Giraud told him an English ship was expected, but when it arrived Wheler had his suspicions that it might not really be English, 'otherwise I had laded more Marbles on it'. Further complications were to follow. Wheler left Athens for home, but two days into his journey was overtaken by a message from Giraud to tell him of another ship: 'whereby I might have the convenience to send my Marbles, and whatever I would else, into *England*'. The letter requested him to return to Athens, which he was reluctant to do: '[I think] it more safe to go by Boat to *Zant*, the same way I came; we having then War with *Tripoli*, and the ship at *Athens* had no Convoy to guard it.' He accordingly sent directions to the long-suffering consul 'for what other Marbles' he would 'have to be sent by the Ship', presumably less careful for his marbles' safety than his own.[213]

There was frequently a physical problem in actually moving statues. Randolph mentioned that on the island of Leros 'are the ruins of a large Castle on a hill, and about 20 very great marble pillars which are entire, and are too far from the Sea to be carryed away'.[214] It is in connection with the island of Delos that we hear most about how statues were moved. Delos was a crucial site for marble-hunters, not only because of its ancient status but because, being barren and almost waterless, it was uninhabited, so that it was all the easier to carry off statues without attracting any unwelcome notice.[215] Sandys, who had seen it early in the century, wrote that

> the ruines of *Apollos* temple are here yet to be seene, affoording faire pillars of marble to such as will fetch them, and other stones of price, both in their nature and for their workmanship; the whole Iland being now uninhabited,[216]

and Robson reckoned that the only reason for visiting the island was 'the vaste reliques of *Apolloes* Temple'.[217] But the person who has left us the most extraordinary account of the considerable lengths to which seekers after antiquities might go is Kenelm Digby, the leader of a privateering expedition in 1628 whose side-line was the fulfilling of a commission from Charles I to find works to fill his galleries. Digby's journal provides a vivid record of the scale of these activities:

> Went to Delphos [Delos] [...] and there I spent my time taking in some marble stones and statues [...] To avayle myselfe of the conveniencie of carrying away some antiquities there, I busied

them [the sailors] in rolling of stones downe to the sea side, which they did with such eagernesse as though it had bin the earnestest businesse that they came out for, and they mastered prodigious massie weightes; but one stone, the greatest and fairest of all, containing 4 statues, they gave over after they had bin, 300 men, a whole day about it [...] But the next day I contrived a way with mastes of shippes and another shippe to ride overagainst it, that brought it down with much ease and speede. In the little Delphos there are brave marble stones heaped up in the great ruines of Apollos temple, and within the circuit of it is a huge statue, but broken in two peeces about the wast, which the Greekes told me was Apollos. It weigheth at least 30 tonnes, and time hath worn out much the softnesses and gentilenesses of the worke, yet all the proportions remain perfect and in grosse; the yieldings of the flesh and the musculous partes are visible, so that it is still a brave noble piece, and hath by divers bin attempted to be carried away, but they have all failed in it.[218]

The piece that he describes as 'containing 4 statues' may well have been a relief, perhaps an altar or pedestal: Peacham recorded that thanks to Digby the king acquired 'marble bases, columns and altars' from Delos.[219] It is worth mentioning that Digby was a young man, still in his mid-twenties, when he commanded this expedition and devised these ingenious arrangements for moving huge stones.

Although some Englishmen, Smith for example, may have thought of themselves as connoisseurs *par excellence* of classical remains,[220] it was not only the English who plundered the riches of Delos. Randolph writes that 'the Ruins are carried away by all ships who come to anchor there, so as part are in *England, France, Holland*, but most at *Venice*'.[221] Wheler is one of those who left a record of his visit to the island. He was particularly intrigued by an oval structure that he thought might have been a place for the staging of sea battles: possibly this was the sacred lake, which was surrounded by buildings in ancient times but in Wheler's day had a wall around it, as it still does. He saw 'a vast heap of admirable white Marble, which we knew

Antiquities, Proto-Archaeologists and Collectors 141

to have been the Temple of Apollo, by the Trunk of his Statue we found among them'. Four to five times life-size, it was too ruined to judge the details of its form, and 'the God himself [was] so ill handled, that he had neither hands, feet, nor head left him, yet what is remaining appeareth still most beautiful'. His landlord on Mykonos told him that it had been upright until three years earlier, when someone (Spon and Wheler disagreed on whether this person was English or Venetian) broke it up in an attempt to carry it away, so if it was the same statue that Digby had seen, human activity as well as time had made its condition worse.[222] While Wheler did not explicitly criticise those who removed statues, the implication of the phrase 'ill handled' is that he did not approve, although his own removal of a bas-relief has been mentioned. As has been discussed in connection with the measurement and exact recording of ancient buildings, attitudes in the 1670s had perhaps shifted a little from those of half a century earlier.

Wheler also commented on pieces that he 'guessed to have been the Lyons, that the Neighbouring Islanders remember to have seen formerly here', and on capitals whose 'Beauty made them esteemed worth carrying away', as well as a female figure and a centaur of the highest quality.[223] Like many of his other comments, this shows Wheler to have had an eye for the aesthetic qualities of Greek sculpture.

It is apparent, therefore, that ancient works of art were collected because of their perceived aesthetic value, even in a damaged state, and there is ample evidence, at least from the 1670s, that visitors admired some works of art that they had no intention of trying to remove. The name of the sculptor Praxiteles, known from Pliny the Elder's account of ancient art,[224] appears in several accounts. Here is Wheler again: 'A great way Eastward [from Cerigo] we discerned Paros, Renowned for its excellent White Marble; which after was so improved by the excellent Workmanship of Phidias and Praxitiles.'

At Eleusis he found part of a colossal statue of Ceres, 'from the head to below the Waste [sic], made of very white Marble, of admirable Work, and perhaps of no less a Master, than *Praxiteles* himself', and at Thyatira a 'remarkable' carving with

Vine Branches, mixed with Figures of several sorts of Creatures, as Beetles and Snails, with two Masques, and a Vessel full of Grapes, trodden by three Men, all excellent work. Without doubt, this was taken from the Temple of *Bacchus*.[225]

This sounds, from its description, to have been a Hellenistic piece, though beetles and snails seem unlikely. For Wheler, however, the acme of beauty in Greek art remained the sculpture of the Parthenon:

We were so impatient to go to the Temple of *Minerva* [...] which is not only still the chief Ornament of the Cittadel; but absolutely, both for Matter and Art, the most beautiful piece of Antiquity remaining in the World.

The frieze contained 'Historical Figures of admirable Beauty', and in the east pediment

The Horses are made with such great Art, that the Sculptor seems to have outdone himself, by giving them a more than seeming Life: such a Vigour is express'd in each posture of their prauncing and stamping, natural to generous Horses.[226]

Veryard too knew the name of Praxiteles, referring to a (no longer extant in his day) statue of Venus by '*Praxateles*' from her temple at Cnidos; and earlier in the century Coryate had seen at Troy a marble sepulchre with some hands so beautifully carved on it that 'it is impossible for Praxiteles or any other that was the most excellent carver in the World to surpass it'.[227] Occasionally, we find an awareness of what might be missing. Sandys, for example, mentions two works of art that were no longer to be seen, a painting by Apelles of Venus rising from the sea, which he knew Augustus had taken to Rome from Cos,[228] and the Colossus of Rhodes, by Chares of Lindos.[229]

Covel demonstrates that it was not only pagan sculpture that was admired. On his trip to Mount Athos, which he is thought to have been the first English traveller to visit,[230] he appreciated the Byzantine treasures he saw, such as jewelled crosses at Iveron and a cupola at Vatopedio covered with 'admirably well done' mosaic.[231] Rycaut, who based his account of Mount Athos on information provided by Covel, introduces a note of envy, saying that the monks sit on their heaps of treasure (vestments, plate, crosses, icons and richly bound manuscripts) like misers. Or is he perhaps implying that such treasures would be better off in the hands of western collectors?[232] Mosaics were appreciated by Veryard, too, who saw Armenian examples in Constantinople 'so fresh as if they had been newly done'.[233] Wheler saw, and commented on, the mosaics in the church of Hosios Loukas, near Delphi, though he did not rate the architectural features as highly as the scorned Guillet had done.[234] Sandys, on his visit to Haghia Sophia, had seen mosaics of 'unexpressible statelinesse', of which he described the method of construction, implying that the medium was not very familiar to western eyes.[235] Evliya Çelebi (1611–c.1684), an Ottoman traveller, described how 12 foreigners, experts in geometry and architecture, bit their fingers in astonishment at what they saw when they visited the mosque of Sultan Suleiman.[236]

Covel's descriptions of the antiquities he saw do not generally convey any strong sense of aesthetic appreciation, but he was intrigued by the detective work required to understand some works of art. In particular, he described in detail a piece of relief carving that he saw at Ephesus, although he was irritated by the fact that his companions were in more of a hurry than he was, and he therefore felt he could not do the job justice and had to rely on his Smyrna friend Jerome Salter for a detailed description. He described the relief as showing men in armour, including one figure pulling a naked corpse by the leg, and women in mourning. He noted that he thought the stones had been rearranged, so that as he saw it it was 'but a patchit peice of work'. He himself thought that the subject represented might have been an incident recorded in Appian involving Mithridates, and strongly rejected another suggestion that the subject was Christian persecution (at the time he saw it, the carved slabs were built into what was known as the 'Gate of Persecutions', the name having been acquired from the conjectural subject of the reliefs), although he was tentative about his own interpretation:

'I offer this as a meer, It may be, and so let it passe.'[237] What is curious is that Covel apparently did not know the suggestion mentioned by Wheler (and also known to Rycaut) that it depicted the dragging of Hector, a story familiar from Homer, though Wheler himself was a little doubtful about this interpretation because of the apparent absence of a chariot.[238] Covel's description is more detailed and accurate than that of the French traveller Monconys, who saw the gate in 1648 and described one of the mourning women as a man in the costume of a senator, scratching his head as if displeased with an object being presented to him.[239] These reliefs in fact come from a Roman sarcophagus, now in the Woburn Abbey collection, that does indeed represent the dragging of Hector.[240] The same gate was seen by Evliya Çelebi, who described it as 'a strange and marvellous, highly wrought ancient gate. Above the arches are a kind of fine depictions [...] that dazzle the eye and puzzle the mind.'[241]

Books and manuscripts

There is a final aspect of collecting to consider, and that is the collecting of books and manuscripts, for which the Constantinople area, and possibly Mount Athos, offered rich pickings. Although there are indications of scholarly interest, a desire to possess – sometimes, as in the case of antiquities, in the guise of concern about the safety of the objects – can almost always be detected underneath. Western travellers believed that there were treasures in the form of Greek and Arabic manuscripts, the latter in many cases translations of classical Greek texts, to be found inside the Sultan's court. This is not unlikely, since there was intermarriage between the sultanate and the Byzantine Greeks in the early days of the Ottoman Empire: for example, the father of Mehmed II, Ottoman conqueror of Constantinople, in 1435 married a Christian who retained her faith and was the protector of Mount Athos.[242] Mehmed II himself appreciated Greek culture: he had a Greek tutor and spoke the language.[243] On the other hand, there was also a belief among visitors that Christian manuscripts had been destroyed by Muslims. According to Finkel, the Sultan's library contained many Greek manuscripts until the early seventeenth century, but the Ottomans

Antiquities, Proto-Archaeologists and Collectors 145

had begun to lose interest in their Byzantine heritage towards the end of the sixteenth, and it is not known what happened to most of the manuscripts.[244] Wheler mentions a manuscript of Livy that was supposed to be in the Seraglio, but this was a misapprehension, as indicated by a Turkish note on the flyleaf.[245] Some manuscripts had certainly already gone abroad: Ogier de Busbecq, ambassador to Constantinople from the Holy Roman Emperor in the sixteenth century, had taken 264 back to Europe with him, and in 1687–8 the French ambassador took 15 Greek manuscripts to Paris.[246]

Arundel's agent, Petty, had been helped by Roe and the Orthodox patriarch Cyril Lucaris to acquire 22 manuscripts from 'the best library knowne of Greece':[247] the library was probably that of the monastery of S. Trinitas in Insula, on the island of Chalcis near Constantinople, the provenance of some of the Greek manuscripts from the Arundel collection, now in the British Library.[248]

Before the Civil War, oriental studies were flourishing in England, particularly in Oxford.[249] In this period Archbishop Laud had even suggested that every returning Levant Company ship should be required to bring back one Arabic or Persian manuscript, though this idea was not taken up enthusiastically by the company.[250] However, two Oxford scholars, Pococke and Greaves, travelled to Constantinople in the 1630s for the express purpose of collecting manuscripts and books. Pococke was to become professor of Arabic at Oxford, and mentor to Covel's predecessor Smith, while Greaves (whose brother Thomas was an orientalist) was a mathematician and astronomer, some of whose notes were later transcribed by Smith.

Sometimes they encountered difficulties in obtaining what they wanted. On 2 August 1638, Greaves wrote to Patrick Young, keeper of the king's library, that he had acquired some manuscripts but had had to give them back in the aftermath of the murder of Lucaris, whose friendly attitude towards England is indicated by his gift of a valuable biblical manuscript (the *Codex Alexandrinus*, now in the British Library) to Charles I:[251]

> For having procur'd out of a [?] and ignorant Monastery, which depended on the Patriarchate 14 good MSS of the Fathers, I was

compelled[?] to restore the bookes, and loose my mony, for feare of a worse inconvenience.[252]

Money was often a problem. Greaves wrote that there were plenty of Arabic mathematical and scientific books available if only he could prevail on the Levant Company to pay for them. In such difficulties he seems to have been willing to resort to theft: the most beautiful piece he had seen was a copy of Ptolemy's *Almagest* in Arabic which had been stolen from the library of the Seraglio by an Ottoman cavalryman, and he thought there might be other such opportunities if ambassadors played their cards right. Even by this method, however, he is unlikely to have acquired anything without paying somebody for it, whether legitimately or otherwise.[253]

Another method suggested by Greaves was exchange, although to what extent he acted on this idea is unclear. In a letter to Pococke of 1636,[254] he suggests that they should take 'good store' of Greek and Arabic books to Constantinople, where there was no printing press, to be exchanged for others. In 1627, Nicolas Metaxa had arrived from England with a press and Greek type, and the press was set up with the approval of Lucaris and under the protection of Ambassador Roe. According to Smith, the French Jesuits were angered by this, feeling that it threatened their influence, and told the Grand Vizier that the alleged religious purposes of the press were a cover for anti-Ottoman political activity. As a result, janissaries destroyed parts of the press and damaged others, so that it could no longer function.[255] In another letter, of 1638, Greaves's tone had changed, and he lamented that the Greeks had either had their books taken from them by violence or been compelled to sell them in order to pay tribute to the Grand Signor, 'so that now there is not anything left of antiquity', and in the course of five months he had seen nothing but some liturgies and a 'few imperfect pieces of the fathers'. The Greeks informed him that there were plenty at Mount Athos, but he was inclined to believe Belon's statement[256] that he had found no manuscripts of 'polite learning' there, and did not carry out his earlier plan to go to Mount Athos in order to catalogue manuscripts and help Laud with editions of Greek texts. He recognised that treasures did turn up from time to time: he had heard of a library of Greek and Egyptian books found three years previously in Cairo, and he believed that the library of the Byzantine emperors 'is to this day kept whole & intire in the Seraglio', if only it could be got out. He did manage to acquire some books in spite of being 'often cheated by the brokers, who are Jews' whom he 'secretly imployed'.[257] In Turkish shops, such things were very pricey and he 'onely knew then, what it was to be poore'.[258] John Sanderson had looked for Greek books for his brother, who had been appointed one of the translators of the Greek New Testament, but a marginal note of his on a letter from Ambassador Lello to Thomas Sanderson about this subject reads 'Much promised in this letter; nothinge performed'.[259]

Books could be useful diplomatic tools. Ambassador Winchilsea, in the 1660s, made a point of sending manuscripts and books as presents to those in high places. Winchilsea referred in a letter of March 1661/2 to 'an antient Greeke Evangelist' given to him by the patriarch of Constantinople, which he proposed as a present to the King. In 1662 he wrote to the Lord Chancellor, Lord Clarendon, to say that he had sent 'the Greek Evangelists, the antientest that the Patriarch of Constantinople could with the most diligent inquisition and scrutiny procure in any of the monasteries or churches of Greece', and in the following January he expressed his wish to furnish the Lord Chancellor with the best manuscripts that the patriarchs of Constantinople and Jerusalem could find for him. In return he had already given the patriarch of Constantinople 'one of our great Bibles of six volumes in diverse tongues',[260] probably the one that had been worked on in London in 1655–7.[261] In February 1664/5, the Lord Chancellor sent a slightly double-edged thank you to Winchilsea for a manuscript of St Gregory's works about which, he wrote, there was disagreement among the learned, one person thinking it fit for a university library, another that it was full of errors.[262]

It is clear that Orthodox clergy played a part in obtaining books and manuscripts, whether illicitly or not. Wheler was shown a text of St Dionysius by the archbishop of Athens, which the French ambassador had been interested in but had found too expensive – a view shared by Wheler, who managed to obtain two other copies of the same work, cheaper and just as pleasing. He also bought 20 or 30 Greek manuscripts from a 'Paper-shop hard by [the patriarch's] Door' in Constantinople.[263]

Wheler may not always have been on the look-out to buy, but was interested simply in seeing what was extant. In a monastery at Penteli, north of Athens, which was under the protection of the Sultan's mother (another instance of a link between Christians and Muslims), he and Spon saw 'a library of Good Books to inform their Minds', though he 'fear[ed] they make but little use of them'. These consisted mainly of the Church fathers, Chrysostom, St Basil, St John Damascene, Gregory Nazianzen, St Cyril, Dionysius the Areopagite and St Macanus. They also saw scriptural manuscripts and Greek liturgies on parchment rolls on the acropolis of Corinth, where treasures were kept safe against the threat of pirates.[264] Covel, who unlike Wheler did make it to Mount Athos, found it to be true as far as he could tell that there were few if any humanist books, and the collections consisted mostly of Church Fathers, though he was frustrated in several monasteries by the absence of the treasurer, who could have shown him what they had. At Simeno, Covel wrote,

> I could not take an account of all their bookes as I design'd; yet I view'd severall 1000ds. and found them all divinity, fathers, councels, evang. old and new Test. in parts, commentators, homilyes. τριῶδιον, μηναῖον. church books. γρηγορίου Theol. Scholia in Basilium, Πρακτικὰ Svae Synodi antiq. MS. [in other words, works concerning the calendar and liturgy of the church as well as texts and commentaries.] I beleive there are noe bookes of humane learning there left.

However, he disagreed with Belon[265] that monks who read humanist books were excommunicated. At the monastery of Iveron he found

> multitudes of Theologicall bookes every where; but in every place ye scevofylaca [i.e. treasurer] abroad: [could] not see their bookes in their towers. was told here all bookes burnt of

humane learning; those concern'd not them. phaps all a pretence, fear'd me.

It is of course possible, as he recognised, that the treasurers were canny enough to absent themselves because they did not want westerners poking about in their libraries and perhaps trying to take books away. The absence of the Iveron treasurer made him 'more grieved missing the MS', but he did see a great deal, including many inscriptions 'in ye Iberian toung. and [...] at least 60 very old MS. in velum in ye same toung. [He] turn'd over about 1000 ms. left out by ye σκευοφυλ. all divine fathers &c.'[266] The 'Iberian' language was not Spanish but Georgian; the name of the monastery, Iveron, has the same etymology. Though not an avid collector of antiquities, Covel acquired a manuscript of Simeon, archbishop of Thessalonica in the early fifteenth century, worth 20 dollars, given to him by the patriarch at the monastery of Lavra.[267] He seems to have been offered a book about 'the procession of the H.G. [Holy Ghost], Greek and Latin', but perhaps the 100 dollars the seller wanted was too much, as he does not appear to have bought it, although it might have been useful for the book he planned to write about the Greek Church.[268] On a journey to Nicaea, however, when he was visiting islands in the Sea of Marmara, in one monastery he found classical texts including a printed edition of two or three of Euripides's plays, as well as Demosthenes, Apollonius Rhodius and Homer.[269] And on one occasion a papas presented him with two manuscripts for which he paid 'in charity' one and a half dollars.[270] There is no doubt that he did make a personal collection over the course of his life, since in a letter to Humfrey Wanley of 5 February 1712/13 he wrote that he made daily use of his Greek manuscripts.[271] It is likely that most of these were acquired while he was living in the Ottoman Empire.

Clearly, antiquities were important to all kinds of travellers, in various ways: Greece's past was a primary reason for their interest in visiting Greece, not only in the case of precursors of the Grand Tourists such as Wheler, but also for others whose ostensible reason for going to that part of the world was quite different.

The post-Restoration travellers demonstrate a shift in attitude: under the influence of a more 'scientific' view of the world, the beginnings of what was to become archaeology began to be seen. This is well expressed by Wheler's comment that on his arrival at the house of Jean Giraud they decided to rest in order that they 'might with the more Care and Exactness, see, view, and compare all things necessary to give an Account of this Place, that might not deserve so much Censure for the Truth of it, as some [before them had done]'.[272]

It was a kind of manifesto for the educated traveller's journey to Greece, and prefigures not only the attitudes of Grand Tourists but also the more scholarly approach to antiquities that would become more widespread in the following century.

CHAPTER 4

AMONG THE GREEKS

As outsiders in the Ottoman Empire, Covel and his contemporaries saw that empire as made up of a mixture of the ruling Turks and their various subject peoples. One of these peoples was the Greek 'nation' – so described by some travellers, though of course a cultural and not a political entity – distinguished by its Orthodox Christian belief and, usually, by its language. In English eyes, however, the Greeks were not the proud people of classical antiquity but a degenerate people, the human counterpart of the ruined buildings that were to be seen all over the landscape. When it comes to the attitude of travellers towards Greece and the Greeks, there is a commonplace that occurs again and again in their writings: this is the idea that Greece had fallen from her former glory. Covel wrote of 'this place and nation of ye greekes, so famous for their learning and zeal in those dayes [is ...] now in a manner meer beasts and the worst of slaves'.[1] Wheler described Athens as 'a City now reduced to near the lowest Ebb of Fortune'.[2] Finch implies a sense of defeat among the Greeks themselves, recording in his journal a conversation with a 'reverend old Greeke' who 'with many sighs' told him that 'they were barbarous now and slaves, who before were the most learned of all Europeans'.[3]

The sentiment that the very people who once called other races barbarians are now barbarians themselves is common. Different writers echo each other's phrases, not necessarily because they had read each other's work, but because the 'fallen glory' idea was a piece of received wisdom that in general needed no justification or explanation, a preconception that in many cases was confirmed by their experience. There does not seem to have been any sense of surprise: conditioned by their classical education, travellers saw with their own eyes what they expected to see, the physical wreck of classical Greek civilisation alongside the ignorance of Greek people; their writings include many comments on both the neglect of monuments and the ignorance of Greeks concerning their own past. The result is a view of the Greeks that combines pity and contempt.

That this view was not so much a reaction to what English-speakers encountered in Greece as an expectation they brought with them is confirmed by the fact that it is also found in the works of men who never went to Greece, for example Heylyn and Howell. As a point of view, it also had the great advantage to classical scholars that it allowed them to see themselves, rather than contemporary Greeks, as the inheritors of Homer and Plato.

The idea of the degeneracy of Greece was not new in the seventeenth century, but had a long history, recurring in different historical periods: even in Hellenistic Greece there was a sense of looking back to the glory days.[4] While Polybius, a Greek writing in Greek in the second century BCE about the rise of Rome, begins his history by describing the superiority of Rome,[5] Plutarch, under the Roman Empire (and also writing in Greek), suggests that statesmen can improve the character of their contemporaries by recounting the acts of Greeks of former times.[6] Goldhill, discussing texts produced in Greek-speaking areas of the Roman Empire in the period of the Second Sophistic (approximately the first to the third centuries CE), describes such attitudes as a 'constant pull backwards towards the glorious traditions of classical Greece'.[7]

A deep ambivalence about the Greeks runs through Roman literature.[8] Cicero, who was to be widely read in England in the early modern period, and held up as a model of prose style, spent time in Athens and greatly admired the Greeks, especially those of earlier generations than his own, but nevertheless criticised them for valuing abstract intellectual discussion over the practical values that he saw as one of the strengths of the Romans.[9] In the letter he wrote to his brother Quintus (proconsul in the province of Asia), he tells him not to rush into friendship with Greeks, apart from those few who are worthy of the old Greece ('praeter hominum perpaucorum si qui sunt vetere Graecia digni'); nowadays, most of them have become too servile, and are jealous of both Romans and fellow Greeks. And yet, everything Cicero has learnt, he has learnt from Greek literature.[10] Pliny the Elder, also popular among English readers, quotes the advice of Cato to his son, that he should dip into Greek literature rather than making a close study of it, on the grounds that the Greeks are a worthless and intractable people ('nequissimum et indocile genus').[11] Juvenal uses the term 'graeculus' to poke fun at those who are too Greek in their habits, as does Cicero.[12] In Plautus, the use of the term 'pergraecari' (to behave like a Greek) is slightly different: here it is associated with loose living, especially drinking, but Plautus uses his mockery of Greeks to laugh at Romans, and to allow them to laugh at themselves. Nevertheless, as one scholar has commented, this strategy depended on the fact that his audience 'knew exactly what a Greek was like: he was their exact opposite'.[13] There may also have been ambiguity in Roman minds over whether their conquest of Greece was a result of Roman superiority or of Greek inferiority – or both – and perhaps there is a parallel here with the seventeenth-century English attitude to Greeks: they were pitied because of their subjection to the Ottomans, but at the same time despised for it.

The attitude of pity verging on contempt also appears in the Middle Ages, in the sermons of Michael Choniates, Metropolitan of Athens in the late twelfth century, who in his first sermon in the city celebrated the fact that he was speaking to the descendants of ancient Athenians, who he thought had the qualities of their forebears with the added advantage of being Christians, but soon lost his illusions: 'O city of Athens, to what depths of ignorance thou hast sunk, thou the mother of wisdom.'[14]

In the eyes of seventeenth-century English visitors, Greek degeneration was primarily a matter of education, but also to some extent of social status, both of which were consequences of political subjection: Rycaut noted that because the Sultan tended to acquire the estates of the prominent Greek families you shall find the Daughters of ancient Greek Houses espoused to Shepherds and Carters, and the ancient Reliques of the noble Families of *Cantacuzeno* and *Palaeoligi*, living more contemptuously [i.e. in a manner worthy of contempt] at *Constantinople* than ever *Dionysus* did at *Corinth*.[15]

This quotation demonstrates the power of the 'fallen glory' attitude to Greece, since in Constantinople at least, where Rycaut spent time as Winchilsea's secretary, the Phanariots, claiming to belong to some of the old Byzantine families such as the Cantacuzeni and the Palaeologi, were in fact increasingly powerful as employees of the Ottoman Porte.[16] There were also prosperous Greek merchants, essential to the Ottoman economy (since the Ottoman elite tended to regard commerce as beneath its dignity) and an important link in the transmission of news, and there were powerful Greek churchmen, bankers and moneylenders.[17] However, apart from church dignitaries, higher-status Greeks seem on the whole to have been less visible to visitors than their poorer, mostly rural-dwelling, compatriots. Even Athens seemed no more than a village. Covel and others travelled widely through the rural areas of Greece and Asia Minor, where the ignorance of villagers reinforced their preconceptions that Greeks were poorly educated.

Ambassador Roe had written to Arundel on 27 January 1620/1 that he had been told by a Greek bishop that 'neither in Greece nor in any other place subject to the Grand Signor, were left so much as the footstepps or ruines of any antient learning'.[18] Here again, Roe's language links the intellectual state of Greeks to the ruined landscape. Roe's bishop himself, on the other hand, is described as 'learned'. It was undoubtedly the case that the lack of educational opportunities in Greece impelled those Greeks who aspired to an education to seek it in Italy. In Rycaut's view,

> whereas now the ancient Structures and Colleges of *Athens* are become ruinous, and only a fit habitation for its own Owle, and all *Greece* poor and illiterate, such Spirits and Wits amongst

them, who aspire unto Sciences and Knowledge, are forced to seek it in *Italy*.[19]

In Protestant eyes, this was a dangerous course, involving the risk that such refugees would be enticed into converting to Catholicism. Lack of historical knowledge among the Greeks, even the monks of Mount Athos, meant that Rycaut himself had to resort to 'Books of ancient History' for information about the holy mountain. At Philippopolis, at least, he felt that local people appreciated what he could tell them: 'with much admiration they hearken to us, when we tell them any thing what our Books relate concerning [the city]'.[20] Here, as so often, English visitors see themselves as keepers of Greece's ancient learning, able to do for contemporary Greeks what they cannot do for themselves. One of the books referred to by Rycaut is Heylyn's *ΜΙΚΡΟΚΟΣΜΟΣ* (first published in 1621 and also used by other travellers), the popularity of which is suggested by the number of editions it ran to.[21] The familiar sentiments about degenerate Greeks are found here too: Greece was once the 'Mother of Arts and Sciences', but was supplanted by her 'Daughter' Italy. Greeks were once brave men, sound scholars, and lovers of virtue and civility; they were famous for government and lovers of freedom. Now, however, they are ignorant, lazy and frequently drunk.[22] Heylyn links this with what he regards as the degeneration of the language itself, and that idea too is echoed by other writers such as Edward Brerewood, who thought that although the carelessness of the Greeks played a part, the main cause of the decline of the language was 'the ordinarie change, which time and many common occasions which attend on time, are wont to bring to all languages in the world'.[23] The spoken language diverged to a greater and greater extent from written Greek:[24] to those with a classical education, it was as if any development of ancient Greek could only be for the worse. Howell wrote of contemporary Greek as 'adulterated by the vulgar, as a bed of Flowers by Weeds',[25] and Henry King, who wrote a poem to celebrate the journey of his friend Blount to the Ottoman Empire, refers to the Greeks as 'In language as in mind, degenerate'.[26] Alexander Mavrocordato, himself from an old Greek family and grand dragoman in the late seventeenth century, showed his contempt for the language of his own day by writing books in classical Greek.[27] Wheler is unusual in wishing that English schools taught contemporary Greek pronunciation.[28]

In Asia Minor, Covel, Smith and Rycaut all found groups of Greeks who had forgotten their language altogether, and spoke Turkish: although their Orthodox Christianity made them definitely Greek in the eyes of these visitors, their loss of their language was a further sign of how far they had fallen.[29] Of course, the very assumption that classical Greek was the 'real' Greek, and that the further the language deviated from that standard the less value it had, meant that some travellers disabled themselves from actually talking to the Greeks they met and prevented them from enlarging their knowledge and understanding the country in which they found themselves. Covel, though he complains about the degeneration of the Greek language,[30] nevertheless throughout his long life maintained a correspondence in contemporary Greek with Greek churchmen.

The emphasis on degenerate language is surprising in that those who had learnt their Greek at grammar school had been taught to a great extent through the Greek New Testament, the language of which is very different from that of fifth-century BCE Athens. I have not come across any comment on this in seventeenth-century travel accounts, though the educationalist Brinsley wrote that St Luke's gospel was the equal of any other work for the 'sweetnesse and purity' of its Greek.[31]

Apart from the fact that it was a commonplace of the time, there are a number of other reasons why visitors to Greece in the seventeenth century so regularly demonstrate the same sentiments. The physical state of Greece, with its many more or less indecipherable heaps of ruins, was visible evidence for the decay of Greek civilisation, and aroused in those who saw it a generally nostalgic attitude, often combined with reflections on the 'instability of humane things'.[32] A general tendency to look back at the past as a golden age may be a factor as well. There is also a moral and religious dimension here which is exemplified by Sandys's view that the fall of once-glorious civilisations offered 'threatening instructions' to his contemporaries, and by Lithgow's comment on Rome, that it was on account of her sins that she was only the 'carkas' of her former self.[33] Travellers in the middle and second half of the century were acutely conscious, because of the English Civil War and the execution of Charles I, of the risk of, in Wheler's words, 'Schism, Rebellion and Civil Discord'.[34] One prevalent idea at the time was that great empires succeeded each other (*translatio imperii*): some thought that this happened in a movement from east to west, so that the succession from Persia to Greece to Rome to Latin Christendom was part of a natural order, an idea that suggests an element of inevitability. Toomer quotes a letter from Huntington, Aleppo chaplain, in which he writes that eastern learning 'hath followed the Motion of the Sun and is Universally gone Westward'. Others thought the movement was cyclical, a pattern into which the Ottoman Empire could more easily be fitted.[35] Covel, at Nicaea, reflected on 'ye strange revolutions that hath been in ye world', and Rycaut, at Ephesus, suggested that God 'casts down one [city], and raises another'.[36] The author of a popular history of the Turks first published at the beginning of the century, Knolles, concluded that the Ottoman Empire would inevitably collapse under its own weight, just as Howell viewed the Roman Empire as having fallen.[37] These ideas led some to be sanguine about the prospects for the fall of the Ottoman Empire: Smith thought that the decline of discipline among the janissary corps was 'a good omen, that the *Turkish* Empire, which has been rais'd to that great pitch and degree of glory, upon the ruin of so many Kingdoms and Governments, grows towards an end'.[38]

The perceived decline of the Greek 'nation' can be seen in the context of these various factors: the entrenched 'fallen glory' idea, the decay of the material remains of the classical past that was so evident to those who were eye-witnesses to the state of ancient sites, and general theories of empire. It has also been suggested that belief in the failure of the Greeks to match up to their ancient ancestors was a convenient way of salving the consciences of those who had little sympathy with contemporary Greeks,[39] but this raises the question of the reason for their lack of sympathy. Whatever its origins, it enabled Britons to see themselves rather than Greeks as the true beneficiaries of the classical heritage, the torch-bearers of the glories of Greek civilisation.

The conditions in which visitors found the Greeks, as subjects of the Ottoman Empire, also provided strong support for their views. In so far as travellers attached blame for this state of affairs, it was the Turks rather than the Greeks whom they held responsible; while this view is generally articulated in terms of the Ottoman conquest being responsible for Greek misery, the subtext is that Greek weakness allowed, or even invited, the Turks to invade. Rycaut quotes Livy in support of the notion that no tyrant can overcome a united people, and attributes the fall of the Greeks partly to religious dissension among themselves.[40] In addition, in the context of religion, the sad condition of the Greeks was often seen as a punishment for backsliding. Smith writes that slavery (in the sense of political subjection to the Turks) had 'broken [the Greeks'] spirits, and quite alter'd their tempers, and taken them off from the natural courage and vigour and love of liberty, wherewith their Ancestors were inspired'.[41]

Another way of looking at the Greek condition was that it was a punishment for a different fault: Sandys translates a passage from the sixteenth-century scholar J. C. Scaliger in which he suggests that a double punishment has been exacted for a double crime:

Old Troy by Greece twice sackt: twice new Greece rued
Her conquering ancestors. First when subdued
By Romes bold Troian progenie: and now
When forc't through Turkish insolence to bow.[42]

Blount, travelling some two decades after Sandys, introduces a rare note of optimism with his suggestion that in time the conquered peoples such as the Greeks would have a civilising effect on Turkish 'fiercenesse',[43] but in this period the only hints of the idea that Greece might be liberated from Turkish oppression are expressed in terms of Christians uniting to defeat Islam. Even then, the purpose of such a plan was seen as being not so much the liberation of the Greeks as the halting of the westerly advance of the Ottomans. Sherley, at the very beginning of the century, saw the possibility of a Greek rebellion: 'This [i.e. that the Greeks would rise if they had arms and leaders] I have learned of divers wyse & wealthye Greekes that doe wyshe for this helpe with teares.'[44] Sherley unfortunately tells us no more about who these wise and wealthy Greeks were.

Outside Constantinople and the big trading centres, many Greeks were extremely poor and ill-educated. In the administrative organisation of the Ottoman Empire different groups were distinguished by their religious affiliation, and freedom of religion was permitted, but Christians remained second-class citizens, heavily taxed and living under a range of restrictions and obligations, such as the need to provide troops for the empire.[45] North writes that the Turkish authorities are apt to 'find a hole in [a Greek's] coat, at which they drain out that which otherwise might have troubled his children to divide',[46] and Wheler gives an account of coming across a group of shepherds in the Morea sitting in a circle around the Turkish official who was responsible for collecting the poll tax from them: he gave each man five pebbles and told them to turn these into dollars within 24 hours or risk being taken into slavery. Presumably the pebbles were intended as a visual aid to the illiterate shepherds, but whether – and how – they were actually expected to come up with the cash is unclear. Perhaps it was simply a kind of bullying.[47] In the earlier part of the seventeenth century, Greeks were still subject to the tax under which children from the subject peoples were taken to Constantinople, converted to Islam and trained as janissaries or seraglio slaves for the Grand Signor.[48] Although it is impossible to gauge how families felt about this, and there were certainly advantages in terms of career for these children, it is hard not to believe that it involved some heartache for their parents. Christians also suffered the legal disadvantage that the evidence of Christian witnesses was not admissible against Muslims.[49] In spite of all this, however, many Christian Ottoman subjects may have preferred Muslim to Catholic (Venetian) rule, for what Mazower has described as the 'hope of political stability, desire for wealth and status in a meritocratic and open ruling system, admiration for the governing capacities of the Ottomans, and their evident willingness to make use of Christians as well as Muslims'.[50]

It should also be remembered that travellers to Greece in this period were making their journeys through dangerous areas and under difficult conditions, often involving pirates at sea and brigands on land;[51] fear of the unknown, and the lack of a common language, may have played a part in forming their views of the indigenous people they met. It might seem that this would apply to Turks even more than to Greeks, but many of the Turks they encountered were in the civilised and cosmopolitan city of Constantinople, where there was also a substantial European community, very different from rural Greece and Asia Minor.

Another important consideration is that under the Ottomans Greece was more isolated from western Europe than it had been under the Venetians, with the result that education and literacy suffered, although schools were kept going to some extent by monasteries and in the cities, and there were also some Catholic schools. Greeks wanting to take their education further found it necessary to travel to Italy to do so, from where they might or might not return. According to Vacalopoulos, Crete, which remained Venetian until 1669, was the only Greek territory where 'political conditions favoured the emergence of writers, lawyers, and physicians'; this was possible because of its links with Venice, where there were Greek printing presses.[52] However, the 'golden age' of Cretan culture of the sixteenth and seventeenth centuries, described by Sugar, is barely noticed by travellers, who were more likely to comment on Cretans' propensity for lying, although Smith recognised their courage.[53] The stereotype of Cretans as liars may also derive from classical literature: the classical Greek verb κρητίζειν means 'to lie'. Wheler was unusual in noticing the 'better sort' of Athenians, who leave the city for the country 'to enjoy the pleasant shades in the heat of summer, to their little Country Houses', but this seems to refer more to means than to education. Salonica, where there was a higher level of learning, is barely mentioned in travel accounts.[54]

As I have suggested, travellers' predominantly classical education was a prime cause of the prevalent attitude towards Greeks. Sandys is an example of someone who was more interested in classical learning than in observation of the contemporary scene or the figures inhabiting it, and Mitsi writes of him that he 'reads the Greeks as ruins'.[55] Here, in other words, is the literate, learned, cultured Englishman reading the Greeks as they cannot read themselves. Such a view gives Englishmen the great advantage that they can regard themselves rather than contemporary Greeks as the inheritors of classical Greek civilisation. One of the most widely read Roman authors was Virgil, whose *Aeneid* has a strong anti-Greek bias, and in this context we come across another strand in the attitude of English-speakers towards Greeks, one that contradicts the 'fallen glory' idea but is nevertheless found in some of the same writers. This is the belief that Greeks are in fact exactly the same as they have always been, that is to say deceitful, wily and untrustworthy. The archetype of this character is Odysseus, whose Homeric epithet πολυμήχανος (resourceful, inventive) tells the beginning of the story. Odysseus was courageous and clever, but those qualities shade into wiliness and deceit, so that in later literature there are at least two diverging traditions: Odysseus the cunning trickster and Odysseus the much-enduring wanderer/pilgrim.[56] His significance for travellers thus involves multiple and conflicting characteristics. Already in the classical period he is sometimes portrayed as a very unpleasant character: in Euripides's *Hecuba*, for example, although he has only a tiny part he leaves the extremely distasteful impression of a man both callous and calculating, probably intended to shock an audience sympathetic to Hecuba throughout the play.[57] In Seneca's *Trojan Women*, while he is portrayed as able to sympathise with Andromache over the impending death of her son, he is still characterised almost exclusively by epithets conveying his cunning, wiliness and deceit.[58] Shakespeare's Ulysses in *Troilus and Cressida* is only one later example of the man who is adept at twisting the arguments.

On the question of Greeks and Trojans, there are several strands that need untangling. In the *Aeneid*, Aeneas leaves the sacked city of Troy and after various adventures arrives in Latium to found a new Troy, Rome. It is possible that their familiarity with Virgil may have inclined English readers to see the fall of Troy to some extent from the perspective of the defeated. Travellers to Constantinople saw the supposed site of Troy as they sailed towards the entrance to the Dardanelles, often having to wait for a favourable wind in order to enter the narrow passage, and it was not unusual to go ashore there. Troy was a site of special significance for visitors, and had been since classical times: if those who came in the seventeenth century had read their Lucan (another popular author at the time), they will have known that Caesar paid his homage there, as Alexander the Great had also done, and indeed even Xerxes.[59] The story of Aeneas raises a further question about attitudes to the Greeks. It may be that even in this pre-empire period of English history, Englishmen had a sense of being inheritors not only (as the Romans were) of the cultural mantle of Greece but also of the imperial mantle of Rome: a complex mindset is involved here. If Englishmen were heirs of Rome, then by hypothesis they were heirs of Troy too, and Geoffrey of Monmouth even traced the British monarchy back to Brutus, grandson of Aeneas.[60] William Camden, as a result of his investigations into Britain's Roman past, saw Britain as the inheritor of Rome not through Brutus but through the Roman colonists of Britannia.[61] In Spenser's *The Faerie Queene*, Troynovant stands for London,[62] and Dryden cast Charles II as Aeneas in his poem *Annus Mirabilis*. The status attached to Troy is indicated by the fact that Giovanni Nanni (Annius) of Viterbo in the fifteenth century traced the ancestry of the European races back through the Trojans to Noah's sons.[63] The antiquarian John Selden, though he did not believe in the idea of Trojan origins, nevertheless understood its attraction: 'That universall desire, bewitching our Europe, to derive their bloud from Trojans.'[64] The ambivalence and paradox involved are highlighted when we consider that, looked at from another angle, the Turks might be seen as the geographical inheritors of Troy,[65] a fact that may help to explain the comparatively sympathetic attitude with which, despite their infidel status, they were regarded by English visitors.[66]

The ambivalence with which the tale of England's Trojan origins was regarded is well illustrated by Coryate's account of the mock knighting ceremony he underwent at the supposed site of Troy, in which he both celebrates and makes a joke of the story. This event and the way its protagonist chose to record it have been illuminatingly analysed by Baker, who unpicks Coryate's relationship to his various audiences – the on-the-spot, uncomprehending Turks as well as the readers at home – and comments that 'a bogus legend underwrites a bogus knighthood'.[67]

To return to the Greeks: frequent repetition of the same vocabulary in travel accounts ('subtle', 'deceitful', 'dissembling', etc.) implies not necessarily that the writers had read each other's books, but that certain stereotypes and the descriptive phrases that go with them were common currency at the time. The use of such words reflects the vocabulary of Virgil himself, who characterises the Greeks by ascribing to them *insidiae* and *doli* (plots, guiles, deceptions).[68] English writers, for example Shakespeare, often give Greeks the epithet 'merry', sometimes simply to indicate cheerfulness and jollity but sometimes with connotations of buffoonery and lack of seriousness, perhaps even of madness. For Heylyn it implied drunkenness.[69] One scholar suggests this term originated in Roman contempt for Greek adventurers;[70] this is speculative, but it is possible that there is a link with the Latin 'graeculus'. The word 'greek' itself in sixteenth-century English meant both 'loose-living' and 'cheating', qualities that are ascribed to contemporary Greeks by Covel, among others.[71] Ambassador Roe early in the seventeenth century complained that he was constantly deceived by 'Greekish promise'.[72] Accusations of lying are common, particularly against the Cretans, in their case perhaps partly because of St Paul's description of them (after Epimenides) in his epistle to Titus.[73] The writer Lucian, in the second century CE, thought that Homer's Odysseus was the teacher of all liars.[74] Rycaut, who usually looked for the middle way, even uses the phrase 'fides graeca' (Greek faith) to mean Greek unreliability, the exact opposite of its literal meaning.[75] There is a sense that classically educated Englishmen felt almost personally betrayed by the failure of contemporary Greeks to live up to the high ideals attributed to the ancient Greeks, though there is also an element of *Schadenfreude;* Greek shortcomings allowed Englishmen to step into the breach as the true heirs of classical values.

Covel's unsatisfactory encounter with an old man on the island of Cervi, when he cites Sinon as an exemplar of the duplicitous Greek, has already been mentioned. Here Covel and the ship's captain collude in following Virgil's Aeneas and Euripides's Iphigenia by encouraging their audiences to tar all Greeks with the brush of Sinon's bad behaviour.[76] Rycaut is similarly uncomplimentary about another apparent manifestation of duplicity, this time involving the monks of Mount Athos, who asserted their poverty, 'which will be a Riddle and Mystery to any person to whom they will shew or expose their Treasure'. He likens them to a miser who is 'miserable and starving amidst the heaps of his Gold'.[77] However, it seems entirely likely that the monks may not have wanted to lay their treasures out for foreigners to see, and perhaps wish to acquire.

Covel's ambivalence about the Greeks is in evidence throughout his only published work, his volume on the Greek Church which appeared right at the end of his long life, many years after his return from the Levant. He bemoans their lack of education and learning, and makes disparaging comments about them: Greeks in general are '*poor Silly Greeks*, quite overspread with *Ægyptian* darkness', while Dositheus, patriarch of Jerusalem, is '*a very perfidious, crafty, true Greek*'. In contrast, he refers to 'the topping Greeks, who still retain their antient Genius and Wit'.[78] They were, in his view, ground between two millstones: '*The Turk hath rob'd them of their Empire,* and, I fear, *The Pope will soon strip them of their Faith*'.[79] As far as relationships between Greeks and Catholics go, however, it has to be remembered that Covel's fiercely anti-Catholic attitude colours everything he says.

In spite of the prevalence of negative feelings about contemporary Greeks, there is also evidence that in their actual encounters with individuals travellers often met with, and acknowledged, kindness and generosity, as well as recognising some of the good qualities that they were so quick to assert had been lost. Learned individuals do crop up from time to time: on one of the islands in the Sea of Marmora, Covel met six or seven Greeks from Alexandria, one of whom had brought an Arabic/Latin Testament with him. Covel reports, 'I made it into greek and he went along wth me in Arab'.[80] Wheler encountered an abbot who understood ancient Greek very well, and was well-versed in philosophy, 'so far as to be esteemed a *Platonist*'. This man gave Wheler lessons in modern Greek.[81] He met a number of other scholars and learned men: a member of the Comneno family on Corfu who had a collection of coins; and a Doctor Bon, a Greek now living in Venice, who 'doth promise the World a Book' about a numismatic puzzle. He heard of, but did not meet, a priest from Crete who 'hath a good Study of Manuscripts'. On Zante he met an Athenian, Demetrio Bernizelo, who knew Greek (ancient and modern), Latin and Italian. It is notable, however, that several of those Wheler mentions have Italian rather than Greek names, and that he also makes a scornful reference to the state of Greek learning: '[Guilletière's] only Talent was to teach to Write and Read: which goes a great way in the Grecian Learning now-a-days'.[82]

Learning was not always undervalued, even on the evidence provided by travellers. Some of the monasteries on Mount Athos competed to buy manuscripts that had belonged to Michael Cantacuzenos (d. 1578) in the sale after his death, so they must have been regarded as valuable possessions.[83] Covel, a page or two before his complaint that the Greeks cannot give an accurate account of their own history, describes an encounter with an 'infinitely civil' priest, and is grateful for the books lent him by the Metropolitan of Adrianople, although the latter was 'not troubled wth too much learning'.[84] When Wheler and his party were endeavouring to identify the site of ancient Delphi, one local inhabitant knew 'by some Book he had read' that Amphissa was the right place; however, 'it is not usual that they know anything of the History of their Country'.[85] The poor (at least in foreign eyes) level of literacy could lead to some comic situations, for example when Robson tried to communicate with a man he met in a church on Mykonos by pointing to sentences in the Septuagint; not surprisingly, the conversation was abortive.[86]

Aside from book-learning, several travellers recognised quick-wittedness among the Greeks they met. Wheler, for example, comments that Athenians retain their 'natural Subtilty, or Wit', and gives several instances of Greek ingenuity, although his compliments are sometimes back-handed. In one Albanian village his party inadvertently lodged with the chief of a 'Nest of Thieves', but came to no harm because their Greek guide was able to persuade the landlord that Wheler was secretary to a high-ranking Turkish official, with whom it would be unwise to tangle; Wheler adds that 'these *Greeks* never want invention to help themselves out at a dead lift'. In northern Greece, he and his companions saw a tomb that was supposed to be that of St Luke, but that Wheler identified by the inscription on it as belonging to one Nedymos. The priest then told them that those who had buried the saint had deliberately disguised whose tomb it was in order to mislead heathens, which showed Wheler 'the quickness of his Wit, and Ignorance, at the same time, but was not satisfactory to us'. On another occasion, Spon and Wheler met a cobbler who had become a physician, with whom Spon exchanged recipes for medicines, and who acted as their guide, together with 'another Quack, but naturally ingenious'.[87] It is to Wheler's credit, however, that he does not seem to have seen himself as superior to contemporary Greeks in the way that so many travellers did: Athenian manners were civil, polished and respectful, and Athenians were able to stand up for themselves against the Turkish authorities. Wheler himself 'went to school at *Athens*'.[88]

The friendliness and cheerful disposition of Greeks are mentioned in several accounts, sometimes characterised by the use of the adjective 'merry'.[89] When Covel was invited to join in wedding celebrations on the island of Lemnos, he seems to have been made welcome by all but one of the other guests: 'a peevish cur yt had a handsome wife rose up and made his wife rise and said he would not stay if we did'. Covel, having been roused from bed by the invitation, tactfully returned there, but was summoned again with the news that 'ye coxcomb yt began ye embroyl was gone'. It was on the same island that he gathered information about the process of wine-making: he tells us that the wine-jars are left for people to help themselves, and that the only people who cheat by not paying for what they take are Turks and strangers.[90] In this case, therefore, Greeks are people of integrity.

Apart from sporadic references to individual instances of friendliness, two Greek qualities are more consistently praised: piety (which will be discussed below, when I consider the Orthodox Church) and hospitality. Lithgow, early in the century, was one traveller to recognise the latter: 'the best sort of *Greekes*, in visiting other, doe not use to come empty handed, neither will they suffer a stranger to depart, without both gifts and convoy'.[91] Of all the travellers discussed in this book, Wheler was the most appreciative of the Greek people he met. He and his party had a letter of introduction to a Turk in Amphissa, but when they found he was not at home 'a Relation of his' sent them to 'an honest, and merry *Greek*':

> [This Greek] made us all the welcome he could, and provided us a Supper, not ungrateful to our travelling Stomachs. But we had like to have over-sawc'd it with Wine; for our good Host would not let the Bowl stand still; it being the *Greek* Mode to make the Cup go round without ceasing: Nor was it Manners on our side to refuse it, or call for Wine out of our turns.[92]

It is noteworthy that the introduction to this Greek household was made by a Turk. Such was Wheler's gratitude for the generosity with which he had been received that in his book on how to run a Christian household (published in 1698 but written some 20 years earlier)[93] he included the following passage in his section on hospitality:

> In *Greece*, where publick places of Entertainment are less frequent, and such as our Inns are altogether unknown; there that part of Hospitality, that is Entertainment of Strangers, is more used than in Western parts of the World. There, everywhere in Towns and Villages, Strangers are received with Kindness into their Houses; and are Lodged and Entertained with such things as they have with much Humanity, as I have

often experimented [i.e. experienced]; and thereby the defect of Inns is very well supplied.[94]

In all the thousands of words written by Englishmen about Greece and Greeks, there are very few about women: not only do women not tell their own stories, but only fragments of their stories are told by men. Several visitors comment that the women of Chios are both better-looking and freer than in other parts of Greece; perhaps it was their comparative liberty that allowed them to dress in a way that made them more noticeable to foreigners. Covel, for example, describes how on his first night on the island someone brought out a fiddle, with the result that all the windows, terraces and leads filled up with women. Also on Chios, he got into conversation with a girl on her way to school; the fact that he saw girls going to school suggests that Chios was unusual, although he also mentions a papas's wife in the Peloponnese who kept a school. The Chian girl wanted to learn English, but the conversation came to an end because he used an English word that she mistook for a rude Greek one: he points out that Chian women are 'extream modest' as well as 'extream free'.[95] Lithgow, on the other hand, thought that the women of Chios were whores whose husbands acted as their pimps.[96]

Teonge's attitude to a woman he met on his voyage home is not entirely clear, but he is probably making a moral as well as an aesthetic judgement when he recalls a Venetian from another ship who 'had brought with him from Smyrna a Greek lady, at vast charge to him': '[he or she] made us happy with her company at our ship at dinner. She was wondrous rich in habit, and counted the beauty of the Levant; but I have seen far handsomer in England amongst our milkmaids'.[97] Lithgow, who is not always a reliable witness, recounts an adventure involving his rescue of a French Protestant from the galleys, for which purpose a Cretan laundress with whom he was 'friendly inward' lent him a dress as a disguise for the Frenchman.[98] Two other examples of women of spirit are found in the Randolph's description of the Greek islands. On Crete he made the acquaintance of a group of 'doctoresses',[99] one of whom skilfully cured him of a bullet wound that he had received in his leg 'by accident'; their skill in curing the plague was not so great, however, as 'several of the Doctoresses were swept away by that disease'. And the women of Mykonos, having been enjoying the spoils of a ship captured by a privateer, were quick and resourceful in hiding both their spoils and their guilty husbands as soon as the authorities appeared on the scene.[100] These glimpses of Greek women are tantalising: they are so often in the background, or only to be seen through men's eyes rather than their own.

The Orthodox Church

There is one area that is crucial to understanding the attitudes of western visitors to the Greeks, namely the fact that despite the enormous differences between them, Anglicans saw themselves as co-religionists with Orthodox Christians. Under the Ottoman Empire, the different Christian sects, and also Jews, as people of the Book, were allowed freedom to practise their religion, both on moral grounds and also because it was in the interests of Turks. The 'millet' system categorised people in the empire according to their religious affiliation, so that each Christian sect had a certain measure of autonomy. North records that 'neither Christian, Turk, nor Jew can curse either's faith, but upon complaint to the magistrate you may have them punished'.[101] Orthodox Christians had recourse to the Patriarch of Constantinople to resolve legal as well as religious questions, since he acted as a tax collector and enforcer of the law for his flock.[102] Tax was of great importance; according to Blount, the Turks understood the principle of *'Sanguis Martyrum Semen Ecclesiae'* ('the blood of martyrs feeds the church'), so that it was preferable to tax Christians heavily rather than preventing them from practising: 'Hee rather suckes the purse, than unprofitable blood'.[103] That is not to say, however, that life for Christians was easy or that they were equal citizens with Turks. In fact, difficulties were numerous, and the state of Christianity as recorded by English visitors was miserable. Aside from the monasteries of Mount Athos, which were accorded special protection, Orthodox communities in the rural areas tended to be desperately poor, sometimes even lacking a priest.[104]

Tolerance went only so far: it was hard for Greeks to build or repair churches, and the ringing of bells was forbidden.[105] Georgirenes writes that Greeks are careful not to show any outward signs of magnificence, for fear of inciting Turkish anger.[106] After a serious fire in the 1660s, the Vani Effendi (a senior religious official) confiscated the land on which 25 churches had stood, and in 1664, not surprisingly, imposed a ban on the ecumenical prayers that were being said throughout the empire in support of the Hapsburgs.[107] Covel heard a story that a Greek who had been put to death for alleging Mohammed was an imposter was subsequently canonised by the Greeks and had his portrait painted on the wall of a church in Asia Minor; perhaps the most unlikely aspect of this is not that he was put to death but that the Orthodox community was able to display his portrait.[108] In 1657, a patriarch was hanged for making detrimental comments about Islam.[109] Priests were nervous that their congregations might defect to Islam, and Rycaut mentions that some Christians even used the indelible juice of a herb to mark the foreheads of their babies with a cross in order to prevent their apostasy.[110] Wheler notes that the Greeks of Corinth, priests included, have a tendency to fall into apostasy and Turkish superstition for want of decent instruction.[111] However, that the traffic was not only one way is indicated by Finch, who describes a repentant renegade returning to the Christian fold and suffering martyrdom, who went to his death 'as merrily as if he had bin to goe to a wedding'.[112] Finch's comment that 'The Turks, Jewes and the Latin Church are all sorry to see the Greekes show such a martyr' demonstrates the vested interests of the various religious groups, and the degree of rivalry among them.

The Orthodox Church was not without its own internal dissensions. Different sources attribute the murder of Cyril Lucaris, patriarch of Constantinople, in 1638 to Turks, Catholics and 'men of his owne Coat'; his successor behaved so badly, excommunicating, imprisoning and murdering other Christians, that the result was 'such a combustion in the Greeke Church [...] the like hath seldome beene'.[113] There were in fact 61 changes of patriarch in the century between 1595 and 1695, and Covel believed that the office could be bought.[114]

It is in the context of Orthodox Christianity that there are frequent comments about the ignorance of Greeks, even of priests and monks, not to speak of ordinary people. Priests were generally literate – according to Georgirenes it was the duty of the Metropolitan to check whether an ordinand could read and write 'without false Pronuntiation, or mis-spelling'[115] – but ordinary people, and even monks, were often illiterate. Even at Mount Athos, where there were monastery libraries, the emphasis was very much on the Church Fathers rather than any wider, humanistic learning, and the books were not always properly looked after: Rycaut tells his readers,

> we must not imagine that these Libraries are conserved in that order, as ours are in the parts of Christendom; that they are ranked and compiled in method on Shelves, with Labels of the Contents, or that they are brushed and kept clean, like the Libraries of our Colleges; but they are piled one on the other without order or method, covered with dust, and exposed to the Worm.[116]

The French traveller Belon, who like Covel had been to Mount Athos himself, thought that monks who read books on subjects other than theology were in danger of excommunication.[117] Greaves was of the opinion that patriarchs had put anathemas on all Greek libraries 'thereby to preserve these bookes from the Latines'.[118] Covel does mention one monastery in Asia Minor where boys went to learn to read, but this seems to have been unusual.[119]

The liturgy was in ancient Greek and was little understood by the flock, even priests sometimes having difficulties with the language.[120] Pronunciation, as well as grammar, syntax and vocabulary, confused the issue. According to the soldier Thomas Gainsford early in the century, their service and language [are] Greeke, and when they write or print it is a reasonable good Character, though farre from the atticke Dialect: and yet I will be bold to say, a good Scholler of our grammer instruction, shall scarce understand the phrase of their common speakers, no more then a southerne man, one borne farre north, or in Scotland.

The unspoken assumption is that a properly educated Englishman knew the right way to pronounce ancient Greek.[121] Wheler records meetings with monks and priests who could read ancient Greek, as well as with others who could not.[122] Rycaut writes that because the Latin mass is shorter than the Orthodox liturgy, some Greeks attend Catholic churches, while retaining their allegiance to the patriarch.[123] Lucaris, as part of his attempt to improve Greek education, had a translation of the New Testament made into 'vulgar' Greek, but there were few copies of it, since it was in manuscript. Knowledge of Christianity was poor.[124] Covel, however, turns the argument about Greek illiteracy on its head: he thought that books were being published by Catholics in 'vulgar' Greek with the intention of converting Orthodox people, whereas if such books had been written in 'learned' Greek, ordinary people would not have been able to read them, and consequently would not have been put into danger.[125]

Whatever their learning or lack of it, monks and priests, like lay Greeks, were found to be extremely hospitable. At the monastery of St Luke Stiriotes, near Arachova,[126] Wheler was so taken with the atmosphere of peacefulness that he was tempted to stay there, but could not 'wean [himself] from the World'. In Athens, the archbishop entertained him and his party with great civility: '[he received] us after the *Eastern* Fashion; that is, making us sit upon a *Sopha*, and drink *Coffee* with him'.[127] Covel visited Mount Athos on his way home from the Levant, enjoying lavish hospitality there while he made notes about the daily life of the monasteries.

In the late sixteenth century, the French naturalist Belon had published his account of visiting Mount Athos, including some information about the number and organisation of the monasteries.[128] In 1659, Henry Oldenburg, secretary of the Royal Society, who acted as an entrepôt for the exchange of information in the European world of science and letters, probably relied on Belon when he wrote to the educational reformer Samuel Hartlib about the Holy Mountain:

> The Greek Christians of Mount Athos, wch are a sort of monks, are reported by all to be of an exemplary external holines, temperance, simplicity; having about 24. Monasteries on yt mountaine, being in number between 5. And 6. thousand, never eating any flesh, and in Lent abstaining from fish yt have blood. They earne their living by their hands, going forth in ye morning very early out of their cloisters, wth their tooles about ym, and a knapsack on their shoulders, stored wth biscuit and onions: working each for the maintenance of their monastery, some digging and dressing vines, some felling trees, other building ships, etc. They doe certainly shame ye Popish monks, who are swarms of idle bellies.[129]

At this date, no Englishman had yet visited the mountain. In the 1630s, Lucaris started to make arrangements for Greaves to go there with the aim of cataloguing and acquiring manuscripts, but Lucaris's murder meant that the plan was aborted, and so the distinction of being the first Englishman to set foot there fell to Covel some 40 years later. The pass allowing him to do so, signed by the French ambassador de Nointel, is still extant among his papers.[130] He also had the blessing of the hegoumenos, or abbot, of the monastery of Great Lavra, whom he had met at Gallipoli on his journey from Constantinople.[131]

On Covel's arrival on the coast at the tip of the peninsula, near Great Lavra, in the spring of 1677, he writes: 'We had everyone his mule furnisht wth carpets, to ride up to ye monastery, which stands about a mile up ye hill from ye shore.' There they were met by the hegoumenos, who took them to the chapel: as they crossed the threshold, because it was between Easter and Pentecost the monks sang 'Christ is risen', and they were then received with 'extraordinary respect' by the retired patriarch Dionysios Bardales, who was still living there. He seated them in armchairs (which Covel calls 'elbow chairs'), also covered with carpets. Over the course of the next ten days, Covel visited the monasteries of Iveron, Stavronikita, Pantokratoros, Koutloumousi, Vatopedi, Karakallou, Philotheou, Esphigmenou and Docheiariou, as well as the village of Karyes.

He tells us a good deal about the organisation of monasteries, but does not make clear whether they were cenobitic, in which absolute obedience is owed to the superior, or idiorhythmic, in which personal property is allowed and meals are sometimes taken individually in cells rather than always in common. In fact, there is some doubt among today's scholars about which type most of the Mount Athos monasteries belonged to in this period. They were largely self-governing institutions, but in civil matters were subject to a Turkish official, who resided in the village of Karyes. Taxes were of course paid to the Porte. From Covel we learn that the office-holders, apart from the hegoumenos, were the person who oversaw the liturgy and the keeping of festivals, 'like our Dean of ye Chappel at White Hall'; the treasurer; the store-keeper; the wardrobe master, with responsibility for carpets, beds and bedding, and for entertainment of visitors; the person in charge of food and wine (anyone was free to help himself to bread, but wine was strictly measured out; tobacco was not allowed); the chief cook; the chief baker; the person in charge of horses and mules; and the monk in charge of external affairs. This last person was the one who managed the travelling monks, who were sent out as what Covel calls 'missioners' to Russia, Wallachia, Constantinople and Smyrna, the Peloponnese and Palestine; Covel met two who had been as far as Archangel. The purpose of these travels was to amass funds, and those who had done their duty in this way had a better chance of being made hegoumenos of their monastery, a post which was held for a year.

Covel also mentions the person who looks after and winds the clocks. He saw one clock that he describes as being like English church clocks, with a big bell, inscribed with Latin characters. Timepieces were rare and highly valued in the Ottoman Empire in this period, and were sometimes brought as gifts to the Porte by western ambassadors; ordinary people would tell the time by the muezzin's call. Covel recalled that on one occasion he timed the duration of some ceremonies in Constantinople by his pulse.[132]

On Athos as elsewhere, his primary interest was not in theology, though he does make occasional comments in this area: for example, he found a book dealing with the question of whether the light surrounding Christ at the transfiguration was created or uncreated, a matter of dispute between the Greek and Latin Churches, and therefore of importance in any negotiations about uniting the Orthodox and Anglican churches. Mostly, however, he was more interested in what he could find in the way of manuscripts and other treasures. This was at times a frustrating quest, because at several of the monasteries the treasurer was away, and he was unable to see the library: it is not impossible that the monks were wary of visitors wanting to look at manuscripts, in case they should attempt to acquire them by some means. However, as described above in the chapter on antiquities, Covel did manage to obtain a few manuscripts for himself.

At Iveron, he saw psalters and crosses set with precious stones, priests' robes 'of inexpressible vallue', and innumerable gold and silver dishes and boxes. He also saw some rich plate at Lavra, as well as an iron collar with a cross that was supposed to have belonged to St Athanasius, the founder of the monastery: it weighed five pounds, and the saint was reputed to have worn it round his neck. Covel comments that anyone doing such a thing in England would be thought a candidate for Bedlam. The staff with which Athanasius drove out the devil was also on view, and Covel was shown the place where the saint had seen a vision of the Virgin, as well as a stone supposed to have been worn down by his knees. Covel was sceptical about this last, but in general he is sympathetic to the life of the monasteries – much more so than Rycaut, who was scathing about their lack of commitment to the ideal of poverty. Rycaut's information came from Covel, but his tone is quite different.[133] Covel records but does not condemn superstitions that he obviously disagrees with, for example that 'there is a cup of jasper stone that they boast many miraculous cures done on them who drink out of it wth faith enough', and he tells a story of an icon of St George that made its own way from Arabia to the port of Vatopedio. After a dispute about what should happen to it, it was put on a mule and taken to the monastery of Zographou. Some Arabian Christians came to worship it and recognised it as the very picture they knew from home.

Covel was impressed with some of the buildings he saw, particularly one of the 19 chapels at Great Lavra that had a floor tiled in black and white checks, a fountain with a 'cupola' over it, of which the basin was eight feet in diameter, and a gallery from which you could look into the choir of the church. He comments more than once on the size and beauty of the fonts, and their use for triple immersion, a custom that he traces back to the cult of Isis and Serapis at Ephesus, another example of his interest in making cross-cultural links. In addition to fonts, he saw basins for holy water, and wondered what happened to all of it: he learned that on every feast day and on the first Sunday of every month all the rooms were blessed with it, as well as every individual.

We also learn a good deal about the daily life of the monasteries. Monks, though not priests, work as tailors, bakers, shoemakers, gardeners, weavers, launderers, coopers and smiths. They make items such as crosses, ropes, clothes, spoons, crucifixes and pietas, which are sold in the Saturday market in the village of Karyes, to which no Turk was allowed without the permission of the resident Turkish official. We learn that many country churches in Greece serve communion wine from spoons made on the mountain. The monks also keep sheep and grow olives and grapes. There are many visitors, particularly at the great festivals, when there may be several hundred at a time, so that the baking of communion bread has to take place twice a week instead of once.

In the past, the Mount Athos monasteries had received revenue from farms on the islands of Lemnos and Imbros, but in Covel's day it was the other way round and these islands were themselves supplied with money and necessaries from the mountain. Covel mentions danger from pirates or corsairs, so that the monasteries allow no one in or out after sunset, and some of them have defensive towers or castles, though he comments that these are of little use since the invention of guns. At Great Lavra there was a drawbridge. At Vatopedio, however, he says that 'Corsairs seldome trouble them but onely for a little wine and bread'.

Covel appreciated the kind reception he received everywhere he went: 'At all places we stay'd a little at ye door, then kindly received.' He arrived at Vatopedio on St George's day, was blessed by the priest and kissed the cross according to the custom. He tells us that the liturgy lasted two hours at least, 'so that it is no wonder that most of the *Greek* Priests [...] are so little acquainted with any other Learning'.[134] The monks are devoted to the Virgin, regarding her as being present at all their meals, so a small piece of bread is always placed in a dish in front of her image. At the end of the meal this is shared by all present, who also drink out of a common cup in her name. The same ceremony is performed for the protection of anyone undertaking a sea voyage. When Covel left any monastery, the words of farewell used by the monks were '*may God keep you and the all-holy Lady*'. More prayers are offered to her than to Christ, and lamps are often burned in front of her image, not only on Mount Athos but all over Greece. Covel adds that the Greek emperors regarded her as their fellow-soldier against the Latins, but adds, 'Poor Lady, it seems she could not save *her self*[,] much less *their Army*.'[135] At Vatopedio, one of the monks had thrown a candle and a picture of the Virgin into a well to keep them safe in 'troublesome times', and both were said to have been recovered unharmed 70 or 80 years later.

Another of Covel's interests was music: in the garden at Great Lavra he saw a room where John Koukouzelis, whom he calls 'the famous inventor or refiner of the now Greek musick' worked and lived.[136] Finally, not least of the pleasures of visiting Mount Athos for Covel was the food he ate and the generous amounts of wine he drank there. Of the former, he lists fish cooked in various ways, octopus, limpets three times as big as English limpets and very tasty, 'caveor' (probably fish roe), salad, artichokes, beet, lentils, herb pies, onions, garlic, olives, cheese and beans, flavoured with salt, pepper and saffron and accompanied by good wheaten bread. The wine was a 'sort of small claret', and there were 'exquisite' preserved oranges to finish with. At the end of his visit, Covel presented the patriarch with gifts of wine, sugar and pepper, and in turn received a manuscript of the work of Simeon, archbishop of Thessaloniki.[137]

Greek piety

If hospitality was one of the qualities for which foreigners praised Greeks, the other notable one was piety. For Wheler, Orthodox Christians demonstrate 'much of the Simplicity and Charity of more Early Times of the Gospel'. He also admired the Christian patience of the Greeks under Turkish rule,[138] and Rycaut recognised the 'Constancy, Resolution, and Simplicity' with which poor Greeks adhered to their faith.[139] Covel provides an example of the regard in which priests were held, by dressing in black and growing his beard, thereby gaining much respect.[140] He was also delighted by the civility of the Armenian priests of Prusa, who called him 'into ye rayles' in the church, amongst themselves.[141] Christianity was kept alive among ordinary people not by doctrine but by observing fasts and feasts,[142] and at this level Christianity and Islam were not entirely separate: Mazower has argued that the Turkish conquest followed a long period of interaction between members of the two religions, and that devotional practice might be shared between them.[143] Many examples of such sharing were documented by Hasluck.[144] Travellers' accounts too provide evidence of this: Smith describes Turks afraid to go to sea until the water had been blessed by Christians,[145] and Covel, not knowing that St George originated in Anatolia, writes that he 'is a great saint even amongst ye Turkes'. Covel also came across a church where 'an old Turk' was buried who was revered as a saint, though unfortunately he does not tell us why.[146] In his book on the Greek Church, he refers to miracles that were accepted by both groups.[147] Bargrave, similarly, came across a chapel named after a Christian saint who was also venerated by Turks, and was considered to be 'in part a Musselman' on account of a miracle he had performed.[148] On the feast of the assumption of the virgin, Christians, Jews and Turks all shared in a ceremony directed to the cure of diseases, and in the church of St Michael in a village near Prusa, on the saint's feast day, Turks as well as Christians gathered in the hope of being cured of their illnesses.[149] Veryard saw a stone in Haghia Sophia that was purported to have been brought from the Holy Land and was revered by Muslims on the grounds that Mary had washed Jesus's linen on it.[150] According to North, 'poor' Christians and Jews get 'a holy man, though a Turk' to read over a sick child.[151] Finally, when Teonge had to bury the boatswain of his ship in the Greek church in Scanderun, the whole town came to watch; the Turks stood away from the grave: '[they] observed, but were not at all displeased, but (as we heard after) commended our way'.[152] This happened in the town where ships with goods destined for Aleppo docked, so the Turkish population was more familiar with foreigners than was probable in the villages.

At the level of folk religion, some visitors comment on the superstition of ordinary people. Covel refers to a miraculous drip of oil as a 'peice of Greekish monkery',[153] and Wheler to a picture of the Virgin that performs miracles as 'a ridiculous jugling'.[154] There is generally a note of scepticism, illustrated by Randolph, writing about a site in Crete where 'they say' St Paul preached and carried out baptisms;[155] but there is also a recognition that Greeks are 'wonderful devout in their professed religion': this observation comes from the virulently anti-Catholic Lithgow, determined to point out how different Orthodox Christians are from Papists.[156] Superstition was of course precisely one of the elements of Catholicism criticised by Protestant visitors to Italy. According to Wheler, the Greeks shared the Protestant hatred of Catholicism, but Covel's book on the Greek Church paints a more complex picture of the relationship between Catholicism and Orthodoxy, which was a matter of church politics as well as of theology or doctrine.[157]

There were links between Islam and Christianity at a higher social level as well, going back through the early sultans to the Byzantine emperors. The emperor Manuel II (late fourteenth to early fifteenth century) composed a dialogue between a Greek and Turk on the subject of religion;[158] the Turkish ruler Murad II married a Christian, Mara, who endowed and protected monasteries on Mount Athos; and his son, Mehmed the Conqueror, spoke Greek and was a collector of icons. Mehmed's admiration for the classics was such that he commissioned a biography of himself, in Greek, on the pattern of Arrian's biography of Alexander the Great.[159] To give thanks for his victory over Constantinople, Mehmed visited Haghia Sophia, a building of which Rycaut wrote two centuries later that it was 'still conserved sacred and separated for use of Divine Service, of the Revenue of which *Mahometan* Barbarism and Superstition hath made no Sacrilegious Robbery, but maintained, and improved, and added to it', although by 1609 all the Christian frescoes had been covered up.[160] Christians also prayed at Mara's tomb in a Constantinople mosque.[161] Wheler visited a monastery in Penteli that was under the protection of the Sultan's mother, and the one he stayed in near Arachova, St Luke Stiriotes, had a Turkish protector, who had to be paid.[162]

Smith tells a story about Mehmed IV, reigning at the time of which Smith was writing: in 1661 or 1662, while out hunting, he stopped at a monastery on the Thracian Bosphorus, where a monk gave him a basket of cherries, 'then which [...] nothing could have been more welcom to him, being thirsty and over-heated with excessive riding'. Mehmed suggested that the monk convert to Islam, but accepted his refusal to do so with good humour, and gave some gold coins to the man and additional land to the monastery.[163] A few years earlier, this same sultan had treated the Quaker missionary Mary Fisher with kindness and courtesy.[164] A monastery on Chalcis, in the Sea of Marmora, was rebuilt by Panagiotes, who had been dragoman at court, and 'so much in his [the Sultan's] favour, that he obtained many Kindnesses for his Fellow-Christians of the *Greek* Church; as the repairing of several of their Churches and Monasteries'.[165] But he kept this a secret, fearing the ill-will of Catholic monasteries in Constantinople: here, as so often, we find a greater antagonism between different Christian sects than between Islam and Orthodoxy or Islam and Protestantism. Rycaut records that during an outbreak of the plague the Greek and Armenian patriarchs were asked to pray for respite, probably on the grounds that it might help and could do no harm.[166] Turkish friendliness did however have its downsides: in Prusa, Turks had apparently rebuilt a church using old materials, so that 'the fair Capitals of the Pillars

[were] set, where the Basis should be; and the Basis where the Capitals; An Emblem of their Tyranny over Christendom, turning all things upside down'.[167] In foreign eyes, at least, the sense of Turkish oppression is never far from the surface, and no doubt Christians had to be careful how they behaved: Browne was grieved to see churches that displayed crescent-tipped crosses on their roofs,[168] probably a diplomatic political act rather than a religious one.

However, although in travellers' accounts the categories of 'Greek' and 'Turk' are generally presented as opposites, there is nevertheless some blurring of the boundaries. Rycaut refers to Greeks and Turks being brought up side by side, 'sometimes under the same Roof', in the Peloponnese.[169] Encounters with Greeks in Asia Minor who had forgotten their original language and now spoke Turkish have already been mentioned; moreover, as will be discussed in the next chapter, it was possible to become a 'Turk' by converting to Islam. It is also worth noting that it is not only within the Ottoman Empire that we find examples of unexpected accommodation between Christianity and Islam: in 1618, a Turkish envoy to James I asked the King to touch his son for scrofula, the king's evil. The King apparently complied, using the sign of the cross over the child but omitting the customary prayers.[170]

During the seventeenth century, there was considerable interest in a possible reunion of the Anglican and the Orthodox Churches. Early in the period, two men who tried to take this forward were the patriarch Lucaris and Ambassador Roe.[171] In the first half of the century, too, a few Greeks found their way to England, but it was only after the Restoration that there was a more organised attempt to link the two Churches. Greek students were sent to study theology in England, and in 1677 the building of a Greek church in London was completed.[172] As far as reunion went, the crucial question from the Anglican point of view was whether the Orthodox Greeks believed in transubstantiation or not: if they did, this would be a deal-breaker. Although Lucaris denied such a belief, it was not a simple matter. The question continued to be discussed and disputed: the overriding concern about it needs to be seen in the context both of anti-Catholic feeling in England and of the controversy on the Continent in the

1660s between the Huguenot Claude and the Catholic and Jansenist Arnauld over this very point.[173] Covel was asked by the dean of St Paul's, Sancroft, and other senior churchmen to investigate transubstantiation and other questions of Orthodox theology during his tenure of the chaplaincy in Constantinople, but the publication of his work was delayed, perhaps because his heart was not in it, and perhaps also because it was not long after the building of the London Greek church that tensions arose there between Anglicans and Orthodox, making reunion less likely.[174] After 1689, the possibility was revived by the non-jurors, one of whom was Smith, Covel's predecessor as Constantinople chaplain.[175] In 1716, the non-jurors sent a document to Constantinople asking for clarification about doctrines, but the reply that eventually arrived in 1721 or 1722 insisted on transubstantiation as an Orthodox belief.[176] It may have been in this context that Covel's work was eventually published. He was not a non-juror, and his conclusions are ambivalent: he seems to say that sensible Greeks do not believe in transubstantiation, but that the beliefs of many have been corrupted by the Catholic Church. It has to be kept in mind that his discussion of theology is never a dispassionate one, but always coloured by his own convictions about right and wrong views, and in particular by his anti-Catholic stance.[177]

Among Covel's contemporaries, Rycaut as well as Smith wrote about the Greek Church, and Wheler was also interested. The latter was unwilling to commit to one side or the other of the transubstantiation question: he refers to the Claude-Arnauld controversy and hopes that 'the World will have an Account one day [...] from Dr *Covel*'.[178] Smith's more confident opinion was that the Catholic Church had forced the doctrine on the Orthodox Church.[179]

There are both theological and political dimensions to the project of possible reunion, one element in the mix being the rivalry between Anglicans and Catholics. According to Smith, Greeks suffered from being '*wrought upon by the sly artifices and insinuations and underhand dealings of the subtile Emissaries of* Rome',[180] and Covel states that the aim of Catholic missionaries was not to convert Muslims but to

'Poison the poor ignorant Christians [...] with their *Latin* inventions'.[181] Describing the circumcision ceremony for converts to Islam, Covel comments,

> it is our shame, for I beleive all Europe have not gain'd so many Turkes to us these 200 yeares; for though the Ch. of Rome boast their Emissaryes here [...] Jesuits, dominicans, franciscans, & c, yet beleive me they have other designes then converting of Turkes.[182]

The 'other designes' being of course the conversion of non-Catholic Christians.

In a period of anxiety about religion, and perceived threats from Catholicism and/or Calvinism, the Church of England appeared to some to be a middle way that might be attractive to people from both extremes. Before the Commonwealth, values of tolerance were subscribed to by Sandys, as they were by his brother Edwin, who was a major influence on him;[183] after it, Rycaut, horrified at the killing of Charles I, which he saw as partly attributable to over-zealous Christians, made a point of being conciliatory, writing that he offered 'nothing [...] out of partiality to the Cause of the Reformed Churches, or prejudice to the Papal Interest'. He is 'rather inclinable to reconcile Differences, than to widen them', having no time for those who tore the 'seamless Coat of Christ', although he too was worried about proselytising by the Roman Church.[184] Smith saw Anglicanism as a middle way between '*Papists*' and '*Giddy Sectaries*'.[185]

At the time when Smith and Covel were travelling in Greece and Asia Minor, in the late 1660s and 1670s, English interest in Orthodoxy was particularly strong,[186] but the main stumbling block was always the question of transubstantiation. In Anglican eyes, evidence of Orthodox belief in this doctrine would make unity impossible. Finch, discussing the Greek church in London (which Georgirenes had helped to build on his visit to the city in 1676)[187] in his diary in February 1678/9, records that the bishop of London required all Greek priests there to 'disown' the doctrine as a condition of their being allowed to officiate.[188] One reason why this was a matter of such anxiety to Protestant travellers is made explicit by Wheler: Turks despise Christians, he says, partly because they believe that Christians eat their God, hence it is our duty to teach them to distinguish between 'the glorious light of the gospel we enjoy and profess, and the Roman Superstition they with so much reason abominate'.[189] Crawford, English resident in Venice, thought questions about the Greek Church of universal concern, and found himself irritated by Finch's dilatoriness in providing him with information; he hoped that Vernon would fill the gap.[190] In 1673, Henry Dodwell of Trinity College, Dublin, wrote to Smith to ask him about the differences between the Anglican and Greek Churches, as well as the relation of the latter to the Catholic Church, with special reference to the Greek attitude to the use of images and to the Eucharist. Looking at it from the Greek point of view, he asks, 'which of our tenets [do] they think, though eroneous, yet tolerable; and what [do] they think so pernicious as to oblige them to separate from us[?]'[191] Anything that reminded Anglicans of the Catholics they so feared at home was apt to cause fear and distrust: on Chios Robson was told that Greek monks read the liturgy without comprehension, on which his comment was, 'I did not wonder at this, calling to minde the history of our Masse-mumbling Priests in Queene *Maries* dayes.'[192]

The theological shades into the political in the view that the lack of unity among Christians is both confusing to Turks and a hindrance to a possible crusade against Islam, for the success of which the help of Christians within the Ottoman Empire would be essential.[193] With the gradual decline of the Ottoman threat to Europe, this idea became less prominent, but in the early years of the century Sherley, who hated the Turks for having held him captive for several years, argued fiercely for a naval expedition for just this purpose:

[Such an expedition] wyll make all the Greekes in Morœa, Epire, & a greate parte of Macedon to revolte, & all the ilandes, soe a man doe commaunde that hath prattique & acquayntans with somme principall Greekes of understandinge & esteeme;

& the action wyll bee the more easye yf God frende the Christian fleete to meete the Turke his gallyes, for yf they bee beaten the Christians shall never neede to drawe one swoorde for the rest.[194]

There is little evidence of missionary activity by Anglicans among Greeks; however, there is one exception to this. Isaac Basire, who had been chaplain to Charles I and who left England during the Civil War,[195] made some efforts at proselytising, with mixed success. He records that he used 'a vulgar Greek translation of our Church catechism' in Zante, but aroused the envy of Catholics there and had to leave for the Morea, where his sermons to the bishops and clergy were 'well taken'. Moving on to Aleppo, he left an Arabic catechism with the patriarch of Antioch. From there he travelled to Jerusalem and on to Mesopotamia, where he intended to provide the Armenian bishops with a Turkish catechism procured through the ambassador to Constantinople, Thomas Bendish. Back in Constantinople, he preached to French Protestants, though he was worried about how long he would be allowed to continue doing this. He also had plans to go to Egypt to study the Coptic Churches and confer with the patriarch of Alexandria. He was clearly interested in the differences between the various sects he encountered – writing, 'I have collated the severall confessions of faith of the several sorts of Christians, Greeks, Armenians, Jacobites, Maronites, & c., which confessions I have with me in their own languages'[196] – and found his medical skills (picked up in Padua en route) as well as his linguistic ones useful on his travels. Perhaps not surprisingly, given his obvious academic interests, his next career move was to a chair in theology in Transylvania, where he taught until he was able to return to England, and to his long-suffering wife, after the Restoration.[197]

There is one final facet of the attitudes of British visitors to the Greek Church that needs examination. When London churches were being rebuilt after the fire of 1666, there was a huge level of interest among architects, led by Wren and then Hawksmoor,[198] in the architecture of the early church, and in the link between Christian doctrine and its architectural expression.[199] There was a desire to return to a simpler, purer form of Christianity, which would be both aided and expressed by a new architecture based on that of the early church. In keeping with Protestant theology, the new churches were places where the congregation might hear scripture being expounded rather than going through processes of ritual – what Doran and Durston have called 'auditory' churches.[200] Because early Christians had used pagan elements in their church buildings, the line of influence goes back beyond the beginnings of the Christian church both to classical temples and to the temple in Jerusalem.[201] As Greene has put it with reference to Palladio, there was 'no concern for any anachronistic disparity between ancient and Christian worship'.[202]

The great interest taken by some travellers – principally Covel, Wheler, Rycaut, Smith and Huntington – in the sites of the seven churches of Asia can be seen in this context. These were men looking for evidence of a church that had not been corrupted as, in their view, the Roman Church had been.[203] Wheler in particular demonstrates his interest in the architecture of the early church: he felt that the cause of Christian unity would be well served by a better understanding of early Christianity, an understanding that might be gained by the study of architecture. He approved of the separation of men and women in church, a practice that was still followed in the Orthodox Church.[204] Alongside the search for uncorrupted Christianity, however, we find a horrified sense of what could happen to Christians who failed to live faithfully: Smith, for example, writes of the state of neglect in which he finds the seven churches, which he attributed to a combination of Greek carelessness and their subjection to the Turks. For him, this state of abandonment and physical neglect was in contrast to Palestine, which had been widely surveyed and was therefore familiar to anyone who had 'but the least gust [taste] for Antiquity, or History, or Travel'.[205] Wheler writes about Ephesus in similar but more personal terms – 'How could I chuse but lament the Ruin of this Glorious Church! To see their Candlestick [of Revelations 2.5], and Them removed, and their whole Light utterly extinguished! These Objects ought to make Us, that yet enjoy His Mercy, tremble' – and urges his readers to repent.[206] Although he does not, as Smith does, specifically blame the Greeks for the state of Christianity in their country, the implication is still that contemporary Greeks are unworthy successors of St Paul's congregations. The idea of punishment and retribution is related to the more general theory that the rise of Islam and the success of the Ottoman Empire in themselves constituted part of God's punishment of backsliding Christianity.[207] The clues to an earlier, purer form of Christianity suggested by the seven churches are in painful contrast to their contemporary condition.

***

Many English visitors to Greece were deeply ambivalent about the Greek people: to a great extent, this is a reflection of their sense of affinity with the Greek past, both pagan and Christian, and the dislocation they felt between their knowledge of that past and the actual experience of their encounters with contemporary Greeks. As (mostly Anglican) Christians, and as men educated in grammar schools where the classics dominated the curriculum, they carried with them a good deal of cultural, religious and educational baggage, with the result that they were not open-minded about the Greeks of their own time.[208] They pitied them for their subjection to Islam, but at the same time could not help seeing that subjection on one level as a punishment, directed either at Greek Christians specifically or at Christendom in general. This also allowed them to see themselves as standing, as educated men and as Christians, where perhaps Greeks ought to have stood. It was possible for Englishmen to see themselves as powerful in relation to Greeks, at the same time as they were visitors to or residents in an empire in which, as they recognised, the power was in the hands of the Ottomans. Layers of experience, at home and abroad, contributed to a complex network of attitudes.

CHAPTER 5

AMONG THE TURKS

When travellers use the word 'Turk', they refer not to an ethnic category but primarily to a religious one, although the name also carried all sorts of connotations about character that will be explored below.[1] If a traveller refers to a person as a Turk we cannot infer anything about that person's ethnicity. The word is synonymous with 'Muslim', and those who 'turned Turk', or converted, were no less 'Turks' in foreign eyes, and no less Muslims in Ottoman eyes, than those born into the faith.[2] Rycaut describes it like this: 'The *English* call it Naturalization, the *French*, Enfranchisement; and the *Turks* call it, becoming a Believer.'[3] A confusion arises, because, for Ottomans, 'Turk' was a pejorative term for an Anatolian peasant.[4] However, I shall use 'Turks' to describe those seen as Turks by English travellers.

Travellers' tales provide evidence of ambivalent attitudes towards Turks as towards Greeks, and of a tension between expectations and actual experience. At home in England, the fundamental assumption was that Turks were infidels: on Good Friday, Christians asked God to

> Have mercy upon all Jews, Infidels and Hereticks, and take from them all ignorance, hardness of heart and contempt for thy word; and so fetch them home [...] to thy flock, that they may be saved among the remnant of the true Israelites.[5]

Such conversion may have seemed like a real possibility from the vantage point of home – but as Matar points out, in the real world things were not as easy as in the 'imaginatively-controlled environments of the theater and the pulpit, [where] Britons converted the unbelievers, punished the renegades, and condemned the Saracens'.[6]

It was particularly clear to those who actually set foot in the Ottoman Empire that Islam had to be treated as 'a powerful civilization which they could neither possess nor ignore'.[7] The crucial word here is 'powerful': within the empire, the balance of power lay with the Ottomans, and that is what makes the situation of travellers vis-à-vis Turks quite different from that in relation to Greeks. There is a contrast here between the old world and the new: in the latter, which was being opened up by Europeans during the same period, power was very much in the hands of the newcomers, and native Americans were the underdogs.[8]

The European consciousness of Ottoman power is graphically illustrated by Covel in his account of an ambassadorial audience at which, the dragoman told him (he himself having been excluded from the audience hall, to his chagrin), the ambassador 'trembled like a leaf'.[9] Yet ambassadors were generally, if somewhat erratically, treated as persons of importance, and presented with gifts: the man who trembled like a leaf in the Sultan's presence was not a nobody. Although the empire may already have been past its heyday, and in the 1660s Ambassador Winchilsea could liken it to 'the prophet's ripe fruite, readie to fall into the mouths of those that shake them first',[10] there may have been an element of wishful thinking in this judgement. Ottoman power was still to be feared, and the advance of the Sultan's armies to the walls of Vienna was still in the future. The frontispiece of Marsh's *New Survey of the Turkish Empire*, published in 1663, shows Mehmed IV as the stereotypical 'terrible Turk' familiar to theatre-goers, with his armies lined up behind him.[11]

Even at home, however, as well as in Ottoman lands, there is some evidence of a more realistic attitude to Turks and Islam than is found on the stage or in the church. James Howell, who in 1650 added to his 1642 book of travel advice an appendix on Turkey, gives the purpose of travel to Turkey as being the understanding of the errors of the Ottoman Empire, Christianity's greatest enemy. The travellers themselves, other than Quakers, rarely show any interest in the conversion of Muslims, in strong contrast to the general attitude towards Jews. Howell himself writes that '*Christians* are more beholden to the *Turk* then to the *Jew*, for he acknowledgeth Christ to have been a great prophet', also advising travellers to be circumspect in their relations with the other travellers they meet, concealing their own religion and becoming 'all to all in point of morall conversation'. Howell even says that Turks 'may be a pattern to some Christian nations in point of common *humanity*', and though the force of this is significantly blunted by the fact that it follows immediately on a description of Turkish methods of torture, he does not appear to be writing ironically.[12] Other works of advice to foreigners in Turkey also suggest that it is best not to take a hard line: Dallington in 1605 cautions them to be willing to learn, rather than sticking to their own native customs, and Gailhard (1678) states that every country has its good and bad citizens, and that travellers should comply with the customs of the country they find themselves in,[13] although neither of these writers is specifically concerned with Ottomans. Cleland, too, recognises that custom varies from place to place.[14]

There were already the beginnings of knowledge and scholarship about the Islamic world in England: from the mid-sixteenth century some continental works of oriental scholarship had been published in English, though the first full English translation of the Qur'an did not appear till 1649. Chairs of Arabic were established in the universities in the 1630s, about a century after the establishment of chairs of Hebrew.[15] The first general history of the Turks, published in 1603, was by Richard Knolles, a schoolmaster, who updated a later edition of his work with the aid of the papers of Ambassador Roe.[16] A traveller who was able to take account of this knowledge and see beyond the condemnation of the Turks as infidels might be able to engage with them on a day-to-day level, so that the balance tipped away from ideology and towards experience and observation; this was perhaps most likely to happen in the case of men whose work involved negotiation and transactions with Turks, that is to say merchants and diplomats in particular.

Of course we encounter a wide range of views about Turks among travellers. At one end of the scale we find Blount, whose book was published in 1636, attempting to assess the Turks on their own terms: 'He who would behold these times in their greatest glory, could not finde a better *scene* than *Turky* [sic].' The Turks are 'the only moderne people', and to an impartial observer 'the *Turkish* way appeare[s] absolutely barbarous, as we are given to understand, or rather an other kinde of civilitie, different from ours, but no lesse pretending'.[17] He expresses strongly his view that it must be judged by its own standards rather than European ones: 'I in remembring the *Turkish* institutions, will only Register what I found them, nor censure them by any rule, but that of more, or lesse *sufficiency* to their ayme, which I suppose the *Empires* advancement.'[18] He regards the Turks as '*Souldier*-like' and 'open' (in contrast to Egyptians and Jews with their 'touch of the *Merchant*') but thinks that just as Roman philosophy was nurtured by the Roman conquest of Greece, so the Turkish Empire will be affected by the cultures of its subject peoples, so that while Turks may retain their 'owne proper *fiercenesse*', in time the conquered countries will '*Gentilize* [Turkey], and infect it with the ancient softnesse *naturall* to those places', and learning, the arts and philosophy will prosper.[19] He constantly emphasises 'civility', which he says follows the sun from east to west. It is perhaps a surprise to find that in Blount's view Turkish mariners are not fierce, but show him 'so ready service, such a patience, so sweet and gentle a way' as to make him wonder 'whether it was a dreame, or reall'.[20] Like many other travellers, Blount admired Constantinople, writing of the fall of the city to the Turks in 1453 that

> in this losse it may be said to gaine; for it is since at an higher glory, then it had before, being made Head of a farre greater *Empire*: of old it was ever baited, by the *Thracians* on the one side, and *Grecians* on the other; but now it commands over both.[21]

When Blount's friend Henry King wrote a poem in praise of him, he included lines lauding Turks for being 'just and free/To inoffensive travellers'.[22] Not all is sweetness and light, however: the empire is based on fear and absolute rule, and Blount quotes Tacitus's phrase 'in pessima republica plurimae leges' to illustrate his view of the way the state is run.[23] To fulfil the precepts of Islam, Turks do charitable works such as building hospitals, and hostels for travellers, but these seem to him to be 'like daintie fruit growing out of a *Dung-hill*'.[24]

It is necessary to look beyond Blount's wordy and discursive style, and his generalised pronouncements, to get any sense of his individual experience, but he does occasionally drop his guard to give us a better idea of what travelling was actually like for him. The story of his first pretending to be a Scot and then speaking ancient Greek has already been told: he clearly enjoyed laughing at those who could not understand what he was saying and had no knowledge of Britain, while at the same time displaying his erudition to his readers back home. Elsewhere, Blount admits to having felt vulnerable among Turks because of his '*Christian*' clothes, until he discussed the matter with 'one of the better sort', and learnt that clothes were regarded as a matter of custom, in which the Turks do not like '*novelties*'. At this point he 'perceived it [the Turkish attitude to his dress] to be a peece rather of *institution*, then *incivilitie*'.[25] While journeying with a caravan, he was worried about being kidnapped, and let it be known that he was a poor man, so that there would be no hope of a ransom payment, but also, as insurance, kept some members of the caravan in 'secret pension', and made friends with people who might be able to help him escape should the need arise. 'Herein was the most expence, and unquiet of my *voyage*: this excepted, the *Turkish* disposition is generous, loving and honest'.[26]

At the other end of the scale of attitudes to Turks are Sandys and Lithgow. In Sandys's eyes, Islam had caused the beauty of Smyrna to be 'turned to deformitie, her knowledge into barbarisme, her religion into impietie',[27] although he does also praise some Turkish qualities. Lithgow took a virulently anti-Islamic stance: the Qur'an is 'execrable', and in it 'one saying oft contradicteth another, both in words, and effect'; Mohammed, by denying that Christ was the son of God and the Messiah, is responsible for 'abhominable and blasphemous heresies'. Perhaps there is a vestige here of the idea found in the early days of Islam that it was not a new religion but a heretical Christian sect.[28] Haghia Sophia has been turned into a mosque 'after a diabolicall manner'. He has no great opinion of Muslim devoutness either, since although Muslims pray five times a day and wash in preparation, they still work on Fridays and sometimes 'abruptly sing the Psalmes of *David* in the *Arabick* tongue, but to no sense, nor verity of the Scriptures'.[29] However, even Lithgow shows signs of ambivalence, telling us that the Turks are not such bad masters for the Greeks — there is freedom of worship, and the 'tax' that took the form of the selection of Christian children to be trained as janissaries (the devshirme) is no longer in force[30] — but this is said in the context of denigrating Greeks for their unreliability rather than of praising the Turks: 'Look to it that you be no more gulled [by Greek tales].'[31] He does also report an encounter involving his rescue by friendly Turks from French-born renegades who had attacked him: '[the] other Infidells standing by said to me, behold what a Saviour thou hast, when these that were Christians, now turned *Mahometans*, cannot abide nor regard the name of thy God'.[32] It is difficult to judge Lithgow's own reaction here, but it appears that he was ashamed and the 'infidels' shocked by the bad behaviour of those who had been his co-religionists and were now theirs.

Most travellers did not really engage with the theology of Islam,[33] though it was recognised that, like Christianity, it was a monotheistic religion.[34] We do, however, have a description of an encounter between the Vani Effendi and Thomas Baines in which they discussed matters of doctrine such as the nature of women's souls and whether they can go to heaven. Baines told the Vani that he believed the Qur'an had been badly translated, and that in his view right-thinking Muslims might go to paradise. The Vani in his turn told Baines he had never before met so Muslim-like a Christian, and urged him to convert to Islam, an offer that Baines tactfully declined, saying he was too set in his ways to change.[35] Baines expressed his taste for theological discussion with Jews, Jesuits and Orthodox Greeks in a letter to Anne Conway (Finch's sister), although he was apt to denigrate his opponents:

> Our Conversation shall be, with the Craftyest and most ingenuous [sic] Jesuitt we can find, with the sobriest and most stayd Patriarchall man of the Greek Church to whome if your Ladyship please to add the arrantest and cunningest knave amonge the Jewes we can light upon, say our Conversation is made compleat.[36]

The reactions of Britons to Turks were complicated by Protestant attitudes to Catholics. Lithgow thought that Catholic idolatry was an obstacle to the conversion of Turks, with their ban on figural representation in mosques, to Christianity, but although he did not mince his words about Muslims any more than about Catholics,[37] others praised the Ottoman Empire specifically in contrast to Catholic countries for allowing religious freedom.[38] Robson, while regarding the Turks as 'profane' and their allegiance to Islam as 'bawling devotion', nevertheless remarks that there is less superstition among them than in Spain and Italy.[39]

When visitors did open their eyes to what was happening around them, what they saw was an extraordinarily diverse society, which Vitkus (referring specifically to the coastal areas) has described as 'a complex and unstable meeting ground for divergent cultural and religious groups'.[40] There was a big difference here between the commercial centres, usually coastal towns, where there were sizable Frank populations, and the remoter country areas. Greeks and other subject peoples made up separate communities, and yet there were surprising examples of interaction, such as a variant of Greek used by Levantine Christians that was written in Arabic script.[41] No people in the world, according to Rycaut, 'have ever been more open to receive all sorts of Nations to them than they', although he adds that one of the corollaries of this is that Turks cannot trace their ancestry back to 'the ancient bloud of the Saracens', because of the frequency of conversions to Islam: 'some of the most [...] desperate in wickedness [...] flock to these Dominions, to become members and professors of the *Mahometan* superstition'.[42] If you open your doors to all sorts, he seems to be saying, all sorts are what you get. Rycaut also comments that Christians have to be much more careful in Asian Turkey than on the European side of the Bosphorus, except in the maritime towns, where the Turks have learnt civility from their trading activities with Franks. Asian Turks, he says, think European Turks have been defiled by too much contact with Christians, and especially by taking up their habit of wine-drinking.[43]

One of the qualities that impressed several visitors to the Ottoman court was the deep silence that prevailed in the presence of the Sultan.[44] Sandys writes with admiration of the way in which the deaf and dumb servants communicate even quite complicated matters by sign language, while officials 'stand like so many statues, without speech or motion'.[45] Covel describes his experience of this silence:

> Amongst so many people it was most wonderfull to see ye order and strange silence [...] amongst these vast multitudes all are as husht and orderly as we are at a sermon; I could not possibly beleive it till I found it alwayes so.[46]

Rycaut tells how, when Ambassador Winchilsea had his audience with the Sultan, 5,000 janissaries waited in absolute silence for their pay: ambassadors' audiences regularly took place on janissaries' pay days, to impress diplomats with the military might and discipline of the empire.[47] Blount mentions that the seraglio is surrounded by an 'infinite swarme' of officials and servants, in 'a *silence*, and *reverence* so wonderfull, as shew'd in what awe they stand of their *Soveraigne*'.[48]

Cleanliness was another admired Turkish quality. As Browne travelled through northern Greece, he was accompanied by an Ottoman messenger or 'chiaus', Osman, 'a stout and faithfull honest person, very clean and neat'. When Browne needed to urinate, he recalled the story of another traveller, who had caused offence, so he asked the messenger where he might 'make water without offence': '[he] answered me grumblingly at first, but afterwards directed me to a place, and stood at a little distance, to secure me from any affront'.[49] In view of this, it is hardly surprising that Turks were apt to revile 'the Christian whom they see pissing against a wall'.[50] The contrast in attitude to Turks and Jews in this respect has been mentioned: Turkish cleanliness is praised, while the fact that Jews wash frequently is seen as a sign that they must be unnaturally dirty.

Browne was also struck by the politeness and hospitality of the Turks, who were quick to offer coffee, tobacco and food to his party. Hospitality is remarked on by other travellers too: Covel found the Turks of the area around Prusa 'extraordinary kind and sumptuous', even though it was Ramadan, and near Nicomedia a friend of the Metropolitan gave him an excellent Turkish supper, with plenty of wine, although the host himself did not drink.[51] Sandys, too, knew about helpful officials, though possibly from hearsay rather than from personal experience:

> Some [janissaries] are appointed to attend on Embassadors: others to guard such particular Christians as will be at the charge, both about the Citie, and in their travels, from incivilities and violences, to whom they are in themselves most faithfull: wary, and cruell, in preventing and revenging their dangers and injuries, and so patient in bearing abuses, that one of them late being strucken by an English man [...] as they travelled along through *Morea*, did not onely not revenge it, nor abandon him to the pillage and outrages of others, in so unknowne and savage a country; but conducted him unto *Zant* in safety, saying, God forbid that the villany of another should make him betray the charge that was committed to his trust.[52]

Veryard thought Turks were 'devout, sober, grave, cunning [here used in a non-pejorative sense], and punctual to their word'. He believed they had built up a more effective empire than the Romans over a shorter period of time. On the other hand, he distinguished, unusually, between 'true' Turks, whom he saw as good, just and charitable, and renegades.[53] The effective Ottoman administration and the quality of Turkish officials were also praised highly by Rycaut.[54] Smith comments on their kindness to the sick, as well as to animals, including dogs, who they believe have souls. This is interesting in that 'dog' was sometimes a Muslim term of abuse for a Christian: Winchilsea recalls that when the French ambassador complained to the Grand Vizier of bad treatment, the Vizier replied, 'Do not I know you, that you are a Ghiaur (which is Infidell), that you are a hogge, a dogge, a turde eater'.[55]

In the story of English travel to the Greek world in this period, women generally appear only fleetingly, on the margins, obscured by men, so it is refreshing to find one who was definitely a protagonist. Mary Fisher was a Quaker, a servant who converted when her master and mistress did so. She had been illiterate, but probably learnt to read from other Quakers who, like her, were imprisoned in York Castle. Before she travelled to Constantinople she had already been to the West Indies and New England as a missionary, suffering severely for her beliefs. In 1657, in her thirties, she set out in the company of five other Quakers for the Levant.[56] When she arrived in Smyrna, the consul put her on a boat back to England, but she disembarked in the Morea.[57] The story was told by Croese in his history of the Quakers, published during Fisher's lifetime:

> There having got this freedom, and regarding neither the circumstances of Nature, nor the weakness of her Sex, being all alone, and ignorant of the Way and the Language, that she might avoid the danger of falling into the hands of Thieves, she Travails on Foot all along the Shoar and Sea-Coast of the *Morea*, *Greece* and *Macedon*; and from thence over the Mountains and craggy places of *Romania*, or *Thrace*, as far as [...] *Adrianople* [...] The Woman was lucky, tho' she did not know it, to alight upon such Men, who tho' they are called by the name of Turks, came not short, in their Kindnesses to Strangers, of any other Nation.[58]

The only extant description of her journey that we have in Fisher's own words refers simply to 'many tryalls such as [she] was never tried with before', and it is likely that by the time Croese's book was published in 1696 the story had been embroidered and acquired the status of myth within the Religious Society of Friends; nevertheless, her feat is an extraordinary one. Arriving in Adrianople, she was admitted to the presence of Mehmed IV, who was still only a teenager. This was a unique outcome, as the typical response of English diplomats to Quakers was to express extreme irritation and put them on the next boat home.[59] But Fisher, with the help of an interpreter, was able to make her attempt to convert Mehmed. As she wrote home, he treated her with kindness:

> I have borne my testimony for the Lord before the king unto whom I was sent, and he was very noble unto me [...] he and all that were about him received the words of truth without contradiction, they do dread the name of God many of them [...] [They are] more near truth then many Nations, there is a love begot [in me] towards them which is endlesse [...] Neverthelesse though they be called Turkes the seed in them is near unto God [...] they would willingly to have me to stay in the country, and when they would not prevaile with me they proferred me a man and a horse to go five dayes journey, it was to Constantinople but I refused and came [?] safe from thence.[60]

On the evidence of her letter, and paradoxically, since she represents the only religious group to send missionaries to the Sultan's court with the specific aim of proselytising, Fisher's Quaker belief that every individual has access to God without the need for mediation by clergy allowed her to intuitively understand and respect the Sultan's own religious feelings. Conversely, a non-trinitarian version of Christianity may have been more acceptable to the Sultan than other versions. According to George Bishop, a fellow Quaker whose work was published in 1661, she was asked in the course of her audience what she thought of the Prophet, to which she replied that she did not know him, but Christ she did know, and that true prophets might be known by whether their words proved to be true.[61] She seems to have been an astute woman as well as a brave one.

Fisher's attitude to Islam is very different from anything we encounter in other travellers, even in Blount, with his recognition of

Turkish 'civility', but it is confirmed by other Quaker writings. Daniel Baker, who travelled to Smyrna in 1661, published a letter sent by Quakers to Ambassador Winchilsea chastising the English community in Constantinople for their treatment of innocent people, that is for expelling the 'Friends and Messengers of Christ' (the Quakers) out of Turkey. These English, according to the letter, are Christians in name only and excelled by the Turks 'in uprightness, steadfastness and temperance in things civil'. '[God] shall awaken [...] the eternal witness [...] in every Conscience, whether *Turks*, *Jews*, *Christians* or *Heathens*, under what name or denomination soever they may be called.'[62]

Evidence of Quaker attitudes is also found in the work of Stephen Smith, who in his early life had been a merchant in Scanderun and who was converted to Quakerism in his forties, after his return to England.[63] Writing towards the end of his life, he praised ordinary Turks ('Plain People') for their courtesy, honesty and fear of God, in contrast to most Christians. He believed that God 'gives [those who do his will] Power to eschew the Evil and to love the Good, of what Nation, Language or Country soever they be of'.[64] He was not alleging that Islam was as valid as Christianity, as his ultimate aim was the conversion of the Turks: his message was that only through truly Christian behaviour would such conversion come about, and examples of 'Christian' behaviour might be found among Turks. There is a generosity of spirit found here that is not apparent in other writings about Muslim beliefs.

Comments on the bad qualities of the Turkish character are perhaps predictable: cruelty and tyranny, pride, greed, hypocrisy, superstition, susceptibility to bribery, lack of learning, suspicion of foreigners, polygamy and subjection of women are all ascribed to Turks by various writers.[65] They are sometimes described in terms of animal imagery, just as Turks sometimes describe Christians as dogs: Rycaut compares Turks to various animals, for example worms and cormorants.[66] Thomas Smith uses the word 'brutishness' to describe Turks, but there is a certain irony here, recognised by Smith himself, since his reference is in the context of the destruction of ancient buildings, and he goes on to compare Turks to the people who destroyed English churches during the Interregnum.[67] Another criticism that crops up frequently, clearly arousing a kind of horrified fascination in most westerners, is that the Turks are excessively lustful and practise sodomy. In Sherley's words: 'For theyre Sodommerye they use it soe publiquely & impudentelye as an honest Christian woulde shame to companye with his wyffe as they doe with theyre buggeringe boyes'.[68] Covel describes actors dressed as animals performing representations of buggery, which he calls 'proeposterous leachery and unnatural lust'. He also gives a gloating account of a lewd puppet show that took place after dark in Ramadan.[69] Blount is unusual in mentioning catamites without condemnation.[70] As Matar has suggested, accusations of sodomy also functioned as a means of allowing Christians to feel morally superior to Muslims.[71]

The Sultan's seraglio, which of course was not accessible to men – Thomas Dallam had nearly got into serious trouble in 1599/1600 when he watched, through a grill, some of the Sultan's women playing with a ball[72] – was also of great interest, and was reckoned to contain hundreds of concubines.[73] It is impossible to judge what the numbers actually were, but the interest does demonstrate the beginning of the idea of the orient as a world of sexual excess that both attracted and repelled westerners. There is one tantalising reference to a visit to the seraglio by the wife of Peter Wych, ambassador to the Porte during the reign of Charles I:

> the *Sultanesse* desired one day to see [her ...] whereupon my Lady *Wych* (accompanied with her waiting-women, all neatly dressed in their great *Verdingals*, which was the Court Fashion then) attended her Highnesse. The *Sultanesse* entertained her respectfully, but withall wondring at her great and spacious Hips, she asked her whether all English women were so made and shaped about those parts: To which my Lady *Wych* answered, that they were made as other women were,

and demonstrated the device of the farthingale by taking it off.[74]

A further characteristic of Turkish society that is criticised, sometimes by implication if not explicitly, is the system of slavery that was prevalent. Smith is perhaps the most outspoken when he writes of the 'horror and confusion of mind' with which he observed the slave market in Constantinople. He also clearly saw it as part of his duty as a chaplain to make efforts, with the help of the ambassador and factors, to ransom Christian slaves.[75] Winchilsea was able by negotiation to obtain the freedom of some members of the crew of the frigate *Anne* who had been captured by Turks while gathering wood on the Peloponnese.[76] Rycaut condemns the practice by his choice of language when he writes that large numbers of slaves are 'daily transported to nourish and feed the body of this great *Babylon*'.[77] However, expressions of concern about slavery, and any actions arising from such concern, were highly selective, since Christians as well as Jews and Muslims used slaves as domestic servants.[78] Covel points out that the lawless people of the Peloponnese habitually capture both Muslim sailors to sell as slaves to Christians and vice versa. He also writes of watching the procession in celebration of the marriage of the Sultan's daughter, in which waxwork gardens were carried by slaves who were 'managed by galley whistle', but he does not overtly condemn the practice.[79] The English were not above condoning slavery, at least in practice: North's brother, who wrote his biography, comments on the poor conditions in which slaves were held, but goes on to say that North himself was served by slaves, and brought two home to England with him. However, it may be that he regarded this as an act of charity, since he had probably rescued them from a worse situation. One was a Pole, whom he sent back to his native country; the other, a Georgian, ran away from North's mother's household, was caught, and was eventually returned to Smyrna. Their respective nationalities suggest that both were Christian.[80] Browne, who expresses pity for slaves working in Turkish households in Greece, also met one who was serving in a post-house near Mount Olympus, and being a slave to the Sultan was 'never to be redeemed': according to Browne, he was extremely dejected on that account. But he also met a Hungarian who had served successively a Turk, a Jew and an Armenian, the last of whom gave him his freedom, so that Browne hoped 'by this time he [was] in his own Country'.[81] Foreigners may have recognised that the Ottoman Empire could not have functioned as it did without the widespread practice of slavery.

In general, as far as views of the Turks go, it is Rycaut who, as so often, provides the voice of reason and charity: they do, he acknowledges, have a reputation for barbarism, but he adds, 'a People, as the *Turks* are, men of the same composition with us, cannot be so savage and rude as they are generally described; for ignorance and grossness is the effect of Poverty'. Like Blount, he accepted that Turks should to some extent at least be judged by their own standards rather than English ones, although he also drew attention to the comparison with England, whose sovereign understood that subjects too have rights. It is significant that Rycaut was writing in the early years after the Restoration, in an atmosphere in which there was a lively sense of rights hard-won from the monarchy.[82]

One interesting question is the extent to which foreigners felt that they could make friends with Turks. Both Covel and Finch refer to friendships with Ottoman officials, but what such relationships meant is hard to gauge, though in these cases it seems to have involved an element of advantage for the visitor: Finch counted the chief customs officer as his 'very good friend', and Covel, who was partial to sherbet, made friends with the official in charge of sherbet at the court.[83] North entertained Turks in his house, but as a merchant he knew that his work and profitability depended on making good personal relationships.[84] He spoke Turkish, and felt that foreigners' misunderstanding of Turkish character was inevitable because of the reluctance of Turks to talk freely to unbelievers.[85] The only suggestion I have found that something more than acquaintance might have been involved is Covel's remark that he ate 'many times' in Turkish houses,[86] but again it is difficult to know what degree of intimacy is implied.

It is also impossible to know whether the Turks with whom foreigners made friends were ethnic Turks or renegades. Matar has listed the three principal types of renegades, usually from Christianity or Judaism, found in English writing as: children forcibly taken to be trained as janissaries; slaves who converted in order to obtain their freedom, though their conversion did not always have the desired effect; and expatriates who gradually adopted Muslim culture.[87] The career opportunities offered by a meritocratic society were considerable, particularly for those who learned Ottoman:[88] for example, two-thirds of grand viziers between 1453 and 1623 were converts,[89] and renegades also frequently became imperial messengers or dragomans, thanks to their knowledge of countries or languages.[90] In the Balkans, many were originally speakers of Greek or Slavic languages.[91] In Greece itself, however, it was only on Crete that there were large-scale conversions.[92] Greene suggests that there were three reasons for this: the social dislocation caused by the long war over the island between Venice and the Turks, resentment of long Venetian/Catholic domination, and the career opportunities in the expanding janissary corps.[93] I have not found any mention in travellers' accounts of conversion occurring as a precursor to, or result of, marriage. Once a person had converted to Islam, he was equal with other Muslims, whatever his origins: 'An Ottoman Muslim might speak Serbian, Arabic, Albanian or Turkish; it made no difference to that person's status in the eyes of his rulers.'[94] Many cases of conversion probably fall into what Bulliet, in the context of the Middle Ages, has called 'social conversion', that is, not an ideological or theological change so much as 'movement from one religiously defined social community to another', which tends to happen in societies such as that of the Ottoman Empire in which social identity and status are defined by religious affiliation.[95] Matar suggests that foreigners of a lower social status were more likely to 'turn Turk' as there was more in it for them.[96]

Aside from such general comments, various travellers write of their encounters with renegades. Randolph ran across one on Euboea whose tale suggests that he was English. This was a man named Muzlee Aga, who had been sold into slavery in Leghorn in 1660, but was freed thanks to an English merchant, and made his way to the house of a certain Richard Langly in Smyrna, where Randolph later stayed. Muzlee Aga was in Euboea in 1679, at the same time as Randolph, and helped him after a robbery.[97] Wheler too, in company with Covel, with whom he was searching out antiquities and manuscripts, crossed the path of an English convert, a surgeon who had been enslaved (we do not hear how) very young, and who showed them his collection of books in English, Italian and Latin, 'and one in *Arabick*', adding, 'how well he understood it, I am no competent Judge'.[98] Covel mentions that the surgeon employed to circumcise the Sultan's son, a ceremony at which 200 proselytes were also circumcised, was himself an Italian-born convert; so too was one Baccareschi, about whom Covel makes several scathing remarks in his diary, an employee of the Sultan's who accompanied Baines and Covel on their visit to the Vani Effendi. Ceremonial fireworks were arranged by Venetian and Dutch renegades.[99]

Randolph also tells how he met a renegade on Crete:

> When I was there in the year 1676, a Renegado was taken; He was a Greek born on the Island of *Candy*; and turned Turk when the *Vizier* was at the Siege of *Candy*; afterwards he married at *Scio* [Chios], and lived very well; but upon some discontent he made his escape from *Scio*, and got to the Privateers of *Malta*, with whom he lived some years; & landing on this Island, he with some others were surprized, and taken. His companions were condemned to the Gallys, but his sentence was to be shott away, out of one of these great Gunns, which was accordingly effected.[100]

As so often, one would like to know more of this man's story.

Travellers are ambivalent in their attitudes to both Greeks and Turks, but there is also a marked contrast, Greeks generally being seen as weak and Turks as strong. On one level, Turks represent a kind of foil for Greeks; to adapt the terms used by Reed in his discussion of Virgil's *Aeneid*,[101] part of their function in travel accounts is to stand for stereotypical 'anti-Greeks', infidel but powerful as opposed to Christian but oppressed. Visitors' consciousness that the Greeks, whose ancient ancestors they revered, were in a state of subjection in the Ottoman Empire directed the focus of their attention towards the power of the Turks.

The Ottoman Empire comprised a huge range of people of varied ethnicity and religious affiliation. The reactions of visitors to those they met, as individuals or as representatives of particular groups, cannot be neatly categorised. Foreigners' responses were affected by their own characters, the backgrounds they came from, and their previously held convictions, as well as the conditions of their sojourns in Greece and Asia Minor. Then, in turn, their experiences of travel and meeting people influenced the way they saw the world and the way they wrote about their journeys: Wheler remembered and many years later published a testimony to the hospitality he had received in Greece, and Covel corresponded with Greek churchmen for the rest of his long life. Sympathy for the Greeks, and admiration for the Turks, mixed with criticism in both cases, are part of the overall picture of English reactions to the Ottoman world. Responses to Catholics and Jews are also part of the pattern: opposition to Catholicism serves to show Islam in a more favourable light, while travellers who might be learned in biblical scholarship came across numbers of individual Jews for perhaps the first time in Turkey. In particular, however, Greeks and Turks functioned as a pair of opposites, against each of which, in the different ways that I have tried to examine, expatriate Englishmen could begin to define themselves both as individuals and as members of a developing nation. I have suggested that there is evidence to demonstrate that consciously or unconsciously many Englishmen in Greece regarded themselves as being the true heirs of the ancient Greeks, although also superior to them in being Christians rather than pagans. This sense of inheritance both influenced their attitude to the contemporary Greeks they met and was reinforced by it. The texts that resulted from their travels, on which the imprint of the classical heritage is so strong, fed in turn into the discourse that was developing at home about nationhood and empire, a discourse in which Britons come to inherit the imperial legacy of Rome in addition to the cultural legacy of Greece. The Ottoman Empire provided for aspiring imperialists an example of what a contemporary empire might look like.

CONCLUSION

What I have tried to demonstrate in this book is the extent to which travellers to the Greek world, both 'passengers' and 'inhabitants' as they are described in the seventeenth-century texts,[1] saw that world through a classically tinted lens. Both Blount and Sandys, for instance, thought that coffee was likely to be the same as 'the old blacke broth used so much by the *Lacedemonians*',[2] while Coryate compares whirling dervishes to bacchantes, and the Grand Signor in procession to Roman triumphs.[3] Sandys's emotional allegiance to the classics is demonstrated by the fact that even his account of the Christian holy places is illustrated by classical rather than biblical allusions. Covel is another striking example of this emotional allegiance. The classical world was for him a kind of default setting: he explains Turkish musical instruments, bolsters and coaches all by classical analogies, making it clear that he is not simply making comparisons but alleging actual survival of classical types.[4] Mentioning Turkish eating habits in a discussion of the Eucharist, he reminds his readers that Xenophon describes bread being broken into pieces and distributed for eating;[5] other points of reference in this discussion are Ovid and Plutarch.[6] He also thought that a ragged old man whom he met on Cervi looked like Hesiod, or a character from Hesiod, risen from the dead,[7] and churches as a cool resting place for the sick or for travellers reminded him that in classical times the sick were accustomed to take refuge in Aesculapian temples.

Conclusion

Adams, identifying a comparable phenomenon, points out that late sixteenth-century engravings of Native Americans by de Bry have a distinct look of classical statues about them.[8] The extent to which a classical bias was part of the mental landscape even of those who were not classical scholars is considerable.

In terms of encounters with people, Greeks, Turks and others, travellers' attitudes were influenced both by their preconceptions and also by meetings with real individuals. There is an additional important element, and that is the way in which religious, political and national identities were being formed at home. At the level of the individual, there is a complex interplay between the eager observer of or participant in foreign affairs and the Englishman conscious of the borders of his own identity, an identity that might be altered or reinforced by his experience abroad. At a national level, the English took home their observations of the Ottoman world, its power structures and the ways in which it was, more or less successfully, held together, expressing them in writings that in turn contributed to the making of England as an aspiring imperial power. The increasingly popular genre of travel writing also helped to make English a more flexible and confident language, a language that in itself was a crucial element in the rise of a sense of English national identity. In English/British culture towards the end of the seventeenth century, the place of the classical world in general, and of the Latin language in particular, was beginning to shift. With the rise of nation states, speaking English or French or whatever was one's native language became a matter of national pride, so that Latin declined as a spoken language. One aspect of the flourishing of written English was the rise of the novel, which was to become such an important genre of English literature,[9] and of which travel writing as fantasy rather than reportage was a significant ancestor. Travel accounts were written to entertain as well as to instruct, and in many cases they were eagerly read at home. As Covel expressed it: 'How naturally do Men listen to Travailers who relate strange and prodigious wonders, which with most of them will settle in their Memory though not fully in their Opinion'.[10] The impression left by the text might become more important than the facts it set out.

At the same time, as geographical knowledge increased, other areas of the world, and especially the new world, competed for the attention of the curious traveller.

In terms of antiquities, there was a change in the post-Restoration period, when scholarly visitors, particularly, tried to look at ancient sites in a more contextual way, by studying remains on the ground more closely and relating them to texts such as the works of Strabo and Pausanias. Covel and his contemporaries, Vernon, Rycaut and Wheler, demonstrate this change. It was a shift that happened alongside the rise of the Royal Society and experimental science at home. An example of the influence of that society can be seen in Wheler's description of finding a dying pelican, identified by reference to Pliny, which he and Spon measured and on which, when it was dead, they conducted an experiment to see how much water its beak could be made to hold.[11] Covel's dissection of a shark has already been mentioned.[12] Both Wheler and Covel carried the principle of empirical observation over into the field of archaeology, or proto-archaeology. The former used Roman coinage to identify – wrongly, as we now know – pedimental figures on the Parthenon. Covel thought that the reliefs he saw at Ephesus could not represent the dragging of Hector, on the grounds that there was no chariot to be seen. In the eighteenth century, science would become closer to what we would now recognise as science, Winckelmann would outline a chronology of ancient sculpture, and excavation would begin to be used as a tool for understanding material remains of the past as historical evidence. An example of this last development is William Stukely (1687–1765), who applied the dissection techniques he had learnt as a doctor to the investigation of Stonehenge. The Royal Society, the Society of Antiquaries and the Society of Dilettanti, with their different emphases, all flourished: the latter, with its interest in taste and aesthetics, sponsored the travels of artists such as Stuart and Revett to Greece.[13] Another important eighteenth-century development was of course the Grand Tour, in which travel to Italy, and sometimes further afield, to Greece and the Levant,[14] became part of the education of a gentleman, in many cases a substitute for, rather than an addition to, a university course. Travellers such as Wheler, with his attention to the aesthetic qualities of ancient sculpture, are precursors of these more self-conscious collectors and arbiters of taste.

In time, America too may have altered travellers' perspectives on their relationship to the classical world. In the mid-eighteenth century, James Caulfeild, Lord Charlemont, noted his reactions on his first sight of Athens:

> Is this the renowned Athens? How melancholy would be the reflection should we suppose, what certainly must come to pass, that in a few ages hence, London, the Carthage, the Memphis, the Athens of the present world, shall be reduced to a state like this, and travellers should come, *perhaps from America*, to view its ruins.[15]

The idea of the rise and fall of empires, which we have noted among seventeenth-century travellers, is behind this comment, but it also suggests a strong element of nostalgia; perhaps this can be linked with the romantic celebration of ruins that is to be found in this period.[16]

Travellers and English society

While the state of England does not figure prominently in travel accounts, there is evidence that it was often in the back of travellers' minds as a matter of both pride and anxiety. On one level, what Sandys referred to as his 'Beloved soile: as in site/*wholly from all the world disjoined*/so in thy felicities'[17] was seen as being the best of all possible worlds, a standard by which other countries were measured and found wanting. The wording on Gainsford's title page makes the same point, referring to England's 'sufficiencie and fulnesse of happinesse'.[18] Biddulph, early in the century, thought that reading about conditions in the Ottoman lands would encourage people of every social status to be thankful for conditions in England.[19] Wheler believed that the state of Greece was a warning to English subjects, while Rycaut valued the combination of island safety with the 'free and open Trade' facilitated by the Levant Company and its worthy ambassadors.[20] In the post-Restoration peace, memories went back to the troubles – Rycaut had been horrified by the execution of Charles I[21] – but even before the Civil War there was uncertainty: Avcioğlu has deconstructed Sandys's frontispiece in terms of the tension in England between self-confidence and worry about Ottoman power, and of the contrast between perceptions of divine right and of tyranny.[22] The execution of Osman II in 1622 was an uncomfortable precedent, and even as early as 1617, Joseph Hall asked prophetically 'Where learned wee [...] the bloudy and tragicall science of King-killing [?].'[23]

After the Restoration, notes of both relief and warning are sounded. Rycaut kept a record of events in the Ottoman Empire in a blank book acquired for the purpose, with the aim of providing '*Examples and Precedents to future Ages*'.[24] He urged his readers to thank God that they were born Christians in 'a Country the most free and just in all the World', where they were protected by the King and did not need to descend to the 'desire of Revolution'. For him, obedience to the monarchy was the key, 'the only bar to all other Enormities and Sins'.[25] The spectre of revolution also haunted Bargrave, who described the 'deplorable Tragedie' of the death of Charles I and compared the janissary revolt to the English rebellion.[26] That religion as well as politics was at issue is made explicit by Smith in his comparison of the behaviour of those who destroyed English churches during the Interregnum to 'Turkish brutishness and barbarousness'. In his view, even the cathedrals of England might easily have become '*confused heaps of stone and rubbish, like* Ephesus *or* Laodecea'.[27] There was both a need to believe that the English monarchy was different in kind from the Ottoman sultanate and also a fear that there might be similarities.

***

The travellers discussed in this book were individuals, and their reactions to the Ottoman-ruled Greek world were individual too, but the texts that were among the fruits of their journeys show that common threads can also be traced. Most of those who made the journey east had had an education based on the Greek and Latin classics and, because of this, they saw both the Greek people and the classical remains of the Greek landscape as ruins of the glorious civilisation that continued to live in their imaginations. This reaction was sharpened by their experiences in the strange and powerful Ottoman Empire, whose culture and institutions, unlike those of Greece, they were unable to read through historical texts and were therefore forced to decode with their own eyes. The contrast between the two emphasised the degradation, in the opinion of travellers, of Greek culture and, in doing so, gave Englishmen the freedom to take on themselves the mantle of ancient Greece. Although they were changed in various ways by their experiences of travel, they nevertheless brought back home again the classical baggage that they had carried out with them. And although, perhaps, few of them were as self-aware as the speaker in Seferis's poem, nevertheless he speaks for them too:

> I woke with this marble head in my hands;
> It exhausts my elbows and I don't know where to put it down.[28]

NOTES

Introduction

1. Harrigan, writing about French seventeenth-century 'récits de voyage en orient', has suggested that the objects brought back for display in cabinets of curiosities are the physical equivalent of the curiosities described by travellers in their written accounts; Harrigan 2003: 49–55.
2. The notion of 'civility' includes all the characteristics that a civilised man should possess, all the qualities that distinguish the civilised from barbarians. It also encompasses ideas of humanist education, culture and good breeding, and was in use in all these senses from the 1530s or 1540s (*OED*).
3. Coward 2003: 282–3; Kishlansky 1997: 231–5; Doran & Durston 1991: 66.
4. MacLean 2007: xi, 245.
5. Yerasimos 1991: 2–3.
6. Blount 1636: 2. 'Civility' here also includes the idea of good government.
7. Lewis (online).
8. Brotton 1997: 35.
9. Parker 1999: 9.
10. Knolles 1603: 'To the reader'. For editions of Knolles's book, see Barbour 2003: 16.
11. In mediaeval allegorical interpretations, Odysseus was also adopted as an archetype of the Christian pilgrim; Stanford 1992: 321; Hall 2008: 49.
12. Herodotus was available in Latin from the middle of the fifteenth century, but the first complete English translation, by Isaac Littlebury, dates from 1709.

13. Cheke's work on Herodotus inspired Roger Ascham to travel; Clarke 1959: 18.
14. [Hall] 1609.
15. Leigh 1671; Cicero, *Tusculan Disputations*: 5.108; Pacuvius, *Teucer*; Aristophanes, *Pluto*: 1151. Cicero tells the story of Socrates, who, asked which country he belonged to, replied that he was a citizen of the world; the same story is told by Plutarch, 'On exile', *Moralia*: 600. There is also a link here with the Stoic notion of world citizenship.
16. Claassen 1999: 20–1, 49–50.
17. Seneca, *Ad Helviam*: 8.1–3, 10.1.
18. One of the works of Hakluyt's successor, Samuel Purchas, is entitled *Purchas His Pilgrimage*, while his *Hakluytus Posthumus* is subtitled *Purchas His Pilgrimes*. In the latter work he describes the whole of human life as a pilgrimage; Purchas 1905–7: vol. 1, 138.
19. Brotton 1997: 21, 31–3.
20. Parker 1999: 6–7.
21. Bacon 1696: 46.
22. Royal Society 1665–6: 140–2.
23. Rubiés 1996.
24. Palmer 1606.
25. Rubiés 1996: 145.
26. This was both practical (coinage, customs, weights and measures, etc.) and historical or mythical. It was too large to be a handy pocket book.
27. Hall 1975: 2.
28. Ibid.: dedicatory epistle.
29. Ibid.: dedicatory epistle.
30. Ibid.: 5, 7. John Covel and his contemporaries, although some of them were employed in the Levant, were very much travellers of curiosity.
31. Ibid.: 12–13.
32. Ibid.: 76, 99.
33. [Hall] 1609: A1v.
34. Hall 1975: 25.
35. Hall 1674.
36. Peacham 1962: 63.
37. Parry 1995: 3; Swann 2001: 2.
38. Fuller 1642: 159.
39. Peacham 1962: 161–2.
40. Fuller 1642: 160.
41. Rycaut 1680: second sequence, 65.
42. Cleland 1607: 261; Neale 1643: 103.
43. E.g. Milton 1973: 58; Veryard 1701: b1v.
44. E.g. Burton 1676: 167; King 1664: 111; Coryate 1611: 'To the reader'.
45. Warneke 1995: 49, 70.

46. Howell 1650: 5. Howell had been the English ambassador in Madrid at the time of the future Charles I's escapade there, in disguise, with the future Duke of Buckingham; Brotton 2006: 85, 87–8.
47. Howell 1650: 17, 27, 108–9, 129.
48. [Heylyn] 1631: dedication.
49. Evans 1993.
50. Essex 1633: 'To the reader'; Leigh 1671: 26; Lassels 1670: preface.
51. Wheler 1682: preface; Rycaut 1679: 31; Veryard 1701: b1r–v.
52. Lassels 1670: a3r. The concept of the physical world as a book was common in early modern England; Walsham 2011: 393.
53. Coryate 1616: 3.
54. Wheler 1682: preface; Wheler 1911: 26.
55. BL MS Add. 22910: 80.
56. Lassels 1670: a4r.
57. Neale 1643: 2.
58. BL MS Sloane 1911–13: 52r.
59. Veryard 1701: 286.
60. Harvey was Covel's first ambassador.
61. HMC 1913: 518.
62. Covel 1722: i.
63. Wheler 1682.
64. BL MS Add. 22910: 37.
65. Leedham-Green (online); BL MS Add. 5821; BL MS Add. 19166.
66. Sandys 1615: 'To the prince'.
67. Grelot 1681: 91.
68. BL MSS Add. 22910, 22911, 22912, 22913, 22914, 57495; BL MS Harley 3778: 98–130; BL MS Harley 6943. MS Add. 22912 is numbered in several different sequences: I have used the folio numbers that run right through the ms. in the top right-hand corners.
69. Covel 1722.
70. BL MS Add. 22912.
71. E.g. a quotation from Alcaeus is attributed to Anacreon; ibid.: 220r.
72. Ibid.: 69–71.
73. Ibid.: 5–74.
74. Ibid.: 175–248.
75. Ibid.: 181v.
76. Ibid.: 247r. Covel consistently misspells words such as 'friend'.
77. BL MSS Add. 22913, 22914.
78. Haynes 1986: 36.
79. Blount 1636: 28.
80. MacLean 2007: 97.
81. Carey 2003: 39–40.
82. Blount 1636: 5.
83. Ibid.: 32–3.

84. The word 'Turk' was used by travellers to describe religious rather than ethnic identity; see Chapter 5.
85. An alternative explanation is that new editions were a way of repackaging not very popular works.
86. BL MS Add. 70485.
87. These owed something to Venetian diplomatic relations; Rubiés 1996: 149–50.
88. Sandys 1615.
89. Rycaut's *Memoirs* were written with the express purpose of providing 'Examples and Precedents to future Ages'; Rycaut 1680: second sequence, 63.
90. Thomas Smith's purpose was to make the reader thankful for his Christianity; 1678: 'To the reader'.
91. Digby 1968.
92. Rubiés 2007: 20.
93. [Biddulph] 1609: 'To the reader'; MacLean 2004: 53–4. It has also been argued that 'Lavender' was the publisher rather than the author; Taylor 2006: 222, 241.
94. Carey 2009: 20, 22–3; Baker 2007: 135.
95. Coryate 1616: his readers may ask whether this is a brave man or a mad one, but their attention is likely to be caught.
96. Lithgow 1632: frontispiece, 417, 455.
97. Chard & Langdon 1996: 24; Chard 1996: 138. Chard is writing here about how Grand Tourists began to see themselves self-consciously as 'tourists': the touristic attitude, she suggests, keeps the possibility of the destabilisation of the traveller's identity as a threat which lurks in the background, 'invest[ing] the foreign with a gratifying drama and excitement'. I think that both Coryate and Lithgow are self-conscious travellers, using their accounts of their experiences to reinvent themselves as characters for their readers and deliberately dramatising their adventures.
98. Adams 1980. See Bosworth on Lithgow (2006: 127–30) and MacLean on Biddulph (2004: 51ff, 114).
99. Yerasimos 1991: 2.
100. Hemmerdinger Iliadou 1967: 537.
101. BL MS Add. 22912: between 187v and 245v.
102. I am very grateful to my brothers, Matthew Robertson and Professor Stephen Robertson, for their help with this.
103. Covel 1998.
104. BL MS Add. 22912: 237r.
105. Ibid.: 190v.
106. BL MS Add. 22910: 81r–v.
107. Peile 1910: 572; Cambridge University Archives, *Books of Subscriptions for Degrees*, vol. 2.
108. BL MS Add. 22910: 122.

Notes to Pages 18-23

109. We hear nothing, either, about whether he ever traded in cloth on his own account, as he had permission to do; Pearson 1883: 52.
110. BL MS Add. 22912: 175r.
111. Royal Society MS 73: 59r.
112. Smith 1678: 160.
113. BL MS Add. 22911: 217, 236, 238.
114. BL MS Add. 22910: 57–9.
115. Rycaut 1680: second sequence, 311.
116. BL MS Add. 22910: 192–5.
117. Rycaut 1680: second sequence, 188–94, 335.
118. BL MS Add. 22912: 240v.
119. Ibid.: 246v–247r.
120. Leedham-Green (online); Covel 1998. There are also some very interesting comments on Covel in Games 2008: 235–7. I am indebted to Dr Leedham-Green for drawing my attention to several sources relevant to Covel. See also BL MSS Add. 5821, 19166.
121. E.g. BL MS Add. 22912: 177r, 177v, 181r, 181v, 182v. In one instance (191v) he uses the East Anglian dialect word 'jibby-horse', a horse decorated for a ceremony.
122. BL MS Add. 22911: 217; HMC 1901: 334–5.
123. Covel 1722: *2v.
124. Runciman 1968: 310–16; Pinnington 2003: 109, 163–4.
125. Hasluck 1910–11: 103–31.
126. Doran & Durston 1991: 31.
127. BL MS Add. 22912: 268v.
128. Ibid.: 220r.
129. BL MS Add. 22910: 164r.
130. Ibid.: 164v; BL MS Add. 22912: 237r; Games 2008: 236.
131. BL MS Add. 22912: 16v.
132. BL MS Add. 22910: 165r.
133. BL MS Add. 22912: 187v.
134. Christ's College, Cambridge, archives, box 21, item 28.
135. BL MS Add. 70485.
136. Mayor 1911: 147.
137. BL MS Harley 7021: 354–418.
138. HMC 1893: 35.
139. BL MS Add. 22914: 33r.
140. Green 2009: 257. By this time it was probably a less inflammatory question than it had been in Erasmus's day; Goldhill 2002: 57.
141. BL MS Add. 22912: 180v; BL MS Add. 22910: 81–2.
142. BL MS Add. 22914: 47r.
143. BL MS Add. 22912: 5r–10v.
144. Peile 1910: 559.
145. BL MS Add. 22914: 60v.

146. HMC 1893: 32–6.
147. BL MS Add. 22912: 249v–250r; Cary's death is also recorded in Wheler 1682: 217.
148. BL MS Add. 22914: 2r.
149. BL MS Add. 22912: 74r; BL MS Add. 70485: 8.
150. Wheler 1682: 217.
151. BL MS Add. 57495.
152. Covel 1722: 65.
153. BL MS Add. 22912: 58r, 270r; BL MS Add. 22914: 36r.
154. BL MS Harley 3778: 98–130; BL MS 22911: 142–212. One account suggests that he remained quite sprightly into old age, looking only 60 when he was into his seventies: Mayor 1911: 147.
155. BL MS Add. 70485; [Covel] 1724.
156. Belon 1554: 33v–43v; Rycaut 1679: 215–29. The year before Rycaut's book came out, the former archbishop of Samos, Georgirenes, now living in London, published an account of Mount Athos. Smith also mentions the mountain, but refers readers to Georgirenes for further information; Georgirenes 1678: 86–111; Smith 1680: 97–8.
157. BL MS Add. 22914: 64r.
158. BL MS Add. 22912: 234v.
159. Covel 1722: xxii, 136.
160. HMC 1893: 32–6.
161. BL MS Add. 22912: 242r.
162. Ibid.: 35r.
163. Ibid.: 188r.
164. BL MS Add. 22914: 30r; Pliny, *Natural History*: 31.6.
165. BL MS Add. 22912: 217r.
166. Ibid.: 160r.
167. Leedham-Green (online).
168. BL MS Add. 22912: 18r.
169. Robson 1628: 5.
170. Covel 1722: 213.
171. [Milles] 1721: 18–19.
172. Covel 1722: 284, 286.
173. Ibid.: 346.
174. Ibid.: lix.
175. BL MS Add. 22912: 163v.
176. Covel 1722: 344.
177. BL MS Add. 22912: 217v.
178. Rycaut 1679: 216; BL MS Add. 22910: 199–200.
179. BL MS Add. 22910: 107–8, 180–1, 387–8; BL MS Add. 22911: 217, 236, 238.
180. E.g. BL MS Add. 22912: 240r, where the ambassador's hand shakes so much in an audience with the Grand Vizier that he keeps spilling his coffee.

181. North 1890: 52, 137.
182. BL MS Add. 22910: 57–8.
183. Ibid.: 122, 192–5.
184. Bray 2003: 140–5; Wilson 1995: 70–83.
185. HMC 1913: 253.
186. North 1890: 79.
187. HMC 1922: 128–9.
188. Covel 1722: 223–4.
189. Thomas 2009: 190–6, 200–7.
190. BL MS Add. 22914: 35v, 55v, 60v–62r.
191. Ibid.: 48r.
192. BL MS Add. 22912: 219r–v.
193. Ibid.: 218v.
194. Ibid.: 266v.
195. BL MS Add. 22910: 164v.
196. Lithgow 1632: 177; Sandys 1615: 91; Gainsford 1618: 30; Veryard 1701: 330. See Maryon 1956: 70–2.
197. [Biddulph] 1609: 25; Sandys 1615: 37. This story goes back to Gilles 2008: 99.
198. HMC 1922: 163.
199. BL MS Add. 22912: 188v–189r.
200. Ibid.: 190v.
201. BL MS Add. 22914: 37v.
202. BL MS Add. 22913: 4v; Randolph 1687: 60–4. The *Plymouth* is mentioned several times by Pepys, but not this incident. On the other hand, a very similar story is told by Evelyn (1959: 460): Charles II presented the Royal Society with the 'horne of a fish' which had holed a ship in the 'India Sea' but prevented it from foundering by sticking in the hole until the ship reached home. Perhaps this is the origin of Covel's and Randolph's accounts.
203. BL MS Add. 22912: 220r.
204. Mansel 2006: 437. The merchant Lewes Roberts in 1638 referred to the city as 'the *Metropolis* of *Greece*'; 1638: 191.
205. Mazower 2001; Vacalopoulos 1976; Woodhouse 1998; Mackenzie 1992; Sugar 1977; Stavrianos 2000.
206. Randolph 1687: 47.
207. Mazower 2001: 17, 51; Livanios 2008: 243.
208. Woodhouse 1998: 102–3.
209. Mazower 2001: 39.
210. Vacalopoulos 1976: 16, 100.
211. Woodhouse 1998: 108; Mazower 2001: 59; Vitkus 1999: 211–12. On the other hand, much of our seventeenth-century evidence for this comes from rabidly anti-Catholic sources, into whose agenda this notion fitted neatly.
212. Covel 1722: 155.
213. BL MS Add. 22912: 201v.

214. HMC 1913: 143, 360, 400; North 1890: 135–6.
215. Covel 1722: 374.
216. Vacalopoulos 1976: 94–6; Braudel 1992: 571; Goffman 1990: 85–7.
217. Mazower 2004: 45, 49, 69; Stavrianos 2000: 90.
218. Glaser 2007.
219. Purchas 1626: 'To the reader'.
220. Games 2008: 50.
221. Grassby 1994: 61–5
222. Pearson 1883: 52; Runciman 1968: 293.
223. Dowling & Fletcher 1915: especially 67–9.
224. Covel 1722: i.
225. Raven 2007.
226. [Covel] 1724; Finch 1986.
227. Green 2009: 57, 64; Coward 2003: 68; Thomas 2009: 18; Mack 2002: 8.
228. Elliott 1963: 175–6. The fact that admonishment was needed suggests, as one would expect, that it was not always easy to make the boys talk Latin among themselves.
229. Oldenburg 1965–86.
230. Hale 1817: 119.
231. Adams 2009: 24ff; Green 2009: 127, 191.
232. Malloch 1917: 53. Malloch quotes from a notebook of Baines, but does not give a clear reference, and I have been unable to discover whether it is still extant anywhere.
233. Kallendorf 2007: II.114–27, V.376; Swann 2001: 14, 153–4; Mack 2002: 44–5.
234. Neuhusius 1658; Dadré 1603.
235. Gailhard 1678: second sequence, 192.
236. Wheler 1682: 329.
237. Baldwin 1944: vol. 2, 419.
238. Clarke 1959: 13–14, 40.
239. Holt 1973: 3, 13.
240. Cook 1917: 14–17.
241. Baldwin 1944: vol. 1, 365.
242. Evelyn 1959: 423.
243. Brinsley 1612: 'To the reader'; Gailhard 1678: 36.
244. Kallendorf 2007: IV.576.
245. Baldwin 1944: vol. 1, 93, 119–22, 129–30, 417, 423, vol. 2, 382; Mack 2002: 14; Watson 1968: 370–3.
246. Elliott 1963: 175.
247. Watson 1968: 487–98, 511–21.
248. Elliott 1963: 175.
249. Peacham 1962: 62.
250. Pepys 1970: 18.
251. Baldwin 1944: vol. 1, 384; Clarke 1959: 36–7; Browne 1852: 426.

252. Holt 1973: 29.
253. Locke 1968: §189.
254. Milton 1973: 51–8.
255. Hobbes 1679: 54.
256. Watson 1971.
257. Green 2009: 66–7.
258. Tinniswood 2007: 302.
259. Games 2008: 17, 21.
260. Twigg 1990: 207.
261. Feingold 1997: 213–14, 391.
262. Ibid.: 227.
263. Lewis 2010.
264. Feingold 1997: 242.
265. Morgan 2004: 512, 514.
266. Momigliano 1950: 292.
267. Costello 1958: 56.
268. Ibid.: 147.
269. Burrow 1997: 81.
270. Twigg 1990: 133–4.
271. BL MS Add. 27606.
272. Tinniswood 2007: 49.
273. Wheler 1911: 13.
274. Costello 1958: 149.
275. Andrich 1892; Stoye 1989: 157–8.
276. Grafton 1992: 222–6; Toomer 1996: 128–9; Hebrew books had been printed at Leiden since Christopher Plantin had moved there from Antwerp in the late sixteenth century.
277. Wheler 1911: 22.
278. Prest 1967: 38–9.
279. BL MS Add. 22912: 5v–8r.
280. BL MS Add. 57495.
281. Stoye 1989: 158–9.
282. Oldenburg 1965–86: vol. 6, 41.
283. Ibid.: vol. 12, 65, 122.
284. Kishlansky 1997: 14.
285. Swann 2001: 55–6, 62, 83–4.
286. Iliffe 1999: 49; Rubiés 2002: 257; Rubiés 1996: 139; Oldenburg 1965–86. Edward Browne was one of those who sent information back.
287. Gillespie 2007: 244; Browne 1852: 442.
288. Barbour 2007: 158–61.
289. Feingold 1997: 229.
290. Quinton 1980: 10, 83–4; Locke 1968: §189.
291. Blount 1636: 4.
292. North 1890: 55.

293. Elsner & Rubiés 1999: 17.
294. TNA, SP 105/145: 301–4. The Smyrna library had been destroyed by fire in 1688, so must have been built up again over 20 years; Anderson 1989: 16.
295. BL MS Add. 22910: 44; BL MS Harley 6943: 1–2.
296. Baker 2007: 129–45.
297. BL MS Add. 22914: 27r.
298. Dalrymple 2006: 13.

Chapter 1   The Logistics of Travel

1. BL MS Add. 22912: 253r.
2. Gallo 2009: 6.
3. BL MS Add. 22910: 80.
4. BL MS Add. 22912: 41r.
5. Covel 1722: i.
6. [Biddulph] 1609: 'To the reader'.
7. The various routes are described in more detail in Yerasimos 1991: 26–58.
8. BL MS Add. 22912: 5r, 13r.
9. Ibid.: 35r–v.
10. Ibid.: 242r.
11. Ibid.: 46r–72r.
12. In April 1674, Covel travelled in the *Dogger* to Smyrna, to oversee the ceremony in which Harvey's body was carried on board the *Centurion* for its passage home; BL MS Add. 22912: 153r.
13. BL MS Add. 22910: 57–8.
14. Brotton 1997: 21, 31–3, 160, 171, 174, 183.
15. BL MS Add. 22912: 175v.
16. BL MS Add. 22914: 249r; Wheler 1682: 3.
17. Wheler 1682: 259.
18. Browne 1673: 78.
19. Mansel 2006: 99, 130.
20. Bargrave 1999: 132; Courthop 1907: 118; Mundy 1907: 52–3; Rycaut 1675: 296; Veryard 1701: 340.
21. BL MS Add. 22912: 187v.
22. Ibid.: 240v.
23. Wheler 1682: 302.
24. BL MS Add. 22912: 261r.
25. Tavernier 1678: 32–5.
26. Covel 1722: 101.
27. Wheler 1682: 224.
28. Ibid.: 74.
29. Dankoff & Kim 2010: 228n.

30. BL MS Add. 22912: 74r.
31. BL MS Add. 70485: 8.
32. BL MS Add. 22912: 180r.
33. Wheler 1682: 79, 256.
34. BL MS Add. 22912: 180v, 242v; BL MS Add. 22914: 33r. The contemporary Ottoman traveller Evliya Çelebi was presented with a spyglass and a watch when he visited Split, and he used a spyglass to look at inscriptions high up in the ruined city of Ahlat; Dankoff & Kim 2010: 135, 166.
35. Anderson 1989: 257; Browne 1673: 73; Blount 1636: 14–15.
36. BL MS Add. 22912: 37r.
37. Rycaut 1680: second sequence, 180–2.
38. BL MS Add. 22912: 234v; BL MS Add. 22914: 40r; Burbury 1671: 178; Games 2008: 72.
39. BL MS Add. 22912: 260r, 261v.
40. Wheler 1682: 429.
41. Brentjes 2010: VIII. 21.
42. BL MS Add. 22912: 247r; BL MS Add. 22910: 81–2; Wheler 1682: 202.
43. Many of these he had probably brought out with him, as there was no printing in Constantinople at this date.
44. HMC 1913: 225; HMC 1922: 65, 80–1, 177; Abbott 1920: 351.
45. Rycaut 1679: 75.
46. BL MS Add. 22910: 115.
47. Wheler 1682: 310.
48. Ibid.: 239.
49. BL MS Add. 22912: 177r; BL MS Add. 22914: 7r.
50. BL MS Add. 22914: 44v. See Chapter 4 for Covel at Mount Athos.
51. Wheler 1682: 226.
52. BL MS Add. 22912: 14r–v, 22r.
53. Ibid.: 72v.
54. BL MS Add. 22914: 8v.
55. Ibid.: 59v, 62v–63r.
56. Ibid.: 39v–40v.
57. Mansel 2006: 173.
58. Longleat House, Coventry Papers, box 69.
59. Purchas 1905–7: vol. 10, 435; Browne 1673: 59.
60. The term 'aga' is used to refer to senior officials.
61. BL MS Add. 22912: 75r, 218r, 219v.
62. Evelyn recorded in his diary that the first person he had seen drinking coffee was the Greek Nathaniel Conopius, a fellow-student at Balliol College, Oxford; 1959: 11.
63. Mansel 2006: 170.
64. HMC 1922: 144–5.
65. BL MS Add. 22914: 8r.
66. BL MS Add. 22912: 262v.

67. Rycaut 1675: 293–4; HMC 1922: 112.
68. BL MS Add. 22914: 8r, 53v.
69. BL MS Add. 22912: 240r.
70. Wheler 1682: 350.
71. Ibid.: 301.
72. BL MS Add. 22914: 35v.
73. BL MS Sloane 3945: 13v; Rycaut 1680: second sequence, 129–30.
74. Wheler 1682: 307, 440.
75. BL MS Add. 22910: 130.
76. Smith 1678: 97–8.
77. Sainsbury 1859: 284.
78. Covel 1722: 247.
79. BL MS Add. 22912: 112v; Wheler 1682: 204.
80. BL MS Add. 22912: 175v. 'Spasso' in Italian means 'walk'.
81. Bargrave 1999: 99–100.
82. Rycaut 1680: second sequence, 131.
83. Wansbrough 1996: 77–8; Dankoff & Kim 2010: 167.
84. Rycaut 1675: 48, 55.
85. BL MS Harley 7021; Games 2008: 231.
86. Toomer 1996: 112.
87. Clark 1894: 17.
88. BL MSS Add. 22910, 22911.
89. E.g. BL MS Add. 22914: 47r; Green 2009: 257.
90. Browne 1852: 426–7.
91. Spon & Wheler 1724: vol. 1, 91–2.
92. Lewis 2004: 24–5.
93. Georgirenes 1678: 28.
94. Wheler 1682: 202.
95. TNA, SP 105/102: 5r.
96. Rycaut 1675: 163. A late seventeenth-century scheme to train Greeks in Oxford did not last long; Wood 1925: 540. The French minister Colbert (1619–83) sent 12 young Frenchmen to the Capuchins in Smyrna to learn Turkish; Abbott 1920: 50.
97. Rycaut 1675: 10; Longleat House, Coventry Papers, box 69, undated letter (September 1677?) to John Finch.
98. BL MS Add. 22912: 236v–237r.
99. North 1890: 131. The precarious position of dragomans was noted by one ambassador, according to whom the yellow shoes of their office made them 'either [...] respected or subject to the scorne of the boyes in the street'; HMC 1913: 418.
100. HMC 1913: 346.
101. Longleat House, Coventry Papers, box 69, 24 February/6 March 1674/5.
102. HMC 1922: 154.
103. BL MS Add. 22912: 190v.

104. Covel 1722: 132.
105. Bent 1893: 83–4.
106. Mazower 2004: 114.
107. Wheler 1682: 201. This Jew was a dragoman named Abram Finch; perhaps he came from the same family as Dallam's guide?
108. BL MS Add. 22912: 219r.
109. HMC 1913: 110, 260.
110. Peile 1910: 559.
111. HMC 1893: 32–6; Mansel 2006: 124.
112. BL MS Add. 22912: 212r, 249v–250r.
113. Merritt 1949: 214.
114. Covel 1722: iv, xi.
115. This was in the context of the controversy between the Catholic Arnauld and the Huguenot Claude; Pinnington 2003: 113.
116. Randolph 1687: 93. According to the *OED* the word 'doctoress' was in use from the late sixteenth century. Evelyn uses it in his letter to Pepys of 12 August 1689; Evelyn 1850–2: 296.
117. Wheler 1682: 247; Teonge 1927: 97–8. Ambassador Edward Barton's tomb could be seen on Chalcis, and the tomb of Edward Wych, brother of ambassador Peter Wych, on Chios; BL MS Add. 22912: 243r–v, 255r.
118. BL MS Add. 22912: 152v–153r.
119. BL MS Add. 22910: 57–8.
120. Essex Record Office D/DHf025.
121. Sanderson 1931: 265, 274–5; Forde 1616; MacLean 2004: 224.
122. HMC 1913: 252–3. This is a very curious story: not only does bacon seem an unlikely cargo, but the risks of being caught removing a body without permission must have been significant.
123. HMC 1922: 162. These examples are not as extreme as the case of the seventeenth-century Italian traveller Pietro della Valle, who carried the embalmed corpse of his wife with him on his travels for some five years: della Valle 1989: xv.
124. Games 2008: 192.
125. Bargrave 1999: 57, 120. In this case the swimming took place in the Atlantic en route to the Levant, and the swimmer was one of Bendish's sons.
126. Burbury 1671: 121; Bargrave 1999: 78.
127. Ravelhofer 2006: 243–6.
128. Games 2008: 325–6.
129. BL MS Add. 22914: 2r; BL MS Add. 22912: 163v, 217v.
130. BL MS Add. 22912: 195v–218r; Covel 1722: 313. The parade of the guilds of merchants and craftsmen is also described by the Ottoman Evliya Çelebi; Dankoff & Kim 2010: 24–30.
131. HMC 1913: 98–9, 459, 461–4, 473, 518.
132. Bargrave 1999: 53.
133. Essex Record Office D/DHf025.

134. The word 'travel' was often spelt 'travail'.
135. Webb 1857: 190–3. Webb describes the whole monument in detail: the section I have quoted is only a small part of the inscription, which also includes various verses, one commemorating Coningsby's 'double pilgrimadge' – in this case the journey of his life and his journeys into foreign parts. It was erected by his half-sister. Coningsby had been a mercenary with the Hungarian army as well as a traveller for pleasure.

Chapter 2   Scholars and Texts

1. Hammond 1998: 143, 148; Grafton 1988: 769; Green 2009: 25, 50.
2. Cleland 1607: 'To the reader'.
3. BL MS Add. 22912: 74r.
4. Royal Society MS 73: 18r–56r.
5. 'Corn now grows where Troy used to be': Ovid, *Heroides*: 1.53. Other travellers who quote this line are [Biddulph] (1609: 14), Roberts (1638: 120) and Coryate (Purchas 1905–7: vol. 10, 408).
6. BL MS Add. 22912: 22v.
7. BL MS Add. 22914: 30v.
8. Oglander 1936: 11. The line was also used of the monastery of Alcester by William Dugdale, and of Malmesbury Abbey by Aubrey; Dugdale 1656: 574; Jackson 1862: 255.
9. Yerasimos 1991: 2.
10. Burrow 1997: 85; *Aeneid*: 1.279.
11. Hardie 1993: 99. Just as the epic poets worried about how the office of emperor might be passed on, so English writers from the 1640s onwards were likely to have been conscious of similar problems, in relation first to Cromwell and subsequently to Charles II and James II.
12. [Baddeley] 1669: 140; Busbecq 1694: 24; Busbecq 1595: 22. The word 'Iliad' could of course be used without any knowledge of the *Iliad*.
13. 'Travellers change their environment, not their nature'; Horace, *Epistles*: 1.11.27.
14. Lithgow 1632: title page.
15. *Aeneid*: 3.104–6. 'Great Jupiter's island of Crete, site of Mount Ida and the cradle of our race, lies in the middle of the sea. The people live in a hundred great cities in that most fertile place.'
16. *Heroides*: 2.113; Rycaut 1675: 369.
17. *Bellum civile*: 7.712–13; Browne 1673: 53–5.
18. E.g. *Iliad*: 15.193; Browne 1673: 54.
19. BL MS Add. 22914: 62v–63r.
20. *Aeneid*: 2.79; BL MS Add. 22912: 37r.

21. Euripides, *Iphigenia in Tauris*: 1205; BL MS Add. 22912: 37r. It is not entirely clear whether the idea was attributed to Euripides by the captain, or whether this is Covel's gloss.
22. *Aeneid*: 2.65–6.
23. 'Wretch that I am! What mountains of water turn over and over; you think they'll touch the sky at any minute'; Ovid, *Tristia*: 1.2.20–1; [Biddulph] 1609: preface.
24. *Aeneid*: 2.3; [Biddulph] 1609: 'To the reader'.
25. That he was not without a sense of humour is shown by his story of the mariner who prayed to God in a storm, saying that he had never prayed before and would never do so again if God would save him just this once; [Biddulph] 1609: 8.
26. 'In spite of his weakness he was my companion in undergoing all the dangers of sea and sky, beyond the strength and lot of old age'; *Aeneid*: 6.112–14; HMC 1922: 128–9.
27. *Aeneid*: 1.278–9, 6.637ff; HMC 1922: 111–12.
28. Gillespie 2007: 249.
29. Neale 1643: title page; Petronius, no. 6 in the Loeb edition.
30. Horace, *Odes*: 1.14; Rycaut 1675: 1.
31. Sandys 1615. Sandys was described in his time as 'a Learned Argus, seeing with the Eyes of many Authors'; Haynes 1986: 61.
32. He had read some Hesiod at school, for example, but at Oxford he did not make much progress in the language; Wheler 1911: 5, 13.
33. *Odyssey*: 7.115–20; Wheler 1682: 34.
34. Wheler 1682: 35–6, 241.
35. Ibid.: 366. Although Aristophanes does not appear in this list, Wheler certainly knew of him; ibid.: 342.
36. Ibid.: 369, 453.
37. See e.g. Leigh 1671 and Cleland 1607. The special relationship of Rycaut and Tacitus is discussed below.
38. Belon 1554; Gilles 1562.
39. Wheler 1682: 409.
40. Babin 1674. For Guillet, see Chapter 2.
41. Spon & Wheler 1724: vol. 2, 42. Jean Giraud was French consul in Athens from 1658 and English consul from some six years later, after a dispute which deprived him of his French post; Collignon 1913: 8–11. We do not know whether the Pausanias was the Greek text or a Latin translation, both of which were available at this time: the first French translation appeared in 1731, the first English one not until the late eighteenth century; Pretzler 2007: 118; Stailos 2007: 80; Guilmet 2007: 88, 120.
42. Momigliano 1950: 292–3.
43. Leigh 1671: A4v–A5r; Habicht 1998: 163; Pretzler 2007: 144. Pausanias himself writes that many statues had been looted, and such sites as Megalopolis in Arcadia reduced to ruins; *Description of Greece*: 8.33.

44. Grafton 1988: 787. Although Pliny was beginning to be discredited by the rise of inductive science, the change was neither fast nor evenly paced; Doody 2010: 31, 36–7.
45. BL MS Add. 22914: 30r; Veryard 1701: 340; Pliny, *Natural History*: 31.16.19.
46. Wheler 1682: 304.
47. Ibid.: 452; Dioscorides, *De material medica*: 1.122.
48. Wheler 1682: 227; Livy, *Ab urbe condita*: 38.15.
49. Smith 1678: 211; Strabo, *Geography*: 13.1.68. Smith's description fits with Strabo's.
50. Rycaut 1679: *passim*.
51. Lithgow 1632: 62; Strabo, *Geography*: 10.2.14; perhaps we should not lay all the blame on out-of-date information, as the identity of Homer's Ithaca is still a matter of dispute today.
52. Veryard 1701: 336; Cicero, *De natura deorum*: 2.193.
53. Veryard 1701: 351, 353, 355.
54. BL MS Add. 22914: 49r–v; Pliny, *Natural History*: 36.19.
55. Blount 1636: 18–20; Caesar, *De bello civili*: 3.84ff.
56. Veryard 1701: 356; Plutarch, *Life of Agesilaus*: 2.2.
57. Wheler 1682: 271.
58. Ibid.: 428; Pausanias, *Description*: 1.38.6. 'pretends' does not necessarily have the modern connotation of deliberately lying, but may imply some ambivalence on Wheler's part.
59. Wheler 1682: 343.
60. BL MS Add. 22912: 46r–72r; Strabo, *Geography*: 14.1.4, 21; Pliny, *Natural History*: 5.31; Pausanias, *Description*: 7.2.4, 7.3.2; Herodotus, *Histories*: 2.10, 5.100; Xenophon, *Hellenica*: 1.1; Homer, *Odyssey*: 5.425, 13.242.
61. They are more detailed than that in Wheler 1682: 253.
62. BL MS Add. 22912: 46v, 68v.
63. BL MS Add. 22914: 13v; Strabo, *Geography*: 12.4.7.
64. BL MS Add. 22914: 30r.
65. Wheler 1682: e.g. 246, 258, 265, 279, 281, 350. Wheler also made use of Francis Vernon's measurements; 1682: 346, 365, 439, 443.
66. There are many derogatory remarks about Guillet, whom modern scholars have recognised as extremely unreliable; see for example 1682: 351, where Wheler says that Guillet's identification of the Temple of Vulcan in Athens is nothing more than 'the product of his fancy'. Spon had read Guillet's book on the voyage between Italy and Greece, passing it on to Vernon and Eastcourt, who were to leave it for him in Athens. Once Spon arrived in Athens, and when he read Vernon's criticism of Guillet, his own view changed; Spon & Wheler 1724: vol. 2, 58–9.
67. Wheler 1682: 266; Strabo, *Geography*: 14.1.1.
68. Wheler 1682: 472.
69. Ibid.: 251.
70. Ibid.: 466–9; Strabo, *Geography*: 9.2.20; Pausanias, *Description*: 9.37.5.

71. Elsner 1992: 22.
72. Pretzler 2007: 140.
73. Wheler 1682: 312–13; Pausanias, *Description*: 1.22.6.
74. Wheler 1682: 295.
75. Ibid.: 359; Pausanias, *Description*: 1.22.6.
76. Wheler 1682: 329; Pausanias, *Description*: 9.39.4.
77. Wheler 1682: 364; Pausanias, *Description*: 1.26.6.
78. Pausanias 1971: vol. 1, 75n; Jenkins 2006: 122.
79. Wheler 1682: 387.
80. Grafton 1992: 58.
81. *Acta eruditorum*, March 1684: 116. Rycaut is praised for following Tacitus in the scale and variety of his subject matter, the concision of his style, and his perspicuity, as well as being compared to the Roman writer in terms of the violence of the times they described. The references in Rycaut's *Greek and Armenian Churches* tend to follow much more the 'topographical' or guide book pattern than the more moralising pattern found in *The Ottoman Empire*.
82. Anderson 1989: 238, 262–3.
83. Rycaut 1675: 3; Tacitus, *Annals*: 3.18.
84. North 1890: 156–7.
85. Rycaut 1675: 46; Tacitus, *Germania*: 13.
86. Rycaut 1675: 136; Tacitus, *Histories*: 1.66.
87. Rycaut 1675: 84; Tacitus, *Histories*: 2.20, *Annals*: 13.19, 30.
88. Rycaut 1675: 15; Tacitus, *Annals*: 3.65.
89. Rycaut 1675: 88; Tacitus, *Annals*: 6.32.
90. This slippage is reminiscent of the different configurations in the ways in which Englishmen saw themselves in relation to Trojans, Greeks (ancient and modern), Romans and Ottomans, which will be explored in Chapters 4 and 5. Besides Tacitus, another author cited by Rycaut is Quintus Curtius Rufus (a rhetorician and historian of the first to the second centuries CE), according to whom 'barbarians' believed that only men of outstanding physical attributes could achieve great deeds; Rycaut 1675: 46; Q. Curtius Rufus, *History of Alexander*: 6.5.29. The question of who were the barbarians in the eyes of Rycaut and his contemporaries is an interesting one.
91. Rycaut 1675: 148; Tacitus, *Agricola*: 21.
92. Rycaut 1679: preface.
93. Rycaut 1675: 88; Tacitus, *Annals*: 4.20.
94. Rycaut 1675: 138; Livy, *Ab urbe condita*: 5.51.5.
95. Knolles 1603: final unnumbered page before index.
96. Rycaut 1679: 52–3, 67. A Roman precedent for the linking of ruins with personal human frailty is found in a letter written to Cicero (an author widely read in grammar schools) by Sulpicius Rufus to console him on the death of his daughter: as the writer sailed from Aegina to Megara, the sight of the 'corpses' ('cadavera') of once-flourishing towns put human death into a different perspective for him; Cicero, *Ad familiares*: 4.5.4.

97. Rycaut 1675: 143.
98. Ibid.: 364; Tacitus, *Annals*: 1.70.
99. Rycaut 1675: 140; Plutarch, *Life of Aratus*: 30.5.
100. Rycaut 1679: 216–17.
101. BL MS Add. 22914: 41v; Herodotus, *Histories*: 7.23.
102. Wheler 1682: 341–2, 422, 453–4, 474; Herodotus, *Histories*: 8.90.
103. Teonge 1927: 99; Veryard 1701: 346.
104. Browne 1673: 45; Finkel 2006: 80, 130.
105. Raby 1983: 18.
106. Baudier 1635: 35.
107. Rycaut 1675: 143.
108. Wheler 1682: 342.
109. Browne 1673: 44; Livy, *Ab urbe condita*: 40.22. The story had been told by Polybius (24.3), but was refuted by Strabo (7.5.1). The first-century CE geographer Pomponius Mela, however, repeated it.
110. Wheler 1682: 343–4, 362, 370–1, 374, 393–4.
111. North 1890: 5.
112. The Roman names for the gods are almost invariably used, rather than the Greek ones.
113. Rycaut 1679: 46.
114. BL MS Add. 22912: 195r. 'Jibby' horse is Suffolk dialect for a horse dressed up for a ceremony. 'Bevis of Southampton' is presumably the fourteenth-century English metrical romance *Bevis of Hampton*.
115. Ibid.: 220v.
116. Anon. 1670: 1.
117. Wheler 1682: 358; Pausanias, *Description*: 1.22.4–5.
118. Wheler 1682: 337–45, 428, 430.
119. Ibid.: 479.
120. Wheler was ordained later.
121. Smith 1678: 206, 274; Rycaut 1679: 30; Wheler 1682: 245, 263, 265; Teonge 1927: 100.
122. Randolph 1687: 56–7; Veryard 1701: 335.
123. E.g. Veryard 1701: 285.
124. Ibid.: 332.
125. Acts 20.17; Rycaut 1679: 54.
126. Wheler 1682: 343, 440.
127. Teonge 1927: 28, 101, 135.
128. Rycaut 1679: 9–11.
129. II Kings 5.9–14; BL MS Add. 22914: 6v.
130. Isaiah 6; BL MS Add. 22914: 56r.
131. Matthew 5.41; BL MS Add. 22914: 47r.
132. BL MS Add. 22912: 220v. Covel is referring to Peter Heylyn of Oxford, 1599–1662.
133. Isaiah 3.18 ('round tires like the moon'); Veryard 1701: 357.

134. Revelations 2.5; Smith 1678: 273–6; Wheler 1682: 441.
135. Teonge 1927.
136. Psalm 104.18; BL MS Add. 22914: 33r.
137. Thomas 2009: 4; Green 2009: 265, 267, 293. For the ambivalence in attitude to pagan art, see Thomas 1995.
138. *Shepheardes Calender*: July, 49. He also made use of aspects of Lucretius (for example his ideas about mutability) which can be harmonised with Christianity; Gillespie 2007: 245–7.
139. Milton, *Hymn on the Morning of Christ's Nativity*: 89.
140. *Paradise Lost* 1–26.
141. Green 2009: 129, 264, 267, 293.
142. Forde 1616.
143. BL MS Add. 22912: 46r–72r.
144. Ibid.: 46v–47r. These reliefs are discussed fully in Chapter 3.
145. This might indicate that an older building had been turned into a Christian one.
146. Rycaut 1679: 30ff.
147. This is in spite of the fact that Covel came from the Cambridge Platonist circle of Henry More and Ralph Cudworth at Christ's. They had moral reservations about Lucretius, for example, on the grounds that his atomism was incompatible with Christian doctrine, as did Thomas Browne. On the other hand, Lucretius's theory was attractive to those who practised the new science, such as Kenelm Digby. Browne 1852: 442; Gillespie 2007: 244.
148. Wheler 1682: 428.
149. Kallendorf 2007: IV.576; Green 2009: 222.
150. Sandys 1615: 284.
151. Spon & Wheler 1724: vol. 1, 194.
152. Green 2009: 257, 350; Bull 2005: 29.
153. Ellison 2002: 18–21.
154. Nicolson 1992.
155. Ayres 1997: xv, 152–3.
156. Green 2009: 307–8.
157. Parry 1995: 34, 259–60.
158. Green 2009: 224.
159. Christian author of the third–fourth century CE.
160. Watson 1908: 373–5. Colet was deeply influenced by Erasmus; Goldhill 2002: 27–8.
161. Green 2009: 307ff.
162. Royal Society MS 73; for example, BL MS Add. 22914: 21v; Wheler 1682: 413, 451; Smith 1678: 266.
163. The Suda, a tenth-century encyclopaedia.
164. E.g. Wheler 1682: 367, 369, 380, 384, 420, 447.
165. BL MS Add. 22912: 180v; BL MS Add. 22910: 181–2. The *Historia Byzantina* was probably that of Michael Ducas, to whom Covel refers by name several times; e.g. BL MS Add. 22912: 92v, 108v, 111v.

166. BL MS Add. 22912: 74r.
167. Ibid.: 232r.
168. BL MS Harley 6943: 89. Covel's library at the end of his life included 21 volumes of *Corpus Byzantinae historiae*; BL MS Add. 70485: 25.
169. Tinniswood 2007: 330.
170. Pearson 1883: 32, 65–6.
171. Games 2008: 113.
172. Anderson 1989: 16.
173. TNA SP 105/145: 301–4. The factory library in Aleppo had over 200 volumes in 1688; TNA SP 105/145: 157–64.
174. Wheler 1682: 199–200.
175. North 1890: 51–2. Elsewhere, without actually saying that they were stolen, Roger North suggests that other papers somehow found their way from North's household to Covel's rooms in Cambridge; North 1890: 137. I have not been able to identify the Turkish dictionary in the list of Covel's library; BL MS Add. 70485.
176. Basire 1831: 115–17.
177. BL MS Harley 6943: 1–2.
178. Smith 1680: 263–70.
179. Leigh 1671: 26.
180. Howell 1650: 17.
181. BL MS Add. 22912: 175v, 183v, 240v, 241v; Wheler 1682: 36–7.
182. Oldenburg 1965–86: vol. 7, 141; Rycaut 1679: '70' (mispaginated section between 80 and 81).
183. Augustinos 1994: 69.
184. Bodleian Library MS Smith 93: 137; BL MS Add. 22914: 41v.
185. Wheler 1682: 422.
186. Published Lyon, 1562.
187. Gilles 2008: xiii–xxii.
188. Purchas 1905–7: vol. 4, 481.
189. BL MS Add. 22912: 175v.
190. Ibid.: 220v; Rycaut 1679: 41.
191. Augustinos 1994: 95.
192. 'With the arrogance of a geographer, thinks he can see and measure the entire world without leaving his office'. Babin 1674: preface.
193. Mossière 1993: 217; Gallo 2009: 9.
194. Wheler 1682: 398, 458.
195. Collignon 1913: 5, 15–16, 18, 25–6.
196. Paris, 1675.
197. Spencer 1974: 131; see also Constantine 1989: 3–4.
198. Wheler 1682: e.g. 340, 346, 350, 363.
199. Royal Society MS 73: 25r–26r; Wheler 1682: 337, 447.
200. Wheler 1682: 341, 405; Selden 1628.
201. Vernon 1676: 579.

202. Wheeler 1901: 221–30. The so-called 'theatre of Bacchus' was in fact the Odeon of Herodes Atticus; Walker 2013: 40.
203. Strachan 1989: 63. Neither Hakluyt nor Purchas appears in the list of the Aleppo or Smyrna libraries.
204. BL MS Add. 70485.
205. Wheler 1682: 177.
206. BL MS Add. 22912: 74v.
207. Wheler 1682: 195.
208. BL MS Add. 22912: 180v, 246v.
209. North 1890: 156–7. The words are Roger North's. Mary Wortley Montagu was another critic of Rycaut's; Montagu 1965: 318.
210. Browne 1852: 466–7.
211. Browne 1928: 145.
212. He did own the poems of Donne and Herbert; BL MS Add. 70485.
213. Prologue to *The Miller's Tale*: 'An housbond shal nat been inquisitif / Of goddes privitee'.
214. Roberts 1638: A4v.

Chapter 3   Antiquities, Proto-Archaeologists and Collectors

1. Howarth 1985: 88–9; Roe 1740: 583.
2. Brotton 2006; Scott 2003.
3. Evelyn 1959: 562.
4. Peacham 1962: 119–20.
5. Hunter 1995: 47, 68, 132–3.
6. Oldenburg 1965–86.
7. Ibid.: vol. 12, 65.
8. By 'coppy' he probably meant 'drawing'.
9. Oldenburg 1965–86: vol. 3, 343–4.
10. Ibid.: vol. 9, 117; Pliny, *Natural History*: 35.13.
11. Parry 1995: 3, 30, 277.
12. Smith 1678: 206–7.
13. 'Every stone has its name'; Lucan, *Bellum civile*: 9.973; Blount 1636: 29.
14. Byron, *Childe Harold*: canto 4, stanza 80. Byron was writing about Rome.
15. Veryard 1701: 333–5, 338.
16. Wheler 1682: 427.
17. Randolph 1687: 93. North, according to his biographer, observed the ruins of ancient structures everywhere in Constantinople.
18. Smith 1678: 236, 245, 274.
19. BL MS Add. 22914: 11r.

Notes to Pages 107–111

20. For example, Jeremiah 9.11, where God threatens to 'make Jerusalem heaps'.
21. Cotton 1660: 9. The vocabulary of 'confusion', 'heaps' and 'ruins' is also found in Thomas Burnet's work on science and religion; Nicolson 1959: 196–7.
22. Aston 1973: 231; Parry 1995: 276; Walsham 2011: 273ff.
23. Lithgow 1632: 500. The person whom Lithgow held responsible for wreaking destruction on Scottish churches was the Protestant reformer John Knox: Lithgow, though a staunch Protestant, was anti-Puritan as well as rabidly anti-Catholic.
24. BL MS Harley 7021: 361r, 373v; Rycaut 1679: 77.
25. Spon & Wheler 1724: vol. 1, 193; Cicero, *Ad familiares*: 4.5.4.
26. Lyne 2001: 90.
27. Sandys 1615: preface.
28. BL MS Add. 22914: 9v–10r.
29. Robson 1628: 10.
30. Sandys 1615: 132.
31. 'Death comes even to stones and names'; Ausonius, *Epitaphia*: 31.10, echoing Juvenal's line 'data sunt ipsis quoque fata sepulcris' ('even tombs have their allotted fate') in *Satires*: 10.146; Colton 1973: 44.
32. Lucan, *Bellum civile*: 9.969.
33. Purchas 1905–7: vol. 10, 408; Rycaut 1679: 67.
34. Veryard 1701: 338.
35. Wheler 1682: 57.
36. Smith 1678: 245–6.
37. North 1890: 36.
38. Wheler 1682: 352.
39. Stuart & Revett 1762: vol. 1, 50–1.
40. Mackenzie 1992: 50; Augustinos 1994: 50; Wheeler 1901.
41. Teonge 1927: 100.
42. Sherley 1936: 16.
43. 'Corn grows now where Troy used to stand'.
44. Roberts 1638: 120.
45. Sandys 1615: 19–23. Both Biddulph and Lithgow thought they were looking at Homeric Troy; Wheler (but not Spon) followed Sandys; Cook 1973: 16–17, 19; Wheler 1682: 67–8. There are scholars today who doubt whether Homer's city has been – or can be – correctly identified.
46. Lithgow 1632: 122.
47. Wheler 1682: 67–71.
48. Veryard 1701: 338.
49. Janowitz 1990: 3.
50. Krautheimer 2000: 199–202.
51. Du Bellay 1994. Janowitz suggests that Spenser was in one sense repairing the ruins of Rome by recording them in eternal poetry, creating a kind of succession of empires from architecture to poetry; Janowitz 1990: 21.

52. That the lasting qualities of both stones and texts are dependent on the responses of viewers and readers is a post-modern understanding; Fowler 2000: 196, 201–2, 209.
53. Ovid, *Metamorphoses*: 871–9; Horace, *Odes*: 3.30.
54. Bacon 1605: 44.
55. Herodotus, *Histories*: 1.86.6.
56. Wheler 1682: A1v.
57. Smith 1678: 273–6. Veryard also described the ruins of Cnidos as 'Emblems of the Instability of all worldly Grandeur'; Veryard 1701: 336, 340. On the Peloponnese, where according to Lewes Roberts 'the injurie of time hath eaten out and consumed' the antiquities, Lithgow too observed monuments defaced by 'the barbarousness of *Turkes* and Time'; Roberts 1638: 188; Lithgow 1632: 72.
58. Wheler 1682: 67; BL MS Add. 22914: 5v, 51v.
59. Smith 1678: 206, 223.
60. Ray 1693: vol. 2, 21–2.
61. Janowitz 1990: 5.
62. BL MS Add. 22912: 251r.
63. BL MS Harley 7021: 369r.
64. HMC 1913: 269–70.
65. Belon refers to the rugged and uneven ground: 1554: 41v.
66. Rycaut 1679: 217–18.
67. BL MS Add. 22912: 342r; BL MS Add. 22914: 45v–46r.
68. Smith 1680: 97–8; Georgirenes 1678: 86–111.
69. Rycaut 1679: 56–7, 77–8.
70. *Iliad*: 3.146–244; Deuteronomy 34.1; Matthew 4.8.
71. Clark 1956: 23; Nicolson 1959: 49–50. Pausanias noted that much of the Peloponnese could be seen from a mountaintop in Arcadia, and Strabo enjoyed the view from Acrocorinth, but these are unusual observations for ancient writers: Pausanias, *Description*: 8.38.7; Strabo, *Geography*: 8.6.21.
72. Referred to in Langdon 1989: 17. Claude's landscapes tend to be painted from a fairly high viewpoint: Barrell 1972: 7–8.
73. Coryate 1611: 99. MacLean, writing about Dallam, links the idea of looking at a prospect from the top of a hill with the English notion of the right to roam: 2007: 233.
74. *OED*.
75. Mitsi 2008: 56; Clark 1956: 17ff. I have not found any use of the word 'picturesque' in this period: according to the *OED*, it was first used in 1705.
76. Bargrave 1999: 129.
77. 'Nature by her own devices had imitated art': Ovid, *Metamorphoses*: 3.158–9 (translated by M. M. Innes).
78. Langdon 1989: 9, 12; Andrews 1989: 3–4. However, much classical pastoral poetry is not so much about the aesthetic qualities of landscape as about lifestyle, and the idea of the happy man living a contented rural life.

79. Sanderson 1658: 6; Peacham 1962: 127–8.
80. When Wheler describes the view, it is usually in the context of mapmaking.
81. Sanderson 1658: 6.
82. Peacham 1962: 129; Peacham 1612: 42–3.
83. Burton 1676: 167.
84. Evelyn 1959: 114; Nicolson 1959: 17–18.
85. Ogden 1955: 8–9, 13.
86. Bargrave 1999: 128; HMC 1913: 247.
87. Hussey 1967: 2.
88. Langdon 1996: 162–3; Andrews 1989: 8.
89. Peacham 1962: 120.
90. Sherley 1936: 15.
91. Randolph 1687: 79.
92. Smith 1678: 214.
93. BL MS Add. 22914: 10v.
94. Randolph 1689: 22; Randolph 1687: 25. The tree is still so described in modern guide-books.
95. 'All that is to be seen are narrow, unpaved streets, houses without grandeur constructed from ancient ruins, decorated only by pieces of marble columns fixed in the walls without design, like ordinary stones, or by marble blocks marked with crosses which were once part of the doors or windows of churches': Babin 1674: 12.
96. Wheler 1682: 462.
97. Sandys 1615: 22.
98. Rycaut 1679: '74–5' (mispaginated section between 80 and 81).
99. BL MS Add. 22914: 11v; BL MS Add. 22912: 242r.
100. Veryard 1701: 340.
101. BL MS Add. 22912: 179v–180r.
102. Oldenburg 1965–86: vol. 3, 606.
103. Esch 2011: 26.
104. Greenhalgh 2011: 75–80; Kinney 2006: 248.
105. Wheler 1682: 76, 231.
106. Allen 2007: 319.
107. Potts 1994: 7, 19; Haskell & Penny 1981: 101–2. It has recently been suggested by Vout that too much stress has been laid on Winckelmann in this respect; 2006: 226.
108. Browne 1673: 47–8.
109. E.g. BL MS Add. 22914: 9v–10r.
110. Wheler 1682: 357.
111. Roe 1740: 154.
112. The French foot was longer; there was also an Athenian foot somewhere between the two.
113. TNA SP 97/11: 168v–169r; Roe 1740: 570–1.
114. Oldenburg 1965–86: vol. 12, 122.

115. BL MS Add. 22912: 58r–v.
116. Wheler 1682: 312.
117. Ibid.: 323.
118. Ibid.: 329.
119. Ibid.: 373.
120. Merritt 1949: 213; Randolph 1689: 23–4.
121. Bodl. MS Smith 93: 3.
122. Sandys 1615: 13.
123. BL MS Add. 22912: 46r–72r.
124. BL MS Add. 22914: 9v.
125. According to the *OED*, the word 'archaeology' was first used by Joseph Hall in 1607, to mean 'ancient history' or 'systematic description of antiquities'.
126. Wheler 1682: 396–7. The Barberini Library is now part of the Vatican Library, but I have been unable to ascertain whether this manuscript still exists.
127. Rycaut 1675, 1680; Knolles 1687. After Knolles's death, his book was updated by Roe and later by Rycaut; Barbour 2003: 16.
128. Collignon 1913; Wheler 1682: e.g. 352.
129. Wheler 1682: 411.
130. Guillet de Saint-George 1675; Constantine 1989: 1–22; Spon & Wheler 1678. The fourth volume of Spon's *Voyage* was separately published in 1679.
131. Wheler 1682: 202.
132. 'Inscriptions, inscriptions'; ibid.: 425.
133. Blount 1636: 18.
134. Beard 2004: 140; Wheler 1682: 361. Wheler, not realising that in ancient times the Parthenon was approached from the east, thought the subject of the west pediment was the birth of Athena. From the Renaissance there had been a strong interest in the physiognomy of famous historical people as supposedly portrayed on coins; Cunnally 1999: 16, 19.
135. Augustinos 1994: 307. Pliny mentions Pheidias as the sculptor of the statue of Athena in the Parthenon; *Natural History*: 34.19. Leigh's reference to Pheidias' horses suggests that he had the Parthenon frieze in mind; Leigh 1671: 11.
136. They sometimes took issue over questions of identification of antiquities (e.g. Wheler 1682: 331), but agreed in this instance.
137. Howarth 1985: 119–20; Camden 1657: 177–91; Parry 1995: 30.
138. Aubrey 1980–2: vol. 2, 976–7.
139. Browne 1669: 21.
140. Scott 2003: 38–9.
141. Evelyn 1850–2: 297–8.
142. Wheler 1682: 5–6.
143. Terence 2001: 3; Wheler 1682: 369–70.
144. BL MS Add. 22912: 183r.
145. Mundy 1907: 20–1.

146. Gilles 1562: 180–1.
147. [Biddulph] 1609: 28.
148. Wheler 1682: 206–7; Spon & Wheler 1724: vol. 1, 136–7. A number of other travellers also mention it: it was evidently a popular place to visit.
149. Andréossy 1828: 335–6, 338–9; Sumner-Boyd & Freely 2003: 496.
150. Bruyn 1725: 176–7.
151. Veryard 1701: 346.
152. Lithgow 1632: 86–7.
153. Randolph 1687: 78–9.
154. Veryard 1701: 284 (mispaginated 281).
155. Belon 1554: 8r. Neither Lithgow nor Randolph nor Veryard refers to Belon.
156. Zuallardo 1587.
157. Sandys 1615: 8.
158. *Cartographica Neerlandica* (online). The story is discussed in Sarton 1954: 131–7.
159. Purchas 1905–7: vol. 10, 391–2.
160. Wheler 1682: 41.
161. Veryard 1701: 358.
162. Parry 1995: 19.
163. Ibid.: 1–2, 18.
164. Momigliano 1950: 300.
165. Green 2009: 66.
166. Smith 1678: 251, 257.
167. Royal Society MS 73: 4v, 25v–26r, 38r–39v.
168. E.g. BL MS Add. 22912: 84v, 246v, 249r; BL MS Add. 22914: 9r–10r, 16r; BL MS Add. 22910: 81–2. His brother Thomas was a surveyor; *Horringer Parish Records* 1900: 294–8.
169. Ray 1693: vol. 2, 23.
170. Oldenburg 1965–86: vol. 12, 123.
171. Wheler 1682: 310–16. According to Spon, their guide said that it was sacrilege to remove an inscription, but Wheler does not mention this, and Spon dismisses the idea; Spon & Wheler 1724: vol. 2, 33. They were wrong about the site of the temple of Apollo; Ecole Française d'Athènes 1992: 15.
172. Wheler 1682: 230.
173. Smith 1678: 223, 226.
174. Wheler 1682: 379, 384.
175. Ibid.: 397–9.
176. Ibid.: 374–5. He noted with approval that Vernon had already measured the stadium 'exactly'.
177. Desgodetz 1969. However, Desgodetz (whose patron was Colbert) spent 16 months in Rome.
178. Wheler 1682: 337–45.
179. BL MS Add. 22912: 46v, 68v.
180. Robertson 1969: 231.

181. BL MS Add. 22912: 58r, 66r; Vitruvius 1999: 11–13.
182. Smith 1678: 218, 259–60, 269.
183. BL MS Add. 22914: 14v–15r.
184. TNA SP 97/13: 155; Roe 1740: 16.
185. Bodl. MS Tanner 88. It was published in one collection of Milton's works, but can hardly be by him (Milton 1938); Poole makes the attractive suggestion that its author may have been Petty, Arundel's agent; Poole 1912: 109–14.
186. Rycaut 1675: 369–70.
187. It should be remembered that collecting had occurred centuries before. Pausanias knew that many treasures had already been looted by his day; Habicht 1998: 163. Pausanias described the ruined state of Megalopolis in Arcadia, for example, in 8.33.
188. Adams 2004 (online).
189. Purchas 1905–7: vol. 10, 404–5.
190. Smith 1678: 218.
191. Laborde 1854: vol. 1, 124–5. The Ottoman traveller Evliya Çelebi agreed that westerners were better guardians of antiquities than Turks, and Busbecq in the previous century had protested against the damage done to ancient statues at Nicaea by Turks; Dankoff & Kim 2010: 366; Gallo 2009: 6.
192. Coryate 1616: 44.
193. Wheler 1682: 422.
194. Smith 1678: 268.
195. Oldenburg 1965–86: vol. 5, 560–1.
196. Wheler 1682: 202.
197. Rycaut 1679: 37.
198. Bodl. MS Smith 88: 51a–b. This was in 1698, after Pepys had stopped keeping his diary.
199. Peacham 1962: 120; Scott 2003: 18.
200. Wotton 1651: 155.
201. Roe 1740: 16.
202. Scott 2003: 15.
203. Haynes 1975: 9–10.
204. Browne 1852: 398, 405.
205. Augustinos 1994: 83.
206. HMC 1922: 154–6.
207. Roe 1740: 386–7, 433–4, 444–5, 511–12; Sainsbury 1859: 284–5; Mango 2000: 181–6; Wheler 1682: 194; BL MS 22912: 83v. Mango describes the reliefs as a 'montage' of antique and Byzantine carvings.
208. Wheler 1682: a2r.
209. Ibid.: 314, 405.
210. Ibid.: 241.
211. Ibid.: 50, 202.
212. North 1890: 29.
213. Wheler 1682: 353, 476.

214. Randolph 1687: 57.
215. Ibid.: 20.
216. Sandys 1615: 11.
217. Robson 1628: 8.
218. Digby 1868: 56–7. These marbles are now in the Ashmolean Museum in Oxford; Michaelis 1882: 564.
219. Peacham 1962: 120.
220. Smith 1678: 207.
221. Randolph 1687: 20.
222. Wheler 1682: 56. The author of Bodl. Tanner 88 suggests that large statues should be cut up for transportation; Poole 1912: 113.
223. Wheler 1682: 57.
224. Pliny, *Natural History*: 35.
225. Wheler 1682: 49, 237, 428.
226. Ibid.: 361.
227. Veryard 1701: 333; Purchas 1905–7: vol. 10, 396.
228. Robertson 1975: vol. 1, 493.
229. Sandys 1615: 91; Strabo, *Geography*: 14.2.19. Strabo makes several references to the removal of antiquities from their original sites, e.g. 6.3.1, 10.2.21, 12.3.11, 13.1.19.
230. Hasluck 1910–11: 103–31.
231. BL MS Add. 22912: 348r, 349r.
232. Rycaut 1679: 224–7.
233. Veryard 1701: 343.
234. Wheler 1682: 322.
235. Sandys 1615: 31.
236. Dankoff & Kim 2010: 16.
237. BL MS Add. 22912: 46v–47r.
238. Wheler 1682: 253–4; Rycaut 1679: 51.
239. Monconys 1677: 416–17. Another French traveller, Tournefort, included an engraving of the sculpture in one edition of his book; Tournefort 1717: between 514 and 515.
240. Angelicoussis 1992: 78–83; Rudolf 1989: 11–19.
241. Dankoff & Kim 2010: 310.
242. Bryer 1998: 55; Mazower 2001: 70.
243. Mansel 2006: 10; Raby 1983: 24.
244. Finkel 2006: 193.
245. Wheler 1682: 181; Raby 1983: 16.
246. Irwin 2006: 63; Raby 1983: 16.
247. Roe 1740: 500.
248. Howarth 1985: 91.
249. Irwin 2006: 90ff.
250. Toomer 1996: 108.
251. Strachan 1989: 175; BL MS Royal 1.D.v–viii.

252. Bodl. MS Savile 47: 45.
253. There is another piece of evidence for a similar theft: the merchant John Kitely, writing to his colleague John Sanderson in May 1609, alleged that the Bishop of Salonica had stolen books out of the library there for Ambassador Henry Lello. However, as there was a long-standing disagreement involving Lello and these two merchants, the truth is in doubt; Sanderson 1931: 264; MacLean 2004: 56–7.
254. Quoted in Ward 1740: 137.
255. Smith 1680: 263–7.
256. Belon 1554: 36v (mispaginated 39).
257. There were many Jewish merchants in Constantinople; Sugar 1977: 268.
258. Bodl. MS Smith 93: 137–8.
259. Sanderson 1931: 217–18, 221, 228, 236.
260. HMC 1913: 227, 233.
261. Irwin 2006: 95–6.
262. HMC 1913: 227, 233, 358.
263. Wheler 1682: 195, 350.
264. Ibid.: 441, 451.
265. Belon 1554: 37r.
266. BL MS Add. 22912: 348r; BL MS Add. 22914: 46v.
267. BL MS Add. 22914: 44v.
268. BL MS Add. 22912: 348r.
269. BL MS Add. 22914: 21v–22v.
270. BL MS Add. 22912: 249v.
271. BL MS Harley 3778: 103–4.
272. Wheler 1682: 335.

Chapter 4 Among the Greeks

1. BL MS Add. 22914: 16v.
2. Wheler 1682: 337.
3. HMC 1922: 159–60.
4. For example, in the echoes of fifth-century BCE sculpture on the Pergamon altar.
5. Polybius, *Histories*: 1.1–3.
6. Plutarch, *Moralia*: 814A.
7. Goldhill 2001: 14.
8. Ibid.: 1–2, 8.
9. Cicero, *Tusculan disputations*: 1.1; *De republica*: 3.3.4–6. In *Pro Flacco*, Chapter 9, too, he expresses ambivalence about the Greek character.
10. Cicero, *Epistolae ad Quintum fratrem*: 1.1.16, 28.

11. Pliny, *Natural History*: 29.7.14. The younger Pliny, advising another Roman official who was being sent to Greece, reminded him that he should respect the ancient glory of the Greeks, even though all that remained of Athens was the name and shadow of freedom; *Letters*: 8.24.
12. Juvenal, *Satires* 3.78; Cicero, *In Pisonem*: 29; *De oratore*: 1.11.47, 1.22.102, 1.51.221. See Dubuisson 1991.
13. Segal 1987: 37. See Plautus, *Mostellaria*: 1.1.22, 1.1.64; *Truculentus*: 1.187.
14. Setton 1975: 190.
15. Rycaut 1675: 127.
16. Mazower 2001: 61; Sugar 1977: 257; Woodhouse 1998: 116–18.
17. Braudel 1992: 496; Sugar 1977: 83–4, 218.
18. Roe 1740: 16.
19. Rycaut 1679: 28–9.
20. Rycaut 1675: 370; Rycaut 1679: 229.
21. At least seven between 1621 and 1639.
22. [Heylyn] 1631: 378–81.
23. Brerewood 1614: 10. Brerewood was unusual in explicitly recognising that languages change naturally over time.
24. Vacalopoulos 1976: 173.
25. Howell 1678: 37–8.
26. King 1664: 111.
27. Mansel 2006: 158.
28. Wheler 1682: 355.
29. BL MS Add. 22914: 15v; Rycaut 1679: 58; Smith 1678: 249.
30. BL MS Add. 22912: 179r.
31. Brinsley 1612: 227. Erasmus had recognised that New Testament Greek was different from classical, but one of the arguments against him was that the New Testament could not be in bad Greek because it emanated from the Holy Spirit; religious allegiances as well as linguistic questions were at issue here; Goldhill 2002: 24, 35.
32. Wheler 1682: A1v.
33. Sandys 1615: preface; Lithgow 1632: 11.
34. Wheler 1682: A1v.
35. Toomer 1996: epigraph; Blount 1636: 85. See also Ferguson 1984: 24–5; Hodgen 1964: 269–71.
36. BL MS Add. 22914: 16v; Rycaut 1679: 53.
37. Knolles 1603: final unnumbered page before index; Howell 1678: 54.
38. Smith 1678: 124.
39. Spencer 1952: 330.
40. Rycaut 1679: 7; Livy, *Ab urbe condita*: 34.49.
41. Smith 1680: 14–15.
42. Sandys 1615: 21. The first sack of Troy by Greece was probably that by Herakles.
43. Blount 1636: 84.

44. Sherley 1936: 9. In France in 1674 Fénélon envisaged the possibility of Greek freedom; Augustinos 1994: 79–80.
45. Bryer 1998: 54; Clark 2007: 14–15; Stavrianos 2000: 105; Sugar 1977: 5; Woodhouse 1998: 113.
46. North 1890: 35.
47. Wheler 1682: 302.
48. Sugar 1977: 55–8; Vacalopoulos 1976: 35–40. According to Ambassador Winchilsea, the custom was revived in the mid-1660s, after a 30-year gap, because of the need for soldiers; HMC 1913: 412.
49. Vacalopoulos 1976: 192–3.
50. Mazower 2004: 25–6.
51. Vacalopoulos 1976: 71–5, 212ff.
52. Ibid.: 153–4, 157, 160–1, 172, 180–3.
53. Sugar 1977: 256–7; Smith 1680: 239.
54. Mazower 2004: 63.
55. Mitsi 2008: 57.
56. Hall 2008; Stanford 1992; Stanford & Luce 1974.
57. Euripides, *Hecuba*: 131–3, 250: Euripides describes Odysseus as a liar. *Hecuba* had been translated into French and Italian, though not English, before 1600; Bolgar 1964: 512–13.
58. E.g. 'nunc advoca astus, anime, nunc fraudes, dolos, / nunc totum Ulixem' ('Now, my mind, call up your cunning, your deceit, your trickery, everything that makes up Ulysses'); Seneca, *Trojan Women*: 613–14.
59. There is some debate about Caesar's attitude to the ruins of Troy as depicted by Lucan, who was certainly himself ambivalent about Caesar; Rossi 2001: 313–26; Hardie 1993: 106–7.
60. Hingley 2000: 62; Kallendorf 2007: IV.575; MacDougall 1982: 7.
61. Ayres 1997: 85–6.
62. Burrow 1997: 86. Coryate also called London 'our new Troy'; Purchas 1905–7: vol. 10, 409.
63. Grafton 1992: 33.
64. Quoted in Parry 1995: 109.
65. Purchas 1626: 279.
66. There was also an erroneous etymological connection made between 'Turci' and 'Teucri'; Spencer 1952: 331. Turks could also be seen as inheriting some of the qualities of imperial Romans, such as military discipline; Blount 1636: 64. For a discussion of Renaissance views on the origins of the Turks, see Heath 1979.
67. Baker 2007.
68. E.g. *Aeneid*: 2.36, 43–4, 65, 196, 252, 309–10.
69. [Heylyn] 1631: 379.
70. Chew 1965: 61.
71. BL MS Add. 22913: 6v.
72. Roe 1740: 495.

73. E.g. Veryard 1701: 285; Epistle to Titus 1.12.
74. Hall 2008: 48.
75. Rycaut 1680: second sequence, 172.
76. BL MS Add. 22912: 37r; Virgil, *Aeneid*: 2.79; Euripides, *Iphigenia in Tauris*: 1205.
77. Rycaut 1679: 224.
78. Covel 1722: vii–viii, x, xli, lii, 104–5.
79. Ibid.: 343.
80. BL MS Add. 22912: 249v.
81. Wheler 1682: 413. The state of Greek intellectual life in this period is discussed in Henderson 1971: 1ff.
82. Wheler 1682: 31, 41–2, 79. One of Spon's aims in his account of his travels, on which Wheler's work was largely founded, was to correct the errors found in Guillet de Saint-Georges's work of 1669. This work purports to be based on the researches of the author's brother Guilletière, but Constantine has shown that this brother was a fiction; Constantine 1989: 3–4. Vernon, Wheler and other visitors to Athens recognised that the work was full of errors.
83. Vacalopoulos 1976: 177.
84. BL MS Add. 22912: 218v, 232r.
85. Wheler 1682: 316.
86. Robson 1628: 9–10.
87. Wheler 1682: 327, 332–3, 347, 468. The word 'quack' was pejorative in the seventeenth century, as today.
88. Ibid.: 353.
89. E.g. by Teonge (1927: 79), writing of the Morea and referring to Philip Sidney. However, this is a matter of literary reference rather than personal experience, as Teonge did not go ashore there.
90. BL MS Add. 22914: 47r, 48r.
91. Lithgow 1632: 88.
92. Wheler 1682: 312.
93. Raphael 1993: 265–6.
94. Wheler 1698: 174.
95. BL MS Add. 22913: 10r; BL MS Add. 22914: 60v.
96. Lithgow 1632: 102–3.
97. Teonge 1927: 179–80.
98. Lithgow 1632: 82–3.
99. According to the *OED*, this word was in use from the late sixteenth century. Evelyn uses it, apparently without irony, in his letter to Pepys of 12 August 1689; Evelyn 1850–2: 296.
100. Randolph 1687: 15–20, 93.
101. North 1890: 34.
102. Sugar 1977: 46, 253–4; Woodhouse 1998: 102–3.
103. Blount 1636: 110.
104. BL MS Add. 22912: 256r.

105. Mazower 2001: 75.
106. Georgirenes 1678: 12.
107. Finkel 2006: 278–9. The Vani himself was an Armenian; Rycaut 1680: second sequence, 154.
108. BL MS Add. 22912: 267r.
109. Mansel 2006: 51.
110. Sandys 1629: 241 (the author of this work was the brother of the traveller George Sandys); Rycaut 1675: 149.
111. Wheler 1682: 441.
112. HMC 1922: 86.
113. Letter of John Greaves, Bodl. MS Savile 47: 45; Smith 1680: a5v, 151; Mansel 2006: 199.
114. Mansel 2006: 49; BL MS Harley 3778: 111r.
115. Georgirenes 1678: 40.
116. Rycaut 1679: 260; BL MS Add. 22912: 348r. Rycaut had not been to Mount Athos himself, but relied on information provided by Covel.
117. Belon 1554: 37r; Augustinos 1994: 69.
118. Bodl. MS Savile 47: 45.
119. BL MS Add. 22912: 266r.
120. Sandys 1615: 81; Rycaut 1679: 257–8. A similar charge was sometimes made against the Catholic Church, that its congregations could not understand the Latin mass, e.g. Robson 1628: 3.
121. Gainsford 1618: 287.
122. Wheler 1682: 321, 323, 350, 355.
123. Rycaut 1679: 339.
124. Smith 1680: a3r–a4r, 17.
125. Covel 1722: viii–ix.
126. Known to today's visitors as Hosios Loukas.
127. Wheler 1682: 321–6, 350.
128. Belon 1554: 36v (mispaginated 39).
129. Oldenburg 1965–86: vol. 1, 269.
130. BL MS Add. 22910: 130.
131. There are two extended sections of Covel's diaries devoted to Mount Athos: BL MS Add. 22912: 335–51; BL MS Add. 22914: 37–46. The relevant sections of both manuscripts have been transcribed in Hasluck 1910–11. There is additional information in Covel 1722.
132. BL MS Add. 22912: 234v.
133. Rycaut 1679: 216–18.
134. Covel 1722: 18.
135. Ibid.: 98, 376.
136. Koukouzelis flourished around 1300.
137. Simeon died in 1429.
138. Wheler 1698: 11; Wheler 1682: 215, 345.
139. Rycaut 1679: 13.

140. BL MS Add. 22914: 64r.
141. BL MS Add. 22912: 253v.
142. Smith 1680: 18–19.
143. Mazower 2001: 55, 69. See also Sugar 1977: 52.
144. Hasluck 1929: vol. 1, 63–97.
145. Smith 1680: 187.
146. BL MS Add. 22912: 184r–v, 220r–v.
147. Covel 1722: xxxix.
148. Bargrave 1999: 127.
149. BL MS Add. 22912: 220r, 264r.
150. Veryard 1701: 341–2.
151. North 1890: 146.
152. Teonge 1927: 98.
153. BL MS Add. 22912: 243r.
154. Wheler 1682: 30.
155. Randolph 1687: 77.
156. Lithgow 1632: 117.
157. Wheler 1682: 40; Covel 1722.
158. Herrin 2007: 282.
159. Bryer 1998: 54–5; Mansel 2006: 6.
160. Rycaut 1675: 202; Mansel 2006: 139.
161. Smith 1678: 313.
162. Wheler 1682: 322, 450.
163. Smith 1680: 105–6.
164. Villani (online); Croese 1696: part 3, 276; Religious Society of Friends, Friends House Library, MS Caton: vol. 1, 164–5.
165. Wheler 1682: 212–13; BL MS Add. 22914: 20v.
166. Rycaut 1680: second sequence, 81–2.
167. Wheler 1682: 216.
168. Browne 1673: 82–3.
169. Rycaut 1679: 14.
170. Finet 1656: 58.
171. Dowling & Fletcher 1915: 65–7, 80–1; Strachan 1989: 222–4.
172. Pinnington 2003: 97; Runciman 1968: 293–6.
173. Runciman 1968: 306–7.
174. Ibid.: 296–9.
175. Pinnington 2003: 164.
176. Runciman 1968: 312–15; Pinnington 2003: 173–4.
177. Covel 1722: 36ff and *passim*.
178. Wheler 1682: 197.
179. Smith 1680: 152.
180. Ibid.: a4v.
181. Covel 1722: 106.
182. BL MS Add. 22912: 201v.

183. Ellison 2002: 1, 7, 12 and *passim*.
184. Rycaut 1679: A4v, preface; 1680: second sequence, 315. The biblical reference is to John 19.23.
185. Smith 1680: A4v.
186. Williams 1868: xii–xv. Others who showed an interest were Robert Huntington, chaplain at Aleppo, and Covel's successor Edward Browne (not the same Edward Browne as Thomas Browne's son).
187. Tappe 1954: 93; Dowling & Fletcher 1915: 46–8. Georgirenes was also involved in the attempt to bring Greeks to study in England, as Lucaris, who had links with Laud, had done earlier; Trevor-Roper 1992: 94.
188. HMC 1922: 148–50.
189. Wheler 1682: 27.
190. Oldenburg 1965–86: vol. 12, 65–6.
191. Bodl. MS Eng. Misc. c.23: 197r.
192. Robson 1628: 10.
193. Rycaut 1679: preface; Warneke 1995: 140.
194. Sherley 1936: 33. A 'pratique' meant a health certificate issued to a ship: presumably Sherley means that the commander needs to be officially sanctioned.
195. Basire 1831: 39, 47.
196. Ibid.: 115–19.
197. Ibid.: 127, 202. Evelyn (1959: 430) describes Basire as 'that greate Traviller, or rather *French Apostle*, who had ben planting the Church of England, in divers parts of the *Levant* & *Asia*'. Robert Huntington, in Aleppo, used an Arabic catechism and liturgy, translated by Pococke, and a Turkish catechism by Seaman, so perhaps he also tried to do some evangelising; Holt 1973: 20–1.
198. Both Wren and Hawksmoor collected travel books; Watkin 1972.
199. Du Prey 1991: xvi.
200. Doran & Durston 1991: 40.
201. Du Prey (1991: 44) has argued that there was a close connection between architecture and the new science; some travellers, as I have argued, were also participators in and contributors to the new science. Both groups were living in the context of new ways of observing the natural and manmade worlds.
202. Greene 1982: 234.
203. Spencer 1974: 87–8.
204. Wheler 1689: 63, 120, 129–30.
205. Smith 1678: 205–7, 273–6.
206. Wheler 1682: 259.
207. Brerewood 1614: 85; Rycaut 1675: 3; Irwin 2006: 86; Vitkus 2001: 49; Pailin 1984: 104.
208. Of course all travellers, to a greater or lesser extent, carry cultural baggage.

Chapter 5 Among the Turks

1. At home in England, the word could be applied to Englishmen who showed 'Turkish' characteristics; MacLean 2007: 8, 127.
2. The term 'Muslim' is not used in this period, 'Mohammedan' or 'Mussulman' being the common adjectives. Purchas does use 'Islam', but not in the modern sense; Purchas 1626: 318. The *OED* gives 1592 as the earliest instance of the phrase 'turning Turk'. For clarity, I use 'Islam' to indicate the religion and 'Muslim' where I want simply to express religious affiliation without the baggage carried by the word 'Turk'.
3. Rycaut 1675: 143.
4. Sugar 1977: 109.
5. *Book of Common Prayer 1549*, collects for Good Friday. MacLean has uncovered anti-Turkish prayers used in the diocese of Salisbury; MacLean 2007: 1–2. To some extent, such phrases are a matter of rhetoric rather than a real recognition of different creeds; George Fox was unusually even-handed in writing that any Jew, Papist, Turk, heathen, Protestant 'or such as worship *Sun*, or *Moon*, or *Stocks*, or *Stones*' should have 'liberty to speak forth his Mind, and Judgment'; 1706: 234.
6. Matar 1998: 20.
7. Ibid. See also Barbour 2003: 5–6.
8. Elliott 1972: 41–2.
9. BL MS Add. 22912: 234v. Covel wrote this comment in code.
10. HMC 1913: 497.
11. Marsh 1663: frontispiece.
12. Howell 1650: 131, 133, 136.
13. Dallington 1605: B1r; Gailhard 1678: second sequence, 28–9, 65.
14. Cleland 1607: 257.
15. Matar 1998: 12, 73, 182. The English Qur'an was translated from the French of André du Ryer.
16. Watson 1971: 61; Strachan 1989: 146; Knolles 1603.
17. 'Pretending' here implies assertion, rather than pretence in its modern sense.
18. Blount 1636: 2, 61–2.
19. Ibid.: 42, 84–5.
20. Ibid.: 75.
21. Ibid.: 24.
22. King 1664: 115.
23. 'The worst state has the greatest number of laws'; Tacitus, *Annals*: 3.27. The text actually reads 'corruptissima republica' ('the most corrupt state').
24. Blount 1636: 87, 92. The hostels were noted by Sandys and Rycaut as well; Sandys 1615: 57; Rycaut 1675: 204.
25. Blount 1636: 32–3, 99.
26. Ibid.: 103.

27. Sandys 1615: 15.
28. Lithgow 1632: 145, 147; Dalrymple 1998: 299; Irwin 2006: 20; Beck 1987: 15. Covel refers to Islam as 'heresy', and suggests that the first words of the Qur'an are borrowed from Christianity or Judaism; BL MS Add. 22914: 16v; Covel 1722: 317.
29. Lithgow 1632: 135, 142–3. It is not clear how Lithgow would have expected to recognise 'sense or verity' in a language he did not speak.
30. It had been used less and less from the beginning of the seventeenth century; Mackenzie 1992: 29–30.
31. Lithgow 1632: 118.
32. Ibid.: 130–1.
33. Matar 1991: 65.
34. See for example Finch, letter to Lord Conway, BL MS Add. 23215: 78v.
35. BL MS Add. 22912: 236v–237r.
36. Nicolson 1992: 368.
37. Lithgow 1632: 150.
38. Matar 1998: 106–7.
39. Robson 1628: 15–16.
40. Vitkus 2003: 8.
41. Matar 1998: 30.
42. Rycaut 1675: 143. The word 'nation' often refers to a community of merchants from one country, e.g. England or France.
43. Rycaut 1679: 23.
44. Ravelhofer 2006: 253.
45. Sandys 1615: 74.
46. BL MS Add. 22912: 195v.
47. [Rycaut] 1661: 9.
48. Blount 1636: 25.
49. Browne 1673: 79–80.
50. Sandys 1615: 64.
51. BL MS Add. 22912: 266v; BL MS Add. 22914: 8v. Covel does not make it clear whether the friend was Greek or Turkish, but the fact that he did not drink suggests the latter.
52. Sandys 1615: 49.
53. Veryard 1701: 312, 347, 349.
54. Rycaut 1680: second sequence, 290.
55. Smith 1678: 104, 195–6; HMC 1913: 406–7.
56. Villani (online).
57. The State Papers have a number of references to the nuisance caused to consuls by troublesome Quakers. Ambassador Bendish's letter to Cromwell of 24 July 1648 is typical; Thurloe 1742: vol. 7, 287.
58. Croese 1696: part 3, 275–6. Croese comments that he himself has experience of the kindness of Turks.
59. HMC 1913: 143, 360, 400; North 1890: 135.

NOTES TO PAGES 198–204   249

60. Religious Society of Friends, Friends House Library, MS Caton: vol. 1, 164.
61. Bishop 1661: 19–20.
62. B. [Baker] 1662: 15, 22, 26.
63. Fox 1911: vol. 2, 446.
64. Smith 1676: 7, 10–11.
65. E.g. Smith 1678: 190–1; HMC 1913: 198. Blount thought that polygamy was a policy for increasing the Muslim population, while Covel wondered whether the Greeks were deliberately encouraged to become monks, and therefore celibate, in order to reduce the Greek population; Blount 1636: 82; BL MS Add. 22914: 20r.
66. Rycaut 1680: second sequence, 262, 314–15.
67. Smith 1678: 'To the reader'.
68. Sherley 1936: 2.
69. BL MS Add. 22914: 62v; BL MS Add. 22912: 204v, 262v.
70. Blount 1636: 14.
71. Matar 1999: 127.
72. Bent 1893: 74.
73. Purchas 1626: 291; Hill 1709: 162.
74. B. [Bulwer] 1653: 547.
75. Smith 1678: 145, 152–5, 163.
76. HMC 1913: 198–9, 226.
77. Rycaut 1675: 147.
78. Mazower 2004: 110.
79. BL MS Add. 22912: 37r, 212v.
80. North 1890: 151–2; Grassby 1994: 186.
81. Browne 1673: 74–5.
82. Rycaut 1675: A3v–A4r, A6r, A8r, 53–4.
83. Longleat House, Coventry Papers: box 69; BL MS Add. 22912: 162v.
84. Grassby 1994: 191, 274.
85. North 1890: 156–7.
86. Covel 1722: 317.
87. Matar 1998: 23–31.
88. MacLean 2007: 64.
89. Braudel 1992: 483.
90. Rycaut 1675: 349.
91. Mazower 2001: 55–6; Sugar 1977: 58.
92. Stavrianos 2000: 106; Braudel 1992: 11; Woodhouse 1998: 112.
93. Greene 2000: 39–42.
94. Clark 2007: 14–15. Clark is writing about a later period, but his statement is equally true of the seventeenth century.
95. Bulliet 1979: 33–4, 41.
96. Matar 1999: 95.
97. Randolph 1687: 2–3.
98. Wheler 1682: 203.

99. BL MS Add. 22912: 196r, 201v, 207v, 236v.
100. Randolph 1687: 2.
101. Reed 2007: 13.

Conclusion

1. Although the distinction is made between those who were visiting or passing through and those who worked in the region for extended periods, I have not found a marked difference in attitudes between the two groups.
2. Blount 1636: 105; Sandys 1615: 66.
3. Purchas 1905–7: vol. 10, 419, 422.
4. BL MS Add. 22912: 175r–v, 189v, 204r, 218r.
5. Covel 1722: 1; Xenophon, *Anabasis*: 7.3.21.
6. Covel 1722: 92, 98.
7. BL MS Add. 22912: 35v.
8. Adams 1980: 187.
9. McKeon 1987: 100.
10. Covel 1722: xxxiv.
11. Wheler 1682: 304.
12. BL MS Add. 22914: 2r.
13. The cultural-archaeological scene was analysed by Hill 2010.
14. Tregaskis 1979.
15. Stanford & Finopoulos 1984: 135.
16. Janowitz 1990: 5, 20.
17. Sandys 1615: 218. He is quoting from Virgil, *Eclogues*: 1.66 ('penitos toto divisos orbe Britannos').
18. Gainsford 1618.
19. [Biddulph] 1609: A2r–v.
20. Wheler 1682: dedication; Rycaut 1675: 379–80.
21. Rycaut 1679: preface.
22. Avcioğlu 2001: 203–26.
23. Hall 1975: 79; MacLean 2007: 217.
24. Rycaut 1680: second sequence, 63.
25. Rycaut 1675: epistle to the reader, A8r, 43, 142.
26. Bargrave 1999: 78, 81–2.
27. Smith 1678: 'To the reader'. It is notable that in this context the only voices we hear belong to Royalist Anglicans.
28. Seferis 1969: 7.

BIBLIOGRAPHY

Manuscripts

Bodleian Library MS Eng. Misc. c.23.
Bodleian Library MS Savile 47.
Bodleian Library MS Smith 88.
Bodleian Library MS Smith 93.
Bodleian Library MS Tanner 88.
British Library MS Add. 5821.
British Library MS Add. 19166.
British Library MSS Add. 22910–22914.
British Library MS Add. 23215.
British Library MS Add. 27606.
British Library MS Add. 57495.
British Library MS Add. 70485.
British Library MS Harley 3778.
British Library MS Harley 6943.
British Library MS Harley 7021.
British Library MS Royal 1.D.v–viii.
British Library MS Sloane 1911–13.
British Library MS Sloane 3945.
Cambridge University Archives, *Books of Subscriptions for Degrees*, vol. 2, 1637–91.
Christ's College, Cambridge, Archives, box 21.
Essex Record Office D/DHf025.
Longleat House, Coventry Papers, box 69.
Religious Society of Friends, Friends House Library, MS Caton, vol. 1.
Royal Society MS 73.
The National Archives (TNA) State Papers 97/11, 97/13, 105/102, 105/145.

Unpublished theses

Adams, M.J. (2009). 'Classical education in English schools, 1500–1842', London University MPhil thesis.

Lewis, Marilyn (2010). 'The educational influence of Cambridge Platonism: tutorial relationships and student networks at Christ's College, Cambridge, 1641–1688', London University PhD thesis.

Materials on the internet

Adams, Steven (2004). 'Quatremere de Quincy and the instrumentality of the museum', *Working Papers in Art and Design* 3, http://www.herts.ac.uk/research/ssahri/research-areas/art-design/research-into-practice-group/production/working-papers-in-art-and-design-journal (accessed 28 January 2014).

Cartographica Neerlandica, map text for Ortelius map no. 217, www.orteliusmaps.com (accessed 21 September 2011).

Leedham-Green, Elisabeth. 'Covel, John (1638–1722)', *Oxford Dictionary of National Biography*, http://www.oxforddnb.com/ (accessed 15 November 2011).

Lewis, Bernard. 'The roots of Muslim rage', http://www.catholiceducation.org/articles/history/world/wh0067.html (accessed 10 Feb 2010).

Villani, Stefano. 'Fisher, Mary (c.1623–1698)', *Oxford Dictionary of National Biography*, http://www.oxforddnb.com/ (accessed 29 September 2006).

Printed materials

Abbott, G.F. (1920). *Under the Turk in Constantinople: A Record of Sir John Finch's Embassy, 1674–1681*, London.

Acta Eruditorum (1682–). Leipzig.

Adams, P.G. (1980). *Travelers and Travel Liars, 1660–1800*, New York.

Allen, Lindsay (2007). '"Chilimnar olim Persepolis": European reception of a Persian ruin', in Christopher Taplin (ed.), *Persian Responses*, Swansea, pp. 313–42.

Anderson, Sonia (1989). *An English Consul in Turkey: Paul Rycaut at Smyrna, 1667–1678*, Oxford.

Andréossy, A. (1828). *Constantinople et le Bosphore de Thrace*, Paris.

Andrews, Malcolm (1989). *The Search for the Picturesque: Landscape, Aesthetics and Tourism in Britain, 1760–1800*, Aldershot.

Andrich, I.A. (1892). *De Natione Anglica et Scota Iuristarum Universitatis Patavinae*, Padua.

Angelicoussis, Elizabeth (1992). *The Woburn Abbey Collection of Classical Antiquities*, Monumenta Artis Romanae XX, Mainz.

Anon. ('One in the service of the Republic') (1670). *A Description of Candia*, London.

Aston, Margaret (1973). 'English ruins and English history', *Journal of the Warburg and Courtauld Institutes* 36, pp. 231–55.

Aubrey, John (1980–2). *Monumenta Britannica*, 2 vols, ed. R. Legg, Sherborne.

Augustinos, Olga (1994). *French Odysseys: Greece in French Travel Literature from the Renaissance to the Romantic Era*, Baltimore.

BIBLIOGRAPHY

Avcioğlu, Nebahat (2001). 'Ahmed I and the allegories of tyranny in the frontispiece to George Sandys' *Relation of a Journey*', *Muqarnas* 18, pp. 203–26.
Ayres, Philip (1997). *Classical Culture and the Idea of Rome in Eighteenth-Century England*, Cambridge.
B.D. [Daniel Baker] (1662). *A Clear Voice of Truth*, London.
B.J. [John Bulwer] (1653). *Anthropometamorphosis*, London.
Babin, J.P. (1674). *Relation de l'Etat Présent de la Ville d'Athènes*, Lyon.
Bacon, Francis (1605). *The Twoo Bookes... of the Proficience and Advancement of Learning*, London.
——— (1696). 'Of Travel', in *The Essays, or Councils*, London.
Baddeley, Richard (1669). *The Life of Dr. Thomas Morton*, York.
Baker, Daniel. See B.D.
Baker, D.J. (2007). '"Idiote": politics and friendship in Thomas Coryate', in Thomas Betteridge (ed.), *Borders and Travellers in Early Modern Europe*, Aldershot, pp. 129–45.
Baldwin, T.W. (1944). *William Shakespere's Small Latine and Lesse Greeke*, 2 vols, Urbana.
Barbour, Reid (2007). 'Moral and political philosophy: readings of Lucretius from Virgil to Voltaire', in Stuart Gillespie and Philip Hardie (eds), *Cambridge Companion to Lucretius*, Cambridge, pp. 145–66.
Barbour, Richmond (2003). *Before Orientalism: London's Theatre of the East, 1576–1626*, Cambridge.
Bargrave, Robert (1999). *Travel Diary... 1647–1656*, ed. M.G. Brennan, London.
Barrell, John (1972). *The Idea of Landscape and the Sense of Place, 1730–1840*, Cambridge.
Basire, Isaac (1831). *Correspondence, with a Memoir of His Life*, ed. W.N. Darnall, London.
Baudier, Michel (1635). *The History of the Imperiall Estate of the Grand Seigneur*, London.
Beard, Mary (2004). *The Parthenon*, London.
Beck, B.H. (1987). *From the Rising of the Sun: English Images of the Ottoman Empire to 1715*, New York.
Belon, Pierre (1554). *Les Observations de Plusieurs Singularitez & Choses Memorables*, Paris.
Bent, J.T. (ed.) (1893). *Early Voyages and Travel in the Levant*, Hakluyt Society Series 87, London.
[Biddulph, William] (1609). *The Travels of Certaine Englishmen... Begunne in the Yeare of Jubile 1600*, London.
Bishop, George (1661). *New England Judged*, London.
Blome, Richard (1670). *A Geographical Description of... the World* and *A Treatise of Travel*, London.
Blount, Henry (1636). *A Voyage into the Levant*, London.
Bolgar, R.R. (1964). *The Classical Heritage and Its Beneficiaries*, New York.
Bosworth, C.E. (2006). *An Intrepid Scot: William Lithgow of Lanark's Travels in Ottoman Lands, North Africa and Central Europe, 1609–21*, Aldershot.
Braudel, Fernand (1992). *The Mediterranean and the Mediterranean World in the Age of Philip II*, tr. S. Reynolds, abridged R. Ollard, London.
Bray, Alan (2003). *The Friend*, Chicago.

Brentjes, Sonja (c.2010). *Travellers from Europe in the Ottoman and Safavid Empires, 16th–17th Centuries*, Farnham.
Brerewood, Edward (1614). *Enquiries Touching the Diversity of Languages and Religions*, London.
Brinsley, John (1612). *Ludus Literarius*, London.
Brotton, Jerry (1997). *Trading Territories: Mapping the Early Modern World*, London.
——— (2006). *The Sale of the Late King's Goods: Charles I and His Art Collection*, London.
Brown[e], Edward (1673). *A Brief Account of Some Travels in... Thessaly*, London.
Browne, Thomas (1669). *Hydriotaphia*, London.
——— (1852). *Works*, vol. 3, ed. S. Wilkin, London.
——— (1928). *Works*, vol. 4, ed. G. Keynes, London.
Bruyn, Corneille de (1725). *Voyage au Levant*, vol. 1, Paris.
Bryer, Anthony (1998). 'The Holy Mountain', *Cornucopia* 3/15, pp. 42–65.
Bull, Malcolm (2005). *The Mirror of the Gods*, Oxford.
Bulliet, R.W. (1979). *Conversion to Islam in the Medieval Period*, Cambridge, Mass.
Bulwer. *See* B.J.
Burbury, John (1671). *A Relation of a Journey... to Vienna... and Constantinople*, London.
Burrow, Colin (1997). 'Virgils, from Dante to Milton', in Charles Martindale (ed.), *The Cambridge Companion to Virgil*, Cambridge, pp. 79–90.
Burton, Robert (1676). *The Anatomy of Melancholy*, London.
Busbecq, O.G. de (1595). *Legationis Turcicae Epistolae Quatuor*, Frankfurt.
——— (1694). *Four Epistles... Concerning His Embassy into Turkey*, London.
Camden, William (1657). *Remaines Concerning Britain*, London.
Carey, Dan (2003). 'Travel, identity and cultural difference, 1580–1700', in Jane Conroy (ed.), *Cross-Cultural Travel: Papers from the Royal Irish Academy Symposium on Literature and Travel... November 2002*, New York, pp. 39–47.
——— (2009). *Continental Travel and Journeys beyond Europe in the Early Modern Period*, London.
Chard, Chloe (1996). 'Crossing boundaries and exceeding limits: destabilization, tourism and the sublime', in Chloe Chard and Helen Langdon (eds), *Transports: Travel, Pleasure and Imaginative Geography, 1600–1830*, New Haven, pp. 117–49.
Chard, Chloe and Langdon, Helen (eds) (1996). *Transports: Travel, Pleasure and Imaginative Geography, 1600–1830*, New Haven.
Chew, S.C. (1965). *The Crescent and the Rose: Islam and England during the Renaissance*, New York.
Claassen, J-M. (1999). *Displaced Persons: The Literature of Exile from Cicero to Boethius*, London.
Clark, Andrew (ed.) (1894). *The Life and Times of Anthony Wood... 1632–1695*, vol. 3, Oxford Historical Society 26, Oxford.
Clark, Bruce (2007). *Twice a Stranger: How Mass Expulsion Forged Modern Greece and Turkey*, London.
Clark, Kenneth (1956). *Landscape into Art*, Harmondsworth.
Clarke, M.L. (1959). *Classical Education in Britain, 1500–1900*, Cambridge.
Cleland, James (1607). *ΗΡΩ-ΠΑΙΔΕΙΑ, or The Institution of a Young Gentleman*, Oxford.
Collignon, Maxime (1913). *Le Consul Jean Giraud et sa Relation de l'Attique au XVIIe Siècle*, Paris.

Colton, R.E. (1973). 'Ausonius and Juvenal', *Classical Journal* 69, pp. 41–51.
Constantine, David (1989). 'The question of authenticity in some early accounts of Greece', in G.W. Clark (ed.), *Rediscovering Hellenism*, Cambridge, pp. 1–22.
Cook, A.K. (1917). *About Winchester*, London.
Cook, J.M. (1973). *The Troad*, Oxford.
Coryate, Thomas (1611). *Coryats Crudities*, London.
——— (1616). *Thomas Coriate, Traveller for the English Wits*, London.
Costello, W.T. (1958). *The Scholastic Curriculum at Early Seventeenth-Century Cambridge*, Cambridge, Mass.
Cotton, Charles (1660). *A Panegyrick to the King's Most Excellent Majesty*, London.
Courthop, George (1907). *Memoirs*, ed. S.C. Lomas, Camden Miscellany 11, London, pp. 95–157.
Covel, John (1722). *Some Account of the Present Greek Church*, Cambridge.
[Covel, John] [1724]. *A Catalogue of the Entire Library of... Dr. John Covel*, London.
Covel, John (1998). *Voyages en Turquie 1675–1677*, ed. J-P. Grélois, Paris.
Coward, Barry (2003). *The Stuart Age*, 3rd ed., Harlow.
Croese, Gerardus (1696). *The General History of the Quakers*, London.
Cunnally, John (1999). *Images of the Illustrious: The Numismatic Presence in the Renaissance*, Princeton.
Dadré, Jean (1603). *Loci Communes*, Cologne.
Dallington, Robert (1605). *A Method for Travell*, London.
Dalrymple, William (1998). *From the Holy Mountain*, London.
——— (2006). *The Last Mughal*, London.
Dankoff, Robert and Kim, Sooyong (2010). *An Ottoman Traveller: Extracts from the 'Book of Travels' of Evliya Çelebi*, London.
Della Valle, Pietro (1989). *The Pilgrim: The Travels of Pietro della Valle*, ed. G. Bull, London.
Desgodetz, Antoine (1969 [1682]). *Les Edifices Antiques de Rome*, n.p.
Digby, Kenelm (1868). *Journal of a Voyage into the Mediterranean... A.D. 1628*, ed. J. Bruce, London.
——— (1968). *Loose Fantasies*, ed. V. Gabrieli, Rome.
Doody, Aude. (2010). *Pliny's Encyclopaedia: The Reception of the Natural History*, Cambridge.
Doran, Susan and Durston, Christopher (1991). *Princes, Pastors and People: The Church and Religion in England 1529–1689*, London.
Dowling, T.E. and Fletcher, E.W. (1915). *Hellenism in England*, London.
Du Bellay, Joachim (1994). *Ruines of Rome {Antiquitez de Rome}*, tr. E. Spenser, New York.
Dubuisson, Michel (1991). 'Graecus, graeculus, graecari: l'emploi péjoratif du nom des grecs en latin', in Suzanne Saïd (ed.), *ΕΛΛΗΝΙΣΜΟΣ: Quelques Jalons pour une Histoire de l'Identité Grecque*, Leiden, pp. 315–35.
Dugdale, William (1656). *The Antiquities of Warwickshire*, London.
Du Prey, P. de la R. (1991). *Hawksmoor's London Churches: Architecture and Theology*, Ann Arbor.
Ecole Française d'Athènes (1992). *La Redécouverte de Delphes*, Athens.
Elliott, J.H. (1972). *The Old World and the New*, Cambridge.
Elliott, R.W. (1963). *The Story of King Edward VI School, Bury St Edmunds*, Bury St Edmunds.

Ellison, James (2002). *George Sandys: Travel, Colonialism and Tolerance in the Seventeenth Century*, Cambridge.
Elsner, Jas (1992). 'Pausanias: a Greek pilgrim in the Roman world', *Past & Present* 135, pp. 3–29.
Elsner, Jas and Rubiés, J.-P. (1999). *Voyages and Visions: Towards a Cultural History of Travel*, London.
Esch, Arnold (*c*.2011). 'On the re-use of antiquity: the perspective of the archaeologist and the historian', in Richard Brilliant and Dale Kinney (eds), *Re-Use Value: Spolia and Appropriation in Art and Architecture from Constantine to Sherrie Levine*, Farnham.
Essex, Robert Devereux, Earl of, et al. (1633). *Profitable Instructions*, London.
Evans, D.R. (1993). 'Charles II's "grand tour": Restoration panegyric and the rhetoric of travel literature', *Philological Quarterly* 72, pp. 53–71.
Evelyn, John (1850–2). *Diary and Correspondence*, vol. 3, ed. W. Bray, London.
——— (1959). *Diary*, ed. E.S. de Beer, Oxford.
Feingold, Mordechai (1997). 'The humanities', in Nicholas Tyacke (ed.), *Seventeenth-Century Oxford*, History of the University of Oxford vol. 4, pp. 211–357.
Ferguson, M.W. (1984). '"The Afflatus of Ruin": meditations on Rome by Du Bellay, Spenser, and Stevens', in Annabel Patterson (ed.), *Roman Images*, Selected Papers from the English Institute 1982, new series 8, Baltimore, pp. 23–50.
Finch, J.S. (ed.) (1986). *A Catalogue of the Libraries of Sir Thomas Browne and Dr Edward Browne*, Leiden.
Finet, John (1656). *Finetti Philoxenis: Some Choice Observations*, ed. J. Howell, London.
Finkel, Caroline (2006). *Osman's Dream: The Story of the Ottoman Empire 1300–1923*, London.
Forde, William (1616). *A Sermon Preached at Constantinople*, London.
Fowler, Don (2000). *Roman Constructions: Readings in Postmodern Latin*, Oxford.
Fox, George (1706). *Gospel Truth Demonstrated*, London.
——— (1911). *Journal*, 2 vols, ed. N. Penney, London.
Fuller, Thomas (1642). *The Holy State*, Cambridge.
Gailhard, John (1678). *The Compleat Gentleman*, London.
Gainsford, Thomas (1618). *The Glory of England*, London.
Gallo, Luciana (2009). *Lord Elgin and Ancient Greek Architecture: The Elgin Drawings at the British Museum*, Cambridge.
Games, Alison (2008). *The Web of Empire: English Cosmopolitans in an Age of Expansion, 1560–1660*, Oxford.
Georgirenes, Joseph (1678). *A Description of the Present State of Samos, Nicaria, Patmos, and Mount Athos*, London.
Gilles, Pierre (1562). *De Topographia Constantinopoleos* and *De Bosphoro Thracio*, Lyon.
——— (2008). *Constantinople*, tr. K. Byrd, New York.
Gillespie, Stuart (2007). 'Lucretius in the English Renaissance', in Stuart Gillespie and Philip Hardie (eds), *Cambridge Companion to Lucretius*, Cambridge, pp. 242–53.
Glaser, Eliane (2007). *Judaism without Jews: Philosemitism and Christian Polemic in Early Modern England*, Basingstoke.
Goffman, Daniel (1990). *Izmir and the Levantine World, 1550–1650*, Seattle.
Goldhill, Simon (2001). *Being Greek under Rome*, Cambridge.
——— (2002). *Who Needs Greek?*, Cambridge.

Grafton, Anthony (1988). 'The Availability of ancient works', in Quentin Skinner and Eckhard Kessler (eds), *The Cambridge History of Renaissance Philosophy*, Cambridge, pp. 767–91.

——— (1992). *New Worlds, Ancient Texts: The Power of Tradition and the Shock of Discovery*, Cambridge, Mass.

Grassby, Richard (1994). *The English Gentleman in Trade: The Life and Works of Sir Dudley North, 1641–1691*, Oxford.

Green, Ian (2009). *Humanism and Protestantism in Early Modern English Education*, Farnham.

Greene, Molly (2000). *A Shared World: Christians and Muslims in the Early Modern Mediterranean*, Princeton.

Greene, Thomas (1982). *The Light in Troy: Imitation and Discovery in Renaissance Poetry*, New Haven.

Greenhalgh, Michael (c.2011). '*Spolia*: a definition in ruins', in Richard Brilliant and Dale Kinney (eds), *Re-Use Value: Spolia and Appropriation in Art and Architecture from Constantine to Sherrie Levine*, Farnham.

Grelot, G-J. (1681). *Relation Nouvelle d'un Voyage de Constantinople*, Paris.

Greville, Fulke (1633). 'A Letter of travell', in *Certaine Learned and Elegant Workes*, London.

Guillet de Saint-George, G. (1675). *Athènes Ancienne et Nouvelle*, Paris.

Guilmet, Celine (2007). 'The dissemination of the Periegesis in print, 16th–17th centuries' and 'The French translation by Nicolas Gédoyn', in M. Georgopoulou, C. Guilmet, Y.A. Pikoulas, K. Staikos and G. Tolias (eds), *Following Pausanias: The Quest for Greek Antiquity*, New Castle, Del., pp. 88–95, 120–4.

Gyllius. *See* Gilles.

Habicht, Christian (1998). *Pausanias' Guide to Ancient Greece*, Berkeley.

Hale, Matthew (1817). *A Letter of Advice to His Grandchildren*, Boston.

Hall, Edith (2008). *The Return of Ulysses: A Cultural History of Homer's Odyssey*, London.

[Hall, Joseph] (1609). *The Discovery of a New World*, London.

Hall, Joseph (1674). *Concerning Travellers, to Prevent Popish and Debauch'd Principles*, London.

——— (1975 [1617]). *Quo Vadis: A Just Censure of Travel*, Amsterdam.

Hammond, Paul (1998). 'Classical texts: translations and transformations', in S.N. Zwicker (ed.), *The Cambridge Companion to English Literature 1650–1740*, Cambridge, pp. 143–61.

Hardie, Philip (1993). *The Epic Successors of Virgil*, Cambridge.

Harrigan, Michael (2003). 'Cabinet and collection in the seventeenth-century "récit de voyage en orient"', in Jane Conroy (ed.), *Cross-Cultural Travel: Papers from the Royal Irish Academy Symposium on Literature and Travel... November 2002*, New York, pp. 49–55.

Haskell, Francis and Penny, Nicholas (1981). *Taste and the Antique: The Lure of Classical Sculpture 1500–1800*, New Haven.

Hasluck, F.W. (1910–11). 'The first English traveller's account of Athos (1677)', *Annual of the British School at Athens* 17, pp. 103–31.

——— (1929). *Christianity and Islam under the Sultans*, 2 vols, ed. M.M. Hasluck, Oxford.

Haynes, D.E.L. (1975). *The Arundel Marbles*, Oxford.

Haynes, Jonathan (1986). *The Humanist as Traveler: George Sandys's 'Relation of a Journey Begun An. Dom. 1610'*, London.
Heath, M.J. (1979). 'Renaissance scholars and the origin of the Turks', *Bibliothèque d'Humanisme et Renaissance* 41, pp. 453–71.
Hemmerdinger Iliadou, D. (1967). 'La Crète sous la domination vénitienne et lors de la conquête turque (1322–1684)', *Studi Veneziani* 9, pp. 535–623.
Henderson, G.P. (1971). *The Revival of Greek Thought, 1620–1830*, Edinburgh.
Herrin, Judith (2007). *Byzantium: The Surprising Life of a Medieval Empire*, London.
[Heylyn, Peter] (1631). ΜΙΚΡΟΚΟΣΜΟΣ: *A Little Description of the Great World*, 5th ed., Oxford.
Hill, Aaron (1709). *A Full and Just Account of the Present State of the Ottoman Empire*, London.
Hill, Rosemary (2010). 'Gentlemen did not dig', *London Review of Books*, 24 June, pp. 25–7.
Hingley, Richard (2000). *Roman Officers and English Gentlemen*, London.
Historical Manuscripts Commission (HMC) (1893 and 1901). *The Manuscripts of the Duke of Portland*, vols 2, 7, London.
Historical Manuscripts Commission (HMC) (1913 and 1922). *Report on the Manuscripts of A.G. Finch*, vols 1, 2, London.
Hobbes, Thomas (1679). *Behemoth*, London.
Hodgen, M.T. (1964). *Early Anthropology in the Sixteenth and Seventeenth Centuries*, Philadelphia.
Holt, P.M. (1973). *Studies in the History of the Near East*, London.
Horringer Parish Records 1558–1850 (1900). Woodbridge.
Howarth, David (1985). *Lord Arundel and His Circle*, New Haven.
Howell, James (1650). *Instructions and Directions for Forren Travel*, London.
——— (1678). *Epistolae Ho-elianae*, 5th ed., London.
Hunter, Michael (1995). *Science and the Shape of Orthodoxy: Intellectual Change in Late Seventeenth-Century Britain*, Woodbridge.
Hussey, Christopher (1967). *The Picturesque*, London.
Iliffe, Robert (1998 and 1999). 'Foreign bodies: travel, empire and the early Royal Society of London', *Canadian Journal of History* 33, pp. 357–85; *Canadian Journal of History* 34, pp. 23–50.
Irwin, Robert (2006). *For Lust of Knowing*, London.
Jackson, J.E. (1862). *Wiltshire: The Topographical Collections of John Aubrey*, Devizes.
Janowitz, Anne (1990). *England's Ruins*, Cambridge, Mass.
Jenkins, Ian (2006). *Greek Architecture and Its Sculpture in the British Museum*, London.
Kallendorf, Craig (2007). *The Virgilian Tradition: Book History and the History of Reading in Early Modern Europe*, Aldershot.
King, Henry (1664). *Poems, Elegies, Paradoxes and Sonnets*, London.
Kinney, Dale (2006). 'The concept of *spolia*', in Conrad Rudolph (ed.), *Companion to Medieval Art*, Oxford.
Kishlansky, Mark (1997). *A Monarchy Transformed: Britain 1603–1714*, London.
Knolles, Richard (1603). *The Generall Historie of the Turkes*, London.
——— (1687). *The Turkish History*, London.
Krautheimer, Richard (2000). *Rome: Profile of a City, 312–1308*, Princeton.
Laborde, L.E.S.J. de (1854). *Athènes au XVe, XVIe et XVIIe siècles*, 2 vols, Paris.
Langdon, Helen (1989). *Claude Lorrain*, Oxford.

——— (1996). 'The imaginative geographies of Claude Lorrain', in Chloe Chard and Helen Langdon (eds), *Transports: Travel, Pleasure and Imaginative Geography, 1600–1830*, New Haven, pp. 151–78.
Lassels, Richard (1670). *The Voyage of Italy*, London.
Leigh, Edward (1671). *Three Diatribes or Discourses*, London.
Lewis, Bernard (2004). *From Babel to Dragomans: Interpreting the Middle East*, London.
Lithgow, William (1632). *The Totall Discourse of the Rare Adventures and Painefull Peregrinations*, London.
Livanios, Dimitris (2008). 'The quest for Hellenism: religion, nationalism and collective identities in Greece, 1453–1913', in K. Zacharia (ed.), *Hellenism: Culture, Identity and Ethnicity from Antiquity to Modernity*, Aldershot, pp. 237–69.
Locke, John (1968). *The Educational Writings of John Locke*, ed. J.T. Axtell, Cambridge.
Lyne, Raphael (2001). *Ovid's Changing Worlds: English Metamorphoses 1567–1632*, Oxford.
MacDougall, H.A. (1982). *Racial Myth in English History: Trojans, Teutons and Anglo-Saxons*, Montreal.
Mackenzie, Molly (1992). *Turkish Athens: The Forgotten Centuries, 1456–1832*, Reading.
McKeon, Michael (1987). *The Origins of the English Novel, 1600–1740*, Baltimore.
Mack, Peter (2002). *Elizabethan Rhetoric: Theory and Practice*, Cambridge.
MacLean, Gerald (2004). *The Rise of Oriental Travel: English Visitors to the Ottoman Empire 1580–1720*, London.
——— (2007). *Looking East: English Writing and the Ottoman Empire before 1800*, Basingstoke.
Malloch, Archibald (1917). *Finch and Baines: A Seventeenth Century Friendship*, Cambridge.
Mango, Cyril (2000). 'The triumphal way of Constantinople and the Golden Gate', *Dumbarton Oaks Papers* 54, pp. 173–88.
Mansel, Philip (2006). *Constantinople: City of the World's Desire, 1453–1924*, London.
Marsh, Henry (1663). *A New Survey of the Turkish Empire*, London.
Maryon, Herbert (1956). 'The Colossus of Rhodes', *Journal of Hellenic Studies* 76, pp. 68–86.
Matar, Nabil (1991). 'Islam in Interregnum and Restoration England', *Seventeenth Century* 6, pp. 57–71.
——— (1998). *Islam in Britain, 1558–1685*, Cambridge.
——— (1999). *Turks, Moors and Englishmen in the Age of Discovery*, New York.
Mayor, J.E.B. (ed.) (1911). *Cambridge under Queen Anne*, Cambridge.
Mazower, Mark (2001). *The Balkans from the End of Byzantium to the Present Day*, London.
——— (2004). *Salonica, City of Ghosts: Christians, Muslims and Jews, 1430–1950*, London.
Merritt, B.D. (1949). 'The epigraphic notes of Francis Vernon', *Hesperia Supplements* 8, pp. 213–27.
Michaelis, Adolf (1882). *Ancient Marbles in Great Britain*, tr. C.A.M. Fennell, Cambridge.
[Milles, Thomas] (1721). *An Account of the Life... of Mr. Isaac Milles*, London.
Milton, John (1938). *Works*, vol. 18, New York.

——— (1973). *Areopagitica* and *Of Education*, ed. K.M. Lea, Oxford.
Mitsi, Efterpi (2008). 'A translator's voyage: the Greek landscape in George Sandys's *Relation of a Journey* (1615)', *Studies in Travel Writing* 12, pp. 49–65.
Momigliano, Arnaldo (1950). 'Ancient history and the antiquarian', *Journal of the Warburg and Courtauld Institutes* 13, pp. 285–315.
Monconys, Balthasar de (1677). *Journal*, Lyon.
Montagu, Mary Wortley (1965). *Complete Letters*, vol. 1, ed. R. Halsband, Oxford.
Morgan, Victor (2004). *A History of the University of Cambridge*, vol. 2, *1546–1750*, Cambridge.
Mossière, J-C. (1993). 'Voyage en orient et le livre d'Athènes', in R. Etienne (ed.), *Jacob Spon: un Humaniste Lyonnais du XVIIe siècle*, Paris, pp. 207–28.
Mundy, Peter (1907). *The Travels of Peter Mundy in Europe and Asia, 1608–1667*, vol. 1, ed. R.C. Temple, Hakluyt Society 2nd series 17, Cambridge.
Neale, Thomas (1643). *A Treatise of Direction, How to Travel Safely*, London.
Neuhusius, Reiner (1658). *Florilegium philologicum*, Amsterdam.
Nicolson, M.H. (1959). *Mountain Gloom and Mountain Glory: The Development of the Aesthetics of the Infinite*, Ithaca.
——— (1992). *The Conway Letters*, ed., rev. S. Hutton, Oxford.
North, Roger (1890). *The Lives of... Francis North, ... Dudley North; and... John North*, vol. 2, ed. A. Jessopp, London.
Ogden, H.V.S. and Ogden, M.S. (1955). *English Taste in Landscape in the Seventeenth Century*, Ann Arbor.
Oglander, John (1936). *A Royalist's Notebook*, ed. F. Bamford, London.
Oldenburg, Henry (1965–86). *Correspondence*, 13 vols, ed. and tr. A.R. Hall and M.B. Hall, London.
Pailin, D.A. (1984). *Attitudes to Other Religions: Comparative Religion in Seventeenth- and Eighteenth-Century Britain*, Manchester.
Palmer, Thomas (1606). *An Essay of the Meanes How to Make Our Travels... the More Profitable and Honourable*, London.
Parker, Kenneth (ed.) (1999). *Early Modern Tales of Orient*, London.
Parry, Graham (1995). *Trophies of Time: English Antiquarians of the Seventeenth Century*, Oxford.
Pausanias (1971). *Guide to Greece {Description of Greece}*, ed. P. Levi, London.
Peacham, Henry (1612). *Graphice*, London.
——— (1962). *The Complete Gentleman*, ed. V.B. Heltzel, Ithaca, New York.
Pearson, J.B. (1883). *A Biographical Sketch of the Chaplains to the Levant Company*, Cambridge.
Peile, John (1910). *Biographical Register of Christ's College*, vol. 1, *1448–1665*, Cambridge.
Pepys, Samuel (1970). *Diary*, vol. 1, ed. R. Latham and W. Matthews, London.
Pinnington, Judith (2003). *Anglicans and Orthodox: Unity and Subversion 1559–1725*, Leominster.
Poole, Rachael (1912). 'A seventeenth-century archaeological explorer and his methods', *Classical Review* 26, pp. 109–14.
Potts, Alex (1994). *Flesh and the Ideal: Winckelmann and the Origins of Art History*, New Haven.
Prest, Wilfrid (1967). 'Legal education of the gentry at the Inns of Court, 1560–1640', *Past and Present* 38, pp. 20–39.

BIBLIOGRAPHY 261

Pretzler, Maria (2007). *Pausanias: Travel Writing in Ancient Greece*, London.
Purchas, Samuel (1626). *Purchas His Pilgrimage*, London.
―――― (1905–7). *Hakluytus Posthumus, or, Purchas His Pilgrimes*, 20 vols, Glasgow.
Quinton, Anthony (1980). *Francis Bacon*, Oxford.
Raby, Julian (1983). 'Mehmed the Conqueror's Greek scriptorium', *Dumbarton Oaks Papers* 37, pp. 15–34.
Randolph, Bernard (1687). *The Present State of the Islands in the Archipelago*, Oxford.
―――― (1689). *The Present State of the Morea*, London.
Raphael, S. (1993). 'The Reverend Sir George Wheler, 1650–1724', in Roland Etienne (ed.), *Jacob Spon: un Humaniste Lyonnais du XVIIe Siècle*, Paris, pp. 257–67.
Ravelhofer, Barbara (2006). *The Early Stuart Masque: Dance, Costume and Music*, Oxford.
Raven, James (c.2007). *The Business of Books: Booksellers and the English Book Trade 1450–1850*, New Haven.
Ray, John (1693). *A Collection of Curious Travels and Voyages*, 2 vols, London.
Reed, J.D. (2007). *Virgil's Gaze: Nation and Poetry in the 'Aeneid'*, Princeton.
Roberts, Lewes (1638). *The Merchants Mappe of Commerce*, London.
Robertson, D.S. (1969). *Greek and Roman Architecture*, Cambridge.
Robertson, Martin (1975). *A History of Greek Art*, 2 vols, Cambridge.
Robson, Charles (1628). *Newes from Aleppo*, London.
Roe, Thomas (1740). *The Negotiations of Sir Thomas Roe... 1621–1628*, London.
Rossi, Andreola (2001). 'Remapping the past: Caesar's tale of Troy', *Phoenix* 55/3–4, pp. 313–26.
Royal Society (1665–6). *Philosophical Transactions*, January 1665/6.
Rubiés, J.-P. (1996). 'Instructions for travelers: teaching the eye to see', *History and Anthropology* 6, pp. 139–90.
―――― (2002). 'Travel writing and ethnography', in Peter Hulme and Tim Youngs (eds), *The Cambridge Companion to Travel Writing*, Cambridge, pp. 242–60.
―――― (2007). *Travellers and Cosmographers*, Aldershot.
Rudolf, Ernst (1989). *Attische Sarkophage aus Ephesos*, Vienna.
Runciman, Steven (1968). *The Great Church in Captivity*, Cambridge.
[Rycaut, Paul] (1661). *A Narrative of the Success of the Voyage of the Right Honourable Heneage Finch*, London.
Rycaut, Paul (1675). *The History of the Present State of the Ottoman Empire*, 4th ed., London.
―――― (1679). *The Present State of the Greek and Armenian Churches*, London.
―――― (1680). *The History of the Turkish Empire from... 1623 to... 1677*, London (includes Rycaut's *Memoirs*).
Sainsbury, W.N. (ed.) (1859). *Original Unpublished Papers Illustrative of the Life of Sir Peter Paul Rubens*, London.
Sanderson, John (1931). *The Travels of John Sanderson in the Levant, 1584–1602*, ed. W. Foster, Hakluyt Society 2nd series 67, London.
Sanderson, William (1658). *Graphice*, London.
Sandys, Edwin (1629). *Europae Speculum*, The Hague.
Sandys, George (1615). *A Relation of a Journey Begun an. dom. 1610*, London.
Sarton, George (1954). 'The death and burial of Vesalius and, incidentally, of Cicero', *Isis* 45/2, pp. 131–7.

Scott, Jonathan (2003). *The Pleasures of Antiquity: British Collectors of Greece and Rome*, New Haven.
Seferis, George (1969). *Collected Poems 1924–1955*, tr. E. Keeley and P. Sherrard, London.
Segal, Erich (1987). *Roman Laughter: The Comedy of Plautus*, New York.
Selden, John (1628). *Marmora Arundeliana*, London.
Setton, K.M. (ed.) (1975). *Athens in the Middle Ages*, London.
Sherley, Thomas (1936). *Discours of the Turkes*, ed. E. Dennison Ross, Camden Miscellany 3rd series 52, London.
Smith, Stephen (1676). *Wholsome Advice*, n.p.
Smith, Thomas (1678). *Remarks upon the Manners, Religion and Government of the Turks*, London.
—— (1680). *An Account of the Greek Church*, Oxford.
Spencer, Terence (1952). 'Turks and Trojans in the Renaissance', *Modern Language Review* 47, pp. 330–3.
—— (1974). *Fair Greece, Sad Relic: Literary Philhellenism from Shakespeare to Byron*, Bath.
Spenser, Edmund. See du Bellay.
Spon, Jacob (1679). *Réponse à la Critique Publiée par M. Guillet*, Lyon.
Spon, Jacob and Wheler, George (1678). *Voyage d'Italie, de Dalmatie, de Grèce, et du Levant*, 3 vols, Lyon.
—— (1724). *Voyage d'Italie, de Dalmatie, de Grèce, et du Levant*, 2 vols, The Hague.
Staikos, K.S. (2007). 'The first edition of Pausanias' Ἑλλάδος Περιήγησις', in M. Georgopoulou, C. Guilmet, Y.A. Pikoulas, K. Staikos and G. Tolias (eds), *Following Pausanias: The Quest for Greek Antiquity*, New Castle, Del.
Stanford, W.B. (1992). *The Ulysses Theme: A Study in the Adaptability of a Traditional Hero*, Dallas.
—— and Luce, J.V. (1974). *The Quest for Ulysses*, London.
—— and Finopoulos, E.J. (1984). *The Travels of Lord Charlemont in Greece and Turkey, 1749*, London.
Stavrianos, L.S. (2000). *The Balkans since 1453*, London.
Stoye, John (1989). *English Travellers Abroad, 1604–1667*, New Haven.
Strachan, Michael (1989). *Sir Thomas Roe, 1581–1644: A Life*, Salisbury.
Stuart, James and Revett, Nicholas (1762). *Antiquities of Athens*, vol. 1, London.
Sugar, P.F. (1977). *Southeastern Europe under Ottoman Rule, 1354–1804*, A History of East Central Europe 5, Seattle.
Sumner-Boyd, Hilary and Freely, John (2003). *Strolling through Istanbul*, London.
Swann, Marjorie (2001). *Curiosities and Texts: The Culture of Collecting in Early Modern England*, Philadelphia.
Tappe, E.D. (1954). 'The Greek College at Oxford, 1699–1705', *Oxoniensia* 19, pp. 92–111.
Tavernier, J.B. (1678). *The Six Voyages*, London.
Taylor, Joan (2006). *The Englishman, the Moor and the Holy City*, Stroud.
Teonge, Henry (1927). *Diary {1675–9}*, ed. G.E. Manwaring, London.
Terence (2001). *Plays*, vol. 1, ed. J. Barsby, Cambridge, Mass.
Thomas, Keith (1995). 'English Protestantism and classical art', in Lucy Gent (ed.), *Albion's Classicism: The Visual Arts in Britain, 1550–1660*, New Haven.
—— (2009). *The Ends of Life: Roads to Fulfilment in Early Modern England*, Oxford.

Thurloe, John (1742). *A Collection of the State Papers of John Thurloe*, ed. T. Birch, London.
Tinniswood, Adrian (2007). *The Verneys: A True Story of Love, War and Madness in Seventeenth-Century England*, London.
Toomer, G.J. (1996). *Eastern Wisedom and Learning*, Oxford.
Tournefort, J.P. de (1717). *Relation d'un Voyage du Levant*, vol. 2, Paris.
Tregaskis, Hugh (1979). *Beyond the Grand Tour: The Levant Lunatics*, London.
Trevor-Roper, Hugh (1992). *From Counter-Reformation to Glorious Revolution*, London.
Twigg, John (1990). *The University of Cambridge and the English Revolution, 1625– 1688*, Woodbridge.
Vacalopoulos, A.E. (1976). *The Greek Nation 1453–1669*, tr. I. Moles and P. Moles, New Brunswick.
Vernon, Francis (1676). 'Letter to the Fellows of the Royal Society', *Philosophical Transactions of the Royal Society* 11/124 (24 April), pp. 575–82.
Veryard, Ellis (1701). *An Account of Divers Choice Remarks*, London.
Vitkus, D.J. (1999). 'Early modern orientalism: representations of Islam in sixteenth- and seventeenth-century Europe', in D.R. Blanks and Michael Frassetto (eds), *Western Views of Islam in Medieval and Early Modern Europe*, New York.
――― (2001). 'Trafficking with the Turk: English travelers in the Ottoman Empire during the early seventeenth century', in Ivo Kamps and J.G. Singh (eds), *Travel Knowledge: European 'Discoveries' in the Early Modern Period*, New York, pp. 35–52.
――― (2003). *Turning Turk: English Theater and the Multicultural Mediterranean*, New York.
Vitruvius (1999). *Ten Books on Architecture*, ed. I.D. Rowland and T.N. Howe, Cambridge.
Vout, Caroline (2006). Untitled review, *Journal of Hellenic Studies* 126, pp. 226–7.
Walker, Matthew (2013). 'Francis Vernon, the early Royal Society and the first English encounter with ancient Greek architecture', *Architectural History* 56, pp. 29–61.
Walsham, Alexandra (2011). *The Reformation of the Landscape*, Oxford.
Wansbrough, John (1996). *Lingua Franca in the Mediterranean*, Richmond.
Ward, John (1740). *The Lives of the Professors of Gresham College*, London.
Warneke, Sara (1995). *Images of the Educational Traveller in Early Modern England*, Leiden.
Watkin, D.J. (ed.) (1972). *Sale Catalogues of Libraries of Eminent Persons*, vol. 4, London.
Watson, Foster (1968 [1908]). *The English Grammar Schools to 1660: Their Curriculum and Practice*, London.
――― (1971 [1909]). *The Beginnings of the Teaching of Modern Subjects in England*, Wakefield.
Webb, John (1857). 'Some passages in the life and character of a lady', *Archaeologia* 37, pp. 189–223.
Wheeler, J.R. (1901). 'Notes on the so-called Capuchin plans of Athens', *Harvard Studies in Classical Philology* 12, pp. 221–30.
Wheler, George (1682). *Journey into Greece*, London.
――― (1689). *An Account of the Churches... of the Primitive Christians*, London.

——— (1698). *The Protestant Monastery*, n.p.
——— (1911). *Autobiography of Sir George Wheler*, ed. E.G. Wheler, Birmingham.
Williams, George (1868). *The Orthodox Church of the East in the Eighteenth Century*, London.
Wilson, Jean (1995). 'Two names of friendship, but one starre', *Church Monuments* 10, pp. 70–83.
Wood, A.C. (1925). 'The English Embassy at Constantinople, 1660–1762', *English Historical Review* 40, pp. 533–61.
Woodhouse, C.M. (1998). *Modern Greece: A Short History*, London.
Wotton, Henry (1651). *Reliquiae Wottonianae*, London.
Yerasimos, Stefanos (1991). *Les Voyageurs dans l'Empire Ottoman (XIVe–XVIe siècles)*, Ankara.
Zuallardo, Giovanni (1587). *Il Devotissimo Viaggio di Gerusalemme*, Rome.

INDEX

[Dates in brackets indicate the dates travellers first arrived in the Levant.]

accommodation, 48–9, 59–60, 117
'Achilles sarcophagus', fig 17
Adams, P.G., 16, 207
Addison, Joseph, 125
Adrianople (modern Edirne), 14, 18, 22, 25, 28, 30, 47, 48, 62, 96, 198
Aegae, 76
Aeneas, 70–2, 160–1, 164
Aeschylus, 73
Aesculapius, 206
Aesop, 36, 86
Agesilaus, 77
Aleppo, 41, 179, 185
Alexander the Great, 68–9, 76, 87–8, 162, 180
Alexandretta, *see* Scanderun
Alexandria, 52
Alexandria Troas, 110–11
Allen, Lindsay, 119
Alonia (modern Paşalimani), 92
Alps, 116
America, *see* new world
Amphissa, 81, 130, 165, 167
Andréossy, A., 126
Anglicanism, 112, 183
 catechism, translations, 185
 Orthodoxy and, 21, 32, 46, 175, 181–5

animals
 attitudes to, 26, 62, 196–7
 imagery, 199
Anne, 201
anthologies, 34
Antiquaries, Society of, 128
antiquities and antiquarian
 studies, 8–9, 11, 104–13, 119–34, 149–50, 156, 208, 211
 see also collecting, ruins *and under* Covel, Wheler
Antony (Mark Antony), 127
Apelles, 105, 142
Appian, 143
Apollo, 89
Apollonius Rhodius, 149
Arabia, 176
Arabic, 23, 34–5, 36, 56–7, 67, 97, 144, 145–6
Arcadia, 92
archaeology, beginnings of, 42, 61, 82, 132, 150, 208
 see also antiquities and antiquarian studies
Archangel, 174
architecture
 Anglican churches, 185–6
 arches, 133

architecture *cont.*
  nomenclature, 133
archon lists, 125
Ariadne, 88, 89, 126
Aristophanes, 5, 36
Aristotle, 37, 67
Armenians, 84, 143, 178
Arnauld, Antoine, 182
Arrian, 75, 87, 180
Arundel, Thomas Howard, 2nd Earl of 8, 55, 104, 106, 120, 136–7
Arundel House, 136–7
Ascham, Roger, 9
Athanasius, St, 66, 175
Athenians, 87–8, 160, 166, 209
Athens, 46, 74, 78, 81, 109, 117, 120, 121, 123, 151, 153, 154, figs 11, 12
  Areopagus, 131–2
  Babin on, 74, 99, 117
  Erechtheum, 81–2
  gymnasium, 121
  Lysicrates monument/Lantern of Demosthenes, 132
  Odeon of Herodes Atticus, 132
  Parthenon, 45, 99, 109, 116, 123, 124, 125, 129, 137, 138, 142, 208, fig 13
  Philopappos monument, 131
  Propylaea, 81
  stadium, 132
  St Paul in, 91
  temple of Nike, 89
  temple of Olympian Zeus, 132
  theatre of Bacchus/Dionysus (supposed), 73, 99–100, 120
  Theseion, 129
  Turks, Venetians and 30, 45
Athos, Mt, 169, 172–3, figs 18, 19, 20
  Belon on, 24, 74, 98, 114, 146, 148, 171, 172–3
  Covel at, 14, 21, 24, 29, 47, 53, 55, 98, 114, 142–3, 148–9, 172–8

libraries, 98, 144, 146, 165, 170, 173, 175
  see also under Rycaut
atlases, *see* maps
Aubrey, John, 124
Augustus, 142
Ausonius, 108
Austria, 45
Avcioğlu, Nebahat, 210
Ayres, Philip, 94

Babin, J.P., 74, 99, 117
Baccareschi, 60, 204
bacchantes, 206
Bacon, Francis, 6, 39, 40, 111–12
Baddeley, Richard, 69
Baines, Thomas (1672), 17, 19, 34, 37, 39–40, 94
  death, 27, 29, 61, 71–2
  Finch and, 27–8, 61, 71–2, 95
  Vani Effendi and, 58, 193–4, 204
Baker, Daniel, 199
Baker, D.J., 42
barbarians, Greeks as, 152
Barberini, Maffeo, 114
Barberini Library, 114, 123
Bardales, Dionysios, 174
Bargrave, Robert (1647), 56, 61–2, 115, 116, 178, 210
Basire, Isaac (1646 or 1647), 97, 185
Baudier, Michel, 87
Belgrade (village near Constantinople), 56, 62
Belon, Pierre, 67, 74, 98, 100, 126
  on Mt Athos, 24, 74, 98, 114, 146, 148, 171,˙172–3
Bendish, Anne (1647), 61, 63
Bendish, Thomas (1647), 63, 185
Bernizelo, Demetrio, 165
Bevis of Hampton, 88
Bible, 66, 90–2, 93
  King James version, 107
  New Testament, 36, 90, 91, 92, 103, 112, 156, 172

INDEX

Old Testament, 91–2
polyglot Bible, 96, 147
Biddulph, William (1600), 15, 29, 71, 97, 125, 209
Bishop, George, 198
Blaeu, Joan, 47
Blome, Richard, 7
Blount, Henry (1629), 40, 76–7, 97, 106, 124, 155, 206
  Turks and, 3–4, 14–15, 158, 169, 191–2, 195, 198–9, 200, 202
Bon, Dr 165
books and libraries, 10, 33, 41, 50–1, 66–7, 95–101, 122, 138, 144–9, 171, 204
  Greek printing, 72, 97, 146
  world as a book, 10
  see also under Athos, Covel
Bosphorus, 61, 98, 125, 180, 195
botany, *see under* Wheler
Bray, Alan, 27
Brerewood, Edward, 155
bribery, 54, 55, 120
Brinsley, John, 35, 156
British Library, 145
Brotton, Jerry, 4
Browne, Edward (Thomas Browne's son, 1668), 11, 48, 54, 101, 104, 195–6
  at Arundel House, 136–7
  interest in history, 70, 87, 88, 120
  library, 33
  slavery and, 201–2
  Vernon and, 36, 57
Browne, Elizabeth, 101
Browne, Thomas, 11, 40, 101, 104, 120, 124–5
Brutus, 162
Buckingham, George Villiers, 1st Duke of 104, 136, 137
Bulliet, R.W., 203
burial, 60–1
Burrow, Colin, 37, 68
Bursa, *see* Prusa

Burton, Robert, 115–16
Bury St Edmunds, King Edward VI School, 12, 33, 35–6
Busbecq, Ogier de, 69, 145
Byron, George Gordon, Lord 106
Byzantine Empire, 144–5, 154, 179–80
  art, 142–3
  imperial library, 147

Cadmus, 90
Caesar, 35, 68–9, 70, 76, 162
Cairo, 147
Calvinism, 183
Cambridge Platonism, 21, 37, 40, 94
Cambridge University, 33, 37–8
Camden, William, 9, 39, 94–5, 105, 124, 162
Candia, *see* Crete
Cantacuzenos, Michael, 165
capitulations (trade agreements), 58
Capuchins, 30, 31, 100, 109
caravanserais, *see* khans
Carrey, Jacques, 123
Carthage, 67, 209
Cary, John, 23–4, 60
Castri, 81, 130
Catholicism
  anti-Catholicism, 3, 155, 179, 181–4, 186, 194, 205
  anti-travel arguments and, 7
  arguments within, 182
  crypto, 3
  in Greek islands, 30
  see also under Covel, Orthodox Church
Cato, 153
Catullus, 36
Cayster, R., 78
Cephallonia, 30, 76, 127
Ceres, 89, 138, 141
Cervi/Cerigo/Cythera, 70, 164, 206
Chalcis (modern Heybeliada), 47
  S. Trinitas monastery, 145, 180
Chard, Chloe, 16

Chares of Lindos, 142
Charlemont, James Caulfeild, Lord, 209
Charles I, 84, 104, 128, 136, 137, 139, 157, 183, 210
Charles II, 6, 10, 107, 128, 162
Chaucer, Geoffrey, 101
Cheke, John, 23, 51, 96
Chios, 30, 122, 168, 184
  see also under Covel
Christianity
  Islam and, 11, 144, 148, 158, 184, 193, 199
  paganism and, 35, 90, 93–5, 186
  persecution of Christians, 143
  punishment of Christians, 83, 103, 112, 158, 186–7
  sects, 185
  see also Anglicanism, Catholicism, Orthodox Church, Quakers, seven churches of Asia *and under* Covel
Christ's College, Cambridge, 12, 37
  Finch/Baines tomb, 27, 61, 95, fig 7
chronology, historical, 119–20, 132, 208
  coinage and, 124–5
Chrysostom, St John, 66
churches, 50
  converted into mosques, 116–17
  English, destroyed in Interregnum, 200, 210
  used by sick, 206
  see also seven churches of Asia
Church Fathers, 96, 147–8, 171
Cicero, 5, 35, 76, 93, 95, 107
  attitude to Greeks, 152–3
  tomb, 127–8
  citation, 6, 13, 35, 65–73, 83, 92–3, 103
civility, 3, 7
  Turkish, 4, 191–2, 195, 199
Clarendon, Edward Hyde, 1st Earl of 147
classical texts, 34–5, 65, 144, 206

development of critical attitude to, 74, 77, 82
poetry, 67–73
prose, 73–86
see also citation, Greek, Latin, *and specific authors*
classics, emotional commitment to, 40–1, 44, 206–7
Claude, Jean, 182
Claude Lorrain, 115, 116
Cleland, James, 7, 66, 190
climate, religion and, 9
clocks, 51, 174–5
clothes, *see* dress
Cnidos, 106, 142
Codex Alexandrinus, 145
coffee and coffee-houses, 54–5, 120, 206
coins and coinage, 104, 105, 124–5, 135, 138, 208
Coke, Thomas, 96
Colet, John, 95
collecting, 134–49
  antiquities, books and manuscripts, 11, 40, 104–6, 122, 144–9
  natural history specimens, 40
  see also under Covel, Wheler
Colossians, 90
commonplace books, 34, 37, 66
Comneno family, 165
Coningsby, Humfrey, 63–4
consolatio, 5
Constantine, 110
Constantinople/Stambol (modern Istanbul), 30, 31, 48, 54, 115, 117–18, 144–5, 154, 160, 174, 191
  English community, 199
  Gilles on, 74, 98–9, 100
  Golden Gate, 137
  Greek press in, 97, 146
  Haghia Sophia, 117, 122, 143, 179, 180, 193
  mosaics, 143
  Pera, 54

INDEX

Seven Towers, 19, 137
slave market, 201
Suleiman's Mosque, 143
conversion, religious, 8, 31, 91, 181, 182–3, 185, 188–90, 194, 199, 202–4
see also renegades
Conway, Anne, 194
Copais, Lake, Boeotia, 80–1
Corfu, 30, 165
Corinth, 91, 92, 115–16, 123–4, 148, 170
Coryate, Thomas (1612), 10, 15–16, 54, 97, 98–9, 114–15, 206
 on Cicero's tomb, 127
 death, 63
 at Troy, 42, 108, 134–5, 142
Cos/Kos, 117, 142
costume, *see* dress
Cotton, Charles, 107
Cotton, Robert, 9, 128, 135
Covel, John (1669/70), 2, 10, 32, 208, figs 1, 2, 4, 5, 10, 15, 16, 18, 19, 21, 23
 books, library and, 15, 22, 23, 24, 33, 50–1, 95–101
 at Carthage, 67
 Catholicism and, 17, 21, 25, 31, 164, 182
 classics, Christianity and, 20, 43, 93–5
 collecting, 11, 12, 135
 code, 17–18, fig 4
 education, 5, 12, 33, 34, 37, 38–9
 'emotional commitment' to classics, 40–1, 44, 206
 food, drink and, 53–5, 177–8, 196
 Greeks/Orthodox church and, 11–12, 20–1, 31–2, 46, 70–1, 151, 154, 156, 163–8, 170–2, 178–9, 182–3, 205
 health, sickness and, 60
 interests, 11, 20, 23–4, 38–9, 56

 antiquarian, 42, 120, 125, 129, 137
 scientific/medical, 11, 23–4, 39, 60, 79
 on Islam, 31
 Jews and, 22, 48
 journeys from Constantinople, 47–50, 107
 Chios, 23, 25, 28, 54, 70, 91, 168
 Cyzicus, 67, 75
 Ephesus, 13, 24, 47, 78–9, 93–4, 120, 121, 122–3, 132, 143–4, 208
 Lemnos, 76
 Nicaea, 14, 47, 79, 107, 108, 118, 123, 133–4, 157
 seven churches, 90, 103, 186
 see also Athos, Mt
 knowledge of languages, 22–3, 36, 56–7
 life and personality, 12, 20, 24–7, 29, 42–4, 45–6, 62
 luggage, 50–2, 66, 95, 96
 Old Testament and, 91
 Orthodoxy and, 11, 12, 20, 21, 31, 32, 46, 60, 164, 170, 182–3
 Ottoman court and, 25, 47, 58, 62, 88–9, 175, 189, 195, 204
 relationships
 expatriates, 19, 20, 24, 26–8, 41, 47, 78, 97, 100–1, 114
 women, 28
 religion and theology, 21–2, 26, 29–30, 175, 179
 on ruins, *spolia* etc, 113, 117, 118
 scenery and, 113, 114
 on sexual morality, 25–6, 27–8, 200
 texts and, 13, 65–6, 73, 74–5, 86, 92, 101
 on travel, 207
 Turks/Islam and, 31, 96, 117, 118, 160, 178, 196, 202
 work as chaplain, 9, 18–19, 46, 61
 writings, 12–21

Crawford, James, 40, 105, 121, 129–30, 184
Crete/Candia, 30, 45, 89, 90, 117, 127, 165, 179
  conversions to Islam, 203, 204
  'doctoresses', 60, 168–9
  labyrinth, 76, 88, 126
Croese, Gerardus, 197
Crow, Sackville, Jr, 38
Crow, Sacville, Sr, 38
curiosities, cabinets of, 9, 92, 104
curiosity as motive for travel, 7–10, 45–6, 94
Curtius Rufus, Quintus, 66
Cythera, *see* Cervi
Cyzicus, 25, 47, 67, 75, 79–80, 112, 118, 135

Dadré, Jean, 34
Daedalus and Icarus, 88, 126
Dallam, Thomas (1599), 59, 200
Dallington, Robert, 190
Dalrymple, William, 43–4
Dardanelles, *see* Hellespont
Darius, 87
death and burial, 60–1
de Bry, Theodor, 207
della Valle, Pietro, 67, 100, 111
Delos, 108, 139–41
Delphi, 52, 81, 121, 130–1, 138, 165, fig 8
Demosthenes, 36, 149
de Nointel, C.F.O., Marquis, 25, 55, 58, 60, 123, 135, 137, 138, 145, 147, 173, 197
Descartes, René, 38
Description of Candia, 89
Desgodetz, Antoine, 132
Devereux, Robert, *see* Essex
Digby, Kenelm (1628), 15, 40, 139–40
Dilettanti, Society of, 208
Diodorus Siculus, 75
Dionysius, St, 147–8

Dionysus of Byzantium, 125
Dioscorides, 67, 75
diplomacy, 9, 19, 51, 55, 57–9, 63, 120, 147, 191, 198
Docheiariou monastery, 174
'doctoresses', 60, 168–9
Dodington, John, 39
Dodwell, Henry, 184
Dominicans, 30, 31
Domitian, 133
Doran, Susan, 186
Dowling, T.E., 32
dragomans, 57–9, 123, 198, 203
drawing, 115–16
dress, 16, 52, 130, 178, 192, 200
Dryden, John, 162
du Bellay, Joachim, 111
Durston, Christopher, 186

Eastcourt, Giles (1675), 60
Edirne, *see* Adrianople
education
  Greek, 32, 154–5, 160, 164–5, 168, 171–2, 177
  Roman, 88
  school, 5, 33–7, 74, 95
  travel and, 9–10, 103, 128, 152, 208–9, 210
  university, 32, 33, 37–8, 57, 75, 97, 145, 190
Egypt, 135, 185
Eleusis, 78, 81, 89, 94, 106, 141
Elgin, Thomas Bruce, 7th Earl of, 135, 137
Elizabeth I, gift to Mehmed III, 59
Elsner, Jas, 41, 81
embalming, 60–1
Emmanuel College, Cambridge, 38
empire
  cyclical nature/*translatio imperii*, 67, 85, 105, 157, 209
  English aspirations to, 3, 4, 85, 208
  see also Byzantine Empire, Ottoman Empire, Roman Empire

England
  antiquities, 105, 124
  anxiety about, 8, 42, 68, 84–5, 157, 209–10
  Civil War, 67, 69, 85, 107, 112, 157, 185, 210
  Commonwealth, 112, 199, 210
  monarchy, 202, 210
  national identity, 3, 42, 205, 207
  perfection, 8, 209–10
  post-Restoration, 2, 3, 68, 107, 128, 181, 202, 210
  society in 3, 209–10
  trade, diplomacy and, 9, 32, 51, 57–9
  see also under empire
English
  as heirs of ancient Greece, 152, 155, 158, 161–2, 164, 187, 205, 211
  as heirs of Rome, 98, 162, 205
  language, 36, 40, 207
  love of antiquity, 105–6
  slavery and, 201
  see also under Greeks
engraving, 115–16
Ennius, 93
Ephesus, 93–4, 105–6, 107, 112, 132–3, 157, 176, 186–7, 210, figs 9, 10
  basilica of St John, 79
  Covel at, 13, 24, 47, 78–9, 93–4, 120, 121, 122–3, 132, 143–4, 208
  Gate of Persecutions, 93, 94, 143–4, 208, fig 17
  St Paul at, 90
  temple of Artemis/Diana, 76, 79, 120, 129
Epimenides, 163
Erasmus, Desiderius, 26, 34, 35
Eratosthenes, 67
Esch, Arnold, 118
Esphigmenou (Simeno) monastery, 148, 174
Essex, Robert Devereux, Earl of, 7, 10

etymology, 78, 91
Euboea, 203
eucharist, 206
  see also transubstantiation
Euripides, 36, 70, 73, 93, 149, 161, 164
Eurocentricity, 4
Evans, D.R., 10
Eve, 89, 91
Evelyn, John, 24, 35, 39, 104, 116, 125
Evliya Çelebi, 143, 144
excavation, 134, 208
exile, 5
Experimental Philosophy Club, 6

Ferrarius, Philippe, 98
Finch, Heneage, *see* Winchilsea
Finch, John (1672), 9, 25, 37, 47, 55, 58, 94
  Baines and, 27–8, 61, 71–2, 95
  character, 29, 39–40, 184
  on coffee, 54–5
  Covel and, 19, 27–8
  on Greeks, 151, 170, 183
  letters/reports, 15, 17
  luggage sent home by, 52
  Turks and, 202
Finkel, Caroline, 144
Fisher, Mary (1657), 180, 197–8
Fletcher, E.W., 32
Florence, Duke of, 39, 138
food, 50, 53–5, 177–8, 196
France
  Greek mss in, 145
  rivalry with England, 32, 106
  trade with Ottoman Empire, 32
Franciscans, 31
Fuller, Thomas, 9

Gailhard, John, 34, 35, 190
Gainsford, Thomas (1607), 29, 171–2, 209
Galata Tower, Constantinople, figs 21, 22
Gallipoli, 55

Games, A., 21
Gate of Persecutions, Ephesus, 93, 94, 143–4, 208, fig 17
Geoffrey of Monmouth, 162
geography, 5, 6, 208
George, St, 89, 176, 177, 178
Georgirenes, Joseph, 57, 114, 170, 171, 183–4
Gerard, John, 98
Giambetti, Francesco, 123
gifts, 51–2, 62, 175
Gilles, Pierre, 67, 74, 98–9, 100, 125
Giraud, Jean, 99, 120, 123, 124, 138–9, 150
Glover, Anne, 61, 93
Glover, Thomas, 29
Goldhill, Simon, 152
Golden Gate, Constantinople, 137
Grafton, Anthony, 82
grammar schools, 33–7
Grand Tour, 150, 208
Granicus, R., 87
Great Lavra monastery, 149, 173, 175, 176, 177
Greaves, John (1638), 11, 12, 52, 97, 98, 122, 145–7, 171, 173
Greaves, Thomas, 145
Greece, 4
   classical ruins/antiquities, 104–13, 156, 211
   under Ottomans, 30–1, 84, 154, 158–60, 178, 180–1
   under Romans, 152–3, 191
Greek language, 37, 57, 96, 155–6, 171–2
   in Arabic script, 194
   in English schools, 33–4, 36, 156
   printing, 72, 97, 146
   verse composition, 35
   see also classical texts
Greek Orthodox Church, *see* Orthodox Church
Greeks
   craftiness, 161

education, 32, 154–5, 160, 164–5, 168, 171–2, 177
   in England, 32, 181–2, 183–4
   English views of, 113, 151–2, 153–61, 163–9, 187
   hospitality/generosity, 164, 167–8, 172, 205
   'merry', 163
   piety, 178, 179
   Roman views of, 152–3, 163
   Turkish-speaking, 156, 181
   Turks and, 31, 167, 178–81, 204, 205
   urban/rural, 154
   women, 168–9
   see also Byzantine Empire *and under* Trojans
Green, Ian, 93, 95
Greene, Molly, 203
Greene, Thomas, 186
Greenhalgh, Michael, 119
Grélois, J-P., 17, 20
Gresham College, London, 40
Greville, Fulke, 7
guides, 120, 123–4
Guillet de Saint-George, G., 66, 74, 80, 99–100, 123, 143, 165

Hadrian, 88, 124, 125
Haemus, Mt, 88
Hakluyt, Richard, 6, 100
Hale, Matthew, 33–4
Halicarnassus, 106
Hall, Joseph, 5, 7–8, 210
Hapsburgs, 86, 170
Hartlib, Samuel, 173
Harvey, Daniel, 11, 19, 27, 47, 61
Hasluck, F.W., 178
Hawksmoor, Nicholas, 185
health and sickness, 23–4, 59–61
Hebrew, 36, 190
Hecate triformis, 94
Hector, 144, 208
Hellespont, 86–7, 172

INDEX

Hemmerdinger Iliadou, D., 16
Heracleia Perinthus, 47
Hercules/Herakles, 80–1, 89, 137
Herodotus, 5, 67, 74, 78, 86, 112
Hesiod, 36, 51, 96
Hesychius, 131
Heylyn, Peter, 6, 10, 92, 99, 152, 155, 163
Hierapolis, 85, 107, 108–9
Hipparchus, 67
Hippocrates, 117
Historia Byzantina, 96
Hobbes, Thomas, 36
Holy Land, *see* Palestine
Homer, 36, 54, 67, 70, 73, 78, 79, 93, 149
   birthplace, 73
   Iliad, 109, 110, 114
   Odyssey, 73
   works written on a dragon skin, 29
   see also Troy
homesickness, 11, 62–3
homosexuality, 27–8
Horace, 35, 69, 72, 111, 115
horses, 45, 49–50, 52
Hosios Loukas (St Luke Stiriotes), 143, 172, 180
Howard, Thomas, *see* Arundel
Howell, James, 7, 9–10, 97–8, 152, 155, 157, 189–90
hubris, 68
Huckle, Robert, 13, 18, 51, 52, 70–1
Huguenots, 182
humanism, 33, 37
Hungary, 135
Huntington, Robert, 41, 97, 135–6, 157, 186

'Iberian' language, 149
Ida, Mt, 115
identity, sense of, *see under* England, travel
Ilissus, R., 132
Imbros, 176

India, 10, 43–4
Inns of Court, 33, 38
inscriptions, 11, 13, 105, 118–19, 124, 125, 129, 131, 136–7, 138
interpreters, *see* dragomans
Isfahan, 67
Isis, 176
Iskenderun, *see* Scanderun
Islam
   alcohol and, 54, 195, 196
   art and, 116, 135
   Christianity and, 11, 144, 148, 158, 184, 193, 199
   Orthodoxy and, 170, 178–81
   western knowledge of, 190, 193–4
   see also Muslims, Turks
Isocrates, 36
Istanbul, *see* Constantinople
Italy, 32, 116, 155, 160, 179, 194, 208
Ithaca, 73, 76
Iveron monastery, 142, 148–9, 174, 175
Izmir, *see* Smyrna
Iznik, *see* Nicaea

James I, 128, 181
Jerusalem, 6, 147, 185, 186
Jesuits, 30, 31, 109, 146, 193–4
Jesus, 114, 193, 198
Jews and Judaism, 31–2, 60, 124, 147, 169, 178–9, 190, 193–4, 196, 205
   Covel and, 22, 48
John the Divine, St, 90
Justin Martyr, 66
Juvenal, 35, 153

Karakallou monastery, 174
Karyes, 174, 176
khans and caravanserais, 48
King, Henry, 155, 192
Kinney, Dale, 119
Kitely, John, 61
Knolles, Richard, 4–5, 85, 123, 157, 190

Kos, *see* Cos
Koukouzelis, John, 177
Koutloumousi monastery, 174
Krautheimer, Richard, 111
Kritoboulos, Michael, 87

Laborde, L.E.S.J. de, 100
Lactantius, 95
Lampsacus, 119
landscape, *see* scenery
Langly, Richard, 203
languages
  Ottoman, 56, 67, 203
  travellers' knowledge of, 6, 10,
    22–3, 36, 56–7, 97, 202
  see also Greek, Latin
Laodicea, 129, 210
Larissa, 70
Lassels, Richard, 10, 11
Latin, 33–6, 37, 207
  see also classical texts
Laud, William, 57, 145, 146
Laurenberg, Johann, 67, 98
Lavandin, Hildegard, 111
'Lavender, Theophilus' 15, 71
Leedham-Green, E., 20
Leiden, 39
Leigh, Edward, 57, 75, 97
leisure activities, 56, 61–2, 88, 125
Lello, Henry, 147
Lemnos, 23, 47, 76, 91, 166, 176
Lepanto (modern Nafpaktos), 60
Leros, 139
Lesbos, 55
Levant, routes to 46
Levant Company, 9, 32, 96–7, 145, 210
Levi, Peter, 82
Lewis, Bernard, 4
libraries, *see* books
literature, classical, *see* classical texts
Lithgow, William (1610), 16, 29, 63,
  69, 76, 97, 107, 126
  at Troy, 16, 107, 110–11
  Turks and, 192–3, 194

Littlebury, Isaac, 74
Livy, 35, 75, 83, 85, 88, 145, 158
Lloyd, Nicholas, 96
Locke, John, 36, 40
London, 162, 181, 182, 183, 209
  church buildings 185–6
London Merchant, 46
Louis XIV, 137
Louvre Museum, 134
Lucan, 35, 68, 70, 93, 106, 108, 162
Lucaris, Cyril, 145, 146, 170–1, 172,
  173, 181
Lucian, 163
Lucretius, 40
luggage, 50–2, 66, 95, 96
Luke, John (1664), 9, 12, 55, 56, 90,
  96, 107, 113
Lysimachus, 78

Macedonia, 87–8
MacLean, Gerald, 14
Maeander, R., 77, 114
Magnesia, 47, 54
Malaga, 26
Mandrupolis, 75
Mansell, Arthur, 38
Manuel II (ruled 1391–1425), 179
manuscripts, 11, 39–40, 97, 122,
  144–9
maps and atlases, 6, 47–8, 109, 115, 129
Mara, wife of Murad II, 144, 179–80
Marathon, 86
Marmara, Sea of, *see* Propontis
Marsh, Henry, 189
Martial, 36
Mary, princess of Orange, 12, 26
Mary, Virgin, 177, 179
Matar, Nabil, 189, 200, 202–3
Mathew, Robert, 35
Mavrocordato, Alexander, 60, 155–6
Mazower, Mark, 159–60, 178
measurement
  of monuments, 105, 120, 121, 129
  scientific, 52

INDEX

Mehmed II (the Conqueror, ruled 1444–81), 87, 144, 179–80
Mehmed III (ruled 1595–1603), 59
Mehmed IV (ruled 1648–87), 180, 189, 198
Memphis (Egypt), 108, 209
Menander, 73
Mercator, Gerardus, 47
Mesopotamia, 185
Metaxa, Nicholas, 146
Meursius, Johannes, 66, 99
Michael Choniates, 153
Milan, 114–15
Miletus, 90
Milles, Isaac, 26
Milton, John, 36, 93
Minutius Felix, Marcus, 94
missionary activity, 185, 197
  see also Basire, conversion, Fisher
Mithridates, 143
Mitsi, Efterpi, 161
Modyford, James, 62
Mohammed, prophet, 170, 193, 198
monasteries, 145, 148, 180
  dissolution, 107
  see also Athos, Hosios Loukas
Monconys, Balthasar de, 144
morality, 35, 95, 103–4
  sexual, 25–6, 27–8, 200
More, Henry, 21, 37
Morea, *see* Peloponnese
Morosini, Francesco, 30
Morton, Thomas, 69
mosaics, 143
Moses, 92, 114
mosques, 109, 116–17
Mundy, Peter (1620), 125
Murad II (ruled 1421–51), 144, 179
music, 177
Muslims, *see* Islam, Turks
Muzlee Aga, 203
Mykonos, 141, 165, 169
myth, 88–90, 123

Naaman, 91
Nafpaktos *see* Lepanto
Nanni, Giovanni, 162
nationhood, England and, 3, 42, 205, 207
Neale, Thomas, 7, 11, 72
neo-Platonism, *see* Cambridge Platonism
Neuhusius, Reiner, 34
new world, discovery and colonisation, 3, 4, 6, 189, 197, 206, 208, 209
Nicaea (modern Iznik), 14, 47, 79, 107, 108, 118, 123, 133–4, 157
Nicomedia, 54, 91, 94, 98, 196
Noah, 162
non-jurors, 21, 182
Norgate, Edward, 116
North, Dudley (1662), 9, 33, 37, 40–1, 58, 109, 138, 159, 169, 179, 202
  Covel and, 26–7, 97, 100–1
  leisure activities, 61–2, 88
  Rycaut and, 83, 100–1
  slavery and, 201–2
North, Roger, 201
nostalgia, 68, 116, 209
novel, rise of, 207

Odysseus, 5, 72, 88, 161, 163
Oglander, John, 67
Oldenburg, Henry, 33, 105, 173
Olympus, Mt, (Macedonia), 70
Olympus, Mt, (Mysia), 45
oracles, 81, 121
orientalism, 4
Ortelius, Abraham, 47, 97–8, 99, 127
Orthodox Church
  Anglicans and, 21, 32, 46, 175, 181–5
  Catholicism and, 164, 170, 171, 179, 180–3, 193–4
  collection of books/mss and, 147
  Islam and, 170, 178–81
  liturgy, 171–2, 177
  in Ottoman Empire, 31, 151, 169–70

Orthodox Church *cont.*
  patriarchs, 31, 147, 169, 170–1, 180
  see also Athos, Greeks (piety)
Osman II (ruled 1618–22), 210
Ottoman Empire, 30
  Byzantine Empire and, 144–5, 154
  court rituals, 58, 62, 189, 195, 206
  see also under Covel
  English perceptions of, 3–4, 8, 15, 42, 157, 158–9, 184, 187, 189, 194–5, 205, 207, 210–11
  grand viziers, 84, 203
  Greece in, 30–1, 84, 154, 158–60, 178, 180–1
  imperial messengers, 48, 195, 203
  janissaries, 157, 159, 195, 196, 203, 210
  languages in, 203
  organisation, 31, 151, 159, 169–70, 205
  religion in, 31, 151, 159, 169–70, 194, 203
  Roman Empire and, 83–6, 87, 196
  seraglio, 145, 146, 147, 159, 195, 200
  slavery in, 201–2
  sultanate, 210
Ottoman language, 56, 67
Ovid, 5, 35, 66, 69–70, 71, 111, 206
  Christian interpretation of, 94
  Metamorphoses, 34, 73, 115
  on Troy, 67–8, 110
Oxford University, 6, 32, 33, 37–8, 57, 138, 145

Pactolus, R., 114
Pacuvius, 5
Padua, 39, 185
paganism, 35, 78, 80, 90, 93–5, 104, 186
painting, 116
Palestine, 6, 41, 174, 186
Palladio, Andrea, 186
Palmer, Thomas, 7

Panagiotes, Nikousios, 58, 180
Pantokratoros monastery, 174
Paros, 76, 141
passports and permits, 55
Patmos, 90
Patras, 81, 113
Paul, St, 90–1, 92, 103, 163, 179
  see also seven churches of Asia
Pausanias, 66, 74–5, 78–82, 89, 94, 119, 122, 130, 131, 208
Peacham, Henry, 7, 8–9, 36, 104, 115, 116, 124, 136, 140
Peloponnese/Morea, 30, 168, 174, 181, 185, 197, 201
Penteli, 148, 180
Pepys, Samuel, 36, 135–6
Pera, *see under* Constantinople
Pergamum, 117, 133, 135
Persia, Persian, 67, 86–7, 97, 129
Persius, 36
'perspective glasses' 51, 80
Petrarch, Francesco, 114
Petronius, 72
Petty, William (1624), 55, 106, 120–1, 137, 145
Phanariots, 154
Pharsalus, 70, 76
Pheidias, 124, 141
Philadelphia, 52
Philip of Macedon, 88
Philippi, 77
Philippopolis (modern Plovdiv), 69–70, 76–7, 134, 155
Philotheou monastery, 174
Phygela, 90
picnics, 56
pilgrimage, 5–6
Pindar, 36
pirates, 148, 160, 169, 176–7
Pisa, 26
plagiarism, 16
plague, *see* health and sickness
Plataea, 86
Plautus, 35, 153

Pliny the Elder, 35, 66, 67, 74–80,
    105, 130, 141, 153, 208
  fons cupidinis, 25, 75
Plovdiv, *see* Philippopolis
Plutarch, 34, 36, 38, 77, 83, 86, 93,
    152, 206
Plymouth, 29
Pococke, Edward (1630), 11, 12, 34,
    57, 145–6
Pola, Croatia, 125
Polybius, 152
Pompey, 70, 125
'Pompey's Pillar', 125–6
Poseidonius, 67
Potts, Alex, 119
Praxiteles, 141, 142
Pretzler, Maria, 81
printing, *see under* Greek language
Propertius, 36
Propontis (Sea of Marmara), 47, 149
Protestantism, 20, 21, 33, 93, 179,
    180, 184, 185, 186, 194
Protogenes, 105
Prusa (modern Bursa), 46, 47, 178,
    180, 196
Ptolemy, Claudius, 47, 67, 74, 77, 78,
    80, 146
Purchas, Samuel, 6, 32, 100
Puritans, 95, 128

Quakers, 11, 31, 180, 190, 197–9
Quarr Abbey, 67
Quatremère de Quincy, A-C., 134
Quintilian, 35
quotation, 6, 13, 35, 65–73, 83,
    92–3, 103
Qur'an, 190, 192–3

Ragusa, 29
Randolph, Bernard (1670), 29,
    30, 41, 117, 122, 139, 140,
    169, 203
  on Crete, 60, 106, 126, 168–9,
    179, 204

Reed, J.D., 204
religion
  climate and, 9
  travel and, 7–9
  see also specific faiths and sects
Religious Society of Friends,
    see Quakers
renegades, 170, 193, 196, 202–4
republic of letters, 33, 71
Revett, Nicholas, 109, 208
Rhodes, 30
  Colossus, 29, 90, 142
Roberts, Lewes (1619), 7, 101–2, 110
Robson, Charles (1624), 26, 108, 139,
    165, 184, 194
Roe, Thomas (1621), 55, 100, 146,
    154, 163, 181, 190
  collecting and, 104, 120, 134, 136,
    137, 145
Romans, 88
  art, 144
  Empire, 83–6, 87, 157, 196, 206
  Republic, 94
  Roman Britain, 84, 95, 162
  views of Greeks, 152–3, 163
Rome, city, 104, 111, 132, 142, 157, 161
Royal Society, 6–7, 27, 33, 39–40,
    105, 128, 208
Rubiés, J-P., 41
ruins, 74, 89, 209, 211
  aesthetic value, 113, 116
  anthropomorphic view, 107
  Greek people as, 151, 154, 161, 211
  identification, 119–34
  moral lessons, 67, 103, 111, 112,
    116, 157
  see also spolia *and under* Greece
Runciman, Steven, 32
Russia, 174
Rycaut, Paul (1661), 9, 19, 55, 57–8,
    180, 208, 209–10
  Athos, Mt, and, 24, 27, 143, 155,
    164, 171, 175
  on Christianity, 91, 183

Rycaut, Paul *cont.*
  classical texts and, 76
    Tacitus, 72, 83–6, 95
  on Greeks, 153, 154, 155, 156, 158, 163, 170, 172, 178, 182
  interests, 12, 21, 87
  Royal Society and, 105
  on ruins, 107, 108, 118, 180–1
  scenery and, 113–14
  on slavery, 201
  travels, 56, 98
    Philippopolis, 134, 156
    seven churches, 10, 52, 88, 90, 94, 131, 135, 157, 186
  on Turks, 188, 194–5, 196, 199, 202
  writings, 15, 65–6, 67, 69–70, 78, 100–1, 123

Sabina (wife of Hadrian), 124
Said, Edward, 4
St Luke Stiriotes, *see* Hosios Loukas
St Paul's School, 95
Salamis, 86–7, 135
Sallust, 35
Salona, 81, 130
Salonica (modern Thessaloniki), 31, 160
Salter, Jerome, 78, 143
salt trade, 91
Sancroft, William, 182
Sanderson, John, 61, 147
Sanderson, Thomas, 147
Sandys, Edwin, 183
Sandys, George (1610), 12, 15, 67, 94, 100, 107, 108, 160–1, 183, 206
  on Cicero's tomb, 127
  on Delos, 139
  England and, 209, 210
  myths repeated by, 29
  quotations, use of, 35, 73
  on ruins, 107, 108, 156–7
  as translator, 35, 73, 95, 158
  at Troy, 110–11, 117
  on Turks, 192, 195, 196
  on works of art, 122, 142, 143

Sanson, Nicolas, 47
Sardis, 107
Scanderun/Alexandretta (modern Iskenderun), 92, 179, 199
scenery, 113–16
scholasticism, 37
schools, *see under* education
science, 105
  experimental, 6–7, 39–40, 82, 105, 208
  scientific instruments, 32, 51, 52
  see also Royal Society *and under* measurement
Scotland, 107
sculpture, 123, 132, 135, 208
  appreciation of, 108, 136, 141, 209
  collecting, 136–7
  Golden Gate reliefs, 137
  transport of, 138–40
  see also Athens (Parthenon), Ephesus (Gate of Persecutions)
Selden, John, 9, 99, 162
Selibria (modern Silivri), 118
Seneca, 5, 38, 161
seraglio, imperial, 145, 146, 147, 159, 195, 200
seven churches of Asia, 10, 21, 85, 90, 92, 94, 103, 107, 112, 113, 186
  see also Ephesus, Laodicea, Pergamum, Philadelphia, Sardis, Smyrna, Thyatira
sexuality, 27–8
Shakespeare, William, 161, 163
Sherley, Thomas (1603), 63, 110, 117, 159, 184–5, 200
sibyls, 94, 122
Silius Italicus, 35
Simeno, *see* Esphigmenou
Simeon of Thessaloniki, 149, 177
Sinon, 70, 164
Sipylus, Mt, 47
Skopje, 120
slavery, 201–4

Smith, Stephen (1640s), 199
Smith, Thomas (1668), 9, 55, 90, 105,
    114, 120, 123, 135, 145, 156,
    178, 210
  classical texts and, 76
  Greaves and, 122, 145
  on Greek church, 21, 183
  on Greek press, 97, 146
  on Greeks, 158, 160
  at Hierapolis, 107, 108–9
  as non-juror, 182
  Orthodoxy and, 21
  on seven churches, 92, 103, 108–9,
    112, 113, 186–7, 210
    Ephesus, 129, 133, 210
    Laodicea, 129, 210
    Pergamum, 117, 135
    Sardis, 107
    Thyatira, 113, 131
    Tripolis, 107
  on slavery, 201
  travels, 76, 90, 103, 107
  on Turks/Ottoman Empire, 157,
    180, 196, 199–200
  work as chaplain, 19
  writings, 67, 80, 100
Smyrna (modern Izmir), 47, 73, 108,
    135, 138, 174, 192, 197, 199
  English 'factory', 41, 52–3, 97, 105,
    133
  tomb of St Polycarp, 135
Sophocles, 36, 73
souvenirs, 52, 134–6
Spain, 194
Sparta, 77
Spenser, Edmund, 93, 111, 162
spolia, 117–19, 180–1
Spon, Jacob, 57, 77, 107, 109, 120, 137
  antiquarian interests, 94, 121, 125,
    128, 130
  editing of Babin, 99
  Covel and, 27, 47, 78
  on Guillet, 123
  plague and, 59–60

  scientific interests, 75, 128
  Wheler's relationship with, 73, 80,
    81–2, 124
  spying, 9, 58, 120
Stambol, *see* Constantinople
Stavronikita monastery, 174
Stonehenge, 208
Strabo, 5, 74–81, 108, 111, 119, 123,
    130, 132, 133
  read by Vernon, 66, 67
Strymon, R., 77
Stukely, William, 208
Stuart, James, 109, 208
succession, problems of, 68
Suda, the, 96, 131
Sugar, P.F., 160
superstition, 29, 175–6, 179, 194

Tacitus, 35, 38, 65, 72, 83–6, 95, 192
Tavernier, J.B., 50
telescopes, 51, 80
temples converted into mosques, 109,
    116–17
Teonge, Henry (1675), 90, 91, 92,
    109–10, 168, 179
Terence, 35, 125
Thame Grammar School, 34
Thebes (Boeotia), 107
Theocritus, 36, 115
Theognis, 36
Theophrastus, 67
Thermopylae, 77
Theseus and Ariadne, 88, 89
Thessaloniki, *see* Salonica
Thévenot, Jean de, 100
Thomas, Keith, 93
Thucydides, 38, 83
Thyatira, 113, 119, 131, 141–2
Tiberius, 84
Tibullus, 36
Timaeus, 76
time, effect on buildings, 112
Tinos, 30
tombstones, re-use, 117–18

Toomer, G.J., 157
trade, 9, 30, 32, 191, 195, 210
　English 'factories', 41, 52–3, 96, 97, 105, 133
Trajan, 133
translatio imperii see under empire
translation, 72
　see also under Sandys
transport
　land, 45, 49–50, 52
　sea, 46, 53
　of sculpture, 138–40
transubstantiation, 20, 32, 46, 60, 181–4
travel
　advice on, 7, 189–90
　ancestry, 5–6
　arguments for and against, 7–8, 9–11
　'armchair', 2
　civility and, 3, 7
　dangers, 11, 63, 160
　education and, 9–10, 103, 128, 152, 208–9, 210
　identity and, 2–3, 14–15, 20, 42, 205, 207
　purposes, 6–11
　religion and, 7–9
travel writing
　popularity, 6
　reliability, 16–17
　types, 14–16
Tripolis, 107
Trojans and Trojan War, 88, 110
　dragging of Hector, 144, 208
　England and, 42, 162–3
　Greeks and, 161
　see also Aeneas, Hector, Sinon
Trophonius, 81
Troy and Troad, 14, 67–9, 87, 98, 106, 109–10, 113, 117, 136
　Coryate at, 42, 108, 134–5, 142
　Lithgow at, 16, 107, 110–11
Turkey, *see* Ottoman Empire

Turkish language, 97
　see also Ottoman language
Turks/Muslims
　classical remains and, 112, 116–19, 134
　definition of 'Turk', 188
　foreigners and, 56, 61, 120, 129, 131, 189–205
　good/bad qualities, 95, 190–202
　Greeks and, 31, 167, 178–81, 204, 205
　renegades, 170, 193, 196, 202–4
　Trojans and, 162
　viewed from England, 188–90
　see also Ottoman Empire
Twigg, John, 38
Tyre, 107

Ulysses, *see* Odysseus
universities, *see under* education

Vacalopoulos, A.E., 160
Valerius Maximus, 35
Vani Effendi, 58, 170, 193–4, 204
Vatopedio monastery, 142, 174, 176, 177
Venice, 32, 127
　Ottomans and, 30, 45, 159–60, 203
Verney, Jack (1662), 37, 96
Verney, Ralph, 38
Vernon, Francis (1675), 12, 19, 36, 60, 113, 120, 121, 122, 123, 129–30, 184, 208, figs 3, 6
　books read by, 66–7, 95–6, 98, 99–100
　death, 57, 63, 129
　knowledge of languages, 36, 57
　Royal Society and, 40, 105
Veryard, Ellis (1686), 10, 11, 92, 108, 126, 142, 143, 179, 196
　on Cicero's tomb, 127–8
　classical texts and, 76, 77
　Colossus of Rhodes and, 29, 90
　at Cyzicus, 75, 118
　at Ephesus, 112

at Halicarnassus, 106
on Troy, 111
Vienna, 135, 189
Virgil, 35, 66, 68, 93, 115
   Aeneid, 69, 70, 71–2, 73, 161–2, 163, 164, 204
   Christian interpretation of, 35, 94
Vitkus, D.J., 194
Vitruvius, 66, 67, 78
Vossius, Isaac, 66

Wadham College, Oxford, 6
Wallachia, 174
Wanley, Humfrey, 24, 149
Watson, Foster, 36
weapons, 51–2, 177
weather, buildings and, 113
Westminster School, 36
Wheler, George (1673), 3, 10, 55, 96, 137, 208, 209, figs 8, 9, 11, 12, 13, 14
   aesthetic sense, 108–9, 141–2, 209
   antiquarian investigations, 12, 88, 106, 113, 117, 119, 130, 131, 144
   in Athens, 74–5, 78, 81, 89, 99, 120, 122, 123, 131–2, 150, 151
   Parthenon, 45, 109, 123, 124–5, 142
   books used by, 96–100
   as botanist, 11, 23–4, 75, 98
   on Cicero's tomb, 127
   classical texts and, 66, 73, 75, 78–82, 89, 94, 111, 122, 130
   collecting, 97, 124–5, 135, 138–9, 147–8
   Covel and, 19, 20, 27, 47
   on Delos, 108, 140–1
   at Delphi, 52, 81, 121, 131–2
   drawings, 132
   education, 38, 39
   on England, 112, 157
   English renegades and, 203–4
   on food and drink, 53, 55
   Greek Church and, 170, 172, 178, 179, 186–7
   on Greek language, 156
   Greek people and, 87–8, 151, 159, 160, 165–8, 205
   at Hosios Loukas, 143, 172, 180
   on learning by heart, 34
   leisure activities, 56
   on lodgings, 49, 59–60, 117
   luggage, 51, 52
   maps and, 48, 98, 132
   myth and, 89–90
   paganism and, 77–8, 80–1, 94
   on St Paul, 91, 92
   Spon and, 78, 80, 81–2, 124
   on transport, 50
   on Xerxes, 86–7
Wheler, Granville, 19, 27
Winchester School, 34–5
Winchilsea, Heneage Finch, 3rd Earl of (1661), 11, 60, 62–3, 116, 189
   diplomatic activities, 58, 61, 147, 195, 197, 199, 201
Winckelmann, Johann, 119, 208
wine, 53–4, 166–7, 177–8, 195, 196
Winterton, Ralph, 51, 96
Woburn Abbey, 144
women, 28, 60, 168–9, 197, 200
Wren, Christopher, 185
writing materials, 51
Wych, Edward, 200
Wych, Jane, 61
Wych, Peter, 200

Xenophon, 36, 206
Xerxes, 86–7, 162

Yerasimos, Stefanos, 3, 16, 68
Young, Patrick, 145

Zante (modern Zakynthos), 30, 127, 165, 185
Zographou monastery, 176
Zuallardo, Giovanni, 127

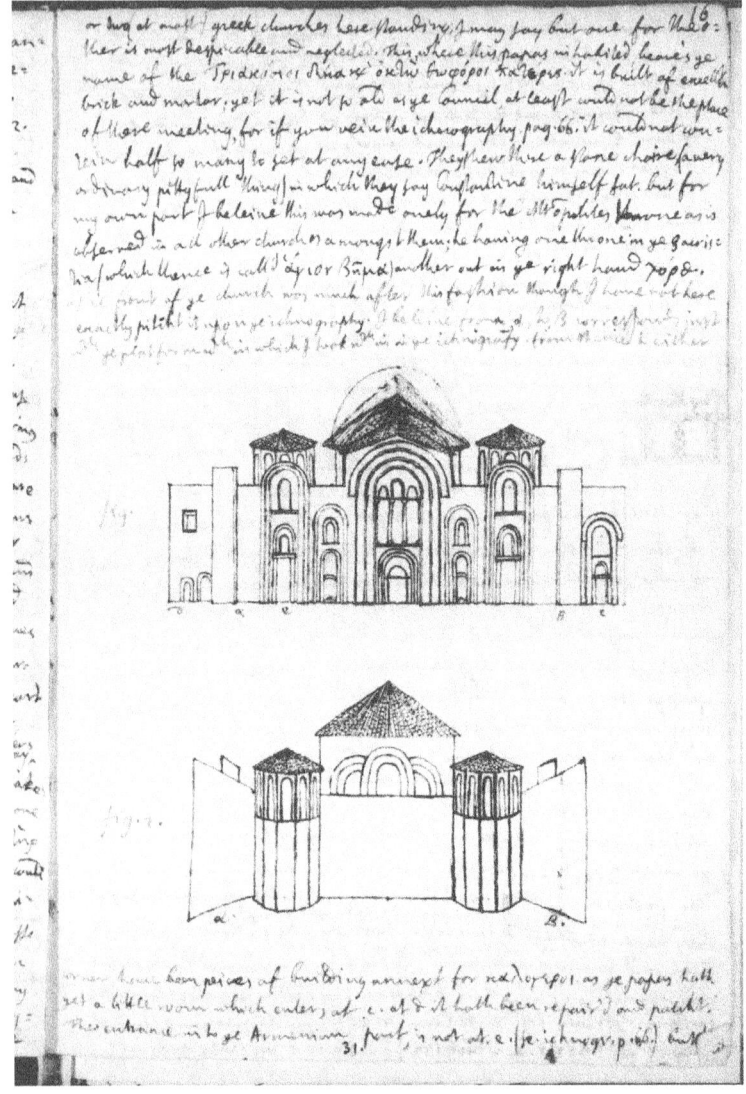

Figure 1 Typical page of Covel's diary, BL MS Add. 22914, 16r (© The British Library Board).

Figure 2 Plant sketch by Covel, BL MS Add. 22914, 44r (© The British Library Board).

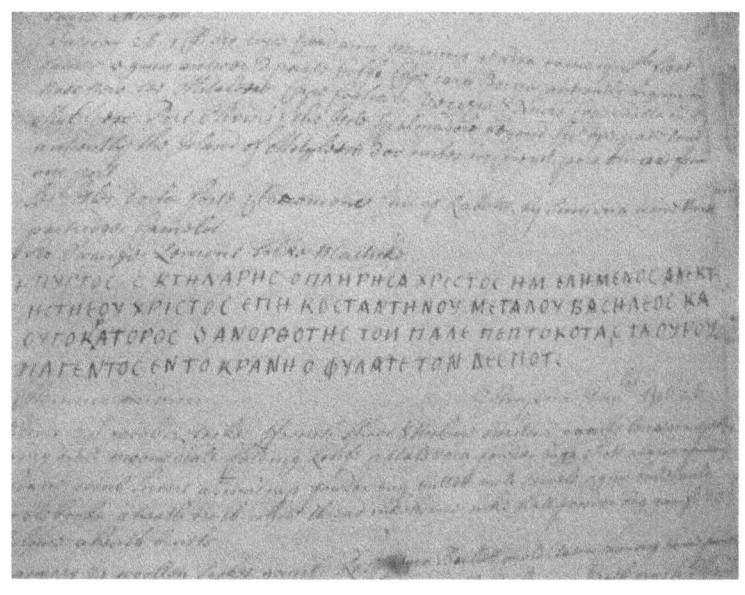

Figure 3 Typical page of Vernon's diary, Royal Society MS 73, 45r (courtesy of The Royal Society).

times of great solemnities as now ye G. Signor sent to them to come and to howe nowe ye circumcision of his son and Marriage of his daughter, they were much confounded not having any precedent left of what ever had been payd before but ye Chiá for Steward or deputy to ye Vizier favour'd them, who a record of what they paid about 30 yeares since in Sult. Morat's time, which saved them much of what they intended to have given. I was very much obliged to him for severall times he took me along with him to see sights and to be treated by ye Turks (for you shall hear anon) even to ye envy of severall of our Company. [coded passage] but enough of that.

May. 19th My Ld had audience wth ye Vizier; for ye ceremony of it, it was ye same wth what is performed here at any audience wth ye Caimacham or Bostangee bashá. we were conducted to his Gallore or Seraglio through the City, two Chiauses furnish't by order and allow ye Janyzaries upon my Ld from Stambol continually led he or hir'ed thither again (each of us and we all following on horse back. we were brought into a pretty large room wth a Soffa (a square raysed about 1½ foot from ye ground) covered wth carpets very rich, and layd upon the 3 sides next ye wall wth narrow quilts or little beds; and great Lystes round, all cover'd wth cloth of gold. At audiences at Stambol we pull of our shoes, but here it would be an affront; as if we were afraid to spoyl the Vizier's goods. the like is before ye G. Signor. you may conceive something of ye businesse by this pittifull figure. A. is ye door where we entered. B. another door where ye Vizier came in. c.c.c.c. is the sofá. o.o. are the squipald wth ye bolsters next ye wall. this fashion is all over Turkey, amongst them and Greeks, Jewes, Armenians &c. and I question not in ye least but it was ye common forme of ye old Tryclinior, but of that I shall talk in some more convenient place and manner. my Lord was placed upon a low stool upon ye Sofá, and we all stood very close at his back round about us stood many Chiauses and other attendants; after about ½ of an hour's stay, in comes ye vizier and drops himself down upon ye couch cross legd at M. my Ld stood was put nearer to him at L. just as he came in all ye waiters cry'd whish, whish &c in token of silence (though I never saw such silence even to admiration) for hereafter shall be sayd without this sign; and at his setting down they all give a great acclamation, as much as God blesse ye G. Signor and hotesse.

Figure 4 Page of Covel's diary showing a passage in code, BL MS Add. 22912, 189v (© The British Library Board).

Figure 5 Covel's sketch of the route from Constantinople to Adrianople, BL MS Add. 22912, 171r (© The British Library Board).

Figure 6 Vernon's sketch map of Greek islands, Royal Society MS 73, 31r (courtesy of The Royal Society).

eloquentiæ tuæ, ...
Principi, Patriæ, atq̃ ecclesiæ Anglicanæ Charissimi,
Ingeniosâ, numerosâ, prosperâq̃ Prole præ cæteris
mortalibus, felicissimi:
Alter D.IOANNIS FINCHII, viri omni laude
majoris Amicus intimus,
Perpetuusq̃, per triginta plus minus annos
Fortunarum ac Consiliorum Particeps
Longarumq̃ in exteras Nationes Itinerationum
indivulsus Comes;
Iste igitur peregrè apud Turcas Vitâ functus
est, nec prius tamen quam alter
A serenissimo Rege Angliæ per Decennium Legatus
præclarè suo functus esset munere,
Tunc demum dilectissimus BAINESIUS suam et Amici
FINCHII simul Animam Byzantij efflavit,
Die V. septembris H.H.I.P.M.A.D. MDCLXXXI. Ætati...LIX
Quid igitur fecerit alterum hoc Corpus animâ Cassum rogare
nuit; sed in amplexus alterius indolait, ingemuit,
ubertim flevit
Solum in loco meas, nisi nos ut qua communis utrisq̃ Anima
...

Figure 7 Detail of the funerary monument for Finch and Baines, Christ's College Chapel, Cambridge (photograph: the author).

Figure 8 Wheler's sketch plan of Delphi, *Journey into Greece*, 313 (photograph: Tam Pollard).

Figure 9 Wheler's plan of Ephesus, *Journey into Greece*, 253 (photograph: Tam Pollard).

Figure 10 Covel's plan of Ephesus, BL MS Add. 22912, 45r (© The British Library Board).

Figure 11 Wheler's plan of Athens from the south, *Journey into Greece*, 338 (photograph: Tam Pollard).

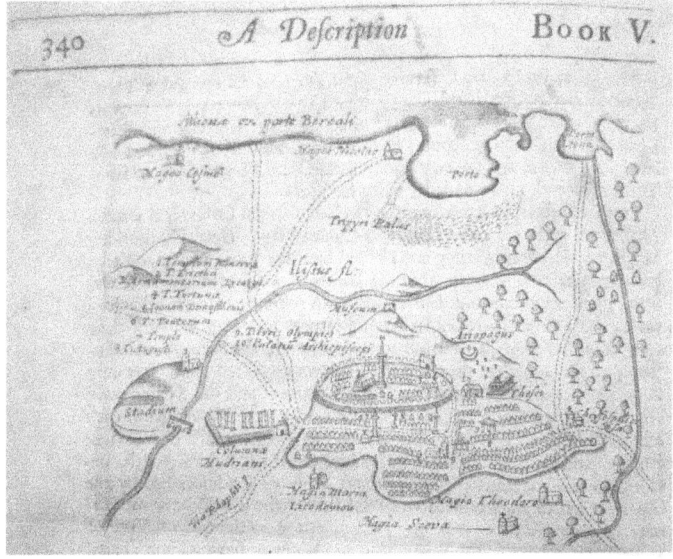

Figure 12 Wheler's plan of Athens from the north, *Journey into Greece*, 340 (photograph: Tam Pollard).

Figure 13 Wheler's drawing of the Parthenon, *Journey into Greece*, 360 (photograph: Tam Pollard).

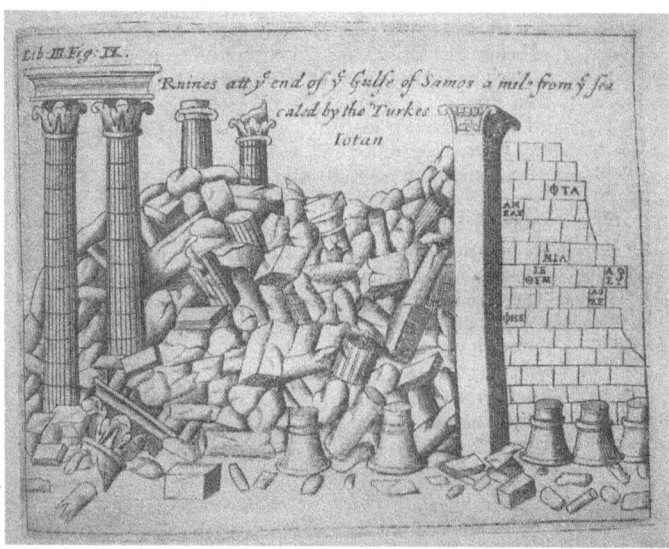

Figure 14 'Heaps of ruins', *Journey into Greece*, 271 (photograph: Tam Pollard).

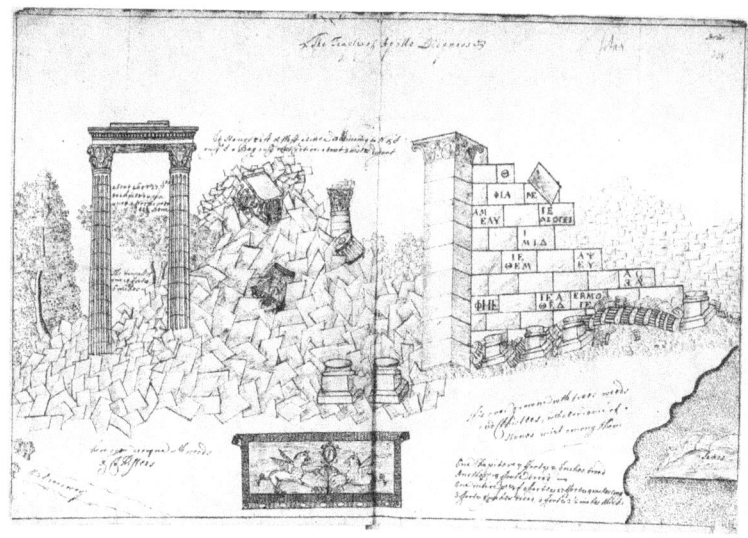

Figure 15 Drawing of Didyma (from Covel's diary but not in his hand), BL MS Add. 22912, 307v (© The British Library Board).

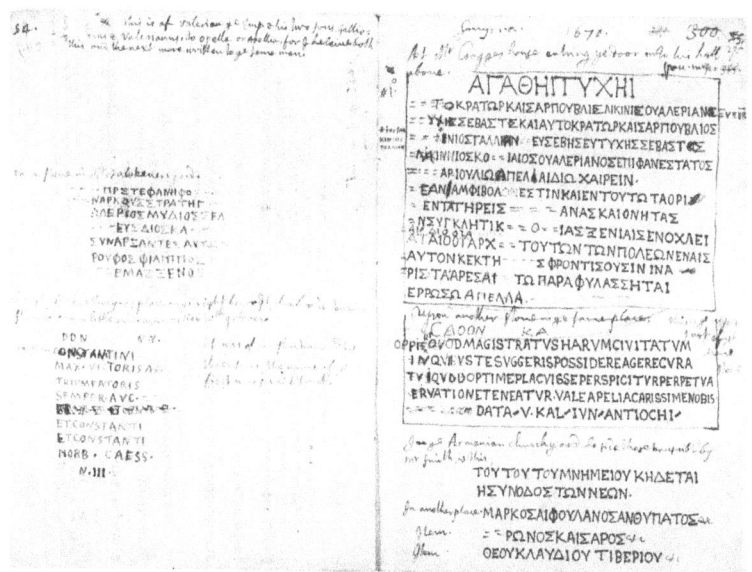

Figure 16 Page of Covel's diary showing his recording of inscriptions, BL MS Add. 22912, 275r (© The British Library Board).

Figure 17 The 'Sarcophagus of Achilles': Covel saw parts of it in the Gate of Persecutions at Ephesus (photograph reproduced by kind permission of the Duke of Bedford and the Trustees of the Bedford Estates).

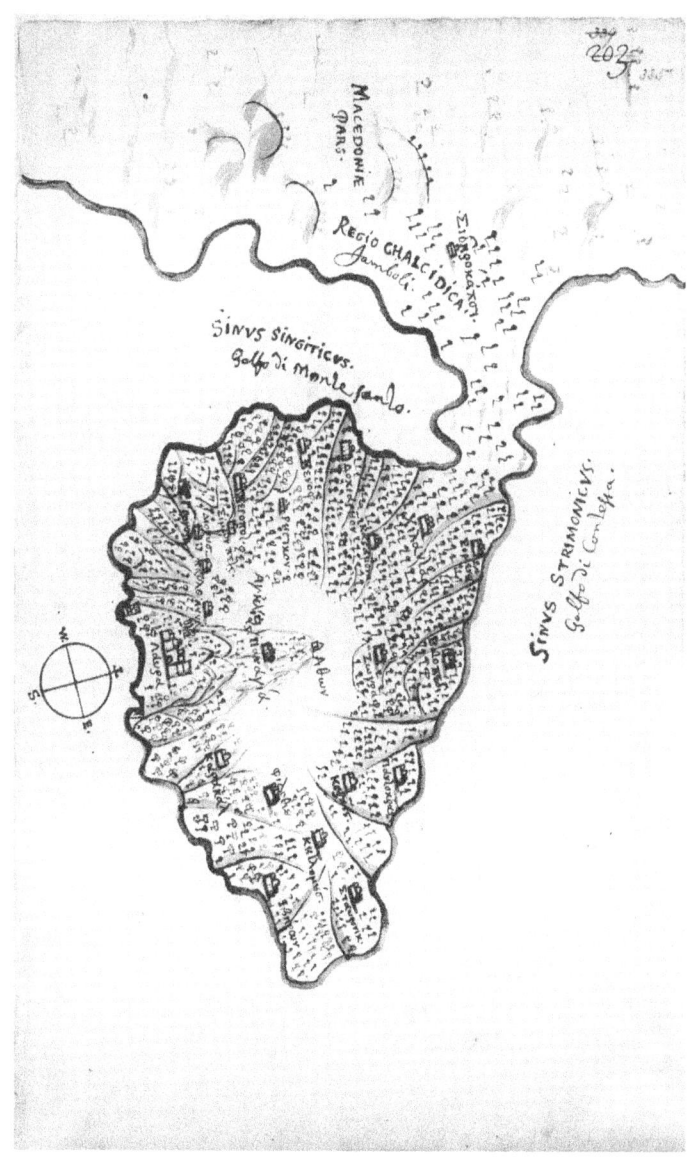

Figure 18 Covel's sketch map of Mount Athos, BL MS Add. 22912, 335r (© The British Library Board).

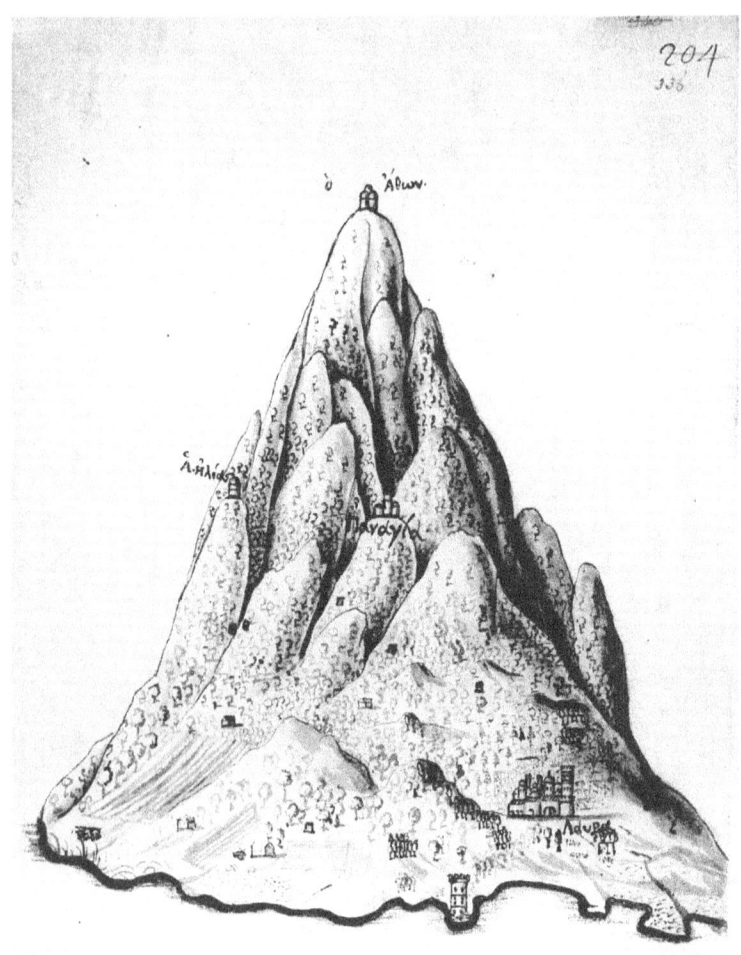

Figure 19 Drawing of Mount Athos by Covel, BL MS Add. 22912, 336r (© The British Library Board).

Figure 20 View of Mount Athos today (photograph: Marcos M. Magarinos).

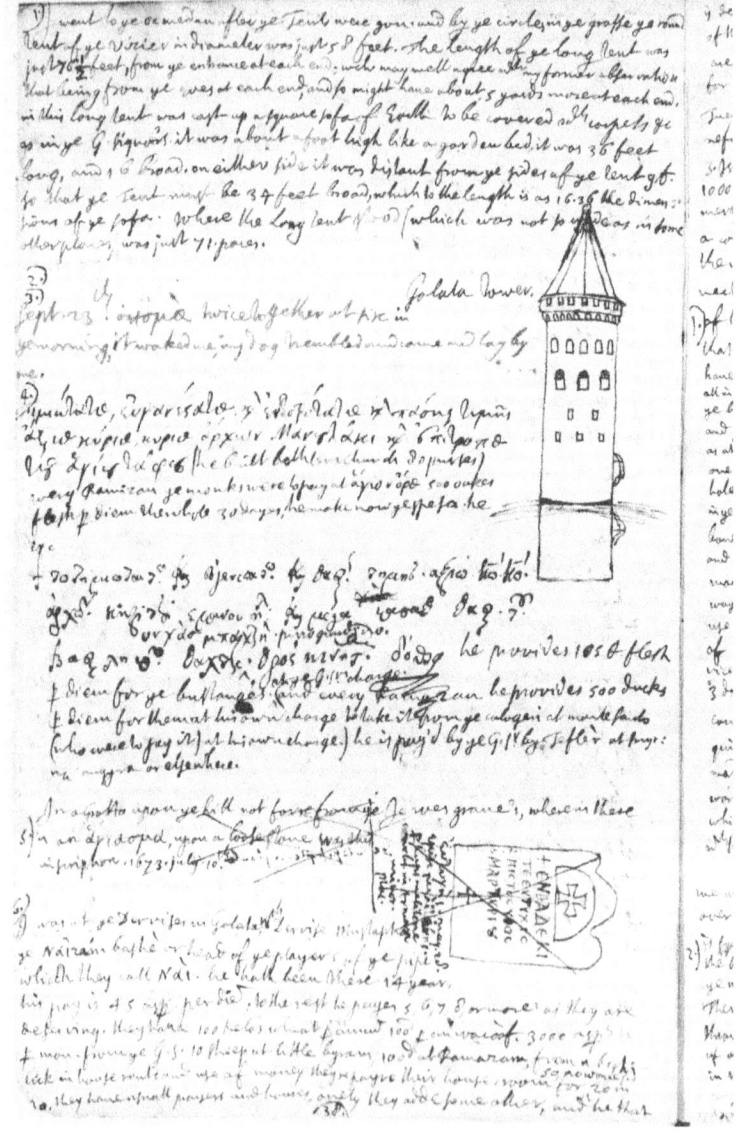

Figure 21 Covel's sketch of the Galata Tower, BL MS Add. 22912, 163v (© The British Library Board).

Figure 22 View of the Galata Tower today (photograph: the author).

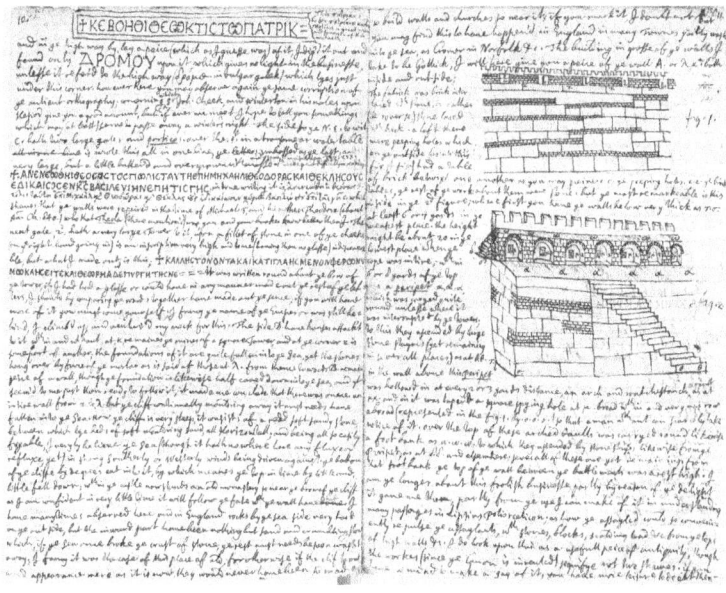

Figure 23 Typical page from Covel's diary, BL MS Add. 22912, 180v–181r (© The British Library Board).

www.ingramcontent.com/pod-product-compliance
Lightning Source LLC
Chambersburg PA
CBHW070017010526
44117CB00011B/1606